AN INTRODUCTION TO FANTASY

Providing an engaging and accessible introduction to the Fantasy genre in literature, media and culture, this incisive volume explores why Fantasy matters in the context of its unique affordances, its disparate pasts and its extraordinary current flourishing. It pays especial attention to Fantasy's engagements with histories and traditions, its manifestations across media and its dynamic communities. Matthew Sangster covers works ancient and modern, well-known and obscure, and ranging in scale from brief poems and stories to sprawling transmedia franchises. Chapters explore the roles Fantasy plays in negotiating the beliefs we live by; the iterative processes through which fantasies build, develop and question; the root traditions that inform and underpin modern Fantasy; how Fantasy interrogates the preconceptions of realism and Enlightenment totalisations; the practices, politics and aesthetics of world-building; and the importance of Fantasy communities for maintaining the field as a diverse and ever-changing commons.

MATTHEW SANGSTER is Professor of Romantic Studies, Fantasy and Cultural History at the University of Glasgow, where he co-directs the Centre for Fantasy and the Fantastic. His other books include *Living as an Author in the Romantic Period* (2021), *Institutions of Literature, 1700–1900* (co-edited with Jon Mee, 2022) and *Remediating the 1820s* (co-edited with Jon Mee, 2023).

AN INTRODUCTION TO FANTASY

MATTHEW SANGSTER
University of Glasgow

Shaftesbury Road, Cambridge CB2 8EA, United Kingdom

One Liberty Plaza, 20th Floor, New York, NY 10006, USA

477 Williamstown Road, Port Melbourne, VIC 3207, Australia

314–321, 3rd Floor, Plot 3, Splendor Forum, Jasola District Centre, New Delhi – 110025, India

103 Penang Road, #05–06/07, Visioncrest Commercial, Singapore 238467

Cambridge University Press is part of Cambridge University Press & Assessment, a department of the University of Cambridge.

We share the University's mission to contribute to society through the pursuit of education, learning and research at the highest international levels of excellence.

www.cambridge.org
Information on this title: www.cambridge.org/9781009429917

DOI: 10.1017/9781009429924

First published 2023

A catalogue record for this publication is available from the British Library.

A Cataloging-in-Publication data record for this book is available from the Library of Congress

ISBN 978-1-009-42991-7 Hardback
ISBN 978-1-009-42994-8 Paperback

CONTENTS

FIGURES

Introduction

In the early 1950s, while attempting to find a publisher for a long, complicated heroic romance he had been developing in various forms for several decades, J. R. R. Tolkien wrote to the editor Milton Waldman to try and explain his ambitions for his work:

[O]nce upon a time (my crest has long since fallen) I had a mind to make a body of more or less connected legend, ranging from the large and cosmogonic, to the level of romantic fairy-story – the larger founded on the lesser in contact with the earth, the lesser drawing splendour from the vast backcloths – which I could dedicate simply to: to England; to my country. It should possess the tone and quality that I desired, somewhat cool and clear, to be redolent of our 'air' (the clime and soil of the North West, meaning Britain and the hither parts of Europe: not Italy or the Aegean, still less the East), and, while possessing (if I could achieve it) the fair elusive beauty that some call Celtic (though it is rarely found in genuine ancient Celtic things), it should be 'high', purged of the gross, and fit for the more adult mind of a land now long steeped in poetry. I would draw some of the great tales in fullness, and leave many others only placed in the scheme, and sketched. The cycles should be linked to a majestic whole, and yet leave scope for other minds and hands, wielding paint and music and drama. Absurd.[1]

[1] J. R. R. Tolkien to Milton Waldman, probably late 1951, Letter 131 in *The Letters of J. R. R. Tolkien*, ed. by Humphrey Carpenter (London: George Allen and Unwin, 1981), pp. 143–61 (pp. 144–5). Quotations

In this letter to Waldman, Tolkien describes his old desire to make another world from art, constructing this world by stitching together a varied (yet specific) range of different forms and styles. In his projected conception, the mixed modes in which he proposed to work would operate synergistically to create both grandeur and verisimilitude. His creations would draw in characteristics he perceived in the world, but they would also engage with forms that only exist in art, compounding, iterating on and extrapolating from longstanding social and cultural traditions in a new imagined space. Tolkien was aware that creating a convincing world does not require making everything in it; in fact, he proposed deliberately to leave room for others to collaborate with him, using forms with which he himself was less adept. Nevertheless, he dreamt of a constellation of artworks that would cohere and connect in manners that would have both an internal aesthetic logic and a wider cultural value. He wanted to create legends that were self-evidently unreal, but which would hold real and powerful meanings for readers.

However, Tolkien's letter encodes a deep uncertainty about whether others would understand or care about the stories he wished to tell. In opening this passage, he frames his ambitions as having been necessarily scaled back. When evoking 'the fair, elusive beauty some call Celtic', he doubts his own ability to conjure this. In closing, he dismisses his dreams as absurd. While

throughout this book reproduce as closely as possible the spelling and punctuation of the original text, with the exception that where single quotation marks would appear within another set of single marks, these have been replaced with double quotation marks for clarity. Editorial amendments and elisions appear within square brackets.

Tolkien had been encouraged by positive reviews of *The Hobbit* (1937) and supportive readings from his family and friends, after ambivalence from the publishing industry, he was sceptical whether his cherished legendarium could find purchase in the hearts and minds of mid-twentieth-century audiences. Was a plunge into the complexities of fabricated romance really something readers desired in the aftermath of war, amidst the burgeoning evidence of modernity? Tolkien was trying to activate and reconfigure resonances rooted in longstanding cultural traditions – including some that were extremely unfashionable at the time he was writing – but the stories he was preparing also sought to do things that were particular and strange. They asked their readers to trust Tolkien and work with him in animating the depths and unfamiliarities of an alternative world. He was unsure how people would respond to this.

The concerns Tolkien expressed were not unjustified; his impassioned account failed to persuade Waldman that Collins should publish the writings that later became *The Lord of the Rings* (1954–5) and *The Silmarillion* (1977). However, as readers of this book will doubtless know, once they were published, Tolkien's audiences found in his idiosyncratic legend-making both the constellations of wonder he had hoped to trace and space for their own imaginations to operate in concert with his richly considered creation. Nevertheless, his works were not universally praised. When the American literary critic Edmund Wilson reviewed *The Lord of the Rings* in *The Nation* in 1956, he denounced it as 'balderdash', describing it as a book that could only be admired by 'certain people—especially, perhaps, in Britain—[who] have a lifelong appetite for juvenile trash'.[2] Wilson bounced off the book, seeing it as indulgent and inadequate by the cultural standards he had internalised and believed should be upheld. Other unsympathetic readers objected to Tolkien's work because they were ideologically uncomfortable with the influence they saw him exerting. One of Tolkien's most notable antagonists was the prolific New Wave fantasist Michael Moorcock, who worried that the models traced in *The Lord of the Rings* were restructuring and restricting what the fantastic imagination might achieve. In an essay entitled 'Epic Pooh', first published in a British Fantasy Society pamphlet in 1978, Moorcock accused Tolkien of promoting a 'fundamentally misanthropic doctrine' that sought to 'dignify the mood of a disenchanted and thoroughly discredited section of the repressed English middle-classes'.[3] For Moorcock, Tolkien's mythology was the wrong one for Britain, promoting complacent, consolatory conservatism, rather than challenging its readers to think better, as he felt the best Fantasy should do. While Moorcock hoped that Tolkien might 'inspire writers who will take his raw materials and put them to nobler uses', he was concerned that if the influence of *The Lord of the Rings* became too dominant, it would crowd out forms of Fantasy that he found more innovative and interesting.[4]

It might be fair to object to the way Moorcock pigeonholes Tolkien. While his is a valid perspective backed by

[2] Edmund Wilson, 'Oo, Those Awful Orcs!', *The Nation*, 14 April 1956, 326–32 (pp. 331–2).

[3] Michael Moorcock, *Epic Pooh*, British Fantasy Society Booklet No. 4 (February 1978), [p. 6].

[4] Moorcock, *Epic Pooh*, [pp. 14, 15].

an evidenced reading, it is far from the only way of interpreting Tolkien's works, which are more complex and multivalent than their critics often admit. However, Moorcock's concerns about *The Lord of the Rings* determining audiences' expectations regarding Fantasy were justified to a certain extent by the genre infrastructures taking shape around the time 'Epic Pooh' was published. Someone like Tolkien pitching a work along the lines of *The Lord of the Rings* to someone like Waldman in the late 1970s would have had a far easier time of it, as they could have placed what they were doing within an increasingly prominent bookshop category that Tolkien's success had played a central role in popularising.

As Tolkien's reputation rose, publishers sought to address hungry audiences who wanted more books like *The Lord of the Rings*. To do this, they turned to new authors, but also to existing works that had the potential to be assembled into a more coherent tradition in light of Tolkien's success. After publishing an authorised United States paperback edition of *The Lord of the Rings* in 1965, Ballantine Books – a pioneering paperback publishing house founded by Ian and Betty Ballantine in 1952 – began seeking out other stories to reprint that might appeal to Tolkien's growing ranks of fans. The Ballantines' first selections included further fiction and poetry by Tolkien, but they accompanied these with major fantasies by E. R. Eddison, David Lindsay and one of Moorcock's own favourite writers, Mervyn Peake, along with two relatively recent novels by Peter S. Beagle: *A Fine and Private Place* (1960) and *The Last Unicorn* (1968).

The success of such works led to the formal inauguration in 1969 of the Ballantine Adult Fantasy series – the

'Adult' in the title serving as both a piece of audience-focused branding and a slightly awkward defensive gesture against snobby dismissals penned by critics like Wilson. The series, edited by Lin Carter, reprinted a complex assembly of authors from a mixed range of backgrounds and traditions.[5] Carter selected fantastical novels by prominent Victorian writers, including George Meredith's orientalist *The Shaving of Shagpat* (1856) and George MacDonald's *Phantastes* (1858) and *Lilith* (1895). He placed William Morris's pioneering secondary-world quest narratives alongside Lord Dunsany's fictional mythographies and his faerie romance *The King of Elfland's Daughter* (1924). James Branch Cabell's playful, ironic metafictions rubbed covers with William Hope Hodgson's dark horror stories and with Hope Mirrlees's delightful *Lud-in-the-Mist* (1926) – an arch, wise rendering of the dance between bourgeois respectability and fairy wildness. Evangeline Walton's books in the series reworked the early Welsh prose fictions of the *Mabinogion*. Walton had originally published her first volume as *The Virgin and the Swine* in 1936, but it had met with a relatively tepid reception. It was only when Ballantine Books republished it as *The Island of the Mighty* in 1970, unaware that Walton was still alive, that she reached out and offered to finish a continuation of the project she had set aside. She eventually contributed four successful volumes to the Ballantine series. Carter's early selections also drew on fantasies that had originally

[5] Carter's canon-making is explored in far greater detail in Jamie Williamson's *The Evolution of Modern Fantasy: From Antiquarianism to the Ballantine Adult Fantasy Series* (New York: Palgrave Macmillan, 2015).

appeared in American pulp magazines such as *Weird Tales* (founded in 1922), *Amazing Stories* (1926–) and *Unknown* (1939–43). Fletcher Pratt, L. Sprague de Camp, H. P. Lovecraft, Clark Ashton Smith and Hannes Bok all published much of their work in such magazines, albeit in very different styles ranging from rousing adventure fiction to playful metafictional comedy to cosmic horror. Carter himself was intimately familiar with the pulp milieu; he had written parodies of Lovecraft and worked on posthumous publications by Smith and Robert E. Howard, the latter most famous as the creator of Conan the Barbarian. Howard's stories appeared in several of the anthologies Carter assembled for the Ballantine series, which included among other things tales by Jack Vance and C. L. Moore and pieces by established literary greats including William Shakespeare, Robert Browning, Edgar Allan Poe and Oscar Wilde. As it built up steam, the Ballantine series brought new authors into print, publishing Katherine Kurtz's debut novel *Deryni Rising* (1970), the first in a long-running series of fantasies modifying historical materials drawn from the medieval British Isles. The series also included the first American edition of Joy Chant's intense, evocative *Red Moon and Black Mountain* (1970), a narrative that grew from a world Chant imagined in her childhood into a vivid story of wonder, balance and responsibility.

The Ballantine series could in some respects be seen as a medium for codifying the kinds of writing Moorcock was concerned about. Carter is name-checked in 'Epic Pooh' and addressed rather ambivalently as someone who 'expresses a distaste for fiction which is not predominantly escapist by charging it with being "depressing" or "negative" if it does not provide him with the moral and psychological comforts he seems to need'.[6] However, Moorcock clearly had a certain amount of time for Carter, and he admired many of the authors included in the Ballantine series. While it commenced under the sign of Tolkien, Carter's editorial processing brought together a disparate range of writers and writing, much of it predating *The Lord of the Rings* by decades or (in the case of some of the works Carter anthologised) centuries. Fantasy was being organised more definitively during the 1970s, in part due to Tolkien's catalysing influence, but it was evolving in manners that created complex social and cultural networks, rather than a single tightly defined lineage. While the fear that fantastic creativity might be reduced to predictable patterns is one that was (and still is) often expressed, in practice, diverse interlocking and jostling fantastic constellations have co-existed for an extremely long time, sometimes fractiously, but very often productively.

Some of the different directions Fantasy framings could take can be seen by glancing at the preoccupations of societies established in the 1960s and 1970s. The Mythopoeic Society was founded in 1967 to study fantastic literature in general, and while it took Tolkien and his fellow Inklings C. S. Lewis and Charles Williams as its 'three core authors', articles in the first ten years of its journal *Mythlore* discussed works ranging from Sumerian myth, Virgil's *Aeneid* and Arthurian material to more recent publications by T. H. White, Dorothy L. Sayers,

[6] Moorcock, *Epic Pooh*, [p. 14].

Lloyd Alexander and Richard Adams.[7] The British Fantasy Society spun off from the British Science Fiction Association in 1971, publishing a newsy *Bulletin* and a magazine, *Dark Horizons*, that contained a fluctuating mixture of articles, fiction, poetry and art relating to Fantasy and Horror.[8] The approaches fostered by the British Fantasy Society often included grimmer visions, vibrant parodies and more urgent forms of politics. As well as Moorcock's essay, the Society's early booklets included a centenary tribute to William Hope Hodgson, a send-up of John Norman's intensely misogynistic Gor books and a brief spoof of Conan-style adventures magnificently entitled *Longbore the Inexhaustible* (1978).[9] In 1975, the World Fantasy Convention was held for the first time in H. P. Lovecraft's hometown, Providence, Rhode Island. At the convention's awards ceremony, Patricia A. McKillip was presented with the inaugural World Fantasy Award for Best Novel for *The Forgotten Beasts of Eld* (1974), a wonderful story of kind creatures, cautious connections and ambivalent magics that had been published when its author was just twenty-six. The award for best short story went to Robert Aickman, a

7 'About the Society', *Mythopoeic Society*, http://www.mythsoc.org/about.htm; *Mythlore Index Plus*, compiled by Janet Brennan Croft and Edith Crowe (2012–), http://www.mythsoc.org/press/mythlore-index-plus.htm.

8 See David Sutton, 'A History of the BFS: The Early Years: 1970–1984', in *Silver Rhapsody*, ed. by John Carter and Jan Edwards, British Fantasy Society Booklet No. 23 (1996).

9 David Sutton (ed.), *William Hope Hodgson: A Centenary Tribute 1877–1977*, British Fantasy Society Booklet No. 2 (1977); 'Norma N. Johns', *Bodoman of Sor*, British Fantasy Society Booklet No. 1 (1977); Adrian Cole, *Longbore the Inexhaustible*, British Fantasy Society Booklet No. 3 (1978).

determinedly individual British writer of 'strange stories'. He received his award for 'Pages from a Young Girl's Journal' (1973), an elegant, creepy Gothic fiction set in early-nineteenth-century Ravenna. This is a narrative with self-consciously literary roots: Percy Shelley and Lord Byron pass through, and the story plays with an awareness that Byron was transformed into one of the first literary vampires by John William Polidori. Best Collection went to Manly Wade Wellman, a veteran of the pulps. Wellman received the award for an anthology of fantastical and horrific stories published by Carcosa, a small press named after an 'ancient and famous' fallen city that was invented by Ambrose Bierce, picked up by Robert W. Chambers and incorporated into the weird tradition by Lovecraft and his circle.[10] Ian and Betty Ballantine won a special professional award for their publishing work, and a lifetime achievement award was presented to Robert Bloch, most famous as the creator of *Psycho* (1959), but a longstanding author of fiction across a wide range of genres.

Something was emerging or changing form in such assemblies, and Tolkien and his works were certainly parts of it, but, as the preceding discussion demonstrates, when organisations began to brand themselves as being concerned with Fantasy, they drew under that umbrella a complicated array of authors, works, audiences and concerns. Some parts of this array related closely to Tolkien – his compatriots in the Inklings, elements of his scholarly

[10] Ambrose Bierce, 'An Inhabitant of Carcosa', in *Tales of Soldiers and Civilians* (San Francisco: E. L. G. Steele, 1891), pp. 241–7 (pp. 244, 247).

interests, some of his influences – but other parts differed considerably from Tolkien's legendarium. Tolkien had written to Waldman that he believed his work should 'be "high", purged of the gross', but this was not the case for many comic or ironic fantasies that preceded or came after him, or for the American pulp tradition. Many fantasies have graphically condemned the brutality of war, drawing on histories and conventions with very different emphases to Tolkien's. The Gothic mode gets its tendrils into almost everything sooner or later: while *The Lord of the Rings* is not straightforwardly a Gothic novel, the Gothic is in play in aspects including the Black Riders' pursuit of the hobbits, the sickly lights of Minas Morgul and Sam and Frodo's encounters with Shelob's webs, stinger and scuttling legs. Readers recognised such affinities at an early stage. Gothic works not only haunt the portals of the house of Fantasy but have regularly been welcomed in as familiar guests.

That Fantasy is a mode that mixes, shifts and combines is undeniably one of its strengths. In this respect, Moorcock was right to be concerned that *The Lord of the Rings* might be taken uncontentiously to be Fantasy's quintessence. There are some parts of Tolkien's manifesto in his letter to Waldman that could be considered as defining general traits of Fantasy – the desire to conjure other worlds, for example, or the importance of collaborations with predecessors and audiences. However, there are also more specific assertions. The conception Tolkien describes draws together the nations of the United Kingdom and the northern European countries on which his scholarly interests principally focused, but this grouping side-lines and at points negatively stereotypes other cultural backgrounds. *The Lord of the Rings* has an enduring worldwide appeal, but, like Moorcock, many recent creators and critics have seen some of Tolkien's positions, developed in his own very particular contexts, as being problematic when afforded too domineering an influence.[11] The northern European medievalist paradigm Tolkien sketched out has sometimes threatened to exclude other modes of fantastic creativity. While Tolkien was seeking in the early 1950s to persuade Waldman that audiences might take to his strange and peculiar works, regardless of how difficult they were to position in terms of mainstream notions of literary value, subsequent writers have often had to fight to convince publishers and readers of the value of fantasies that differ greatly from the expectations his works established.

Nevertheless, the nature of Fantasy as a form that places reappropriation and reconfiguration at its heart means that Tolkien's words have rarely been treated as the last ones. Junot Díaz's novel *The Brief Wondrous Life of Oscar Wao* (2007) spends a lot of time playing with Tolkien as a touchstone valued in different ways by different people. Díaz's creative use of *The Lord of the Rings* sometimes leans into stereotypes, rather than hewing strictly to the fine details. When his narrator Yunior asserts that 'At the end of *The Return of the King*, Sauron's evil was taken by "a great wind" and neatly

11 See, for example, Dimitra Fimi, *Tolkien, Race and Cultural History: From Fairies to Hobbits* (Basingstoke: Palgrave Macmillan, 2009) and Helen Young, *Race and Popular Fantasy Literature: Habits of Whiteness* (New York and Abingdon: Routledge, 2016).

"blown away", with no lasting consequences to our heroes', he employs a pretty loose definition of 'end' and offers a rather debateable reading of Frodo's fate.[12] However, Díaz's novel is not trying to be absolutely faithful in reporting Tolkien's plots (Yunior himself is not a big fan). Instead, it seeks to activate readers' familiarity with the forms and affects of the stories Tolkien is famed for telling. When Yunior asserts that the dictator Rafael Trujillo 'dominated Santo Domingo like it was his very own private Mordor', the analogy communicates immediately and powerfully.[13] The sorts of creative (mis)readings Díaz employs might be evoked to answer some of Moorcock's objections: while Tolkien was in many respects conservative as a person, and there are indubitably elements in his works that can be read as endorsing conservative positions, these do not constitute the whole story. Readers and reconfigurers do not receive *The Lord of the Rings* as an immutable block of ideology. Instead, it has proved to have a great deal of 'scope for other minds and hands' to rework it, expand it, critique it and make it their own.

This is not to say that Tolkien's works are infinitely appropriable. While Díaz makes powerful use of Tolkien's novel, he is sharp on how its specificities can act to exclude. While Díaz's title character, Oscar Wao, loves *The Lord of the Rings*, his first reading of the book (at the age of nine, on the recommendation of 'his favourite librarian') is derailed when Tolkien's world-building

[12] Junot Díaz, *The Brief Wondrous Life of Oscar Wao* (London: Faber and Faber, 2007), p. 156.
[13] Díaz, *Life of Oscar Wao*, p. 224.

appears to place those like him on the side of evil: 'Got through almost the entire trilogy, but then the line "and out of Far Harad black men like half-trolls" and he had to stop, his head and heart hurting too much'.[14] This experience of rejection does not prevent Oscar from wishing to become a 'Dominican Tolkien', but his sense that a Dominican *Lord of the Rings* would need to be substantively different highlights the fact that Tolkien's fantasies imaginatively accommodate some readers more easily than others. Nor is this an unintended consequence of Tolkien's design. The letter to Waldman sets up a series of implicit hierarchies when Tolkien states that he intended to produce a work redolent of an air which is not that of 'Italy and the Aegean' and 'still less [that of] the East'. Tolkien's heroes, extrapolated from his perceptions of northern climes, are associated with whiteness (relatively straightforwardly) and with masculinity (in a more complicated manner, with approved manly behaviour taking in a range of virtues beyond the martial – Gandalf's wily wisdom, Sam's down-to-earth steadfastness, Aragorn's herblore and so on). Many critics have noted imaginative gaps or absences in Middle-earth, and many of those who engage creatively with Tolkien's work have sought to address these lacunae. As Una McCormack has documented, creative-critical responses to Tolkien in fanfiction circles have given considerable time and space to 'establishing female presences, queer presences, and urban

[14] Díaz, *Life of Oscar Wao*, p. 307. This passage is discussed further by Una McCormack (see reference below) and by Maria Sachiko Cecire in the fifth chapter of *Re-Enchanted: The Rise of Children's Fantasy Literature in the Twentieth Century* (Minneapolis: University of Minnesota Press, 2019).

working class presences in a text chiefly concerned with the masculine and the heroic', working to 'negotiate and repair representational gaps'.[15] Some readers are offered numerous straightforward surrogates in Middle-earth; for others, further imaginative work is needful. However, such work has been done rewardingly and well, creating an extensive body of playful, contradictory, hospitable lore and legend that has become far larger than any single mind can fully encompass.

While fans often have powerful attachments to Tolkien's original modes of framing, this does not render him beyond reproach in their eyes. Nor does it prevent them from enjoying modifications, parodies and critiques of his designs. Tolkien's works create a space, but his own high seriousness does not constrain or determine all the possible modes of interaction within that space. *The Lord of the Rings* is complete in itself, but it has been built upon many times and in numerous different directions: by its own author in his further writings; by readers through their personal contexts, juxtapositions, affinities and resistances; by publishers through reworkings and processes of association; and by adaptations in numerous forms, from modified retellings including Peter Jackson's film trilogy (2001–3) and its legacies (see Figure 0.1), to direct (if formally complex) reworkings such as Reiner Knizia's *Lord of the Rings* board game (2000), to creative expansions such as Monolith Productions' video game *Middle-earth: Shadow of Mordor*

[15] Una McCormack, 'Finding Ourselves in the (Un)Mapped Lands: Women's Reparative Readings of *The Lord of the Rings*', in *Perilous and Fair: Women in the Works and Life of J. R. R. Tolkien*, ed. by Janet Brennan Croft and Leslie A. Donovan (Altadena, CA: Mythopoeic Press, 2015), pp. 309–26 (pp. 310, 311).

FIGURE 0.1 Bilbo and Frodo Baggins's Bag End, as built on the Hobbiton movie set where parts of *The Lord of the Rings* (2001–3) and *The Hobbit* (2012–14) trilogies were filmed.
Alex Livesey/FIFA via Getty Images.

(2014), to the vast plethora of subsequent works that have taken Tolkienian elves or quest forms or languages as inspirations or provocations. This is at the heart of Tolkien's achievement as a creator of Fantasy. What he wrought is not his alone; rather, it belongs in a plethora of different ways to tens of millions who have engaged with it seriously or casually, with love or with hatred, with devotion to its details or an eye towards changing them. While we commonly attribute works of Fantasy to particular authors, a large part of the secret of their success is the ease with which they can become ours.

* * *

The preceding sketch has, I hope, given a sense of some of the main areas this book will engage with. Its chapters will examine Fantasy's ability to shape the ways we construct societies and beliefs with language; the advantages and problems inherent in Fantasy's iterative processes; its deep roots in diverse forms of art and storytelling; its role as a parallel or alternative to realist and rationalist models of culture and understanding; the vast potential of its multimedia world-building; and its status as the common property of communities who engage with loving devotion and clear-eyed criticality, often simultaneously. However, in beginning with this overture, I have been taking an elliptical approach to a major challenge. I have been using the word 'Fantasy' to characterise certain works, cultures and affects, but in doing so, I have avoided stipulating exactly what I mean. There are reasons for this avoidance (reasons I hope I will establish as being good ones), but at this point, the question must be asked. If this book sets out to introduce Fantasy, what precisely is it that it presumes to introduce?

This is a question that is both ostensibly straightforward and irresolvably intricate in its implications. The word 'fantasy' can denote a wide range of things: an 'image impressed on the mind by an object of sense' or a hallucination; a true mental representation or a deceptive figment; tastefulness and ingeniousness or capriciousness and falsity.[16] It means and has meant these things with different levels of intensity in different contexts and in changing historical circumstances. Its more specialist uses in discussions of culture have also fluctuated considerably.

[16] Terms taken from the various definitions in 'fantasy | phantasy, n.', *Oxford English Dictionary*, 3rd edition (Oxford: Oxford University Press, 2000–), https://www.oed.com/view/Entry/68119.

When writing to Waldman in the early 1950s, Tolkien could not easily call on the word 'fantasy' to describe his work, although the term lurked in longstanding byways of literary-critical discussion, serving variously as a label for narratives of the strange and otherworldly and as imagination's other.[17] The word also appeared in the names of periodicals like *Fantastic Adventures* (1939–53), *The Magazine of Fantasy & Science Fiction* (founded in 1949) and *Science Fantasy* (published under that name from 1950 to 1966), although Tolkien's sense of what he was doing did not really align with the stories in such magazines. However, twenty-five years later, Fantasy was a term that could be used to brand book series and organise traditions, serving as a concept around which people could gather in societies to celebrate what it described.

One way of proceeding with this introduction would be to continue in a cultural-historical vein by examining modern genre communities, their canons and their concerns. However, while this is a mode I will return to at various points, for me, an account constructed solely in this manner would fail to recognise the full range of things that Fantasy might mean. As the inclusions in the Ballantine series show, the sharpened sense of Fantasy that emerged in the 1960s and 1970s extended backwards in time to take in older creations, making them legible in new and powerful ways. What Fantasy means now is entangled with a deep heritage of works, social fashionings and cultural traditions. The easiest ways into much

[17] I discuss the binary between imagination and fantasy or fancy in Chapter 4.

older art and literature for contemporary audiences are along trails blazed backwards by modern fantasies. While the shape of Fantasy as we now understand it coalesced relatively recently, it has drawn in myriad pasts and remade them in versions of its image.

Such two-way processes of definition and redefinition are not exclusive to the ways that Fantasy operates. Laurence Sterne's mischievous, metafictional novelty *The Life and Opinions of Tristram Shandy*, first published between 1759 and 1767, was eagerly claimed as a post-modern work in the latter half of the twentieth century, providing a new way to engage with its intricacies. It might be (and has been) objected that calling *Tristram Shandy* postmodern is anachronistic, and in a technical sense, this might be correct. However, just because a particular name was not current at a given time does not mean that the affects and structures it later came to signify could not be perceived. The unconscious existed as word, reality and feeling before the work of Sigmund Freud gave rise to its modern inflections and prominence. While eighteenth-century readers of *Tristram Shandy* would not have called its prose postmodern, they nevertheless recognised its self-conscious playfulness, theatricality and referentially: forms of engagement very similar to those later practised by postmodern writers. The connection is a valuable one in that it lets us say useful things about how *Tristram Shandy* works while also destabilising our sense that a postmodern sensibility only inheres in a particular chronological moment. Humans have enjoyed exposing the mechanisms of stories for a very long time; they have also enjoyed and profited from imagining deities, magic and alternative worlds. Just as the connection between *Tristram Shandy* and postmodernism can be reciprocally revealing, so too can a long history of Fantasy.

This is particularly true because Fantasy is a form obsessed with pasts and how these might have turned out differently. Fantasy narratives are commonly set in a historical past or in a world that resembles a historical past in many respects (although crucially not all). When fantasies are set in the contemporary world, they often deal with the intrusions of ancient monsters, fairies or old gods. Like epics, fantasies commonly begin *in medias res*, or (like *The Lord of the Rings*) towards the end of a long succession of ages. Events in Fantasy narratives often turn out to be contingent on past events, the facts of which are slowly uncovered as the story progresses. Fantasies enjoy plots that echo and loop, but they are also often keen to show that while the present is shaped by the past, it is not wholly in thrall to it. Prophecies in Fantasy are rarely as transparent or as foolproof as they first appear. Stories that seem to be repetitions turn out to have new twists. Fantasy creators find pleasure and wisdom through reworking myths, legends, fairy tales and archetypes, but such processes constitute transformative revivifications rather than simple repetitions, taking older materials and making them speak differently to later moments. It is therefore unsurprising that Fantasy as a form is more self-consciously contingent on what has come before than many other kinds of artistic fashioning.

Some scholars have sought to differentiate a longer fantastic cultural tradition from more recent developments in order to articulate processes of change. Brian Attebery has drawn a useful distinction between mode, genre and formula, which, while reductive in certain respects, is nevertheless a helpful tool for clarifying and differentiating. In my view, Attebery's earlier work is unduly dismissive when it comes to formula, describing Fantasy in this guise as 'a form of popular escapist literature that combines stock characters and devices [...] into a predictable plot in which the perennially understaffed forces of good triumph over a monolithic evil'.[18] Attebery identifies fantasy-as-formula with the modern bookshop category, describing it as 'essentially a commercial product' that is 'restricted in scope, recent in origin, and specialized in audience and appeal'. By contrast, he argues that the broadest definition would consider Fantasy to be 'a sophisticated mode of storytelling characterized by stylistic playfulness, self-reflexiveness, and a subversive treatment of established orders of society and thought'.[19] Attebery sees this mode as operating throughout cultural history, often as an artistic impulse ostensibly set in opposition to descriptive or mimetic representations of reality, but in fact intimately entangled with such representations. His third frame – genre – sits between the mode and the formula, selecting more discerningly and taking in a longer history than the bookshop category without pushing out too far into the expansive territory of the mode, which in its broadest sense might be said to

[18] Brian Attebery, *Strategies of Fantasy* (Bloomington and Indianapolis: Indiana University Press, 1992), p. 1. Attebery's more recent criticism nuances his position regarding formula significantly: see, for example, *Stories about Stories: Fantasy and the Remaking of Myth* (Oxford: Oxford University Press, 2013).

[19] Attebery, *Strategies*, pp. 2, 1.

encompass almost everything. Attebery's distinctions can helpfully be linked with historical markers: the mode emerged along with human cultures; the genre became distinct at the point when self-consciously realistic forms began to be defined against it; and the modern formula is the most recent innovation, emerging as the sum of Moorcock's fears in the 1960s and 1970s. As Attebery recognises, this picture does not fully account for the difficulties of delineating what is and is not Fantasy, but it does show that what people mean when they say Fantasy depends a great deal on how terms are set, and on who sets them.

Attebery was far from the first to grapple with the issue of definition, although, as I will discuss shortly, his thinking provided some important breakthroughs in picturing where Fantasy begins and ends. Attempts at definition appeared in many of the earliest critical writings on Fantasy. Subsequently, the difficulty of providing a neat summation has become one of Fantasy scholarship's enduring clichés. In his 1986 *Critical Terms for Science Fiction and Fantasy* (a book that, like much early research on genre fiction, places Fantasy as a secondary concern), Gary K. Wolfe provided a helpful summary of the definitions available at the time he was writing. While there was considerable variation, he identified several points of commonality that indicate core positions upon which numerous commentators have agreed.

Among the critics Wolfe surveyed, there was a strong consensus that the quintessential characteristic of works of Fantasy is that they deal with the impossible. In 1953, Rosalie Moore and Reginald Bretnor described Fantasy as 'Imaginative fiction in which no logical attempt is made, or needed, to justify the "impossible" content of the story.'[20] In 1975, Colin Manlove, author of one of the earliest book-length studies of Fantasy fiction, offered an exacting technical definition, arguing that a fantasy was '*A fiction evoking wonder and containing a substantial and irreducible element of supernatural or impossible worlds, beings or objects with which the mortal characters in the story or the readers become on at least partly familiar terms.*'[21] In 1979, Roger C. Schlobin provided a concise possibility: 'That corpus in which the impossible is primary in its quantity or centrality.'[22] Wolfe himself suggested that a fantasy is a 'fictional narrative describing events that the reader believes to be Impossible', although he rightly notes that this definition places a great deal of weight on a reader's understanding rather than on 'structural or thematic characteristics'.[23] He also notes that 'impossible' is a rather imprecise term, and one that is potentially hugely capacious, taking in a great quantity of Science Fiction and Horror (although this is not necessarily a problem; as we

[20] Rosalie Moore, 'Science Fiction and the Main Stream', in *Modern Science Fiction: Its Meaning and its Future*, ed. by Reginald Bretnor (New York: Coward-McCann, 1953), pp. 91–118. (p. 95). In her essay, Moore writes that she concurs with a definition Bretnor proposed. The words are sometimes attributed directly to Bretnor. In some later citations, a mischievous typo has crept in, creating the phantom Fantasy critic Reginald Eretnor.

[21] C. N. Manlove, *Modern Fantasy: Five Studies* (Cambridge: Cambridge University Press, 1975), p. 1.

[22] Roger C. Schlobin, *The Literature of Fantasy: A Comprehensive, Annotated Bibliography of Modern Fantasy Fiction* (New York: Garland Publishing, 1979), pp. x–xi.

[23] Gary K. Wolfe, *Critical Terms for Science Fiction and Fantasy* (New York, Westport, CN and London: Greenwood Press, 1986), p. 38.

have seen, Fantasy communities have often been keen to encourage such takings in).

While impossibility has some issues as a criterion for defining Fantasy – not least the problem of subjectivity that Wolfe raises – it generally makes good sense when it is used for drawing lines. A fire is not intrinsically fantastical for most modern audiences, whereas a talking fire is. A person shooting a gun is not fantastical; an elven wizard summoning an air elemental is. Within any given work, there will, of course, be a balance between realistic evocation and fantastic elaboration. Even when it veers from reality in certain respects, a fantasy will commonly cleave closely to it elsewhere, mixing the quotidian and the fantastical to achieve hybrid effects. Similarly, even strictly realist works often draw on fantastic artifices when they employ metaphors and dreams, as well as when they use habituated conventions. Few people speak in the ways characters in novels usually speak, but we commonly parse novel dialogue as realistic, having internalised its forms of artifice so that we decode them unthinkingly as being natural. However, realist works tend to keep their fantastic flourishes at the level of language or in their characters' minds. By contrast, works of Fantasy bring impossible things brazenly into their worlds.

While definitions based around impossibility identify Fantasy based primarily on how readers view its content, other definitions place more emphasis on describing its affect or functions. In 1973, Ursula K. Le Guin described Fantasy somewhat polemically as 'a different approach to reality, an alternative technique for apprehending and coping with existence. It is not antirational but pararational; not realistic, but surrealistic, superrealistic, a heightening of reality.'[24] In 1981, Rosemary Jackson's pioneering psychoanalytic study *Fantasy: The Literature of Subversion* stated that its subject was 'a literature of desire, which seeks that which is experienced as absence or loss.'[25] In 1984, Kathryn Hume characterised Fantasy as 'the deliberate departure from the limits of what is usually accepted as real and normal'.[26] In all these definitions, Fantasy serves a contrastive and implicitly critical function. By showing us other worlds, it highlights what our own takes for granted or lacks. We might add to such definitions José B. Monléon's contention that 'one of the basic mechanisms of the fantastic is to question the premises of the natural' and China Miéville's related assertion that 'No matter how commodified the fantastic in its various forms might be, we need fantasy to think the world, and to change it.'[27] Monléon and Miéville are writing from Marxist perspectives, and both are somewhat conflicted regarding Fantasy's revolutionary potential. Monléon argues that fantastic works acted in the nineteenth century to 'help modify hegemonic discourse in order to justify the survival of bourgeois society' (a suspicion similar to Moorcock's regarding Tolkien), while

[24] Ursula K. Le Guin, 'From Elfland to Poughkeepsie', in *The Language of the Night: Essays on Fantasy and Science Fiction*, ed. by Susan Wood (New York: Putnam, 1979), pp. 83–96 (p. 84).

[25] Rosemary Jackson, *Fantasy: The Literature of Subversion* (New York and London: Methuen, 1981), p. 2.

[26] Kathryn Hume, *Fantasy and Mimesis: Responses to Reality in Western Literature* (New York and London: Methuen, 1984), p. xii.

[27] José B. Monléon, *A Specter is Haunting Europe: A Sociohistorical Approach to the Fantastic* (Princeton, NJ: Princeton University Press, 1990), p. 9; China Miéville, Editorial Introduction to *Symposium: Marxism and Fantasy*, *Historical Materialism*, 10.4 (2002), 39–49 (p. 48).

Miéville's hope that Fantasy offers chances to rethink the world is balanced by fears about the ease with which it can be incorporated into the flow of capitalist systems.[28] Nevertheless, both recognise Fantasy's power for rendering evocative alternatives. Not for nothing does Monléon remind us that *The Communist Manifesto* (1848) opens by asserting that 'A spectre is haunting Europe'.[29]

In these conceptions, Fantasy has something in common with the philosophical thought experiment, in which a hypothetical situation is posited so that its potential consequences can be worked through. However, while philosophical thought experiments can often be rather concise or austere, fantasies commonly indulge in playful elaborations. Fantasy has long served as a creative space within which those not comfortable with the status quo can imagine different possibilities, but precisely because the space Fantasy opens is creative and generative, it seldom lends itself to the straightforward transmission of a single ideology. While some fantasies directly examine philosophical problems or posit considered political alternatives, this is rarely everything a work of Fantasy does. This sometimes proves frustrating for those who would prefer that texts be clear what they are about, but it reflects the fact that any given fantasy is 'made of multiple writings, drawn from many cultures and entering into mutual relations of dialogue, parody, contestation'.[30]

[28] Monléon, *A Specter*, p. 14.

[29] Karl Marx and Friedrich Engels, *The Communist Manifesto*, ed. by David McLellan (Oxford: Oxford University Press, 2008), p. 2

[30] Roland Barthes, 'The Death of the Author', in *Image Music Text*, translated by Stephen Heath (London: Fontana, 1977), pp. 142–8 (p. 148).

This is itself a political proposition (as most propositions are), but it is not only political. Many fantasies make their most powerful interventions by approaching problems subtly or obliquely. People's tolerance for being lectured is sharply limited when compared with the enjoyment of seeing a world anew and being asked to play a role in its imaginative creation and interpretation.

Short definitions can be helpful for sketching out things that Fantasy can do, include or be, but in trying to capture the quintessence of Fantasy in a pithy sentence or two, they tend either to express a critical preference or describe a rich form blandly. Partly as a result, some critics have chosen to focus on building toolsets for analysis, constructing frameworks rather than laying out prescriptive rules. Farah Mendlesohn is particularly notable in this regard for her work examining 'the means by which the fantastic enters [...] narrated world[s].' In *Rhetorics of Fantasy* (2008), she argues that fantasies can helpfully be divided into four categories: 'the portal-quest, the immersive, the intrusive, and the liminal'.[31] These are useful terms, so it is worthwhile pausing briefly to unpack them so they can be employed as this book proceeds. In a portal-quest, characters from our world travel into a fantastic realm. This is particularly common in children's fantasies and perhaps most familiar from stories like C. S. Lewis's *The Lion, the Witch and the Wardrobe* (1950), although the technique also underpins a lot of earlier fantastical narratives such as Lucian's satire *A True Story* (second century CE) or Jonathan Swift's

[31] Farah Mendlesohn, *Rhetorics of Fantasy* (Middletown, CT: Wesleyan University Press, 2008), p. xiv

Gulliver's Travels (1726). In an immersive fantasy, the story takes place entirely within a secondary world imaginatively posited as complete in itself: this is a mode that lends itself to long-form storytelling like Robin Hobb's Realm of the Elderlings books (1995–2017) or Robert Jordan's Wheel of Time series (1990–2013), although there are numerous shorter fantasies that make effective use of worlds imagined to be separate from our own. In an intrusion fantasy, fantastical elements impinge on our world and must be resisted or accommodated. This is a form that has particularly strong affinities with Horror and Gothic; examples might include *Buffy the Vampire Slayer* (1997–2003) or (from certain viewpoints) Susanna Clarke's *Jonathan Strange & Mr Norrell* (2004). Finally, liminal fantasies are those in which 'we are invited to cross the threshold into the fantastic, *but choose not to do so*', leading to the unfurling of a 'seemingly ordinary story' that '*feels* like fantasy'.[32] Liminal fantasies are rarer birds and tend to be most prevalent in media where considerable work is left for the audience to do; liminality often is easier to conjure with the gaps between words or comics panels than in a more totalising medium like film (although evoking liminality in film is far from impossible). The examples of liminal Fantasy Mendlesohn gives include M. John Harrison's *The Course of the Heart* (1992) and John Crowley's *Little, Big* (1981), but liminality also forms a part of audiences' relationships with many fantastical works, as they experience the hesitation between uncanny reality and the genuinely marvellous that characterises Tzvetan Todorov's description of the effects of

[32] Mendlesohn, *Rhetorics*, p. xxiii.

the fantastic.[33] One of the effects of Fantasy is to suspend its audiences between two worlds; for Todorov, this is an unsettling experience, but it may also be a delightful, rapturous or nostalgic one. One of the strengths of Mendlesohn's taxonomy is that by thinking about such relations, it models many of the key sensations that arise when reading fantasies, as well as common conventions that structure Fantasy narratives.

While Mendlesohn's system is both analytically powerful and commendably flexible, she is clear-eyed about its limitations, dedicating a fifth chapter of *Rhetorics of Fantasy* to irregular fantasies that operate in ways that subvert her taxonomy. As with most attempts to categorise Fantasy, certain examples and characteristics remain very difficult to pin down. This is partly inherent in the form: it is not in the nature of fantasies to fit neatly into boxes constructed by Enlightenment-inspired classification systems. However, this does not mean that the attempt is meaningless. Fantasies love applying patterns and systems as well as contradicting them. While structuralist accounts like Vladimir Propp's *The Morphology of the Folktale* (1928) or Joseph Campbell's much-cited *The Hero with a Thousand Faces* (1949) are better at tracing commonalities than accounting for the weird specificities that make a particular work of fantasy worthwhile and engaging, critics looking for repeated forms and archetypes in Fantasy will find them in abundance. However, they will also find those forms and archetypes subverted,

33 Tzvetan Todorov, *The Fantastic: A Structural Approach to a Literary Genre*, translated by Richard Howard (Ithaca, NY: Cornell University Press 1975).

remodelled and discarded as Fantasy's traditions play, twist, reconfigure and innovate.

Prescriptive definitions and categorical systems can be useful for delineating strands or mechanisms of Fantasy, but they often find it a slippery subject that refuses to remain within hard borders. Consequently, some critics have developed looser, more descriptive approaches. Attebery has helpfully suggested that genres 'may be approached as "fuzzy sets," meaning they are defined not by boundaries but by a center'.[34] While a binary definition demands that we determine whether or not a given work is Fantasy, a fuzzy set invites us to think about degrees of resemblance. If we had to class Bram Stoker's *Dracula* (1897) as belonging to a single genre, we would probably be more likely to choose Gothic or Horror than Fantasy, but the impossible actions of its eponymous villain would certainly allow it to be placed within a fuzzy set of Fantasy – probably not at the centre, but certainly within a field of influence. When thinking through this concept, Attebery conducted an informal survey of friends to try and suggest what might lie closest to the centre of a fantastical fuzzy set, asking his participants to rate a series of works on a seven-point scale, where one was '*quintessentially* fantasy' and seven was '*by no means* fantasy'.[35] It will probably come as no surprise that the text Attebery's participants identified as being closest to a quintessential Fantasy was *The Lord of the Rings*, a result repeated every time I have conducted the same kind of exercise with students. However, this reflects an Anglophone bias. Readers in other languages would be likely to configure

[34] Attebery, *Strategies*, p. 12. [35] Attebery, *Strategies*, p. 13.

a fuzzy set of Fantasy differently. The configuration of a given community's fuzzy set is also likely to change over time. Around 1990, Attebery's participants placed Roger Zelazny's Amber series (1970–91), E. R. Eddison's *The Worm Ouroborus* (1922), Lewis Carroll's *Alice's Adventures in Wonderland* (1865) and Ursula Le Guin's Earthsea books (1968–2001) close to the centre of the set he sketched. One imagines that if a large-scale survey was conducted now, some of those texts might be pushed further out, displaced by modern juggernauts like George R. R. Martin's A Song of Ice and Fire (1996–), its TV adaptation *Game of Thrones* (2011–19) or J. K. Rowling's Harry Potter books (1997–2007). Fuzzy sets are by their nature less stable than hard definitions, but this is one of the things that makes them useful for registering transformations. They can also be used to map subgenres and consider counterfactuals. What would sit at the centre of a fuzzy set of Young Adult Fantasy, or how might a set look if we chose to make its focal point a work like Michael Ende's *The Neverending Story* (1979) or Ben Okri's *The Famished Road* (1991) or CD Projekt Red's Witcher games (2007–) or CLAMP's *X/1999* (1992–)?[36] Our ability to imagine such reconfigurations suggests that Fantasy is not an eternal verity, but rather a cultural formation in dynamic motion, shaped and reshaped by the questions asked by its creators and audiences.

[36] Farah Mendlesohn has conducted an interesting thought experiment along these lines while considering the status of Mervyn Peake. See 'Peake and the Fuzzy Set of Fantasy: Some Informal Thoughts', in *Miracle Enough: Papers on the Works of Mervyn Peake*, ed. by G. Peter Winnington (Newcastle-upon-Tyne: Cambridge Scholars Publishing, 2013), pp. 61–74.

Considering these active interventions moves us towards a more sociological approach to Fantasy. One of the earliest definitions of Science Fiction is Damon Knight's: he claimed pragmatically that Science Fiction 'means what we point to when we say it'.[37] One way of reading this is as a democratic descriptivist position. In this respect, it has a lot to recommend it. It is an attractive truth to think that the meanings of words and concepts are best determined by communal use, rather than through authoritarian assertions about the forms that usage should take. While to assert that fantasies are the things that people call fantasies is somewhat circular, it is also powerfully true. I have a lot of time for approaches along these lines, which is why I began this introduction by looking at some of the things certain communities have brought together under the rubric of Fantasy, rather than with the definition question. However, there are also some ambiguities in Knight's definition, the most important being who his 'we' signifies. In practice, the make-up of this 'we' is likely to be a complex array of interpreters across different cultures, ranging from the publishing industry and institutions to authors and fandoms, and from broad general populations to individual readers. Opinions within this array will be far from monolithic. Different communities and groupings will not necessarily share a consensus regarding Fantasy, and different individuals are likely to be aligned with a series of overlapping consensuses, subscribing to some more wholeheartedly than others. While Knight's definition is accurate, it is

[37] Damon Knight, *In Search of Wonder: Essays on Modern Science Fiction* (Chicago, IL: Advent, 1956), p. 1.

also incomplete, failing to acknowledge the roles played by discussion, negotiation, experience and persuasion. We are never exactly of one mind, and stating that something is so does not make it so for others (except in certain fantasies, which usually dwell on the dystopian implications of such a power).[38] While things might be made fantasies by naming them as such, some namings will be hotly contested, and not all will necessarily stick.

I lay out these approaches and complications to make it clear that this book intervenes in a continuing conversation in which a wide range of different critics, audiences and institutions have voiced opinions. This conversation would become something fundamentally different and far less valuable if it stopped being a conversation and became a series of diktats or edicts. This is why I have called this book ***An Introduction to Fantasy***, rather than ***The** Introduction to Fantasy*. It will suggest approaches I hope will be interesting and useful, but it will be adding a voice to ongoing discussions. I will present consensuses where I identify them, but the communities with which I intersect are not the only ones with stakes in the meaning of Fantasy, and, despite my efforts, there will inevitably be perspectives I overlook. While I hope this book's discussions will be broadly applicable, and while I will try and pick examples from a wide range of forms, types and traditions, the nature of my selections will be partly determined by my cultural framing and particular experiences. I have my own views and prejudices, and these will

[38] Ursula K. Le Guin's *The Lathe of Heaven* (New York: Avon Books, 1971) and Ann Leckie's *The Raven Tower* (London: Orbit, 2019) are two good books that engage with this conceit.

inevitably colour my account. Most of my examples will be things I personally find interesting or take joy in; your mileage may vary. In Attebery's terms, the conception of Fantasy I will trace has most in common with the mode: a playful, self-reflexive and subversive cultural form traceable throughout cultural history that evokes the unreal and impossible in ways that call into question received truths. However, I will also be arguing that Fantasy creates messier and more entangled relationships between histories, creators and audiences than a focus on form readily accounts for. While works of Fantasy are the easiest of its manifestations to discuss, it is the ways that Fantasy works in communities and cultures that ultimately constitute its greatest contributions.

Enough theorising for the moment. Rather than continuing to postulate, it seems better at this point to give examples of the kinds of works this book will examine under the rubric of Fantasy. I will relate these to Tolkien as an accepted common reference point, but my intention will be to show how different in form, content and approach works can be while still existing meaningfully in networks of fantastic relations.

We might first consider *Sir Gawain and the Green Knight*, the fourteenth-century Middle English romance that Tolkien edited early in his professional career. This is a poem that looks in many respects like Fantasy to modern eyes. It features courts, combat, magic and high-stakes moral encounters. Ostensibly, it takes the form of a quest-narrative, and in some respects quite a traditional one. Read in the context of Tolkien, it can serve to highlight some of his formal innovations. The people who quest in older romances are usually knights like Gawain, or nobles, or princes, not bourgeois individuals like Tolkien's hobbits, who see themselves as being temperamentally unsuited to such actions. While a 'minstrel of Gondor' eventually celebrates the triumph over Sauron by singing of 'Frodo of the Nine Fingers and the Ring of Doom', we have been on a long journey through different realms and registers of language by the time we reach that point.[39]

By contrast, *Sir Gawain and the Green Knight* opens in an environment considerably more rarefied than the 'dear old Shire', commencing at the court of King Arthur on the eve of the new year. The king's celebrations are unexpectedly interrupted by a giant green man, described in Tolkien's translation as the 'mightiest on middle-earth in measure of height' ('On þe most on þe molde on mesure hyghe' (line 137)).[40] The intruder bears a huge axe and suggests a festive game: he will allow any knight present to strike him as hard a blow as they can with the axe, as long as that knight will allow him to do the same a year and a day hence. Sir Gawain takes up the challenge and beheads the Green Knight, but the Green Knight surprises the watching court by picking up his own severed head and leaving, reminding Gawain of his promise and telling him to seek him out at the Green Chapel for a 'nimble knock in return' (line 453). These supernatural events move the story decisively into the fantastic mode for many modern readers.

39 J. R. R. Tolkien, *The Lord of the Rings* (London: Grafton, 1992), p. 990.

40 Middle English text as given in J. R. R. Tolkien and E. V. Gordon (eds.), *Sir Gawain and the Green Knight* (Oxford: Clarendon Press, 1925). Modernised version as given in J. R. R. Tolkien, *Sir Gawain and the Green Knight, Pearl, and Sir Orfeo* (London: George Allen and Unwin, 1975).

Sir Gawain is a traditional knightly quester in that he sets out on his own – 'without fellowship' (line 714) in Tolkien's version. The adventuring party of fractious but complementary talents that has become an integral element of much modern Fantasy storytelling from Tolkien to *Dungeons & Dragons* to *Avatar: The Last Airbender* (2005–8) is less common in earlier literature (although there are important examples, from Tang Sanzang's companions in *Journey to the West* (sixteenth century) to the group that coalesces around Mina Harker in *Dracula*). Gawain quests as a lone individual, venturing forth into rough lands to do battle with the perilous obstacles that they throw up:

> So mony meruayl bi mount þer þe mon fyndez,
> Hit were to tore for to telle of þe tenþe dole.
> Sumwhyle wyth wormez he werrez and with wolues als,
> Sumwhyle wyth wodwos þat woned in þe knarrez,
> Boþe wyth bullez and berez and borez oþerquyle,
> And etaynez þat hym anelede of þe heȝe felle;

> So many a marvel in the mountains he met in those lands
> that 'twould be tedious the tenth part to tell you thereof.
> At whiles with worms he wars, and with wolves also,
> at whiles with wood-trolls that wandered in the crags,
> and with bulls and with bears and boars, too, at times;
> and with ogres that hounded him from the heights of the fells. (lines 718–23)

There are further consonances here with Tolkien's writing – the *Gawain* poet's wandering wood-trolls and hounding ogres resonate with antagonists that Bilbo and the dwarves encounter in the early chapters of *The Hobbit*. Interestingly, though, the *Gawain* narrative skims over such encounters, indicating both that such fights were already clichéd enough that a fourteenth-century audience could be expected to fill in the details and that such combats were not really the main point of interest in the story.

The denouement of *Sir Gawain* demonstrates that the form of the quest has always been more complex than a simple journey to a discovery or confrontation. Gawain is ultimately tested not in his ability to do violence but rather in his ability to keep his word. Arriving exhausted at a splendid castle, Gawain makes a bargain with its lord: they will exchange whatever they gain on three days during which the lord will hunt while Gawain rests. After flirting ambivalently each day with Sir Bertilak's supposed wife, Gawain passes on her kisses without betraying their source, fulfilling the terms of his agreement and keeping to a code of courtly discretion. However, on the third day, the lady presses upon him a girdle of green silk that she claims will protect him from harm. Afraid of the impending encounter with the Green Knight, Gawain does not reveal that he has accepted the girdle. When he reaches the Green Chapel, events transpire so that the Green Knight takes three swings at Gawain's neck, missing twice and nicking the skin with the final blow. The knight is revealed to be Gawain's erstwhile host, transformed by the magic of Morgan Le

Fay. While Bertilak is impressed with Gawain's conduct, Gawain is mortified by what he perceives to be his failure, which he admits on his return to court. He proposes to wear the green girdle as a mark of shame. Arthur – in this version of the story an excellent diplomat and moralist – proclaims that all his knights will wear such a badge, taking it as a mark of honour. Fantasy in *Sir Gawain* thus begins as a form of mystification, but eventually operates as a mechanism for revealing character. The circumstances of Gawain's tests are bizarrely out of the ordinary, but their emotional reality has a great deal to say about how people react under pressure and about the relative nature of good conduct. *Gawain and the Green Knight* thus uses the abstracting power of a fantastical device to stage important questions about how we feel and how we should act.

Sir Gawain and *The Lord of the Rings* are both written narratives that tell relatively linear stories, but this is far from the only form that fantasies can take. As an example, we might take a game with Fantasy in its name: *Final Fantasy VII* (1997). Like *The Lord of the Rings*, this is a story centred on a tight-knit questing group who work together to save the world, a story beloved enough to justify numerous expansions and reworkings (see Figure 0.2). It shares ecological themes with Tolkien, as well as the facility he discusses in his letter to Waldman for moving between world-shaking events and smaller-scale personal interactions. However, *Final Fantasy VII* presents a world with trains, factories, metropolises and guns, all produced by an industrial base that has developed far further than Sauron and Saruman manage. (One wonders how the ents would have fared if the armies

Figure 0.2 Gamers play a pre-release version of *Final Fantasy VII: Remake* (2020) beneath a giant banner of Cloud and Aerith at gamescom, Cologne, August 2019.
MiRafoto.com/Alamy.

of Orthanc had access to airships.) While magic in Tolkien's world is subtle and lightly defined, restricted to a small number of relatively mysterious characters, *Final Fantasy VII* employs systems that the player can manipulate, in which combinations of materia equipped to weapons and armour can achieve predictable results – damaging enemies, applying status effects, resurrecting party members and so on. The game uses an array of further systems to reward and challenge its players. While Tolkien's characters learn and grow as the narrative develops, in *Final Fantasy VII*, progress is tracked in more concrete and material terms as the game clock ticks on, experience points climb and items accumulate. *Final Fantasy VII* is more self-consciously referential than Tolkien's works. Its flashy summons draw their names and aspects of their characterisations from a wide range of mythologies. Beings called Odin and the Knights of the Round (Table) can be summoned in the same battle as Shiva, Hades and Bahamut. There are also considerable and necessary differences in narrative shape and rhythm. While Tom Bombadil was excised from the *Lord of the Rings* films to streamline the story, the nature of video games means that sub-games and side quests can proliferate to enhance the richness of the world and provide further scope for player choice. There is no point in *The Lord of the Rings* where Aragorn settles down to breed giant colourful riding birds, but this is a fantasy that *Final Fantasy VII* allows the player to indulge in, despite the notional pressure of an imminent apocalypse. Few would deny that the Final Fantasy series presents fantasies (although some might qualify the games' aesthetic as being Science Fantasy). However, the fantasies that such games present are very different in their affordances from the prose narratives that often spring first to mind when Fantasy is mentioned.

A film like Guillermo del Toro's *Pan's Labyrinth* (2006) operates differently again. Like Tolkien, del Toro's film draws on longstanding cultural traditions, but *Pan's Labyrinth* takes more from fairy stories and myths than from legend and romance. While Tolkien is keen that his reader be able to invest wholly in the worlds he creates, *Pan's Labyrinth* enjoys keeping its viewers guessing. Its heroine, Ofelia, travels through portals, but fairy creatures also share the screen with characters in the film's real world, presenting the possibility of intrusion or of a larger interconnected whole. The film takes pains to leave space for a viewing in which the supernatural entities

FIGURE 0.3 In the absence of other comforters, the mysterious, menacing Faun (Doug Jones) embraces Ofelia (Ivana Baquero) in Guillermo del Toro's *Pan's Labyrinth* (2006).
© Estudios Picasso/Tequila Gang/Esperanto Filmoj; Picturehouse/ Everett Collection/Alamy.

Ofelia encounters are figments of her imagination. This is a fantasy about longing for meaning, but also one about the dangers of belief, resonating with the ways in which fairy tales can both promise happy endings and distil unpleasant realities. *Pan's Labyrinth* blurs together a real-world situation (the Falangist conflict with the Maquis in the aftermath of the Spanish Civil War) with a fantastic narrative of royal exile and potential return. Ofelia is told by the sinister Faun – whose wonderful design is a key element of the film's creepy enchantment (Figure 0.3) – that she is the reincarnation of a princess and must perform three tasks to regain her immortality and return to her real parents. However, the things she is asked to do are difficult, disgusting and at points morally challenging.

The film is structured around a series of complex doublings: one of these parallels Ofelia (who is prepared to question authority and weigh her options) and her tyrannical stepfather Captain Vidal (for whom the end can always be used to justify the means). The film's pairings and mirrorings multiply, lending a plot that is commendably clear and legible – like the tales it echoes – the vivid complexities of implication that make such tales worth repeating. It is a film that makes powerful creative use of scene tints, animatronics, considered shot framing, clever sound design, the uncanny movement skills of Doug Jones and the committed performances of its cast to create a beautiful, involving, disturbing meditation on conflict, integrity and belief.

While Kelly Link's 'Magic for Beginners' (2005) depicts a world that flirts at times with being magical, its most fantastical element is the enchanting power of a television show that really chimes with you. The story's teenage characters are bound together by their love for a mysterious TV series called *The Library*. As a result of their mutual enthusiasm, 'the five are inseparable; invincible. They imagine that life will always be like this—like a television show in eternal syndication—that they will always have each other. They use the same vocabulary. They borrow each other's books and music.'[41] Link has been open about how the story's evocation of shared passions 'was based on the experience of watching *Buffy the Vampire Slayer*'. In 'Magic for Beginners', she 'wanted to write something that would capture the way it feels to

41 Kelly Link, 'Magic for Beginners', in *Magic for Beginners* (Northampton, MA: Small Beer Press, 2005), pp. 189–236 (p. 197).

be a fan and a member of a fandom', showing how fantasies work for those who love them.[42]

It would certainly be possible to read Link's story as not being technically Fantasy at all. The world in which *The Library* is watched is simultaneously wonderfully normal and charmingly peculiar, but it only touches on the impossible in ways that leave the door open for more quotidian explanations. However, *The Library* itself – with its marvellous, changeable protagonist Fox – infuses the lives of Jeffrey Mars, his friends and his family with the vertiginous excitement of the fantastic. Snatches of episode description capture both a delight in surprises and the joy of sharing frames of reference that feel like a secret language:

> The pirate-magicians lured Prince Wing into a trap so obvious that it seemed impossible it could really be a trap, on the one-hundred-and-fortieth floor of The Free People's World-Tree Library. The pirate-magicians used finger magic to turn Prince Wing into a porcelain teapot, put two Earl Grey tea bags into the teapot, and poured in boiling water, toasted the Eternally Postponed and Overdue Reign of the Forbidden Books, drained their tea in one gulp, belched, hurled their souvenir pirate mugs to the ground, and then shattered the teapot, which had been Prince Wing, into hundreds of pieces. Then the wicked pirate-magicians swept the pieces of both Prince Wing and collectable mugs carelessly into a wooden cigar box, buried the box in the Angela Carter Memorial Park on the seventeenth floor of The World-Tree Library, and erected a statue of George Washington above it.

[42] Quoted in Emily Temple, 'Ten Famous Writers on Loving *Buffy the Vampire Slayer*', *LitHub*, 10 March 2017, https://bit.ly/41DWq1Y.

> So then Fox had to go looking for Prince Wing. When she finally discovered the park on the seventeenth floor of The Library, the George Washington statue stepped down off his plinth and fought her tooth and nail. Literally tooth and nail, and they'd all agreed that there was something especially nightmarish about a biting, scratching, life-sized statue of George Washington with long, pointed metal fangs that threw off sparks when he gnashed them. The statue of George Washington bit Fox's pinky finger right off, just like Gollum biting Frodo's finger off on the top of Mount Doom. But of course, once the statue tasted Fox's magical blood, it fell in love with Fox. It would be her ally from now on.[43]

Both the wildly creative fantasies described in 'Magic for Beginners' and the ways in which the story evokes the experience of shared love spoke powerfully to Fantasy audiences. It won a bushel of awards, including the 2006 Nebula Award for Best Novella, the 2005 British Science Fiction Association Award for Short Fiction and the 2006 *Locus* magazine award for Best Novella. It seems likely that the story was acclaimed because it captures so well how fantasies operate socially. They are not simply solitary experiences, but the glue that holds together friendship groups and communities, forming bonds that unite creators with audiences. As a form, Fantasy is notable for the ease with which creators and audiences can switch positions. When someone who sounds like Fox asks Jeffrey Mars over the phone to play a role in the continuation of her story, this is a version of the request to collaborate that all fantasies make, asking their readers to discover how the play of the impossible can have

[43] Link, 'Magic for Beginners', p. 194.

meanings for them. In the kinds of interaction Link depicts, Fantasy operates as a larger social formation, drawing people together through shared knowledge, enjoyment and belief.

In seeking to encompass all these works, and many others, I am suggesting a broad view of what counts as Fantasy, but I think this broad view reflects how Fantasy is understood in cultures and in the world. Narrow definitions often operate counterproductively to exclude. Arguing for a tight definition that accords with her interests in Marxism and psychoanalysis, Rosemary Jackson opines that 'As a critical term, "fantasy" has been applied rather indiscriminately to any literature which does not give priority to realistic representation: myths, legends, folk and fairy tales, utopian allegories, dream visions, surrealist texts, science fiction, horror stories, all presenting realms "other" than the human.'[44] However, as I have shown, Fantasy is a form that is constitutionally open to history, influence and mutation. I would be happy to consider all the things Jackson lists as part of a broad fantastic tradition. While she uses the word 'indiscriminate' to suggest that uses of Fantasy as a critical term have lacked precision, being too keen to rule things out can lead to considering certain distinctive kinds of tree at the expense of the forest. Introducing *The Cambridge Companion to Fantasy Literature* (2012), Edward James and Farah Mendlesohn contend that after departing from the accepted common ground that Fantasy is about 'the construction of the impossible', critics often 'generate definitions of fantasy which include the texts they value

[44] Jackson, *Fantasy*, pp. 13–14.

and exclude most of what general readers think of as fantasy'.[45] There is quite a lot of criticism ostensibly about Fantasy that actually explores very specific subsets of canonical literature. James and Mendlesohn are right to resist the exclusions that arise in such criticism, which can move into the realm of idiosyncratic prescription, rather than seeking to understand the broad range of things Fantasy audiences care about and value.

However, while James and Mendlesohn's collection is wide-ranging and interesting, it has little to say about a vast number of works integral to what Fantasy has become for modern audiences. Their book acts as a companion to Fantasy *literature*, discussing books, stories, authors and readers, but only glancingly acknowledging directors, actors, artists, designers, players and fans. Much of the scholarship on Fantasy has been written by literary critics, who unsurprisingly privilege fiction in their discussions. This presents only part of a larger picture. Fantastic roots can be discerned in a broad range of art-forms, including sculpture, heraldry, architecture and cartography. Lineages of Fantasy art can be traced both through particular painters, such as Hieronymus Bosch and Richard Dadd, and through groupings and movements like the Pre-Raphaelites and Surrealism. Some of the earliest narrative films, such as Georges Méliès's *A Trip to the Moon* (1902; see Figure 0.4) and *The Impossible Voyage* (1904), are fantasies, and Fantasy has

45 Edward James and Farah Mendlesohn, Introduction to *The Cambridge Companion to Fantasy Literature*, ed. by Edward James and Farah Mendlesohn (Cambridge: Cambridge University Press, 2012), pp. 1–4 (p. 1).

FIGURE 0.4 The Man in the Moon suffers an unfortunate landing in Georges Méliès's *A Trip to the Moon* (1902).
Apic/Bridgeman via Getty Images.

had an enduring, flickering presence on the silver screen. Fantasy is arguably the dominant paradigm in animation, which allows for the easy depiction of strange bodies and wild magics. It has a strong presence in games – both traditional and digital – and in comics. While large-scale televisual adaptations of medievalist fantasies have only met with widespread acclaim relatively recently, shows as various in tone as *The Twilight Zone* (1959–64), *Bewitched* (1964–72), *Xena: Warrior Princess* (1995–2001) and *Galavant* (2015–16) might be evoked as examples of Fantasy, although these are hybrid series, mixing the fantastic with the conventions of other genres.[46] Fantasy manifests in complex arrays of fan practices, including

[46] On the generic mixings that tend to occur in fantasies for the small screen, see Catherine Johnson, *Telefantasy* (London: BFI, 2005).

writing, art and cosplay, as well as in myriad more fragmentary forms – references, jokes, metaphors, conceits, icons and serendipities. Some of these forms are difficult to capture or discuss, but it nevertheless seems worthwhile to acknowledge that Fantasy is not just something that dwells between covers, but rather a range of traditions and sensibilities that live with us and within us.

Essentially, my suggestion would be that we should modify Attebery's sense of what the fuzzy set of Fantasy includes to move beyond texts. Rather than simply being a grouping of works, Fantasy is a complex assemblage of creators, audiences, languages, forms, conventions, tropes, communities, institutions, histories and traditions.[47] This is true of other forms and genres, of course: opera is Maria Callas and La Scala and the Three Tenors' stadium audiences as well as Wolfgang Amadeus Mozart's *Don Giovanni* (1787), Georges Bizet's *Carmen* (1875) and Dmitri Shostakovich's *Lady Macbeth of Mtsensk* (1934). However, it seems to me that this is particularly true of Fantasy, which remains engaged with cultural traditions stretching back to our earliest records while also operating promiscuously in cutting-edge forms of new media and serving as an invaluable site for discussions regarding pressing social issues. Fantasy is a form predicated on

[47] My use of the term 'assemblage' echoes ideas posited by Giles Deleuze and Felix Guattari and developed further by Manuel DeLanda, although here I need only the sense that an assemblage is 'a multiplicity which is made up of many heterogeneous terms and which establishes liaisons [and] relations between them' (Gilles Deleuze and Claire Parnet, *Dialogues II*, revised edition, translated by Hugh Tomlinson and Barbara Habberjam (New York: Columbia University Press, 2007), p. 69).

sharing, on memory, on reconfigurations and revivals, on the ability of listeners to become tellers and viewers artists. This is the thing I am keenest to explore in this book: the ways that Fantasy connects us into networks across time and space, serving as a means of explaining ourselves to each other, of sharing enjoyments, negotiating difference, imagining alternatives, constructing histories and forging cultures within which we can agree, disagree, imagine, reimagine and iterate in manners that speak both of ourselves as individuals and of our fears, aspirations, dreams and desires as groups and collectives.

* * *

In closing the introduction to my *Introduction*, it will be useful briefly to address and dismiss one charge commonly levelled against Fantasy: that it is essentially an escapist form. This has always seemed to me to be a peculiar accusation, both in its being framed as a criticism and in its ignoring the ways in which culture actually works. Le Guin, who can always be relied on to puncture received cant, points out in one of her late essays that escaping from strictures currently dominant in the world can be both liberating and moral:

> Escape from real life, responsibility, order, duty, piety, is what the charge [of escapism] implies. But nobody, except the most criminally irresponsible or pitifully incompetent, escapes to jail. The direction of escape is towards freedom. So what is "escapism" an accusation of?
>
> "Why are things as they are? Must they be as they are? What might they be like if they were otherwise?" To ask these questions is to admit the contingency of reality, or at least to

allow that our perception of reality may be incomplete, our interpretation of it arbitrary or mistaken.[48]

The societies we have built are not utopias: there are good and healthy reasons why people might want to use Fantasy to be somewhere else for a while, occupying an imaginative space that is kinder, or starker, or easier to parse, or simply and mercifully different. However, as Le Guin goes on to show, while the move into a different space allows contrasts to be drawn, we do not remain floating in such spaces, untethered and unconcerned. Fantasies are modified echoes of the world, and like echoes, they bounce back. In Mervyn Peake's grand and beautiful conception, the purpose of the artist is

> to create one's own world in a style germane to its substance, and to people it with native forms and denizens that never were before, yet have their roots in one's experience. As the earth was thrown from the sun, so from the earth the artist must fling out into space, complete from pole to pole, his own world which, whatsoever form it takes, is the colour of the globe it flew from, as the world itself is coloured by the sun.[49]

While Peake valued creation in a heroic and Romantic sense, he also knew that works of art rely both on the artist's particular experiences and on the wider patterns and conventions of the world. A plunge into Fantasy might ostensibly seem like turning one's back on cold realities, but we always come back, and often with new

[48] Ursula K. Le Guin, 'It Doesn't Have to Be the Way It Is', in *No Time to Spare: Thinking about What Matters* (Boston and New York: Houghton Mifflin Harcourt, 2017), pp. 80–84 (p. 83).

[49] Mervyn Peake, *Drawings by Mervyn Peake* (London: Gray Walls Press, 1949), p. 11.

ways of seeing and understanding the people and environments around us. When we return, we may be better equipped to ask Le Guin's questions, and if the answers are not to our liking, we can work to change things, drawing inspiration from the alternative perspectives revealed through our access to the fantasies of others.

Fantasy creators know intimately that fantasies inevitably exist in dialogue with the world. Tolkien is one of the authors most devoted to the idea of constructing a deep, consistent and immersive secondary world, but he knew that to have meaning, the journey into Fantasy must necessarily include a return. In his essay 'On Fairy-stories' (1947), he took pains to assure his readers that the nature of Fantasy depends on its auditors recognising its unreality:

> Fantasy [. . .] does not destroy or even insult Reason; and it does not either blunt the appetite for, nor obscure the perception of, scientific verity. On the contrary. The keener and the clearer is the reason, the better fantasy will it make. If men were ever in a state in which they did not want to know or could not perceive truth (facts or evidence), then Fantasy would languish until they were cured. If they ever get into that state (it would not seem at all impossible), Fantasy will perish, and become Morbid Delusion.
>
> For creative Fantasy is founded upon the hard recognition that things are so in the world as it appears under the sun; on a recognition of fact, but not a slavery to it.[50]

While Tolkien acknowledges that Fantasy can 'be carried to excess' or 'can be ill done', he also asserts that it 'remains

[50] J. R. R. Tolkien, 'On Fairy-stories', in *On Fairy-stories*, ed. by Verlyn Flieger and Douglas A. Anderson (London: HarperCollins, 2008), pp. 25–84 (p. 65).

a human right'. In his Catholic conception, this right is an inheritance from God. However, we need not follow Tolkien's religious beliefs to concur that everyone, having seen the world as it is, should have the right to imagine things differently. Many of the infinite circular paths into and out of Fantasy will be taken unremarked, leaving little trace upon the world. However, some will be shared in conversation or in writing or in art, and some will be mapped by individuals and groups in networked collaborations and made available as part of our common cultural property. Not all fantasies speak to everyone, but Fantasy as a form gives us the tools to speak ourselves and others better, as we expand and reconfigure a vast constellation of alternative possibilities that can entertain, inform, enlighten, inspire and – ultimately – create change.

1

Fantasy, Language and the Shaping of Culture

When one considers where Fantasy begins, there is a strong argument for going a very long way back. We can think of Fantasy in its broadest sense as a kind of constructive, questioning potential inherent in human sociality and language. In his book *Sapiens*, Yuval Noah Harari locates the beginnings of humanity in a posited event he calls the Cognitive Revolution, which he frames as the point when 'history declared its independence from biology'.[1] For Harari, the Cognitive Revolution was made possible by the development of linguistic forms that could refer to things not literally present or extant, such as concepts, figments and fantasies:

> [T]he truly unique feature of our language is not its ability to transmit information about men and lions. Rather, it's the ability to transmit information about things that do not exist at all. As far as we know, only Sapiens can talk about entire kinds of entities that they have never seen, touched or smelled.
>
> Legends, myths, gods and religions appeared for the first time with the Cognitive Revolution. Many animals and human species could previously say, 'Careful! A lion!' Thanks to the Cognitive Revolution, *Homo sapiens* acquired the ability to say,

[1] Yuval Noah Harari, *Sapiens: A Brief History of Humankind* (London: Vintage, 2019), p. 42.

'The lion is the guardian spirit of our tribe.' This ability to speak about fictions is the most unique feature of Sapiens language.[2]

Harari argues that the inductive and associative powers of symbolic language play key roles in making us distinctively human. His essential contention is that shared fictions are fundamental to the creation of cultures and self-conceptions. This argument for the crucial importance of constructing stories has obvious relevance to Fantasy, a form of storytelling that wears its fictional status on its sleeve.

Before proceeding further, it is important to note a slip in Harari's terms: one that potentially complicates his assertion, but which also indicates the seriousness of the discourses in which Fantasy intervenes. Harari calls what his imagined *Homo sapiens* does 'speak[ing] about fictions'. This might be justified from a modern position of disbelief, in which the supernatural can only be fictional. One might also take a poststructuralist position and argue in concert with Jacques Derrida that 'language is originarily metaphorical'.[3] According to this view, all language necessarily operates by logics similar to fiction, unable ultimately to escape its own referentiality and indeterminacy. However, in the context that Harari imagines, the statement 'The lion is the guardian spirit of our tribe' is likely not to have been received as a fiction of either kind, but rather as a literal statement, or an expression of a

[2] Harari, *Sapiens*, p. 27.

[3] Jacques Derrida, *Of Grammatology*, translated by Gayatri Chakravorty Spivak, corrected edition (Baltimore, MD, and London: Johns Hopkins University Press, 1997), p. 271.

belief, or an articulation of a determined ethos, or a combination of these things. While Harari sees the guardian spirit lion as a convenient unifying construct from his own sociohistorical perspective, the society he imagines is likely to have seen it as a social, mystical or cultural reality.

However, in practice, the distinctions laid out in the previous paragraph are fuzzier than they might first appear. There is a spectrum between recognising things as fictions and holding them as beliefs that allows for middle positions to be adopted, and it is these middle positions that structure many of our sociocultural niceties. Few adults literally believe in Santa Claus, but many people act as if they do for the benefit of children. The qualities and rituals embodied in Santa Claus thus determine the behaviour of a considerable part of the world's population around Christmas. When 176,632 census respondents in England and Wales declared their religion as Jedi Knight in 2011 (down from 390,127 in 2001), it is unlikely that many of them thought they could wield the Force.[4] It is more likely that they considered claiming to hold to values espoused in *Star Wars* either a funnier or a truer answer than the other options available. Nevertheless, Jedi being notionally the seventh-largest religious denomination in England and Wales clearly demonstrates that beliefs and fictions often share sociocultural positions and codes. In the modern world, many old beliefs have become the stuff of Fantasy, and this is not a complete transformation in kind. The extent to

[4] For data, see the Office of National Statistics website: www.ons.gov.uk/census.

which individuals buy in to a given cultural locus will vary considerably, but this does not necessarily compromise its communicative potential. It is fairly easy for someone who holds something to be true and someone who believes it to be a fiction to use their shared sense of that thing as a point of connection and understanding, if not of agreement. Language binds us together, but it also serves as a means for recognising and negotiating difference: a particular speciality of fantastic usages.

Harari argues that the ability to imagine, induce, abstract and thereby collaborate is vital for letting societies function at scale. In his words, 'fiction has enabled us not merely to imagine things, but to do so *collectively*'. As a consequence, 'Sapiens can cooperate in extremely flexible ways with countless numbers of strangers.'[5] This seems to me to be powerfully true. To understand and work together, we rely heavily on shared mythologies and conceptualisations, along with assumed truths, rules of thumb, ascriptions of authority and (more problematically) stereotypes. Many of these mutual conceptions rely on the fantastic ability of language to refer to things that do not literally exist. The conventions that underpin morality, ethics and social relations have developed through processes of negotiation into the accepted building blocks of our worlds, but they depend on notions that were first postulated as ideals, beliefs or dreams. Much of what humans have become as we have constructed increasingly complex social mechanisms results from the evolution of the stories we have learnt to tell about

[5] Harari, *Sapiens*, p. 28.

ourselves. These often-fantastical stories shape what we are and what we might be in fundamental ways.

It is not overreaching to claim that societies are structured in considerable part by collective beliefs and shared fantasies. Some take the form of narratives or characters that can be used to negotiate or renegotiate certain kinds of meaning – Romulus and Remus and the wolf, King Arthur, Dick Whittington, Pope Joan, Thomas the Rhymer, Anansi, Cinderella, Coyote, Blue Beard's wife, Baba Yaga, the Slender Man. As we tell and retell stories about figures like these, we also posit ideals, social specifics and modes of interaction. Other unifying concepts are more essentialising: *Liberté*, *Égalité*, *Fraternité*; chivalry; national identity; Manifest Destiny; human rights; the dream that one day Martin Luther King's children 'will not be judged by the color of their skin but by their character'.[6] Obviously, not all these things are equally important, specific or current as communicative norms. Some are local, liminal or subcultural, while others constitute or have constituted core principles for numerous cultures. Roles shift as times change and identities are renegotiated. Some cultural norms are founded on principles of inclusion and fellowship, while others draw divisions which provide excuses for elitism, ostracisation and violence. Structuring ideals can often be double-edged swords, guaranteeing freedom for some at the expense of others. The fact that King had to dream of a future where his children would have the same opportunities as others rebuked a nation that began with the promise that

[6] Martin Luther King, from the 'I Have a Dream' speech, given on the steps of the Lincoln Memorial in Washington DC on 28 August 1963.

'We hold these truths to be self-evident, that all men are created equal, that they are endowed by their Creator with certain unalienable Rights, that among these are Life, Liberty and the pursuit of Happiness.'[7] The stories cultures tell about themselves intermingle and challenge one another as some people seek to hold the existing spoken and unspoken conventions of the social world in place while others look to redefine them.

When we talk with each other, we do not speak the world objectively as it is, but rather as we have agreed to frame it, or as we render it through shared or novel abstractions, or as we would like to believe it to be, or as it might be, or as we would have it be. In speaking thus, using shared speculations, we open the possibility for collaborations that reify ideals that begin as fantasies, bringing these ideals into our cultures as beliefs, conventions, systems and forms of resistance.

Fantasy creators of numerous stripes – makers and remakers of fictions inevitably derived from the languages and customs of our world – are fascinated by the processes through which language, fantasy and belief collaborate to define and redefine the parameters of culture and imagination. Consequently, we can find numerous versions of the kinds of argument Harari makes in works of Fantasy. One of the most compelling renderings is Terry Pratchett's in *Hogfather* (1996). Towards the end of the story, Death (who on Pratchett's Discworld takes the classic form of a skeleton in a black robe WHO SPEAKS LIKE THIS) is debating human nature with his eminently

[7] United States Declaration of Independence, signed in Congress on 4 July 1776.

practical granddaughter, Susan. Susan is exasperated by people's tendency to believe in things that she sees as being ridiculous, such as the Discworld's analogue for Santa Claus. This is an especially acute problem on the Discworld, where belief literally shapes reality: a process that over the course of the novel has spawned explanatory beings such as the Eater of Socks (to solve where the missing half of the pair goes), the Verruca Gnome and Bilious, the 'Oh God' of Hangovers. Death, who is characterised in Pratchett's conception by his genial if sometimes uncomprehending fascination with humanity, his occasional frustrations with his role and his sense of responsibility, argues that the ability to believe in unreal things is crucial for societies to function. He also contends that fantasies and beliefs are not straightforwardly separable:

> "All right," said Susan, "I'm not stupid. You're saying humans need...*fantasies* to make life bearable."
>
> REALLY? AS IF IT WAS SOME KIND OF PINK PILL? NO. HUMANS NEED FANTASY TO BE HUMAN. TO BE THE PLACE WHERE THE FALLING ANGEL MEETS THE RISING APE.
>
> "Tooth fairies? Hogfathers? Little—"
>
> YES. AS PRACTICE. YOU HAVE TO START OUT LEARNING TO BELIEVE THE *LITTLE* LIES.
>
> "So we can believe the big ones?"
>
> YES. JUSTICE. MERCY. DUTY. THAT SORT OF THING.
>
> "They're not the same at all!"
>
> YOU THINK SO? THEN TAKE THE UNIVERSE AND GRIND IT DOWN TO THE FINEST POWDER AND SIEVE IT THROUGH THE FINEST SIEVE AND THEN *SHOW* ME ONE ATOM OF JUSTICE, ONE MOLECULE OF MERCY. AND YET YOU ACT AS IF THERE IS SOME...SOME *RIGHTNESS* IN THE UNIVERSE BY WHICH IT MAY BE JUDGED.

"Yes. But people have *got* to believe that, or what's the *point*—"

MY POINT EXACTLY.[8]

Pratchett is making a big claim here, but one that Death does a good job of justifying. While certain people and institutions embody or instantiate juridical roles, these are social performances rather than manifestations of scientifically measurable forces. The Code of Hammurabi and the Napoleonic Code set out laws that purport to be just, but such codes are particular and time-bound legal strictures that can be superseded and modified, undercutting any implicit claims to be eternal verities. Unlike Pratchett's Death, people who work as police officers or judges are not anthropomorphic personifications. If they are accorded judicial authority, this is a function of social consensus. Justice itself remains elusive. The alignment between individuals' fantasies of justice and the practices of those who claim to be reifying them is seldom seamless. Judicial institutions can be deeply unjust. Nevertheless, the notion of justice as something desirable and attainable – the fantasy we can share regarding its nature and value – can be activated powerfully against institutions that have arrogated the authority of the ideal and can be held accountable should they fail to live up to it. Justice does not exist tangibly as a table or a cat does, but we have developed a consensus that it should be socially real, and through our belief it becomes so, although its precise nature remains necessarily contested.

[8] Terry Pratchett, *Hogfather* (London: Victor Gollancz, 1996), pp. 335–6.

In this respect, as in many others, Pratchett's Discworld, 'world and mirror of worlds', is a mirror that exaggerates to reveal, rather than one that deceptively distorts.[9] While our beliefs and stories do not create gods as literally as they would on the Discworld, they nevertheless produce the value systems by which we live and the language through which we frame our aspirations. In a very real sense, society is held together by linguistic fantasies that describe shareable beliefs, knowledges or structures of feeling. Conversely, societies can be divided when ideals around which consensuses have been built are thrown into doubt, or when different groups' fantasies about how the world should work seem to be or become irreconcilable.

This all means that the creators of works of Fantasy are playing with heady stuff when they highlight the constructedness of language and belief by staging impossibilities that posit plural or alternative values and understandings. This is perhaps why some thinkers have been keen to draw a very sharp distinction between Fantasy and fiction as cultural forms and the shared beliefs that underpin societies. A famous early example of this argument is made by Plato (via Socrates) in the *Republic* (c. 375 BCE): a work we might see as constructing a fantasy of a better society, although its author might dispute this description. In Book X, Socrates spends a considerable time arguing that the ideals created in art are by their very nature misleading, indulgent and potentially destructive:

[9] Terry Pratchett, *Moving Pictures* (London: Corgi, 1992), p. 9.

> be aware that hymns to the gods and eulogies of good people are the only poetry we can admit into our city. For if you admit the honeyed Muse, whether in lyric or epic poetry, pleasure and pain will be kings in your city instead of law and the thing that has always been generally believed to be best—reason.[10]

Socrates advocates against fantasising that might (in his view) deceive the community away from the pursuit of virtue. He places law as part of a different order of meaning to poetry, arguing that while law relates to a consensus regarding an ideal truth, poetry is both essentially imitative and likely to lead to corrupt forms of divisive individualism. In a thought experiment like Plato's, ostensibly based on the predicate that an ideal society is achievable, the alternatives presented through different artistic prisms are seen as misleading distractions rather than as part of a valuable social negotiation.

However, the *Republic* is not entirely consistent regarding the perversity of fictions. In Book III, Socrates hesitantly endorses the use of a 'noble lie' designed to make the Just City's inhabitants 'regard the other citizens as their earthborn brothers'.[11] Socrates admits that the tale he proceeds to weave is false, but argues that it might be justified through its creating a positive effect. This, however, is a matter we might dispute, as the implications of Socrates's tale are less benign than he claims:

> when the god was forming you, he mixed gold into those of you who are capable of ruling, which is why they are the most honorable; silver into the auxiliaries; and iron and bronze into

[10] Plato, *Republic*, translated by C. D. C Reeve (Indianapolis, IN, and Cambridge: Hackett Publishing, 2004), p. 290 (607a).

[11] Plato, *Republic*, pp. 99 (414c), 100 (414e).

the farmers and other craftsmen. For the most part, you will produce children like yourselves; but because you are all related, a silver child will sometimes be born to a golden parent, a golden child to a silver parent, and so on.[12]

In imaging people as being constituted by ingredients that differ starkly, Socrates provides a fictional justification for a rigid class structure that is difficult to challenge if the unverifiable assumptions of the story that underpins it are largely accepted. While the myth allows for social mobility across generations, Socrates's language implies that this will be a rare occurrence. His founding fiction also grants the gold-endowed rulers the right and responsibility to judge individuals' metallic constitutions, rather than distributing agency among the populace at large. Those less invested than Plato in the idea of absolute truth might well characterise this arrangement as inherently autocratic, with the 'noble lie' serving to entrench a hereditary nobility granted authority through an abstract model of virtue, the terms of which they themselves largely determine.[13]

Plato's dialogue thus demonstrates the danger of hiding the fact that the stories we tell to make societies are often purposeful constructions. In the *Republic*, the imaginative creations of the poets are to be shut out so as to maintain the authority of a law defined by those considered by convention and by themselves to be the wisest. This aligns

[12] Plato, *Republic*, p. 100 (415a-b).

[13] For an affectionate deconstruction of Plato's ideas and influence, see Jo Walton's *The Just City* (New York: Tor, 2015), which imagines a group of Plato fans from across history being brought together by Athene and Apollo to put the precepts of the *Republic* into practice.

with Joseph Laycock's assertion that 'It is in the interests of any hegemonic institution [...] to discourage imagination. Hegemony can be resisted only if we can imagine new possibilities.'[14] In our stuttering growth as ethical beings, imaginative space has been crucial for realising that laws and long-established practices can be fundamentally unjust. We are no longer comfortable with the divine right of Plato's golden children, or with slavery, which was an accepted part of the Athenian social order, and we are no longer comfortable with these things precisely because people have used the imaginative and creative affordances of language to communicate, empathise, condemn and then construct alternative social systems.

Works of Fantasy sometimes share Plato's fascination with higher truths and perfect archetypes, expressed powerfully in the Allegory of the Cave (Figure 1.1), which holds that in our everyday lives we experience only shadows of genuine forms. This is an idea drawn on implicitly by many Fantasy worlds that look to seem truer or more intense than our own, and one that is sometimes evoked quite specifically, as in C. S. Lewis's true Narnia at the end of *The Last Battle* (1956). However, while it can be deeply interested in questions regarding fundamental forms, modern Fantasy is essentially relativist, made so by virtue of its impossibilities' friction with the known attributes of the world. While Plato's Just City ostensibly aspires to find the best way of doing things and then close off other ways of thinking by barring its gates against

[14] Joseph P. Laycock, *Dangerous Games: What the Moral Panic over Role-Playing Games Says about Play, Religion, and Imagined Worlds* (Oakland: University of California Press, 2015), p. 215.

FIGURE 1.1 Illustration by Edmond Lechevallier-Chevignard of Plato's Allegory of the Cave, from *Le Magasin pittoresque* (July 1855).
Chronicle/Alamy.

them, most works of Fantasy do not seek to monopolise truth. A work that describes itself as Fantasy admits at the outset that it is making tacit or brazen use of impossibilities. When a work of Fantasy seeks to persuade, it does so by postulating a clearly fictional alternative and asking whether we might want to veer the world towards or away from it, or whether we might understand others better by recognising this as something that they might dream. Fantasies are by no means necessarily radical in what they propose – there are strong strands of conservatism in many fantastic works – but, as Plato recognised, their nature tends towards the multiplicative and disruptive, calling the current social facts of the world into question through shamelessly imagining alternative positions and propositions.

Thus far in this chapter, I have been dwelling mainly on large-scale social fantasies. Most political philosophies turn on converting observed qualities into applicable strictures for effective governance. In the second book of the *Analects*, for example, Confucius offers the following advice to those who would seek to rule justly: 'Guide them by edicts, keep them in line with punishments, and the common people will stay out of trouble but will have no sense of shame. Guide them by virtue, keep them in line with the rites, and they will, besides having a sense of shame, reform themselves.'[15] This dictum lays the ground for a society that is bound together by shared ideals, rather than coerced into co-operation by the threat of violence. There is, however, a

[15] Confucius, *Analects*, II.3, as given in *The Analects*, translated by D. C. Lau (London: Penguin, 1979), p. 63.

certain amount of realpolitik in this conception: the purpose remains to keep the common people in line by encouraging them to self-police. In this respect, shared social beliefs might be seen as means of imposing limitations on individual autonomy. Such beliefs determine the baselines for what being human entails in a given culture, and deviations can serve to place individuals beyond the pale.

While beliefs set or perpetuate conventions, fantasies provide some of our most powerful means of individually and collectively projecting alternatives to those conventions. Such articulations can be demonstrative and public, but they can also be (and often begin as) deeply personal reflections. As well as imagining large-scale structuring processes, fantasies can manifest intensely private explorations of possibility and desire. Fantasies comprise major parts of our mental action: projected parallels, pondered potentialities, speculative situations, imaginative recombinations, playful alternatives and painful returns. Fantasy is what we use, often necessarily, to fill in the gaps between things. When we are faced with an intractable problem, we play out different fantasy scenarios to try and work out the best solution. When we are parted from our lovers, we spend part of our time in dialogue with the versions of them who dwell in our heads (and perhaps – probably – our fantasy versions of ourselves act in manners that are kinder or more absolute or more eloquent than we can usually achieve in the world). Through fantasy as a mental process, we live fractions of the many other lives we might have lived. Through Fantasy as a cultural form, we access lives we could never live due to the limitations of the world and the very particular windows that our individual bodies, locations and self-conceptions provide. Fantasies play important roles in binding us together, but they are also means by which we can reflect on those bindings and determine whether they are empowering associations or coercive restraints.

One of Fantasy's most potent tools for reflecting on the shaping power of language is abstraction: literalising metaphors to explore the concepts they embody or constructing the mechanics of a projected world to bring ideas into focus. This imbues many works of Fantasy with a degree of self-reflexivity, as their content reflects on the processes that constitute it. Many writers have followed the Bible's lead by literalising the importance of language, depicting worlds created through speech acts. In Ursula K. Le Guin's Earthsea, *The Creation of Éa* describes Segoy raising the islands of the archipelago from the ocean by naming them in the True Speech. Other Fantasy worlds are born from different forms of art. In C. S. Lewis's *The Magician's Nephew* (1955), Aslan sings Narnia into being, his deep voice joined in harmony by the 'cold, tingling, silvery voices' of the stars.[16] At the beginning of *The Silmarillion* (1977), Tolkien's Eä is also sung into existence: 'the voices of the Ainur [. . .] began to fashion the theme of Ilúvatar to a great music [. . .] and the music and the echo of the music went out into the Void, and it was not void'.[17] In Robert Jordan's Wheel of Time series (1990–2013), the titular wheel is a seven-spoked cosmic loom made by the Creator that weaves the Great Pattern

[16] C. S. Lewis, *The Magician's Nephew* (London: Collins, 2009), p. 120.

[17] J. R. R. Tolkien, *The Silmarillion*, ed. by Christopher Tolkien (London: HarperCollins, 1999), p. 29.

that constitutes and underpins existence, using lives as its threads. Over the course of the *Dark Souls* games (2011–17), the player character encounters the painted worlds of Ariamis and Ariandel, the first created to house things the gods feared, the second a snowy dreamscape that harks backwards to earlier moments in the games' cycle of cycles and hints towards the possibility of a new world, or an old one refreshed through art, or a merciful release. These artistic workings presented within fantasies reflect the processes through which their creators construct. Le Guin maps the islands of Earthsea in language and ink. Lewis writes Narnia even as Aslan sings it. Tolkien composes and sets down the many songs of Arda. Jordan weaves the loops and reiterations of his long epic, reminding readers as he opens each new volume about the turning of the Wheel and the nature of endings and beginnings. Hidetaka Miyazaki and his team at FromSoftware conceptualise, design, paint and render a world into being, using new digital technology to build fantastic visions of decaying glory and employing old techniques of fragmentation, elision and implication to seed remnants of mysterious histories in monuments, provenances and gnomic utterances.

Sometimes such entanglements are principally playful. However, such self-reflexive processes are also commonly means of reflecting on the ways in which we construct our own social and cultural worlds. Language and magic are tightly entangled in works of Fantasy, with discussions of magic serving as meditations on how we exercise power. In Le Guin's Earthsea books, the True Speech used by wizards can compel action and obedience: a literal shaping of the world, but one that mirrors the metaphorical shapings that all languages accomplish. Le Guin, deeply aware of this resonance, is careful throughout the Earthsea books to consider what constitutes a judicious use of authority. As the series goes on, she carefully reconfigures her presentation of magic to renegotiate inherited exclusionary assumptions that had informed her earlier work, reflecting her own changing understanding.

However, even in the first Earthsea book, *A Wizard of Earthsea* (1968), magic is depicted as being linguistically constrained in revealingly social manners. Early in his magical education at the School on Roke, Ged is sent to study with the Master Namer, Kurremkarmerruk, 'a name that had no meaning in any language'.[18] Ged's task is to discover and memorise names that will grant him the power he seeks, but his time among the rustling books is also about learning the limits of language and the authority it can allow him to wield. In Le Guin's conception, naming something correctly is neither easy nor arbitrary. As Kurremkarmerruk explains,

> The sea's name is *inien*, well and good. But what we call the Inmost Sea has its own name also in the Old Speech. Since no thing can have two true names, *inien* can mean only "all the sea except the Inmost Sea". And of course it does not mean even that, for there are seas and bays and straits beyond counting that bear names of their own. So if some Mage-Seamaster were mad enough to try to lay a spell of storm or calm over all the ocean, his spell must say not only that word *inien*, but the name of every stretch and bit and part of the sea through all the

[18] Ursula K. Le Guin, *A Wizard of Earthsea* (Harmondsworth: Penguin, 1971), p. 58.

Archipelago and all the Outer Reaches and beyond to where names cease. Thus, that which gives us the power to work magic, sets the limits of that power.[19]

While Le Guin is writing about an invented magical language, everything she says is also true of conventional languages, which move between ideal forms or general descriptors and particular instances or specifics, all of which matter in rendering our perceptions of the world. In the Old Speech, 'there is no end'; consequently, it is unknowable in its entirety (at least by humans). Again, this echoes more conventional languages, which are almost infinitely flexible in their referential power, but which are also constantly changing and which inevitably fail in encompassing the fullness of the things to which their words refer. The limits of Le Guin's magic system are a kind of literalisation of Ludwig Wittgenstein's seventh proposition, 'Whereof one cannot speak, thereof one must be silent.'[20] Language is a powerful means of abstracting the world into forms we can reconcile with one another, but as a set of agreed conventions, it necessarily deflects away from the exact qualities of what it describes. In Le Guin's world, this means that magic requires both a strong grasp of general communicative principles and careful attention to particularities of circumstance. To overrule the usual operations of the world requires that these first be known and understood, at least in part.

[19] Le Guin, *Wizard of Earthsea*, p. 60.

[20] Ludwig Wittgenstein, *Tractatus Logico-Philosophicus*, translated by C. K. Ogden with F. P. Ramsey (London: Kegan Paul, Trench, Trubner & Co., 1922), p. 90.

While magic systems in Fantasy are often practical tool kits, they are also commonly systems of ethics. Le Guin does not permit her wizards to rewrite reality without consequences. A core part of formal and informal magical education on Roke consists of recognising and coming to terms with what should not be done. Frustrated by the subjects he is initially permitted to study, Ged asks the Master Hand, who teaches illusion, whether it is possible to move from making something appear to be a diamond to making that thing an actual diamond. His question is answered more fully than he initially realises:

> The Master Hand looked at the jewel that glittered on Ged's palm, bright as the prize of a dragon's hoard. The old Master murmured one word, '*Tolk*,' and there lay the pebble, no jewel but a rough grey bit of rock. The Master took it and held it out on his own hand. 'This is a rock; *tolk* in the True Speech,' he said, looking mildly up at Ged now. 'A bit of the stone of which Roke Isle is made, a little bit of the dry land on which men live. It is itself. It is part of the world. By the Illusion-Change you can make it look like a diamond – or a flower or a fly or an eye or a flame –' The rock flickered from shape to shape as he named them, and returned to rock. 'But that is mere seeming. Illusion fools the beholder's senses; it makes him see and hear and feel that the thing is changed. But it does not change the thing. To change this rock into a jewel, you must change its true name. And to do that, my son, even to so small a scrap of the world, is to change the world. It can be done. Indeed it can be done. It is the art of the Master Changer, and you will learn it, when you are ready to learn it. But you must not change one thing, one pebble, one grain of sand, until you know what good and evil will follow on that act. The world is in balance, in Equilibrium. A wizard's power of Changing and of Summoning can shake the balance of the world. It is dangerous, that power.

It is most perilous. It must follow knowledge, and serve need. To light a candle is to cast a shadow...'

He looked down at the pebble again. 'A rock is a good thing, too, you know,' he said, speaking less gravely. 'If the Isles of Earthsea were all made of diamond, we'd lead a hard life here. Enjoy illusions, lad, and let the rocks be rocks.'[21]

Before he learns much of naming, Ged has thus been told gently that he should think very carefully before editing creation. While Le Guin's world is one in which language can reshape reality, this can be read as a literalisation of the ways that more commonplace uses of language work to change how we perceive. For example, when we name certain plants as weeds, or certain materials rubbish, or certain people criminals or vagrants, we reconfigure their ontological statuses and provide ourselves with excuses to reject or marginalise them. The power to apply a name to something is a kind of authority claim. Consequently, it should be exercised with care. This is a lesson Ged initially struggles to understand. The main action of *A Wizard of Earthsea* is triggered by Ged performing an unwise and excessive magical act to try and impress his fellow students. He spends the rest of the novel seeking to undo the consequences of this act (or perhaps reconcile himself to them). Only by learning to use his power to recognise and protect others, rather than imposing on them, does Ged come to be worthy of his magical gifts, and of other gifts later freely granted.

While Le Guin's Earthsea literalises language's power in its magic, Ted Chiang's more introspective 'Story of

[21] Le Guin, *Wizard of Earthsea*, p. 56

Your Life' (1998) explores how language constructs our capabilities and self-conceptions. Chiang's narrative is ostensibly science fictional, telling the story of a linguist, Louise Banks, who is part of a team that initiates first contact with an alien race, the heptapods. However, the way that the heptapods register reality is a fantastical one from a human perspective. Rather than experiencing time sequentially, heptapods experience all the events of their lives simultaneously. This determines how they write, with all parts of the sentence established at once, and also determines the essential qualities of their language. Through speaking with heptapods, Louise acquires something of their perception of the universe. The nature of her consciousness changes as she acquires new means to articulate it, a process that Chiang sketches effectively using simile and metaphor:

> Before I learned to think in Heptapod B, my memories grew like a column of cigarette ash, laid down by the infinitesimal sliver of combustion that was my consciousness, marking the sequential present. After I learned Heptapod B, new memories fell into place like gigantic blocks, each one measuring years in duration, and though they didn't arrive in order or land contiguously, they soon composed a period of five decades. It is the period during which I knew Heptapod B well enough to think in it, starting during my interviews with Flapper and Raspberry and ending with my death.
>
> Usually, Heptapod B affects just my memory: my consciousness crawls along as it did before, a glowing sliver crawling forward in time, the difference being that the ash of memory lies ahead as well as behind: there is no real combustion. But occasionally I have glimpses when Heptapod B truly reigns, and I experience past and future all at once; my consciousness

becomes a half-century long ember burning outside time. I perceive—during those glimpses—that entire epoch as a simultaneity.[22]

A cold way of describing Chiang's story would be to characterise it as an exploration of the Sapir–Whorf hypothesis: the idea that a language fundamentally structures its speakers' cognition, perceptions and worldview. This approach sees language not just as a functional tool, but as a shaping force that determines the conditions of speech, our forms of perception and what we can know. Differences between the core tools of understanding possessed by heptapods and humans initially make meaningful communication almost impossible. However, Chiang's fantasy of first contact is ultimately an optimistic or benevolent one, in which careful acts of observation and alignment can open the door for tentative modes of mutual understanding.

While Chiang's story is ostensibly about overcoming difference in an encounter with the radically other, it is also about meaning-making more generally, and about how we value our time. While the nature of heptapod language is the story's big reveal, the emotional pay-off comes as the reader assembles the non-sequential fragments of the future revealed to Louise through her acquisition of Heptapod B and slowly realises that the relationship the story focuses around is not all wine and roses. Chiang cannot fully bring his reader into the space of simultaneous understanding he imagines for Louise, but his mastery of prose allows him to gesture towards

22 Ted Chiang, 'Story of Your Life', in *Stories of Your Life and Others* (Easthampton, MA: Small Beer Press, 2010), pp. 91–145 (pp. 140–1).

how that state might feel. In this respect, the subject of the story and its medium are tightly aligned. Chiang cannot make us think like Louise is imagined to think, but he can bridge us towards a sense of her perceptions by making her own understanding less absolute than that of the heptapods, and more like our own experiences with non-sequential reading. Chiang's story shares something with experimental fictions like B. S. Johnson's book-in-a-box *The Unfortunates* (1969) – in which all but the first and last chapters are supposed to be shuffled and read in a random order – or Nanni Balestrini's *Tristano* (1966 and after), which in its fully realised version randomises paragraph arrangements to 'enact the variegations of the human heart'.[23] However, it is also an intensification of the lived experience of reading more generally, in which we approach books with preconceptions and impressions, and might easily skip a page, or take a break, or sneakily read the ending first. Such forms of reading (which can be encouraged by certain forms of writing, and by forms like lore wikis) let us break free of theoretically dominant linear assumptions. While such experiences are by no means exactly equivalent to the ones Chiang imagines for Louise, the affinities work relationally to suggest how different the world would become if we were not bound by temporalities that are partly a function of our biological apparatus, but which also arise from the ways that we have assimilated and conceptualised dominant forms of perception as organising principles of our cultures.

[23] Nanni Balestrini, *Tristano*, translated by Mike Harakis (London: Verso, 2014), back cover copy.

At the story's conclusion, Louise thinks that she 'would have liked to experience more of the heptapods' world-view, to feel the way they feel. Then, perhaps I could immerse myself fully in the necessity of events, as they must, instead of merely wading in its surf for the rest of my life.'[24] Our relation to Louise as readers is in many respects equivalent to hers to the heptapods. This is also a relation that resonates more generally with our predicament *vis-à-vis* other humans. We can only touch on the perceptions of others in mediated forms: we can never see exactly as others see, with their complex and unique arrays of frames and experiences. However, the affordances of written and visual languages – the abilities of these languages to abstract, suggest and differentiate – mean that we can come closer to imagining (or fantasising) how it would be to think differently, know differently or be differently. A story of a life is not a life, but stories (and fantasies) have the advantage that they can be shared and reflected upon, serving as revealing and affecting correlatives.

Chiang's story is in part about accepting that all forms of perception come with restrictions, but fantastic narratives are often deeply suspicious of the ways that language can bind us into certain modes of behaviour. We might think of the deal in Hayao Miyazaki's film *Spirited Away* (2001) by which the central character, Chihiro, gives up a character from her name when she places herself in the service of the witch Yubaba. The change from Chihiro to Sen – from 'a thousand questions' to 'one thousand' – makes an enquirer into a number. While Chihiro maintains enough of herself to neutralise this threat of

[24] Chiang, 'Story of Your Life', p. 144.

FIGURE 1.2 The witch Yubaba, compelled by Chihiro's request for work in Hayao Miyazaki's *Spirited Away* (2001), considers how to turn the circumstances to her advantage.

commodification, Yubaba's gesture bespeaks a desire to control people by controlling meanings. Language works through agreements, and Yubaba takes advantage of this by striking deals that allow her to accumulate the wealth that adorns her office through the labour of those who sign contracts and give up aspects of their autonomy (Figure 1.2). Miyazaki does not tend to enjoy motiveless or incomprehensible evil. While Yubaba's bathhouse models some of the excesses of capitalism, she herself can be constrained by language. She is magically obligated to provide employment to those who ask and is bound by the terms of the contracts she signs. She is also overburdened and not completely lacking in empathy. Those she employs can pool their knowledge to find spaces of freedom and means to negotiate. The film enjoys hinting darkly that there will be severe consequences should such ploys fail, but language's potential for connection ultimately takes precedence over its power to constrain.

Other fantasies are less sanguine regarding language's ability to mediate rationally. While Miyazaki's works have affinities with Lewis Carroll, Miyazaki's filmic imaginaries are generally kinder and less dependent on alienation effects than Carroll's books. At the trial in *Alice's Adventures in Wonderland* (1865), communications continuously misfire as the rules of the court are arbitrarily enforced and rewritten. *Through the Looking-Glass* (1871) takes this conceit even further in the person of Humpty Dumpty, who claims absolute control over his language:

> "I don't know what you mean by 'glory,'" Alice said.
>
> Humpty Dumpty smiled contemptuously. "Of course you don't—till I tell you. I meant 'there's a nice knock-down argument for you!'"
>
> "But 'glory' doesn't mean 'a nice knock-down argument,'" Alice objected.
>
> "When *I* use a word," Humpty Dumpty said in rather a scornful tone, "it means just what I choose it to mean—neither more nor less."
>
> "The question is," said Alice, "whether you can make words mean so many different things."
>
> "The question is," said Humpty Dumpty, "which is to be master—that's all."[25]

This is a fantasy much loved by post-structuralists, who contend that language's meanings are culturally determined and inevitably slippery. While Alice rightly rejects Humpty Dumpty's arbitrary insistence that he alone controls the meanings of language, the episode highlights the unavoidable gap between what one person thinks they

[25] Lewis Carroll, *Through the Looking-Glass, and What Alice Found There* (London: Macmillan, 1872), p. 124.

have said and what another person understands. While language's role is to be a common frame of reference, we develop our own languages idiosyncratically based on our particular circumstances. While my vermillion and your vermillion will both mean a deep red if the two of us know and accept the common definition, mine will be coloured subtly differently by the contexts in which I have encountered the word. However, we might never know this unless I ask you to buy curtain fabric for me and the difference becomes visible. We trust language to carry our meanings, but Carroll, like many fantasists, is acutely aware of the inevitability of transmission failure. Humpty Dumpty's confidence in his verbal power is ultimately misplaced. His arrogant certainty dooms him to be misunderstood. His closing remark that Alice is 'so exactly like other people' that he will not remember her is a condemnation both of his narcissism and of his inability to accommodate others' idiosyncrasies.[26]

Even language used with accommodating intentions will still inevitably reshape what it describes, causing it in part to miscarry. When we forge concepts and histories to bind societies together, we inevitably simplify and elide. Fantasies – obsessed as they are with the flickerings and failures of attempts to communicate from the past – are commonly fascinated by what is lost or altered in historicising processes. One of the chapter epigraphs from Steven Erikson's *The Bonehunters* (2006), the sixth volume of his long series the Malazan Book of the Fallen (1999–2011), neatly captures some of the processes and problems that arise in forging cultural memory:

[26] Carroll, *Through the Looking-Glass*, p. 135.

> Who can say where divides truth and the host of desires that, together, give shape to memories? There are deep folds in every legend, and the visible, outward pattern presents a false unity of form and intention. We distort with deliberate purpose; we confine vast meanings into the strictures of imagined necessity. In this lies both failing and gift, for in the surrender of truth we fashion, rightly or wrongly, universal significance. Specific gives way to general; detail gives way to grandiose form, and in the telling, we are exalted beyond our mundane selves. We are, in truth, bound into greater humanity by this skein of words. . .[27]

The full irreducible specifics of any individual life are ultimately incommunicable. We can only speak or write parts of what we are and feel, and our means of communicating rely on fitting our experiences into the general shapes that language and culture provide. Our shared values are often rather abstract. When we call for integrity, we align ourselves with what is in most cultures a laudable quality, but the precise actions we demand are more ambiguous. When we record histories, we name events and characterise individuals in manners that both impose narrative logics and inevitably edit. Haydon White has argued along similar lines to Erikson's epigraph that 'the historical field is constituted as a possible domain of analysis in a linguistic act which is tropological in nature'.[28] To put that more straightforwardly: we inevitably use pre-established forms to couch explanations. In

[27] Steven Erikson, *The Bonehunters*, Malazan Book of the Fallen 6 (London: Bantam, 2007), p. 584.

[28] Haydon White, *Metahistory: The Historical Imagination in Nineteenth-Century Europe* (Baltimore: Johns Hopkins University Press, 1975), p. 430.

White's view, writing history is a process of tracing patterns and arguing for their meaningfulness, but the patterns we are most likely to trace are heavily determined by existing cultural preoccupations and technologies of organisation. This is true of fantasies also, and Erikson's epigraph acknowledges this fact while simultaneously suggesting that engaged and active reading might allow other kinds of meaning to emerge.

While the epigraph deals in large-scale abstractions, its source in Erikson's world gives it more specific inflections. These words are written by a former priest and historian called Heboric, who readers first encounter in chains several books earlier. Heboric enters the story as a victim of a distortion with deliberate purpose. After '[c]arefully triggered riots, looting and slaughter', the Empress Laseen has sought 'to round up malcontents and unaligned academics, to close the fist of military presence on the capital, drumming the need for more troops, more recruits, more protection against the treasonous scheming of the noble class'.[29] The evocation of a necessity that is at least in part imagined has allowed Heboric – a man who wrote a treatise that 'called [the Empress] a murderer, and then had the gall to say she bungled the job' – to be swept up in the purge.[30] Appeals to a form of academic freedom and the support of an official imperial historian have both proved insufficient to protect him from condemnation as a traitor. He thus first appears to us as someone who has very good reasons

29 Steven Erikson, *Deadhouse Gates*, Malazan Book of the Fallen 2 (London: Bantam, 2001), p. 33.

30 Erikson, *Deadhouse Gates*, p. 31.

to be suspicious of the truth claims of official narratives. Subsequent events only serve to exacerbate his epistemological uncertainties.

While Heboric is a character in *The Bonehunters*, it is not entirely clear when the epigraph appears whether it represents his view at a point roughly contemporaneous with its placement in the narrative, or comprises part of one of his past writings, or represents a projection back from a vantage point in the future. We are told that it forms part of the introduction to a work called *Among the Consigned*, but the nuances of interpretation are left to us. Should we read the tone as clinical, or portentous, or slightly pompous, or as indicating a tentative speculation in progress? Does the framing signify that this is a kind of answer, or an irresolvable problem, or both? What precisely to make of these words is left as a personal choice for readers (or potentially as one that can be negotiated in an interpretive community). This is one way that Erikson seeks to slip away from the problems of editorialising he identifies in histories, using the affordances of Fantasy to suggest a world of complex, intersecting lives and stories that it would be a form of violence to neaten into one dominant line. His books' bulk allows space for a huge range of voices to be heard. The ethics of the series mean that it refuses to resolve these voices definitively for the reader, insisting on the importance of contradictory specifics and digressions, as well as the grand sweep accomplished over ten books and more than 3.3 million words. Vast histories loom up, ambiguous magics are employed and the thoughts of key figures are deliberately withheld. While some purposeful operations are successful, people regularly die pointlessly due to accidents and misunderstandings. However, the series is far from being deliberately abstruse. At the end of the third book, one character asserts that '*Compassion is priceless in the truest sense of the word. It must be given freely. In abundance.*'[31] The series itself mirrors this assertion in its compassionate excess, which provides characters and readers with ample space to develop a spectrum of understandings. Fantasy's generous imaginative extravagances can make it immensely accommodating, as the vibrant online communities that have sprung up around Erikson's work attest.

While Erikson imagines a world in which meanings, significance and deities are necessarily negotiable, other fantasies explore more totalising imaginative and linguistic impositions. In his story 'Tlön, Uqbar, Orbis Tertius' (1940), Jorge Luis Borges imagines the disconcerting experience of discovering books that appear to document unknown civilisations. The first is a fugitive entry in an encyclopaedia describing Uqbar, which appears only in certain rare editions and which describes a land whose literature was 'one of fantasy' in which 'epics and legends never referred to reality, but to the two imaginary realms of Mlejnas and Tlön'.[32] While Mlejnas is not mentioned again, Tlön comes to dominate the ensuing narrative when happenstance places into the narrator's hands the eleventh volume of *A First Encyclopaedia of Tlön*, covering subjects from Hlaer to Jangr. This volume provides a

31 Steven Erikson, *Memories of Ice*, Malazan Book of the Fallen 3 (London: Bantam, 2002), p. 1130.

32 Jorge Luis Borges, 'Tlön, Uqbar, Orbis Tertius', translated by James E. Irby, in *Labyrinths* (London: Penguin, 2000), pp. 27–43 (p. 29).

tantalising snapshot of a society organised around a fascination with mutability, rejecting fixed and definitive thingishness in favour of the play of perceptions and the creation of pleasing fictions:

> The metaphysicians of Tlön do not seek for the truth or even for verisimilitude, but rather for the astounding. They consider metaphysics a branch of fantastic literature. They know that a system is nothing more than the subordination of all aspects of the universe to any one such aspect.[33]

While the book purports to be from another world, later in the story it is revealed that the encyclopaedia has been fabricated by a secret society of idealists with the intention of replacing existing culture with something more decorous and comprehensible. Borges imagines the licence granted by the invented ideologies of Tlön to be far more comfortable than ways of knowing derived from the contingencies of real history or from the sometimes-unpleasant realities observed by scientists. 'Tlön is surely a labyrinth,' he writes, 'but it is a labyrinth devised by men, a labyrinth designed to be deciphered by men.'[34] As a consequence, at the conclusion of his story, the carefully constructed ethos of Tlön overwrites existing ways of understanding and organising culture and society:

> The contact and the habit of Tlön have disintegrated this world. Enchanted by its rigor, humanity forgets over and again that it is a rigor of chess masters, not of angels. Already the schools have been invaded by the (conjectural) 'primitive language' of Tlön; already the teaching of its harmonious history (filled with moving episodes) has wiped out the one which

[33] Borges, 'Tlön', p. 34. [34] Borges, 'Tlön', p. 42.

governed in my childhood; already a fictitious past occupies in our memories the place of another, a past of which we know nothing with certainty – not even that it is false.[35]

In the end, Borges imagines that the world's previous cultures will be replaced with the culture of Tlön, which arose from them, but which has selected their most tempting abstractions as its organising values. While this seems absurd in some respects, Borges's conclusion reminds us that it is very easy to edit the world down to what we are interested in, ignoring things that seem too complex, troubling or contradictory. 'I pay no attention to all this,' his narrator asserts, 'and go on revising, in the still days at the Adrogué hotel, an uncertain Quevedian translation (which I do not intend to publish) of [Sir Thomas] Browne's *Urn Burial*.'[36] In his peculiar obsession with another's peculiar obsession, Borges's narrator reminds us that the things that strike us as being truest and most valuable are often compelling fabrications.

Borges's story imagines relatively absolute forms of overwriting, but other fantasies deal with competing notions of cultural value that dip into and out of one another. In such fantasies, what has been suppressed almost inevitably bubbles back into view. In Hope Mirrlees's *Lud-in-the-Mist* (1926), an age of superstition has ostensibly been forced to make way for a polite and commercial society. However, older practices prove more difficult to dismiss than the rulers of the Free State of Dorimare would wish. Mirrlees uses the country's two rivers to map an interrelation of influences:

[35] Borges, 'Tlön', pp. 42–3. [36] Borges, 'Tlön', p. 43.

The Dawl was the biggest river of Dorimare, and it became so broad at Lud-in-the-Mist as to give that town, twenty miles inland though it was, all the advantages of a port; while the actual seaport town itself was little more than a fishing village. The Dapple, however, which had its source in Fairyland (from a salt inland sea, the geographers held) and flowed subterraneously under the Debatable Hills, was a humble little stream, and played no part in the commercial life of the town. But an old maxim of Dorimare bade one never forget that *The Dapple flows into the Dawl*. It had come to be employed when one wanted to show the inadvisability of despising the services of humble agents; but, possibly, it had originally another application.[37]

By the time the novel opens, the established commercial interests in Dorimare have overthrown an older feudal order, the last representative of which was 'Duke Aubrey, a hunchback with a face of angelic beauty, who seemed to be possessed by a laughing demon of destructiveness', who 'had been known, out of sheer wantonness, to gallop with his hunt straight through a field of standing corn, and to set fire to a fine ship for the mere pleasure of watching it burn'.[38] While other stories of the Duke record moments of kindness and geniality, these more positive aspects of his reputation did not prevent 'grim merchants, obsessed by a will to wealth' from provoking the people against him, bloodily unseating the old nobility and the priesthood. The Duke subsequently vanished into Fairyland and the newly established legislature placed a taboo on the acknowledgement of fairy things.

[37] Hope Mirrlees, *Lud-in-the-Mist* (London: Gollancz, 2008), p. 9.
[38] Mirrlees, *Lud-in-the-Mist*, p. 10.

However, the novel establishes that it is inevitable that the old order will mix into the new. Traces of the ducal regime linger in the town: one of the taverns is the Duke Aubrey Arms; the Duke's songs and stories remain potent in cultural memory; and the forms of metaphorical and allegorical language the inhabitants of Dorimare use often refer to fairy things. While the new mercantile order has sought to establish its legitimacy by constructing a rational system of laws to replace the arbitrary exercise of feudal power and the corrupting influence of fairy fruit, the father of the novel's hero is unconvinced that the two are as different as has been claimed:

> Master Josiah Chanticleer [. . .] who had been a very ingenious and learned jurist, had drawn in one of his treatises a curious parallel between fairy things and the law. The men of the revolution, he said, had substituted law for fairy fruit. But whereas only the reigning Duke and his priests had been allowed to partake of the fruit, the law was given freely to rich and poor alike. Again, fairy was delusion, so was the law. At any rate, it was a sort of magic, moulding reality into any shape it chose. But, whereas fairy magic and delusion were for the cozening and robbing of man, the magic of the law was to his intention and for his welfare.
>
> In the eye of the law, neither Fairyland nor fairy things existed. But then, as Master Josiah had pointed out, the law plays fast and loose with reality – and no one really believes it.[39]

Here, Josiah Chanticleer points out that all modes of social organisation require buy-in. In seeking to confine feudalism to the realm of fiction and replace it with a

[39] Mirrlees, *Lud-in-the-Mist*, p. 13.

more democratic means of organisation based on general laws, the merchants of Dorimare have rationalised their culture in manners that exclude certain kinds of people and certain kinds of feeling. This contradiction is embodied in the novel's deeply respectable protagonist, Nathaniel Chanticleer, a 'stay-at-home and steady' man who is nevertheless haunted by a 'plangent, blood-freezing and alluring' musical 'Note' that he himself played and which he can never unhear.[40] He loves aspects of the decorous town in which he dwells, but the inexplicable Note with its alien resonances has raised in him a kind of dissatisfaction and a fear that order could quickly slip away.

The plot of the novel serves to bear out Josiah Chanticleer's view on the magical affinities of the law when Nathaniel Chanticleer is declared legally dead in order to strip him of his mayoral title:

[W]e ordain that nothing but death alone shall have power to dismiss the Mayor of Lud-in-the-Mist and High Seneschal of Dorimare before the five years of his term of office shall fully have expired. But, the dead, being dumb, feeble, treacherous and given to vanities, if any Mayor at a time of menace to the safety of the Dorimarites be held by his colleagues to be any of these things, then let him be accounted dead in the eye of the Law, and let another be elected in his stead.[41]

As a consequence, Nathaniel Chanticleer, who remains very much alive in body, is forced to take the law into his own hands as a means of challenging the encroachments

[40] Mirrlees, *Lud-in-the-Mist*, p. 5.
[41] Mirrlees, *Lud-in-the-Mist*, pp. 145–6.

of Fairyland. However, he also comes to realise that just as the Note dwells in him, so should the wilder impulses of Fairyland, with their double-edged but liberating potential, have a presence in the town. Fairy is a disorganising principle in *Lud-in-the-Mist*, but one that provides a crucial space of possibility for the oppressed, dispossessed and bored, who (contra Josiah Chanticleer) can freely partake of fairy fruit and the alternative understanding it brings. While those who go into Fairyland or eat fairy fruit may be changed, sometimes brutally, change is often necessary. Cultures that foreclose the possibilities of memory and transformation impoverish those who depend on these for making meanings. Modern Dorimare is better served by engaging with its history than suppressing it.

The idea that myths and fantasies can act as forms of resistance lies at the heart of one of the greatest novels of the fantastic, Mikhail Bulgakov's *The Master and Margarita* (written in the 1920s and 1930s; published 1966–7). Bulgakov's story opens with Mikhail Alexandrovich Berlioz, the 'editor of a fat literary journal and chairman of the board of one of the major Moscow literary associations', trying clandestinely to shape an official line on Jesus.[42] He is in the company of Ivan Nikolaevich Ponyrev, a young poet who writes under the pseudonym Homeless. Berlioz has commissioned a 'long anti-religious poem' from Homeless, but in Homeless's poem, Jesus has come out 'completely alive, the once-existing Jesus, though, true, a Jesus furnished

[42] Mikhail Bulgakov, *The Master and Margarita*, translated by Richard Pevear and Larissa Volokhonsky (New York: Penguin, 2016), p. 3.

with all negative features'. This does not suit Berlioz's purposes. In their discussion at Patriarch's Ponds, Berlioz wants to persuade Homeless that 'the main thing was not how Jesus was, good or bad, but that this same Jesus, as a person, simply never existed in the world, and all the stories about him were mere fiction, the most ordinary mythology'.[43] For Berlioz, textual evidence of a historical Jesus should always be taken as 'a later spurious interpolation'.

However, Berlioz's attempt to impose a controlled official line is swiftly challenged by a mysterious foreign professor, Woland, who dismisses man's attempts to create rational order due to the brevity of human lives. '[H]ow can man govern,' Woland argues, 'if he is not only deprived of the opportunity of making a plan for at least some ridiculously short period—well, say, a thousand years—but cannot even vouch for his own tomorrow?'[44] Woland prophesies accurately that Berlioz will die later in the evening. He also asserts not only that Jesus existed, but that he was personally present when Jesus was condemned to death by Pontius Pilate, a scene he describes vividly, with considerable beauty and deep sympathy.

While Berlioz seeks to impose an official language and understanding, language turns out to be wilder and less controllable than he had hoped. In his initial conversation with Homeless, Berlioz casually invokes the Devil as a figure of speech, but this gives the Devil – taking the form of Woland – an excuse to respond by appearing. The alternative meanings and possibilities in language – the

[43] Bulgakov, *Master and Margarita*, p. 5.
[44] Bulgakov, *Master and Margarita*, p. 10.

Figure 1.3 Appreciative fan graffiti adorns the stairwell of an apartment building where Mikhail Bulgakov lived: the inspiration for the odd flat in which Woland and his company reside (now the Bulgakov Museum in Moscow).
Wojtek Laski via Getty Images.

ungovernability, arbitrariness and wonder that Woland's interpellations evoke – are literalised in the rest of the novel through the actions of the Devil and his hellish companions: the loquacious giant cat Behemoth, the manipulative valet Koroviev, the sinister Azazello and the vampiric Hella. Woland's quarrelling company establish themselves in a tenement flat (Figure 1.3) and cut a swathe through Moscow as they befuddle its authoritarian systems and tempt its inhabitants to express their hypocrisies. While the officials of the city are used to lives of comfortable graft – albeit haunted by the threat of state violence – the exploitative order they are accustomed to is revealed repeatedly to be intensely vulnerable when things happen that it cannot explain. When a corrupt theatre director who has denounced others to gain advantages for himself is inexplicably teleported to Yalta, or when a key official disappears, leaving his animated suit to continue his work, the system's blinkeredness and inadequacy is made starkly apparent.

Woland and his merry band are not the only forces that disrupt Soviet attempts to rationalise and control. While much of the novel describes the Devil's chaotic impact on contemporary Moscow, scenes that subtly repoint the gospel account of Pontius Pilate and the last days of Christ (called Yeshua in this telling) continue to appear throughout the book, their limpid clarity a stark contrast to the sound and fury of Satan's minions. Who the accounts are attributed to varies, but their ultimate source is one of the title characters, the master, whose writings have been suppressed brutally by the state and who has subsequently sought refuge in a psychiatric clinic. After Woland assists the master's lover, Margarita, in liberating him, the master admits somewhat diffidently that he has written 'a novel about Pontius Pilate':

> Woland burst into thunderous laughter, but neither frightened nor surprised anyone. Behemoth applauded for some reason.
>
> 'About what? About what? About whom?' said Woland, ceasing to laugh. 'And that—now? It's stupendous! Couldn't you have found some other subject? Let me see it.' Woland held out his hand, palm up.
>
> 'Unfortunately I cannot do that,' replied the master, 'because I burned it in the stove.'
>
> 'Forgive me, but I don't believe you,' said Woland, 'that cannot be: manuscripts don't burn.'[45]

[45] Bulgakov, *Master and Margarita*, p. 287.

While Berlioz sought to create a single official line, Woland asserts that language itself resists such attempts at control – a point the novel has already demonstrated, as we have been reading the master's tale interwoven with Woland's throughout. The novel enjoys the cunning play of intertexts: Satan himself is borrowed; Berlioz is named for the composer of *The Damnation of Faust* (1845); and Margarita is filched from Johann Wolfgang von Goethe's *Faust* (1808/1832), among other places. However, the novel weaves from these sources a story that is very much itself, showing how language and culture can re-inflect established meanings to make something by turns appallingly grotesque and eloquently beautiful. As Woland argues, people may die, causing their schemes to go awry, but the play of cultures remains, outliving us in unruly, mutable, irrepressible ways.

Through most of the novel, the master's feat of imaginative empathy is unveiled in chapters separate from those detailing the Devil's party in Moscow. However, the end collapses the two plotlines together when Woland and his troupe encounter Yeshua's disciple Matthew Levi. Matthew Levi is not partial to Woland, calling him 'spirit of evil and sovereign of shadows'. Woland does not deny this characterisation, but argues that his interlocutor's scorn is ill-advised:

> You uttered your words as if you don't acknowledge shadows, or evil either. Kindly consider this question: what would your good do if evil did not exist, and what would the earth look like if shadows disappeared from it? Shadows are cast by objects and people. Here is the shadow of my sword. Trees and living beings also have shadows. Do you want to skin the whole earth,

tearing all the trees and living things off it, because of your fantasy of enjoying bare light?[46]

The Devil in Bulgakov is not an evil to be cast out, but a means of proffering alternative forms of meaning, a manifestation of the creative and disruptive powers inherent in language and culture. This allows him to expose hypocrisy – and he often permits his minions a certain cruelty when doing so – but it also allows him to gauge fine distinctions, as when he asserts that the master 'does not deserve light, he deserves peace'.[47] In the master's novel, Pilate regrets that his legal role and what Yeshua has admitted to saying mean that they cannot continue their conversation. In Bulgakov's encircling narrative, and in its reception, that space of generative, generous possibility is not foreclosed.

Those who want a simple world are often quick to use fantasy as an accusation or a diagnosis. Conservative commentators often accuse their opponents of living in a liberal fantasy. In a more self-aware manner, China Miéville contends that '"Real" life under capitalism is a fantasy: "realism", narrowly defined, is therefore a "realistic" depiction of "an absurdity which is true" [. . .] but no less absurd for that.'[48] As Miéville recognises, we spend much of our time living in fantasies: fantasies which are to a limited extent our own, but which are for the most part constructed for us by the slow accumulations of our languages and cultures. However, while fantasies can lull,

[46] Bulgakov, *Master and Margarita*, p. 360.
[47] Bulgakov, *Master and Margarita*, p. 361.
[48] China Miéville, Editorial Introduction to *Symposium: Marxism and Fantasy*, *Historical Materialism*, 10.4 (2002), 39–49 (p. 42).

they can also provoke. Many of the ways our societies operate are determined by things we have chosen to believe. Language holds great power, but also the possibility of power's undoing. One of Fantasy's most significant cultural roles is to provide testing grounds for new kinds of language and belief, through which individuals can access alternative perspectives and recognise our collective power to fashion a world in which difference is acknowledged, respected and available as a force of liberation.

2

The Value of Iteration

One of the most common objections to Fantasy can be introduced in the exasperated words of Hugo Dyson. Dyson was a longstanding member of the Inklings, the literary circle formed in Oxford around C. S. Lewis and J. R. R. Tolkien. While he was generally a fan of their critical conversations and pubbish sociability, he was a more reluctant participant in some of their writerly activities, finding that his tastes did not align well with certain colleagues. Consequently, while listening to a reading from the drafts of *The Lord of the Rings*, Dyson – in some accounts lying despairingly on a couch – was unable to restrain himself from exclaiming, 'Oh God, not another fucking elf!'[1]

Variations on Dyson's objection are commonly lodged by those who find works of Fantasy awkward fits for their sensibilities. To such auditors, Fantasy appears to do the same things over and over again, endlessly proliferating, rather than striking out in bold and original directions. This is an impression that Fantasy sections in bookshops

[1] The principal source of the anecdote is Christopher Tolkien; the precise wording is discussed in Philip Zaleski and Carol Zaleski, *The Fellowship: The Literary Lives of the Inklings* (New York: Farrer, Strauss and Giroux, 2016), p. 358. Diana Pavlac Glyer provides illuminating remarks on Dyson and the Inklings in *The Company They Keep: C. S. Lewis and J. R. R. Tolkien as Writers in Community* (Kent: The Ohio State University Press, 2007), pp. 87–8. Dyson's objection is, of course, rather unfair, as Tolkien's elves very rarely fuck.

can give to those who have not read much of what they contain. Long series of fat paperbacks display serried ranks of the same author names, many employing elaborate fonts and Tolkienian initials (see Figure 2.1). Titles employ repeated patternings. The first three books in George R. R. Martin's A Song of Ice and Fire series are *A Game of Thrones* (1996), *A Clash of Kings* (1999) and *A Storm of Swords* (2000); *A Feast for Crows* (2005) and *A Dance with Dragons* (2011) vary the formula, but only slightly. Robin Hobb's trilogies employ linking words to unite their constituent volumes: *Assassin's Apprentice* (1995), *Royal Assassin* (1996), *Assassin's Quest* (1997); *Fool's Errand* (2001), *The Golden Fool* (2002), *Fool's Fate* (2003). The final Realm of the Elderlings books combine titles from earlier books in the series: *Fool's Assassin* (2014), *Fool's Quest* (2015), *Assassin's Fate* (2017). The crossings-over in these titles make potent promises to those who know something about Fitz and the Fool, but for the casual observer, they can make it seem as if the books are potentially interchangeable. Fantasy book covers often employ generic patterns, styles and situations. Stereotypical touchstones for such designs in cultural memory reflect the predilections of Frank Frazetta, whose covers commonly featured muscle-bound warriors, scantily clad women and dynamic beasts in situations that – by his own admission – often bore little relation to the book's contents. While modern tastes have moved away from the lurid drama of the pulp tradition, shared tropes remain prevalent. In the United Kingdom, A Song of Ice and Fire's mid-series switch to covers with a single principal colour and an iconic item in the centre (a sword, a crown, a helmet, a cup) has been much imitated. Similar

FIGURE 2.1 Series by Sarah J. Maas and George R. R. Martin among other books in the Sci-Fi & Fantasy section of Waterstones, Sauchiehall Street (Glasgow).
Author's Photo.

impressions regarding proliferation and replication can be given by multi-shelf runs of long manga series, vast archives of fan fiction or the numbered instalments of prominent Fantasy video game series such as The Elder Scrolls, Dragon Age or Shin Megami Tensei. All these works openly advertise their affinities, self-consciously positioning themselves as associates, responses, instalments, expansions or modifications.

For critics like Dyson, this networked propagation can prove exasperating. Tolkien's sprawling family trees of related elves were based on assumptions quite different from those that underpinned the literary canons he himself studied. Writing on the authors of the eighteenth and early nineteenth centuries, Dyson was keen to value the 'wild eccentricity and strangeness' and the 'oddity and extravagance' of men like Jonathan Swift, William Blake and Percy Shelley.[2] This kind of selective rhetoric posits great writers as peculiar one-offs, contending implicitly that the more conventional majority can safely be ignored. While Fantasy is certainly a field that can comfortably accommodate eccentricity, its base assumptions are predicated on a different view of cultural and aesthetic production, one that I would contend is more accurate, more democratic and – at least potentially – more inclusive. Rather than denying relations of lineage and influence, fantasies often joyfully acknowledge such connections, building iteratively on existing tropes and systems, reaching new positions through incremental processes of variation and modification. This is an element of

[2] H. V. D. Dyson and John Butt, *Augustans and Romantics, 1689–1830*, revised edition (London: Cresset Press, 1961), p. 39.

Fantasy creativity that is often demeaned or undervalued. However – as I hope to show – it is fundamental to many of the most powerful effects that fantastic forms achieve.

To establish the value of Fantasy's iterative approaches, it will help first to introduce some more developed versions of Dyson's objection. The idea that Fantasy – or, at least, certain kinds – can be mindlessly repetitive is not uncommon even among its ardent defenders. For Brian Attebery, repetition is one of the qualities likely to make a work what he terms a formula fantasy, 'a form of popular escapist literature that combines stock characters and devices – wizards, dragons, magic swords, and the like – into a predictable plot in which the perennially understaffed forces of good triumph over a monolithic evil'.[3] While he argues that wondrous and original works can be created from components of the formula, he implies that all too often it is employed stringently and lazily, resulting in derivative stories that are easily parodied. Diana Wynne Jones, herself an immensely inventive creator of atypical fantasy worlds, took great pleasure in poking fun at Fantasy stereotypes in *The Tough Guide to Fantasyland* (1996). Written in the form of a gazetteer, the book principally consists of an alphabetised compendium of familiar tropes, which Jones skewers one by one. Her entry for 'Quest' sets out what she considered to be some of the common predictabilities of the generic Fantasy plot:

Quest. Many, possibly most, Tours are organized as a Quest. This is like a large-scale treasure hunt, with clues scattered all

[3] Brian Attebery, *Strategies of Fantasy* (Bloomington and Indianapolis: Indiana University Press, 1992), p. 1.

over the continent, a few false leads, MYSTICAL MASTERS as game-show hosts, and the DARK LORD and the TERRAIN to make the Quest interestingly difficult. The Management selects a QUEST OBJECT (of which the Tourists are normally informed either at their STARTING POINT or no later than six INCIDENTS after) then adds the various INCIDENTS, CONFRONTATIONS and FIGHTS [...] The Rule is that Tours will always succeed in a Quest, so the Management will give you hints if you go off in the wrong direction (see PROPHECY). In order to be assured of your future custom, the Management has a further Rule: Tourists, far from being rewarded for achieving their Quest Object, must then go on to conquer the Dark Lord or set about SAVING THE WORLD, or both. And why not? By then you will have had a lot of practice in that sort of thing and, besides, the Quest Object is usually designed to help you do it.[4]

This passage will probably raise smiles of familiarity from those who have read fantasies of a certain vintage. However, while there are numerous works that include some – or even most – of the predictable elements Jones sets out, there are very few that employ tropes as unthinkingly or exactingly as her satire implies. Like composers of classical music, fantasy creators enjoy elaborating on themes, but in doing so, they can produce near infinite variety. Fantasy creators are often avid Fantasy consumers, and when they produce their works, they do so in knowing, adaptive dialogue. Works of Fantasy deliberately take advantage of their audiences' knowledge to sketch quickly using a shared symbolic language. However, the same works will often innovate in other areas by taking

[4] Diana Wynne Jones, *The Tough Guide to Fantasyland* (New York: DAW Books, 1996), pp. 205–6.

something familiar and making it new and strange, changing inflections, modifying contexts or questioning underlying assumptions.

Rather than mindlessly regurgitating, Fantasy creators work to reanimate, reconfigure and subvert the conventions of the form, increasing the diversity of its manifestations, rather than toeing a uniform line. If Dyson had listened more carefully, he might have appreciated the ways in which Tolkien distinguishes his elves from one another. Legolas and Galadriel are very different beings, made so by circumstances, histories, knowledge and predilections. The central conceit of *The Silmarillion* (1977) is that while they share an origin, the elves became differentiated as individuals and as peoples based on their particular experiences, creating the space for dissention and for meaningful acts of loyalty. Just as Tolkien's elves become characters rather than archetypes as we see more of them, works of Fantasy justify themselves by breathing unique and specific lives into common forms, in doing so subtly modifying the forms themselves in ways that change what they can do for future users.

Fantasy's creative possibilities thus inhere in processes that interweave adherence to and divergences from established patterns. This was something that Jones acknowledged when she followed *The Tough Guide to Fantasyland* with *The Dark Lord of Derkholm* (1998). *The Dark Lord of Derkholm* is a novel that fully literalises the concept of adventuring parties as tour groups that Jones had developed in the *Tough Guide*, but it elaborates extensively on the conceit to explore how tourists could negatively affect a fantasy world to which they travelled. The two books share certain conceptual frameworks, but *Dark*

Lord of Derkholm is far from being a derivative repetition or a laborious satirical instantiation of the *Tough Guide*. Towards the end of the novel, its antagonist, Mr Chesney, a dictatorial organiser of package tours and a voracious exploiter of what for him are off-world resources, asserts that he has fundamentally shaped the world he preys upon, claiming of one of the characters

> He's not real life. None of these people are. They're all just the way they are because I turned their world into a theme park. If they didn't happen to be under contract to me, they'd be nothing – just rough types in a world that happens to have some magic to it.[5]

Jones can get away with this villainous rant because she is confident her audience will not believe it. By the time readers reach this point, she has marshalled the full force of her considerable art to make her characters far more than simply rough types. While the wizard Derk has reluctantly taken up the mantle of Dark Lord so he can be repeatedly defeated by Chesney's tour groups, he is essentially a benign and gentle soul who has been deliberately selected by those more adept at conspiracy and revolution as a probable incompetent who is likely to mess up the tours, helping to break Chesney's hold. However, Derk has proved curiously adept in many respects, leading him to unexpected successes and causing those who banked on his ineptitude to incorporate into their plans new opportunities brought into play by his talents. Clever women have strategically manipulated the roles into

[5] Diana Wynne Jones, *The Dark Lord of Derkholm* (London: HarperCollins, 2013), p. 498.

which they have been cast, undermining Chesney's malignant infrastructures while also rebuking complacent patriarchs who have gone along with their oppressors rather than seeking loopholes or modes of resistance. Derk's children – two humans and five griffins – have played important roles in uncovering Chesney's perfidy, but the book also tells stories of their personal growth. They are not simply functions of Jones's central plot, but rather characters given individual hopes, dreams, limitations and lives. Chesney is sure that he can control how everything works, a certainty backed up in Jones's fiction by a demonic binding, the advantages granted by knowing the mechanics of two different worlds and a degree of arrogant personal inflexibility. However, Jones is not interested in telling a story in which things go according to Chesney's neat plans. If the *Tough Guide* is about the tyranny of generic expectations, *Dark Lord of Derkholm* shows how in practice such tyranny is defeated in fantastic constructions by heteroglossic combination and fictional play. Larger cultural patterns are refracted by creators into characters, plots and circumstances that may share a family resemblance, but which are indisputably themselves.

In this respect, Fantasy differs from other forms of cultural production mostly in gracefully acknowledging its entanglements with the larger patterns and structures that underpin any form of meaningful communication. One of the unfortunate legacies of artistic Romanticism is the lingering idea that true art is made by unique geniuses who channel something that has never previously existed into the world. This ideal still has considerable cultural purchase even though in its strong form it is self-evidently contradictory. Innovations do not arise fully formed from the ether; rather, they build on previous achievements. This is a foundational attitude in the sciences, expressed powerfully in Isaac Newton's famous comment to Robert Hooke: 'If I have seen further it is by standing on the sholders of Giants.'[6] While certain theorists and authors have made outsize claims for the creativity of individuals, what Newton says of himself is true of every pioneer and inventor. This is not to say that there is nothing new under the sun, but rather to emphasise that in any given work newness arises mainly from unexpected combinations or modifications of pre-existing elements, whether these be words, images, tropes, structures, technologies, cultural practices or social norms. Visual and verbal languages do not function without repetition, and the novelties they produce are relative, rather than absolute. Following Sigmund Freud, Rosemary Jackson has argued that 'Fantasy is not to do with inventing another non-human word: it is not transcendental. It has to do with inverting elements of this world, re-combining its constitutive features in new relations to produce something strange, unfamiliar and *apparently* "new", absolutely "other" and different.'[7] We cannot articulate how something is different from something else without a point of contrast. Fantasy creators know this, joining a conversation in which the achievements and

[6] Isaac Newton to Robert Hooke, 5 February 1675 [likely actually 1676], Historical Society of Pennsylvania, Box 12/11, Folder 37, https://discover.hsp.org/Record/dc-9792/.

[7] Rosemary Jackson, *Fantasy: The Literature of Subversion* (New York and London: Methuen, 1981), p. 8.

failures of previous fantasies provide pathways to new expressive possibilities.

Thinking about how works exist relationally is particularly important when we consider genres. John Rieder has written, following Hans-Robert Jauss, that 'there cannot be a first example of a genre, because the generic character of a text is precisely what is repeated and conventional in it'.[8] Horace Walpole's *The Castle of Otranto* (1764) has often been called the first Gothic novel, but as Anne H. Stevens has pointed out, it was not until after the publication of Clara Reeve's *The Champion of Virtue* (1777), the flourishing of further Gothic novels in the 1780s and the turbo-charging of the formula by writers like Ann Radcliffe and Matthew 'Monk' Lewis in the 1790s 'that the gothic becomes a recognizable and indeed flexible genre or family of genres'.[9] In a similar fashion, the works we now call Fantasy have acquired their generic meanings relationally. Their innovations come into focus in the context of wider cultural patternings.

It is also important to recognise that even putative origin claims usually send us tumbling further back. *The Castle of Otranto* takes pains to point out that it draws extensively on older traditions. The first edition was published anonymously, with a spurious translator's preface that declared that the book's source was 'found in the library of an ancient Catholic family in the north of

[8] John Rieder, *Science Fiction and the Mass Cultural Genre System* (Middletown, CT: Wesleyan University Press, 2017), p. 20.

[9] Anne H. Stevens, 'Circulating Libraries as Institutional Creators of Genres', in *Institutions of Literature, 1700–1900*, ed. by Jon Mee and Matthew Sangster (Cambridge: Cambridge University Press, 2022), pp. 120–34 (p. 124).

England' and 'printed at Naples, in the black letter, in the year 1529.' Rather than pretending to be a new story, the first edition purported to be an old one, although the safely disguised Walpole could not resist gesturing towards more modern sensibilities by congratulating himself on what he perceived to be the narrative's emotional plausibility: 'Though the machinery is invention, and the names of the actors imaginary, I cannot but believe, that the ground-work of the story is founded on truth.'[10] We might see many works of Fantasy as operating in a similar manner, employing a shared groundwork drawn from cultural traditions to combine the wonder of the new with the plausibility of the familiar.

After being assured of his story's success, Walpole unmasked himself and added a further preface to the second edition in which he elaborated on his method. Walpole described *Otranto* as 'an attempt to blend the two kinds of Romance, the ancient and the modern'.[11] In acknowledging the combined influence of contemporary novels and older fictions, and in claiming to have been directly inspired by Shakespeare, Walpole argued that a successful work is most likely to arise from cleverly modifying established forms:

I might have pleaded, that having created a new species of romance, I was at liberty to lay down what rules I thought fit for the conduct of it: But I should be more proud of having

[10] [Horace Walpole], 'Preface to the First Edition', in *The Castle of Otranto*, ed. by Nick Groom (Oxford: Oxford University Press, 2014), pp. 5–7 (p. 5).

[11] Horace Walpole, 'Preface to the Second Edition', in *The Castle of Otranto*, pp. 9–14 (p. 9).

imitated, however faintly, weakly, and at a distance, so masterly a pattern, than to enjoy the entire merit of invention, unless I could have marked my work with genius, as well as with originality.[12]

While Walpole gestures towards kinds of genius that can leap beyond the need for imitation, he affects to admit that he does not believe he can access these registers. Nevertheless, this has not stopped him from writing or from seeing his writing as a part of a productive conversation. Later in the second preface, he challenges Voltaire's predilection for neat divisions between different forms, discussing how he has mixed registers and social classes to produce naturalistic contrasts between sublimity and naiveite. The extent to which Walpole is deemed to have been successful in imitating nature will vary from reader to reader. What interests me here is not so much what Walpole does in *Otranto*, but rather the way he positions what has been claimed by others to be a wellspring as a joining of the waters. Walpole's newness does not come from nothing, but from a considered critical engagement with older works and forms.

Imitation for Walpole is not merely a sincere form of flattery but rather a worthy alchemical process that can create new gold from materials both exalted and base. In titling this chapter, I have preferred 'iteration' to Walpole's 'imitation' mainly because the meaning of 'imitation' has slipped in the past two hundred years so that, in Colin Burrow's words, 'being an imitator is generally regarded as less good than being whatever else it is that

[12] Walpole, 'Preface to the Second Edition', pp. 13–14.

we are supposed to be—"original" or "ourselves" or "creative" or "whacky" or "unusual" or "generative" or "productive" or "inspiring"'.[13] However, this modern sense of imitation as duplication at best or fakery at worst seems narrow when the wider historical context is considered. Productive, generative imitation has been recognised as a crucial feature of artistic practice across centuries and cultures. For the writers Burrow considers – a cast that includes Lucretius, Virgil, Petrarch, Ben Jonson, John Milton and Alexander Pope – to imitate was not uncritically to replicate, but rather consciously to modify by building upon and veering from the familiar achievements of others. Considering imitation as a process that inevitably reshapes, Burrow presents it as a practice 'which enables change, which also contains within itself the possibility of a derivative authority which interrogates that of the source. An imitator does not need to mimic what is admirable in an imitated text, but can reflect back a sinister double of its failings'. For Burrow, this makes imitation 'potentially a tool of psychological and also political resistance' while rendering it 'inescapable even for those who resist it'.[14] Discourses vested in the authority of Romantic originality might be uncomfortable with this, but Fantasy generally has little problem with adverting to older notions of imitation, in practice if not by name. In doing so, fantasies muster similar forms of creativity and critical engagement to those practised by the writers

[13] Colin Burrow, *Imitating Authors: Plato to Futurity* (Oxford: Oxford University Press, 2019), p. 2.

[14] Burrow, *Imitating Authors*, p. 28.

Burrow considers, reshaping and remaking cultural forms for new ages, media and audiences.

In looking for further analogies for the way Fantasy operates, we might also consider Linda Hutcheon's theorisation of adaptation. Writing against a 'morally loaded discourse of fidelity' that judges adaptations based on how closely they resemble what they adapt, Hutcheon argues that a good adaptation is 'a derivation that is not derivative—a work that is second without being secondary'.[15] For Hutcheon, the best adaptations are those sensitive not only to the work being adapted, but also to the affordances of the media in which the adaptation will operate and the intricacies of the social and cultural contexts within which the adapted text will circulate. Hutcheon contends that while an adaptation has acknowledged sources, these place no limits on what it can achieve as part of a cultural conversation and as a work in its own right:

> because each adaptation must also stand on its own, separate from the palimpsestic pleasure of doubled experience, it does not lose its Benjaminian aura. It is not a copy in any mode of reproduction, mechanical or otherwise. It is repetition but without replication, bringing together the comfort of ritual and recognition with the delight of surprise and novelty. As adaptation, it involves both memory and change, persistence and variation.[16]

[15] Linda Hutcheon with Siobhan O'Flynn, *A Theory of Adaptation*, 2nd edition (London: Routledge, 2013), pp. 7, 9.

[16] Hutcheon, *A Theory of Adaptation*, p. 173. 'Benjaminian' here refers to Walter Benjamin's essay 'The Work of Art in the Age of Mechanical Introduction' (1935), which argues, among many other things, that

What Hutcheon says of adaptation also works well for Fantasy, which takes a similar joy in the interplay of recognisable elements and moments of defamiliarisation, uncertainty and productive questioning.

Fantasy, then, can be used to say things starkly and powerfully precisely because its forms and symbols resonate and clash with previous uses. Sometimes fantastic resonances serve as relatively straightforward enrichments, adding colour by alluding to a shared reference point. 'She glared like Medusa' communicates something quick and specific if the listener knows who Medusa is. Between certain people, it might also carry overtones of misogyny or strength-claiming arising from their knowledge of details, criticisms and reappropriations of the myth.[17] Other resonances transmit through more complex and critical webs and weaves. Mikhail Bulgakov's *The Master and Margarita* (1966–7) produces its originality through dialogues with earlier Russian literature and with previous literary devils. Bulgakov's Woland is striking and effective because he both is and is not like John Milton's Lucifer, Johann Wolfgang von Goethe's Mephistopheles, Hector Berlioz's Méphistophélès and Charles Gounod's Méphistophélès. A reader does not need to know all these other devils to enjoy Woland, but knowing them enhances rather than detracts from the experience of Bulgakov's book as the resonances create a rich tissue of allusion and surprise. The novelty of fantasies is self-consciously

unique works of art have an aura that arises from their authenticity and their singular placement in time and space.

[17] See Hélène Cixous, 'The Laugh of the Medusa', translated by Keith Cohen and Paula Cohen, *Signs*, 1.4 (1976), 875–93.

relative. However, like imitations in the broad sense Burrow revivifies and like the adaptations Hutcheon examines, this does not mean that fantasies uncritically accept older forms and values, or that they cannot make repurposed materials powerfully new.

Even stories told as many times as the key narratives of the Arthurian corpus can be given new meanings and inflections with relatively simple alterations. T. H. White's Lancelot in *The Ill-Made Knight* (1940) draws heavily on Thomas Malory's depiction in *Le Morte d'Arthur*. However, White's Lancelot is a man whose 'face was as ugly as a monster's in the King's menagerie', and this changes the meaning of every event that follows.[18] Malory's handsome Launcelot has relatively little explicit interiority – we are told what he does, but only rarely what he thinks. Conversely, we are given qualified access to White's Lancelot's mind from the outset, making his internal struggles and uncertainties key aspects of the story. When we meet the young Lancelot, we are told that 'He was trying to find out what he was, and he was afraid of what he would find.' Malory's Launcelot has a confidence that matches his abilities, but White's is haunted by doubts:

> The boy thought that there was something wrong with him. All through his life—even when he was a great man with the world at his feet—he was to feel this gap: something at the bottom of his heart of which he was aware, and ashamed, but which he did

[18] T. H. White, *The Ill-Made Knight*, in *The Once and Future King* (London: Collins, 1958), pp. 325–544 (p. 329). *The Ill-Made Knight* was first published in 1940 and revised for its inclusion in *The Once and Future King*; the revised text is used here.

not understand. There is no need for us to try to understand it. We do not have to dabble in a place which he preferred to keep secret.[19]

Of course, while White claims that we do not have to dabble in Lancelot's heart, this is precisely what the book proceeds to do. What Lancelot does in White's retelling is very similar to what he does in Malory. At times, White refers the reader to Malory to fill in the details, remarking at one point that 'There is no need to give a long description of the tourney. Malory gives it.'[20] However, what Lancelot feels in White's hands is very different from what he is depicted as feeling by Malory. White's version compels by revivifying and contextualising the action of an old romance while simultaneously telling a more novel story inside its characters' heads.

An obvious example of the originality in White's depiction is the relationship between Lancelot and Guenever. In Malory, we are told early in the narrative that Merlin 'warned the kyng covertly that Guenyver was nat holsom for hym to take to wyff' because of the destined course of her affections.[21] We are also told that 'quene Guenyvere had [Launcelot] in grete favoure aboven all other knyghtis, and so he loved the queen agayne aboven all other ladyes days of his lyff, and for hir he dud many dedys of armys and saved her frome the fyre thorow his noble chevalry'.[22] However, while their passion is written convincingly at

[19] White, *The Ill-Made Knight*, p. 327.
[20] White, *The Ill-Made Knight*, p. 364.
[21] Thomas Malory, *The Works of Thomas Malory*, ed. by Eugène Vinaver, revised by P. J. C. Field, 3rd edition, 3 vols. (Oxford: Clarendon Press, 1990), 1:97, ll. 29–31 (Book III Chapter 1).
[22] Malory, *Works*, 1:253, ll. 15–19 (Book VI Chapter 1).

various points – particularly in their sad final parting – we are never really told why they feel the ways they do. Malory's characters live in their mature actions. By contrast, White is fascinated by the formations of characters and feelings, as the story of Arthur's education in *The Sword in the Stone* (1938), the antics of the young Orkney faction in *The Witch in the Wood* (1939) and the discussion of Lancelot's upbringing all demonstrate. White spends considerable time exploring how Guenever and Lancelot's mutual love for Arthur initially leads them into conflict. It is in a rather quotidian moment that Lancelot comes to a realisation that both sets the story on its predetermined tracks and changes utterly the inflection of its events:

> The jerfalcon was in a foul temper, and Lancelot caught its mood. Guenever, who was not particularly good with hawks and had no special interest in them, was frightened by his frowning brow, and, because she was frightened, she became clumsy. She was sweetly trying her best to help, but she knew that she was not clever at falconry, and there was confusion in her mind. Very carefully and kindly, and with the best intentions, she wound the creance up quite wrong.
>
> He took the wretched ball away from her with a gesture which was almost rough.
>
> "That's no good," he said, and he began to unwind her hopeful work with angry fingers. His eyebrows made a horrible scowl.
>
> There was a moment in which everything stood still. Guenever stood, hurt in her heart. Lancelot, sensing her stillness, stood also. The hawk stopped bating and the leaves did not rustle.
>
> The young man knew, in this moment, that he had hurt a real person, of his own age. He saw in her eyes that she thought he

was hateful, and that he had surprised her badly. She had been giving kindness, and he had returned it with unkindness. But the main thing was that she was a real person.[23]

White's major innovation is to make Arthurian figures into real people using technologies of prose and understanding that had developed between Malory's time and his own. White's Guenever sees more in his Lancelot because there is more to see. While Malory's Launcelot quests for fame because this is what knights do, in White's version, we are told that Lancelot's quests 'were an attempt to escape from Guenever. They were his struggles to save his honour, not to establish it.'[24] White's Lancelot longs to be good, but he is convinced that he is lacking, haunted by the certainty he can never achieve the forms of purity he aspires to. Both Malory's Launcelot and White's Lancelot demur initially when asked to try and heal Sir Urre, but while Malory's Launcelot refuses out of chivalrous respect for his fellow knights who have failed, White's Lancelot heads to the task convinced that he is irrevocably tainted, filled with fear, 'ugly as ever, self-conscious, ashamed, a veteran going to be broken.'[25] Malory's Launcelot's success is proof of his devoutness and devotion. White's Lancelot sees his success very differently: 'This lonely and motionless figure knew a secret which was hidden from the others. The miracle was that he had been allowed to do a miracle.' When we reach the final sentence of White's book – '"And ever," says Malory, "Sir Lancelot wept, as he had been a child that had been

[23] White, *The Ill-Made Knight*, p. 348.
[24] White, *The Ill-Made Knight*, p. 355.
[25] White, *The Ill-Made Knight*, p. 543.

beaten."' – we re-join Malory's words, but with a transformed understanding of the psychology of this reaction.[26]

White's novel is an easy test case as it very deliberately adapts and comments on a particular source text. There are far more radical reworkings of Lancelot that might be considered, from John Cleese's affably awkward engine of violence in *Monty Python and the Holy Grail* (1975) to the hedgehog antagonist-turned-ally in *Sonic and the Black Knight* (2009). However, rather than dwelling further with Lancelot, it seems more helpful to move out from this specific character to some looser kinds of creative reworking.

Many older representations of Death are violent, threatening or sinister. We might think of the scythe-wielding skeleton on the red horse in the foreground of Pieter Bruegel the Elder's painting *The Triumph of Death* (1562–3) or of the Red Death, who holds 'illimitable dominion over all' at the end of Edgar Allan Poe's 'The Masque of the Red Death' (1842).[27] We might also think of Antonius Block's relentless, moon-faced chess opponent in Ingmar Bergman's *The Seventh Seal* (1957), who claims he has nothing to tell and that nothing escapes him.[28] Poe's and Bergman's Deaths wear their unfathomability prominently. By contrast, Neil Gaiman's Death in *The Sandman* (1989–96) appears first as a cheerful goth

[26] White, *The Ill-Made Knight*, p. 544.

[27] Edgar Allan Poe, 'The Masque of the Red Death', in *Selected Tales*, ed. by David Van Leer (Oxford: Oxford University Press, 2008), pp. 129–34 (p. 134).

[28] Although if this is the case, why does he allow Jof and Mia to slip away when Block seems to distract him? Is this Death fallible, merciful or simply assured that all will come to him in time?

girl. Her initial dialogue with her sullen brother Dream (the Sandman of the title, also called Morpheus, among many other things) contains a long riff on how much she likes *Mary Poppins* (1964). Her perky practicality is very different from the apocalyptic version of Death Gaiman wrote with Terry Pratchett in *Good Omens* (1990). She also differs from Pratchett's genial, skeletal Death in the Discworld series, although the two share a capacity for kindness and a sense of duty. It is not hard to imagine Pratchett's Death responding to the question of whether living fifteen thousand years is 'pretty good' with 'YOU GOT A LIFETIME. NO MORE. NO LESS', or Gaiman's Death responding to the question of what makes life worth living with 'Cats [. . .] Cats are nice.'[29] Death in *The Sandman* is not an unfathomable cosmic force, but someone who is aggressively and genuinely relatable.

Gaiman's Death is a very deliberate subversion of expectations. Cleaving to sinister archetypes would have resulted in a Death rather too close in character to Dream, and it is clear that Gaiman wanted to differentiate the Endless from each other, both to make for a better story and to challenge conventional understandings of the concepts they represent. In rewriting Death as practical, good-humoured and benevolent, Gaiman shifts the stakes of the series away from the Christian notions of sin that underpin in different ways the visions of Bruegel, Poe and Bergman. This is not to say that such notions have no place in *The Sandman*: the comic

[29] Neil Gaiman et al., *The Sandman*, Volume 7: *Brief Lives* (New York: Vertigo/DC Comics, 1994), chapter 3, p. 5; Terry Pratchett, *Sourcery* (London: Corgi, 1989), p. 16. Fonts transposed in these two quotations for demonstration purposes, so Gaiman's Death speaks in Pratchett's Death's distinctive small caps.

visits a viscerally unsettling Hell in its fourth issue and explores its implications extensively in the *Season of Mists* story arc (1990–91). In Gaiman's imagined universe, though, Death rarely judges, and as personified, she is not someone to be afraid of. There are far more terrifying things in the world of the Endless than endings. While sad and sudden deaths occur in the series, Death herself tries to be a catalyst for healthy moving on.

In making a contemporary Death who swerves away from traditions of terror, Gaiman nevertheless finds deep roots to draw upon. While accompanying Death, Dream reflects that humanity's 'attitude to [his] sister's gift is so strange' and recalls the words of a 'forgotten poet' who he believes 'understood her gifts':

> Death is before me today:
> Like the recovery of a sick man,
> Like going forth into a garden after sickness.
>
> Death is before me today:
> Like the odor of myrrh,
> Like sitting under a sail in a good wind.
>
> Death is before me today:
> Like the course of a stream;
> Like the return of a man from the war-galley to his house.
>
> Death is before me today:
> Like the home that a man longs to see,
> After years spent as a captive.[30]

30 Neil Gaiman et al., 'The Sound of her Wings' (issue 8), in *The Sandman*, Volume 1: *Preludes and Nocturnes* (New York: Vertigo/DC Comics, 1995), pp. 229–30.

This text is not original to the comic; rather, it is an English translation of part of an Egyptian text of the Middle Kingdom that Gaiman found quoted in Joseph Campbell's *The Masks of God* (1959–68).[31] *The Sandman*, as a story about dreams, is often deliberately allusive, taking magpie-like delight in tangling bright fragments of other stories in its constructions. However, while this fragment is a lovely diversion in itself, it also echoes through the comic's larger assemblage of stories, establishing a tone to which the narrative will at several points return. Morpheus's liking for the poem says something about death, in general, and Death as *The Sandman* imagines her, in particular, but it also says a lot about Dream, presenting an early foreshadowing of themes that will become increasingly prominent as the threads of fate tighten through the series.

I have been calling the character I have been discussing Gaiman's Death, but while he is her primary author, she is also the product of the comic's artists, inkers and letterers, all of whom add further resonances to the interpretation. In her first appearance, she is punky, scratchy and expressive in Mike Dringenberg's pencils and Malcolm Jones III's inks. Her conventional speech bubbles with their neat standard font contrast deliberately with Dream's dramatic white-on-black voice, a contrast rendered throughout the series in Todd Klein's careful lettering.

[31] Joseph Campbell, *The Masks of God: Oriental Mythology* (New York: Viking Press, 1962), p. 138; Neil Gaiman, *journal.neilgaiman.com*, 5 March 2002, https://bit.ly/3Lh1TpV. The lines are an interpretation of part of Papyrus Berlin 3024, usually titled either 'The Dispute Between a Man and his Ba' or 'The Debate Between a Man and his Soul'.

While Death's font remains consistent, her appearance varies considerably as different artists iterate upon her established image. She shows different faces when she is drawn chibi-style by Jill Thompson in a flashback to the younger days of the Endless and when she is rendered in Marc Hempel's expressive lines in *The Kindly Ones* (1994–5). Thompson's child version of Death can be unabashedly cute, and her interpretation of the character in general emphasises her playfulness and charm, which works particularly effectively when sibling dynamics are depicted. There is a lovely scene in the Thompson-illustrated *Brief Lives* (1992–3) where a skinny, elbowy Death upbraids Dream with sisterly insightfulness and snark while he towers in awkward, ineffectual stillness above her.[32] In *The Kindly Ones*, the stark grace that Hempel's inks lend Death is well suited to the role she is required to play. While the character maintains a core identity, part of her success lies in her ability imaginatively to be extended in further stories and re-versionings. She changes subtly when her words are voiced with cheeriness and lightness by Kat Dennings in the audio adaptation, and when embodied empathetically by Kirby Howell-Baptiste in the TV series, and when cosplayed and refracted by thirty years of fans who have taken on her blacks and ankh and aspects of her attitude. Appropriately for a representation of a universal concept, Gaiman's Death travels well between comics narratives, adaptations and wider cultures. Unlike her brother, she can easily accommodate change.

[32] Gaiman et al., *The Sandman*, Volume 7: *Brief Lives*, chapter 6, pp. 19–20.

Anthropomorphic personifications of Death are relatively common in works of Fantasy, but there are presences far more ubiquitous. While certain modern fantasies have swerved away from dragons, seeing them as the quintessential tired Fantasy cliché, they remain among the most beloved of monsters, in part due to their flexibility and power as characters and narrative devices. Dragons have deep roots in numerous cultures. Sticking with Anglophone imaginaries initially, we might look first at the dragon in the work often considered to be the first major English poem:

> Ǣr hī þǣr gesēgan   syllicran wiht,
> wyrm on wonge   wiðerræhtes þǣr
> lāðne licgean;   wæs se lēġdraca
> grimliċ, gry(refāh)   glēdum beswǣled.
> sē wæs fiftiġes   fōtġemearces
> lang on leġere;   lyftwynne hēold
> nihtes hwīlum,   nyðer eft ġewāt
> dennes niosáịan;   wæs ðā dēaðe fæst,
> hæfde eorðscrafa   ende ġenyttod.[33]

To many readers, these words from *Beowulf* will appear incomprehensible. Fortunately, we have modern versions to help interpret the language. In translating, such versions also iterate, subtly differing from one another in their emphases. Seamus Heaney's translation offers a relatively straightforward transposition, but one that displays 'a prejudice in favour of forthright delivery', accentuating the things about the poem he finds most attractive:

[33] *Beowulf*, ll. 3038–46, as given in *Klaeber's Beowulf*, ed. by R. D. Fulk, Robert E. Bjork and John D. Niles, 4th edition (Toronto, Buffalo, NY, and London: University of Toronto Press, 2008), p. 103.

> What I had always loved was a kind of foursquareness about the utterance, a feeling of living inside a constantly indicative mood, in the presence of an understanding that assumes you share an awareness of the perilous nature of life and are yet capable of seeing it steadily and, when necessary, sternly. There is an undeluded quality about the Beowulf poet's sense of the world which gives his lines immense emotional credibility[.][34]

In line with this manifesto, Heaney renders the lines on the death of the dragon thus:

> But what they saw first was far stranger:
> The serpent on the ground, gruesome and vile,
> Lying facing him. The fire-dragon
> Was scaresomely burnt, scorched all colours.
> From head to tail, his entire length
> Was fifty feet. He had shimmered forth
> On the night air once, then winged back
> Down to his den; but death owned him now,
> He would never enter his earth-gallery again.[35]

However, Heaney's unflinching eye is only one of many possible viewpoints on the poem. Approaching the same scene, Maria Dahvana Headley's Hugo-Award-winning translation genders the dragon differently, offering a more sympathetic image of a corpse 'scathed and sooted by her own song'.[36] Headley's punkier, more slangy translation is interested in probing the poem's constructions of

[34] Seamus Heaney, *Beowulf* (London: Faber & Faber, 1999), pp. xxvii–xxviii.

[35] Seamus Heaney, *Beowulf*, ll. 3038–46.

[36] Maria Dahvana Headley, *Beowulf: A New Translation* (London: Scribe, 2021), l. 3041.

masculinity. When Wiglaf mourns Beowulf in Headley's version, he bemoans the fact that

> No councillor could convince
> our king, our old and beloved protector,
> that he shouldn't come at the guardian of this gold,
> but instead let her dream unmolested, drowsing
> alongside her beloved hoard, ground-nested,
> until world's end.[37]

Heaney's translation approaches the same moment rather differently:

> Nothing we advised could ever convince
> The prince we loved, our land's guardian,
> Not to vex the custodian of the gold,
> Let him lie where he was long accustomed,
> Lurk there under the earth until the end of the
> world.[38]

Both translators present effective versions of this oration, but in chaining together Beowulf as his people's beloved and the hoard as the dragon's, Headley favours a more emotive register that places both those slain as capable of degrees of feeling. While Heaney's dragon lurks, Headley employs the more comfortable 'ground-nested'. Heaney's dragon is irritable, assumed to be easily vexed in a way that Headley's translation smooths. In Heaney's translation, Beowulf is the guardian of the land, while the dragon is a custodian of gold, a term that implies the assets held are ultimately for others to reclaim. In Headley's translation, 'protector' and 'guardian' are closer synonyms. The translators' divergent approaches demonstrate how the dragon hits differently for different

[37] Headley, *Beowulf*, ll. 3079–84. [38] Heaney, *Beowulf*, ll. 3079–83.

readers. Heaney's dragon is 'gruesome and vile' in his ruin. By contrast, Headley presents the corpse as a 'wrathful wonder / A sky-dragon become ground-ghost.'[39] Heaney follows a more traditional line, seeing the dragon ultimately as a monstrous foe. Headley displays a reaction that has become more common as we have grown more used to dragons: imagining ways that they might be somewhat like us.

It could be argued that as sympathetic monsters are a relatively modern concern, Heaney's translation takes a more faithful approach. However, Headley's reflexively drawing out the story's inherent ironies might garner support from an influential interpreter. In 'Beowulf: The Monsters and the Critics', Tolkien is keen for dragons to be valued as dragons, contending that 'the dragon in legend is a potent creation of men's imagination, richer in significance than his barrow is in gold'.[40] However, he also argues that the significance of such figures is continuously remade. For him, *Beowulf* is a poem that responds self-consciously to shifting histories and traditions:

> *Beowulf* is not a 'primitive' poem; it is a late one, using the materials (then still plentiful) preserved from a day already changing and passing, a time that has now for ever vanished, swallowed in oblivion; using them for a new purpose, with a wider sweep of imagination, if with a less bitter and concentrated force. When new *Beowulf* was already antiquarian, in a good sense, and it now produces a singular effect. For it is now

39 Headley, *Beowulf*, ll. 3038–9.

40 J. R. R. Tolkien, 'Beowulf: The Monsters and the Critics', in *The Monsters and the Critics and Other Essays*, ed. by Christopher Tolkien (London: HarperCollins, 2006), pp. 5–48 (p. 16).

to us itself ancient; and yet its maker was telling of things already old and weighted with regret, and he expended his art in making keen that touch upon the heart which sorrows have that are both poignant and remote.[41]

While *Beowulf* is often invoked as a first work, Tolkien points out that – like Walpole's *Otranto* – it is only a purported origin point. The dragon in *Beowulf* might be claimed as the earliest extant in English, but others came before, and both these and those that came after shape how readers encounter the Geatish monarch's final foe.

In Tolkien's own legendarium, dragons appear as villains, made as tools of war by Morgoth, the Luciferian evil in the cosmology of Eä. In *The Silmarillion*, Glaurung's might, malice and hypnotising gaze rain down misery on elves and men. The quest in *The Hobbit* (1937) centres on wresting back the treasures of the dwarves from Smaug's fearsome clutches. Sneaking into the dragon's lair, Bilbo finds a sight that is terrifying and unfamiliar to him, but which shares a number of elements with *Beowulf*:

There he lay, a vast red-golden dragon, fast asleep; thrumming came from his jaws and nostrils, and wisps of smoke, but his fires were low in slumber. Beneath him, under all his limbs and his huge coiled tail, and about him on all sides stretching away across the unseen floors, lay countless piles of precious things, gold wrought and unwrought, gems and jewels, and silver red-stained in the ruddy light. [. . .] Bilbo had heard tell and sing of dragon-hoards before, but the splendour, the lust, the glory of such treasure had never yet come home to him.[42]

[41] Tolkien, 'Beowulf', p. 33.

[42] J. R. R. Tolkien, *The Hobbit* (London and Sydney: Unwin Paperbacks, 1981), pp. 205–6.

However, unlike the dragon Beowulf fights, Smaug is an eloquent conversationalist, possessing hauteur and considerable subtlety. Tolkien codes Smaug's greed and possessiveness in quite particular manners, describing his anger after a cup is stolen from his hoard as 'the sort of rage that is only seen when rich folk that have more than they can enjoy suddenly lose something that they have long had but have never before used or wanted'.[43] If *Beowulf*'s dragon is a beast, Smaug is more of a rotten aristocrat: proud, acquisitive and capable of both psychological manipulation and spectacular violence. By the time Tolkien was writing, dragons were considerably smarter, capable of tangling with heroes verbally as well as with tooth and claw.

Smaug as Tolkien presents him has a relatively traditional appearance for a Western dragon. However, images of dragons have long taken varied forms. A thirteenth-century bestiary depicts a rather cheerful-looking feather-winged creature adorned with brilliant colours (Figure 2.2). One drawn by Leonardo da Vinci has a long serpentine neck and weird, hairy, muscle-bound back legs (Figure 2.3). It lacks the front legs or arms common in the shape that became the default, its anatomy resembling that which would later be ascribed to wyverns. Leonardo's dragon is a nightmarish predator, tangling with another stalwart of heraldry in heated combat. If Leonardo's dragon strikes us as in some respects strange, other old images present more familiar designs, like the fighting pair found in the fifteenth-century *St Albans Chronicle* (Figure 2.4). Neither

[43] Tolkien, *The Hobbit*, p. 208.

FIGURE 2.2 A page on dragons from a thirteenth-century bestiary. J. Paul Getty Museum, Los Angeles, Ms. Ludwig XV 3, fol. 89.

Leonardo's dragon nor those in the *St Albans Chronicle* are as large as fully-grown modern Fantasy dragons tend to be. However, both images are clearly recognisable as dragons, showing the reach and persistence of the

FIGURE 2.3 Sketch by Leonardo da Vinci of a fight between a dragon and a lion (original held in the Uffizi Gallery, Florence).

archetype and the ways in which different minds and hands can rework context, scale and plausibility.

Some forms of art have historically accommodated dragons more easily than others. Manushag N. Powell records that while dragons were largely absent from eighteenth-century novels, audiences had access to them in the Bible and apocrypha, in botany and natural philosophy, and in 'popular musical culture' such as 'verse satires, ballads, harlequinades, and pantomimes', as well as in older romances and folklore. She pays particular attention to *The Dragon of Wantley* (1737), 'a travesty send-up of the St. George story, in which the triumphant knight is a drunken buffoon who kills his dragon with a lucky kick to its anus'. A work that is 'simultaneously grandiose and silly, high and low', *The Dragon of Wantley* reflects how

FIGURE 2.4 King Vortigern and Merlin watch a conflict between red and white dragons. *St Albans Chronicle*, MS6, f43v. Image courtesy of Lambeth Palace Library.

new audiences and cultural proliferation can reconfigure older symbols in manners that are simultaneously affectionate and satirical.[44] Theatrical audiences were glad to see a figure of legend made manifest with stage magic, but

[44] Manushag N. Powell, 'The Legacy of Stage Dragons and the Monstrous Eighteenth Century', *Eighteenth-Century Fiction*, 32.3 (2020), 485–504 (pp. 487, 491).

they also enjoyed seeing a heraldic symbol of nobility being taken down a peg or two.

Powell sees the travesty as a work that links 'serious political dragons like Geoffrey of Monmouth to the singing dragons and childhood memories of Edith [Nesbit] and Kenneth Grahame'.[45] However, these later dragons are also political in their ways, speaking to the operations of power in worlds no longer dominated by a nobility justifying itself with codes of chivalry. By exposing knights and dragons to ridicule, *The Dragon of Wantley* undercuts the romance tradition that had worked to legitimise certain forms of aristocratic authority and behaviour. Later dragons in children's writing have a similar interest in remaking assumptions that older dragons were employed to enforce.

Kenneth Grahame's 'The Reluctant Dragon' (1898) depicts a creature typical in its physical form, but utterly undragonish in temperament. The adults in the story initially react with fear and suspicion, employing inherited knowledge rather than trusting the evidence of their eyes:

He was sticking half-way out of the cave, and seemed to be enjoying of the cool of the evening in a poetical sort of way. He was as big as four cart-horses, and all covered with shiny scales—deep-blue scales at the top of him, shading off to a tender sort o' green below. As he breathed, there was that sort of flicker over his nostrils that you see over our chalk roads on a baking windless day in summer. He had his chin on his paws, and I should say he was meditating about things. Oh, yes, a peaceable sort o' beast enough, and not ramping or carrying on or doing anything but what was quite right and proper. I admit

45 Powell, 'Legacy of Stage Dragons', p. 498.

> all that. And yet, what am I to do? *Scales*, you know, and claws, and a tail for certain, though I didn't see that end of him—I ain't *used* to 'em, and I don't *hold* with 'em, and that's a fact![46]

Grahame's child protagonist, though, is more open to new experiences, befriending the benevolent dragon and engineering a conciliation by employing St George. The dragon slayer is initially unwilling to believe that this dragon is different from those he usually encounters. When told that the dragon is good, he interprets this based on his preconceptions: 'A good *dragon*. Believe me I do not in the least regret that he is an adversary worthy of my steel, and no feeble specimen of his noxious tribe.'[47] However, conversation brings St George round, and he eventually agrees to stage a combat to reconcile the dragon and the local residents. Rather than a villain to be defeated, Grahame's dragon is a benign presence who can be accepted and integrated into the community.

'The Reluctant Dragon' is one of many modern works in which the boundaries between dragons and people prove to be fuzzy. In C. S. Lewis's *The Voyage of the Dawn Treader* (1952), Eustace, who begins the story as a selfish and irritating character, suffers an unfortunate change as a result of his acquisitiveness: 'Sleeping on a dragon's hoard with greedy, dragonish thoughts in his heart', he becomes a dragon himself.[48] Lewis's inspiration is probably the thirteenth-century *Völsunga Saga*, in which Fáfnir turns

[46] Kenneth Grahame, 'The Reluctant Dragon', in *Dream Days* (London and New York: John Lane, 1898), pp. 179–245 (pp. 191–2).

[47] Grahame, 'The Reluctant Dragon', p. 213.

[48] C. S. Lewis, *The Voyage of the Dawn Treader* (London: HarperCollins, 2009), p. 105.

into a dragon in order better to guard his accumulated treasure. However, while Fáfnir's permanent transformation makes him into a monster even his brother conspires to slay, Eustace's distressing experience leads to a more fruitful kind of growth. The shock of his vast new form, the difficulties posed by his inability to speak and the sympathy and kindness of his companions all make him reconsider the ways he has previously acted. Lewis writes that Eustace's character 'had been rather improved by becoming a dragon', describing how he explores the island, brings back goats to feed the Dawn Treader's crew, and tears up and transports 'a great tall pine tree' that can 'be made into a capital mast'.[49] Lewis enjoys thinking through the physical prowess of the dragon, imagining the capabilities of a vast scaly body that can somehow still manage to take to the air (magic is usually invoked here as a reasonable justification in the context of Fantasy). However, Lewis also thinks carefully about the psychological impact of Eustace's transformation:

> The pleasure (quite new to him) of being liked and, still more, of liking other people, was what kept Eustace from despair. For it was very dreary being a dragon. He shuddered whenever he caught sight of his own reflection as he flew over a mountain lake. He hated the huge batlike wings, the saw-edged ridge on his back, and the cruel curved claws. He was almost afraid to be alone with himself and yet he was ashamed to be with the others.[50]

Eustace's draconic transformation thus triggers dysphoria and dysmorphia. Lewis sometimes takes a rather

[49] Lewis, *Voyage of the Dawn Treader*, pp. 115–16.
[50] Lewis, *Voyage of the Dawn Treader*, p. 116.

distressing joy in cruel punishments, but here Eustace's vulnerability brings the reader closer to a character who was previously pretty unsympathetic. Looking through a dragon's eyes is a process of change for both Eustace and the reader, causing both to see the world of Narnia and those who quest there in a new light.

While many Fantasy stories include a single dragon, others integrate complex lineages and ecosystems. *Dungeons & Dragons* has developed a vast panoply of draconic types that Dungeon Masters can use to populate their worlds. The core arrangement splits dragonkind into species of chromatic dragons (usually malevolent) and metallic dragons (more likely to be benevolent). The 'exceptionally vain' and arrogant red dragons breathe fire in the classic manner and tend to make their lairs in the mountains. Smaller, 'more animalistic' white dragons 'dwell in frigid climes' and breathe ice, while 'cunning and treacherous' poison-breathing green dragons scheme amidst 'the ancient forests', seeking to manipulate other creatures and bend them to their wills.[51] While the dragons of *Dungeons & Dragons* are magical creatures, their design shows the mixed influence of medieval bestiaries and modern understandings of biology and ecology. The game takes care to gesture towards realism by entangling creatures with their environments. A green dragon's legs are described as being 'longer in relation to its body than with any other dragon, enabling it to easily pass over underbrush or debris when it walks'.[52]

[51] *Dungeons & Dragons: Monster Manual*, 5th edition (Renton, WA: Wizards of the Coast, 2014), pp. 99, 102, 95.

[52] *Monster Manual*, p. 95.

The dragons of *Dungeons & Dragons* are also entangled with the game's internal frameworks for building and playing characters. Copper dragons, characterised as 'incorrigible pranksters, joke tellers and riddlers', are described as being 'particularly fond of bards', a player character class with similar affinities.[53] *Dungeons & Dragons* relies on the essential legibility of the dragon – dragons are right there in the title as one of the game's main selling points – but its rules and lore take pains to elaborate on the basic concept, providing a rich toolbox of adversaries and allies that can be further modified in the improvisations of play.

Rather than seeing humankind and dragonkind as inevitably opposed, modern fantasies often imagine symbiotic or companionable relationships. Anne McCaffrey's Pern stories (commenced in 1967) are one of the earlier examples, depicting lifelong bonds between dragonriders and dragons that are essential to humanity's survival on a planet where dragonfire is a principal means of fighting back deadly Thread falls. In a similar vein, the film *How to Train Your Dragon* (2010; adapted from Cressida Cowell's 2003 book) depicts a Viking-inspired society in which humans and dragons must work together as a precondition for prosperity. Ursula K. Le Guin's dragons begin her Earthsea books seeming like villains. One of Ged's first great feats in *A Wizard of Earthsea* (1968) is preventing the ravages of the Dragon of Pendor. However, as the series develops, the picture becomes considerably more complicated, with dragons in *The Farthest Shore* (1972) assisting Ged in his struggle to restore the balance

53 *Monster Manual*, p. 112.

between life and death. In the final two novels, this is taken further. In the words of Taylor Driggers, 'dragon lore rears its head as the return of a suppressed counter-discourse that disorganizes human doctrines and logics.'[54] In exalting their own power and wisdom, albeit for ostensibly altruistic ends, Earthsea's male wizards have foreclosed possibilities for a more equitable world. It takes the careful interventions of women and dragons, as well as listening and tolerance, to undo the failed experiment of the Dry Land and allow those wronged to find forms of transformation and release.

Robin Hobb's Realm of the Elderlings books contain one of the most sustained and interesting treatments of dragons in recent fiction. They are a fleeting presence in the first trilogy, largely consigned to the past, but the second trilogy considers their life cycle and their entanglements with human traders, whose actions have inadvertently impeded draconic reproduction. As the series continues, dragons establish a more forceful presence as the symbiotic relationships they used to enjoy with their Elderling servants are tentatively re-established with new human associates. Hobb's dragons are often proud and vain, but not without cause. They possess great physical strength, flight, telepathy and – all being well – the transmitted memories of their ancestors. Those who choose to associate with dragons (or who are encouraged to do so by coercion, or who lack other options) encounter beings who are convincingly different in their

[54] Taylor Driggers, *Queering Faith in Fantasy Literature: Fantastic Incarnations and the Deconstruction of Theology* (London: Bloomsbury Academic, 2022), p. 179.

outlooks. Dwelling and thinking with dragons is a liberating experience for many characters in the later books, allowing long-running undercurrents of queer desire a fuller expression within the world. Reflecting on the fact that in Bingtown 'it would be a scandal for two young men to be so openly passionate', one character gives credit to empathy learnt through draconic encounters: 'Perhaps once one realised how deeply one could bond with a creature as foreign as a dragon, all forms of human love seemed more acceptable.'[55] Rather than fiery opponents who must be defeated, dragons in Hobb and Le Guin serve as loci for exploring ethical and ecological issues. Both writers contend that mutual apprehension and care can lead to genuine flourishings.

Fantasy writers have often explored more unusual draconic forms and characters. In Lucius Shepherd's 'The Man Who Painted the Dragon Griaule' (1984), the titular creature is enormous, 'grown to stand 750 feet high at the midback, and from the tip of his tail to his nose he was six thousand feet long'. However, a wizard's spell 'flown a mortal inch awry' has placed Griaule is in a peculiar, suspended state: his 'heart had stopped, his breath stilled, but his mind continued to seethe, to send forth the gloomy vibrations that enslaved all who stayed for long within range of his influence'.[56] The plan to paint him is a literal one, based on the principle that this will slowly

[55] Robin Hobb, *Blood of Dragons* (New York: Harper Voyager, 2013), p. 129.

[56] Lucius Shepherd, 'The Man Who Painted the Dragon Griaule', in *The Dragon Griaule* (London: Gollancz, 2013), pp. 1–30 (p. 2).

poison him with pigments, but over the long course of the process, the dragon infiltrates his painters as much as the paints infiltrate his vast body. The mythology of Jeff Smith's comic series *Bone* (1991–2005) features a similarly vast dragon queen, Mim, who nurtures the dreams of the world, but who has been turned to stone by her fellow dragons after possession rendered her dreams nightmares. The story's central draconic character, the Great Red Dragon, has a personality that belies his name's connection with William Blake's Revelation-inspired paintings and Thomas Harris's villain Francis Dolarhyde, serving as a guide and guardian who is by turns benign, playful, intense and cryptic. Jo Walton's *Tooth and Claw* (2003) presents Anthony Trollope-inspired dragons who inherit by consuming the corpses of deceased family members, placing huge draconic forms at the centre of a comedy of manners. In Aliette de Bodard's Dominion of the Fallen series (2015–19), river-dwelling Vietnamese dragons slowly decay in the capital of their country's angelic oppressors, their sickness a result of and a synecdoche for the corrosive effects of colonial oppression. In the science-fantasy *Shadowrun* universe (1989–), dragons have reappeared along with other magical races; they can take human form and often acquire the wealth and influence they crave by occupying positions of power in the mega-corporations that largely control the world. In the...

I could easily go on. However, I assume by this stage I have made my point: while many Fantasy creators include dragons in their creations – and while the dragons they include may share helpful family resemblances – they are never exactly the same. Varying dragons can make them suit a vast range of purposes and achieve a plethora of effects and affects. So can varying *around* dragons: in Martin's A Song of Ice and Fire, the dragons are in many respects quite conventional, but their integration into the specific history, politics and magic of Westeros and Essos means that Martin's Targaryens are very different from McCaffrey's Weyr-dwellers or Hobb's dragon keepers. Fantasies often return to old ideas, but this is to build, rather than to repeat. Early magic schools like those in Le Guin's Earthsea series and Jill Murphy's Worst Witch books (1974–2018) spring from realist school stories; are developed in institutions like Hogwarts in J. K. Rowling's Harry Potter books (1997–2007), the University in Patrick Rothfuss's Kingkiller Chronicle (2007–) and Cyoria's Royal Academy of Magical Arts in Domagoj Kurmaic's *Mother of Learning* (2011–20); and are subverted in grimmer environs such as Brakebills in Lev Grossman's Magicians books (2009–14), the Gowpenny Academy of Arcane Arts in Dimension 20's *Misfits and Magic* (2021) and the sinister, mind-bending Institute of Special Technologies in Marina and Sergey Dyachenko's *Vita Nostra* (2007). To appreciate how Fantasy excels as a site of delight and critique, we need to get better at celebrating such chains of inspiration, rather than insisting that works are only worthwhile if we cannot think of any others they resemble.

Gauging how Fantasy moves and teaches us might involve articulating more nuanced value systems than those inherited from devotees of the originality myth. Terry Brooks's *The Sword of Shannara* (1977) is often denigrated for being a shot-for-shot rework of *The Lord of the Rings*; Lin Carter notoriously described it as 'the single most cold-blooded, complete rip-off of another book that I have ever read'.[57] Carter is certainly not wrong in tracing Tolkien's obvious influence. During a second-chapter exposition scene, Brooks's Flick spies on Shea and Allanon just as Tolkien's Sam does on Frodo and Gandalf. Many – although not all – of the members of the Fellowship of the Ring have direct equivalents in Brooks's novel, and many important plot beats display marked similarities. At times, *The Sword of Shannara* displays more exact equivalences than direct adaptations: while Peter Jackson cut Tom Bombadil from his film trilogy, Brooks retains a similar figure in the form of the King of the Silver River. However, in dismissing Brooks's novel as a corrupt and inferior imitation, Carter is being somewhat lazy as a critic. The patterns he recognises license him to stop looking, meaning he neglects relatively obvious differences. While *The Lord of the Rings* is just over 480,000 words in length, *The Sword of Shannara* is relatively sprightly at around 225,000 words. This entails a significant register shift, transforming the rhythms of Tolkien's portentous epic into something more action oriented. While *Lord of the Rings* begins slowly with Bilbo's birthday party, in *Sword of Shannara*, a Skull Bearer (Brooks's equivalents of the Nazgûl) flies overhead within the first few pages.[58] By contrast with the long processes of return after Sauron's defeat in *The Return of the King*, Brooks wraps up the story in a couple of short chapters once his Warlock Lord has been successfully overcome.

[57] Lin Carter, *The Year's Best Fantasy Stories: 4* (New York: DAW Books, 1978), p. 207.

[58] Terry Brooks, *The Sword of Shannara* (London: Orbit, 2006), p. 9.

Brooks was certainly iterating on Tolkien's conceptions, but rather than copying wholesale, he hybridised Tolkienian elements with other stories he liked and with some new ideas of his own. Discussing his relationship with Tolkien, Brooks writes that he was 'searching for a format in which to set an adventure story on the order of the ones written by Alexandre Dumas, Robert Louis Stevenson, Joseph Conrad and Arthur Conan Doyle'. Reading *Lord of the Rings* provided inspiration for an environment in which he might embed such a narrative:

> I would set my adventure story in an imagined world, a vast, sprawling, mythical world like that of Tolkien, filled with magic that had replaced science and races that had evolved from Man. But I was not Tolkien and did not share his background in academia or his interest in cultural study. So I would eliminate the poetry and songs, the digressions on the ways and habits of types of characters, and the appendices of language and backstory that characterized and informed Tolkien's work. I would write the sort of straightforward adventure story that barrelled ahead, picking up speed as it went, compelling a turning of pages until there were no more pages to be turned.[59]

This is a pretty accurate description of the experience of reading Brooks's novel: one that differs markedly from Tolkien's slow unfoldings. Where Tolkien's book conjures moral weight, Brooks is more interested in pacy thrills. Tellingly, one of Brooks's main additions is a character directly inspired by the dashing Rupert of Hentzau from Anthony Hope's *The Prisoner of Zenda*

[59] Terry Brooks, 'On the Trail of Tolkien', in *Sometimes the Magic Works: Lessons from a Writing Life* (London: Earthlight, 2003), pp. 185–94 (p. 188).

(1894). Brooks admits that he has 'a soft spot for rogues and reprobates who do the right thing in the end'.[60] This is not an archetype Tolkien liked: charismatic rogues are a conspicuous absence in his works, unless you somehow count Bilbo, whose charm is rather different from that of dubious fast talkers like Cugel the Clever or Locke Lamora.[61] In a similar vein, Menion Leah – introduced as the 'biggest wastrel in the entire Southland' – reads more like an Errol Flynn role than a Tolkien character.[62] Allanon sometimes sounds like Gandalf, but he is a far less genial figure. While Gandalf will withhold information when he deems it necessary, it is hard to imagine him keeping secrets for their own sake or addressing Frodo with either a 'mocking smile and ill-concealed sarcasm' or 'barely controlled fury'.[63] It is not difficult to trace lines of influence between these characters, but to call them the same does both Brooks and Tolkien a disservice.

To say that Brooks iterates on rather than simply duplicates Tolkien is not to claim that *The Sword of Shannara* is as good as *The Lord of the Rings*. It is not, and there are losses entailed in Brooks's revisioning. The titular sword – an object of truth rather than of deception – is less interesting as a quest object than the One Ring. Brooks's loose Gollum equivalent, Orl Fane, feels far less integral to the plot and the moral thrust of the story.

60 Interview with Terry Brooks, *TheOneRing.net*, 22 May 2000, https://bit.ly/3opgNS3.

61 Cugel the Clever is an antihero in Jack Vance's Dying Earth stories; Locke Lamora is the protagonist of Scott Lynch's Gentleman Bastards series.

62 Brooks, *Sword of Shannara*, p. 44.

63 Brooks, *Sword of Shannara*, pp. 29, 33.

While Brooks's imagined history touts the replacement of science with magic – his is a later Earth, rather than Middle-earth – the premise remains underdeveloped. When he wrote *Sword*, Brooks was a far less practiced writer than Tolkien, and this comes through in some formulaic and clunky uses of language, particularly when colouring dialogue and characterising sentiments. However, the book has pleasures of its own and contains some nuances *The Lord of the Rings* lacks. While Tolkien's orcs are inevitably bound to the cause of evil, Brooks imagines benevolent gnomes and a heroic troll, as well as members of these races who serve as foot soldiers of the Skull Kingdom. The success of *Sword* also provided Brooks with foundations for further development. His second novel, *The Elfstones of Shannara* (1982), is far better than *Sword*. As he elaborated his fictional world, he made fuller use of his interesting post-apocalyptic premise and became a dab hand with horrifying pursuers and heart-wrenching sacrifices. Brooks's sales also provided an early success for the new DAW Books list, helping to build the genre momentum that would see dedicated Fantasy bookshop sections populated.

Brooks's approach in *The Sword of Shannara* is hardly an unusual one for new writers, who often learn by imitating and combining, just as visual artists develop their skills by copying models and designers can learn to build games through modifying (modding) existing ones. Expanding upon, rewriting or hybridising existing works is a key element of fan fiction, the form in which many modern Fantasy creators first find their feet and their communities. Like Fantasy itself, a long history can be traced for fan fiction. Some of Geoffrey Chaucer's

Canterbury Tales (1387–1400) rewrite stories by Giovanni Boccaccio, and the structure of Chaucer's work echoes that of Boccaccio's *Decameron* (c. 1353). The Brontës' youthful writings incorporating the Duke of Wellington and Napoleon might be considered as early real person fiction (RPF), as might some of the literary responses to Byron. Jane Austen has been frequently rewritten and extended, and there are myriad reworkings of Sherlock Holmes. However, the accessibility and communicative power of fan writing has been vastly increased by the advent of the Internet. Stories that might previously have been shared between small groups can now be published openly to audiences of hundreds, thousands or millions who can comment, catalogue, creatively respond and collaborate.

Fan fiction is sometimes seen by its detractors as a lesser form of writing. On his website, George R. R. Martin advises would-be authors that they should not 'write in my universe, or Tolkien's, or the Marvel universe, or the Star Trek universe, or any other borrowed background. Every writer needs to learn to create his own characters, worlds, and settings. [. . .] If you don't exercise those "literary muscles," you'll never develop them.'[64] This might strike us as rather rich coming from the author of an enormously successful Wars of the Roses fanfic, but Martin is not ill-intentioned. He also has a point insofar as writing that uses existing characters and environments can skip over certain kinds of establishing work, relying on readers' existing familiarity. However, Martin, like some of the other writers and critics we have discussed, is seeking to

[64] George R. R. Martin, 'FAQ', *georgerrmartin.com*, https://georgerrmartin.com/for-fans/faq/.

draw an inaccurately hard line between the kinds of writing he sees himself as doing and a form he sees as lacking in originality. In practice, fan fiction is tightly networked with other kinds of cultural creativity, rather than nestling gloweringly in a separate box.

The empowering potential of fan fiction is evident from the number of successful Fantasy writers who started out in fan-fiction circles and who return to those circles as testing grounds. N. K. Jemisin, the first writer to win the Hugo Award for Best Novel three years on the trot, is an obvious example. As Julie Beck writes while introducing fan fiction's potential to readers of *The Atlantic*,

> Jemisin started writing fan fiction [. . .] while in grad school for counseling. "I was miserable and lonely. I didn't have a lot of friends, or stress relief," she told me. "Around then was when I became internetted, and one of the first communities I discovered was a fan-fic community." Through talking with other authors and writing her own stories about *Dragon Ball Z* (among other things), she found friends, got feedback, and, as she put it, "blew the cobwebs off writing abilities I hadn't used since college."
>
> For instance, this writing helped her hone her ability to hold readers' interest. "Fan fiction tends to have a built-in hook because it's written in a world you're a fan of; you're predisposed to like it," she said. "You have to find a way to make it not just the world that people are tuning in to read, so they are interested in your story." To this day, Jemisin said, she still writes fan fiction, and treats it as a way to try out new genres and skills, such as using the second person[.][65]

[65] Julie Beck, 'What Fan Fiction Teaches that the Classroom Doesn't', *The Atlantic*, 1 October 2019, https://bit.ly/3A7AgJp.

Obviously, not every writer of fan fiction goes on to write a ground-breaking Fantasy series, but Jemisin's testimony gives the lie to hard distinctions between fan fiction and other kinds of writing. Fan fiction taught Jemisin things about storycraft, audiences and iteration that would have been impossible to learn in splendid isolation.

The central relationship Jemisin writes in her first published novel, *The Hundred Thousand Kingdoms* (2010), nuances a romance dynamic that is commonly explored in fan fiction circles. When blogging about her process, she happily traces one of the chains of influence that inspired her:

> At the time I was very enamored of dark-haired, dark-magic-wielding, just generally dark characters of a certain type seen often in anime/manga; see Vampire Hunter D and Ashura-Ou from Rg Veda as examples (a more recent example is Hagi, from Blood +). Was also very fond of dark-natured (though not necessarily -haired) anti-heroes in Western fiction, such as Gerald Tarrant from C. S. Friedman's Coldfire trilogy, Tarod from Louise Cooper's Time Master trilogy, and Azhrarn from Tanith Lee's Flat Earth stories. I'm not sure why characters like this have such enduring power in fiction on both sides of the pond (the, uh, Western and Japanese pond, apparently), but regardless, Nahadoth was the natural outgrowth of all this.[66]

Jemisin's Nahadoth was created in part as her own version of a brooding, dramatic character archetype that she and other readers enjoyed. Joseph Crawford, tracing the genealogy of paranormal romance, stresses the importance of a compelling outsider figure who is 'at once

[66] N. K. Jemisin, 'Character Study: Nahadoth', *nkjemisin.com*, 5 April 2010, https://nkjemisin.com/2010/04/character-study-nahadoth/.

attractive and fearsome: attractive to the extent that we long to share their freedom or alleviate their loneliness, and fearsome to the extent that we dread that freedom being used against us.'[67] This rather neatly describes the way that Yeine, Jemisin's protagonist, reacts to Nahadoth. However, for Jemisin, as for most writers of Fantasy, archetypes were starting points rather than end goals. In her blog post, she writes that the character 'changed — deepened — as I developed the whole cosmology'. To iterate is to modify, or, in Jemisin's terms, to grow out from (and in some instances outgrow) the figures that sparked initial ideas. Jemisin displays a greater sensitivity to problematic power dynamics than many of the writers who inspired her, a sensitivity that plays out over the Inheritance Trilogy as a whole. Most of the characters Jemisin lists as inspirations guard their independence fiercely, so her decision to begin her series with Nahadoth bound in service establishes powerful tensions with far-reaching consequences. As she proceeds, Jemisin's world-building introduces new questions about Nahadoth, depicting him as a protean force of change, as a character with a complex gender identity and as a parent, all of which push against the steely, masculine solitude radiated by more conventional dark-natured antiheroes.

Rather than feeling constrained by previous uses of an archetype she enjoyed, Jemisin took this archetype as a jumping-off point for making something new. Other creatives have found deliberately engaging with Fantasy's

[67] Joseph Crawford, *The Twilight of the Gothic?: Vampire Fiction and the Rise of the Paranormal Romance* (Cardiff: University of Wales Press, 2014), p. 7.

existing lexicons similarly empowering. Mark Rosewater, the head designer for the collectable card game *Magic: The Gathering* (1993–), enjoys the axiom 'Restrictions breed creativity', and *Magic* itself is an excellent example of how the affordances of Fantasy and the structures of games can generatively align.[68] The rules its original designer, Richard Garfield, created for *Magic* are quite involved, but in its simplest form it is a duelling game in which two players taking the roles of powerful magic-users compete to reduce each other's life totals from twenty to zero. This is usually done by summoning creatures and attacking with them to deal damage and by playing spells that manipulate the game state in advantageous ways. Creatures and spells are divided among five colours: white, associated with co-operation and order; green, associated with growth and nature; red, associated with aggression, impulsiveness and passion; black, associated with ruthlessness and self-interest; and blue, associated with intelligence and manipulation. Players start with a hand of seven cards and take alternating turns, generally drawing one card each turn from the decks they have constructed. To play most creatures and spells requires mana drawn from land cards. Once mana is drawn from a land, it becomes tapped, the card being rotated to indicate this. Tapping is a core game mechanic, clearly indicating which cards have attacked or been used. A player's cards are untapped again at the start of their turn. Only a single land can be played each turn; more powerful creatures

[68] In many places, but see for example Mark Rosewater, 'Twenty Years, Twenty Lessons—Part 3', *magic.wizards.com*, 16 June 2016, https://bit.ly/3mUU6oe.

FIGURE 2.5 Llanowar Elves, with art by Anson Maddocks, from *Magic: The Gathering* (1993).
© Wizards of the Coast.

and spells tend to cost more mana and therefore become available later in the game. A lowly goblin or elf (like Figure 2.5) might cost only a single mana and have a power and toughness of one each, dealing a single point of damage when it successfully attacks and dying when it receives a single point of damage. The game's earliest iconic creature, Shivan Dragon (Figure 2.6), costs six mana and has a power and toughness of five; more mana can be spent each turn to pump its power further, representing its draconic fire-breathing ability. It also flies,

FIGURE 2.6 Shivan Dragon, with art by Melissa Benson, from *Magic: The Gathering* (1993).
© Wizards of the Coast.

meaning that ground-bound creatures an opponent controls can only gaze in awe as it comes swooping in.

The card Shivan Dragon thus translates an inherited idea into game rules, with the card's identity as a dragon providing players with an accurate picture of what to expect from it and the game's rules facilitating the pleasure of imagining summoning and commanding such a creature. *Magic* communicates best when Fantasy identities and game effects evocatively align. Straightforward red spells such as Fireball and Lightning Bolt deal damage directly to creatures or players.[69] Blue spells associated with studying or inspiration can draw additional cards, and tricksy blue mages can also counter an opponent's spells as they are being cast. Much of the game's fun arises from cards becoming more powerful in combination. Tapping a Time Vault provides an extra turn – a very strong effect – but the artifact enters play tapped and can usually only be untapped by skipping a turn first. However, other cards can untap Time Vault without making the payment, in some cases repeatedly. Assembling a repeatable means of untapping Time Vault allows a player to take a theoretically infinite number of turns, achieving almost unlimited power within the rules the game lays down. Interactions like this can be satisfying on both a ludic level (providing a sense of accomplishment from setting up a powerful combination) and a narrative one (representing clever feats of magecraft within the world the game imagines). The Time Vault example is deliberately extreme – the game's most satisfying moments usually arise from close-fought interplay, rather than one player winning out of nowhere – but it suffices to show how rules and fantasies can intertwine to enrich and explain one another.

Magic is a fine example of the enormous ground iterative development can cover. Since the first set disappeared swiftly from store shelves in 1993, over one hundred further expansions containing more than 20,000 different cards have been created. Some sets are inspired by existing fantastic material; the first expansion drew on

[69] For individual cards, see the Gatherer database: https://gatherer.wizards.com/Pages/Default.aspx.

the *Arabian Nights*, and subsequent themes have included legendary heroes, a city of clashing guilds, gothic horror, Greek mythology and *kaiju*-like beasts. However, the game has also created sprawling lore of its own. In its relatively early years, it told the story of the crew of the Weatherlight across numerous sets, but the continuing epic asked a lot of those who wished to follow it. Consequently, the game developed new narrative strategies, highlighting planeswalkers who can travel between different realms, thereby combining a superhero-style recurring cast with more discrete world explorations. As it has aged, *Magic* has invested in developing its own worlds, revisiting and enriching the planes depicted in its most popular sets. An iterative approach has also been applied to rules and card designs. New mechanics have been introduced to alleviate some of the disruptive randomness inherent in the mana system and the relative power of creatures and spells has been adjusted to improve game balance. Decades of sustained development have created a vast and complicated multiverse by refining and building on the core concepts of Garfield's design. *Magic* draws on the shared commons of Fantasy, but it also gives back to it, providing new worlds for its audiences and developing rules and lore that have inspired a plethora of physical and digital card games, as well as numerous other forms of fantastic creativity, including fiction, cosplay, articles, videos and podcasts.

The foregoing discussion has sought to establish that works of Fantasy are often resonant and interesting *because* they iterate, repeat and revisit, rather than *despite* their doing these things. Critics have been unwilling to give iterative works of Fantasy full credit in part because of the ways realism has become confounded with originality. However, reductive modes used to discuss Fantasy also share some blame for the stereotypes. I am thinking particularly of archetype-based criticism, which seeks to identify common patterns and tropes. At its best, such criticism provides helpful means for comprehending norms and explaining a toolkit of shared approaches. However, archetypal approaches can be dangerously reductive if taken to explain more than they actually do.

Opening *The Morphology of the Folktale* (1928), Vladimir Propp writes that 'it is precisely questions of a general character which, more than all others, awaken interest. Their resolution is the aim of scholarship'.[70] Consequently, Propp proposes to describe common elements underpinning folktales as a body. To do this, he identifies thirty-one key functions, which he sees as operating and intersecting in complex manners:

> identical forms adapt themselves to different functions. A certain form is transferred to a different position, acquiring a new meaning, or simultaneously retaining an old one. [...] [T]hese phenomena complicate the analysis and require special attention when being compared to one another.[71]

While I would quibble with Propp over whether general questions are always the most interesting or urgent, for me, this passage helpfully and frankly acknowledges the limits of archetypal criticism. Such criticism can provide productive frameworks, but these frameworks generalise

[70] Vladimir Propp, *The Morphology of the Folktale*, 2nd edition, translated by Laurence Scott, revised by Louis A. Wagner (Austin: University of Texas Press, 1968), p. 3.

[71] Propp, *Morphology*, p. 70.

rather than accurately accounting for the pleasures and achievements of any given work. Reading breakdowns of plot devices on *TV Tropes* is fun and often illuminating, but a list of a work's conventions rarely exhausts its interest.

Where archetypal criticism becomes more problematic is when it posits itself as the end, rather than a means. In place of a conclusion summarising his propositions, Propp cites a passage by Alexander Nikolayevich Veselovsky that contends that all cultural production will eventually be reducible to core functions:

> when the synthesis of time, that great simplifier, in passing over the complexity of phenomena, reduces them to the magnitude of points receding into the distance, then their lines will merge with those which we are now uncovering when we look back at the poetic traditions of the distant past—and the phenomena of schematism and repetition will then be established across the total expanse.[72]

The sweeping, flattening effect achieved in this passage reminds me of the conclusion of a story I have already mentioned: Edgar Allan Poe's 'The Masque of the Red Death':

> [O]ne by one dropped the revellers in the blood-bedewed halls of their revel, and died each in the despairing posture of his fall. And the life of the ebony clock went out with that of the last of the gay. And the flames of the tripods expired. And Darkness and Decay and the Red Death held illimitable dominion over all.[73]

This is a kind of conclusion that delighted H. P. Lovecraft; it is employed particularly effectively in one of his

[72] Quoted in Propp, *Morphology*, p. 116.
[73] Poe, 'The Masque of the Red Death', p. 134.

briefest but most resonant fictions, 'Nyarlathotep' (1920):

> Beyond the worlds vague ghosts of monstrous things; half-seen columns of unsanctified temples that rest on nameless rocks beneath space and reach up to dizzy vacua above the spheres of light and darkness. And through this revolting graveyard of the universe the muffled, maddening beating of drums, and thin, monotonous whine of blasphemous flutes from inconceivable, unlighted chambers beyond Time; the detestable pounding and piping whereunto dance slowly, awkwardly, and absurdly the gigantic, tenebrous ultimate gods—the blind, voiceless, mindless gargoyles whose soul is Nyarlathotep.[74]

These two passages might be classed as functionally similar – both complete a withdrawal that leaves the storyworld in darkness. However, the details are very different. Poe suggests a broad applicability, but Lovecraft encompasses the whole cosmos. While Poe's conclusion touches on the inevitability of death, the story's specifics rebuke immoral excess in the face of want. By contrast, Lovecraft suggests a universe that is the plaything of utterly amoral forces. Lovecraft and Poe might both be seen as imagining more negatively what Veselovsky imagines positively – time and scope as great levellers – and for me, their passages highlight the dystopian implications of Veselovsky's vision. In his imagined future, the bright complexities of a million stories will be systematised into lines and points, their specific beauties lost beneath the sweep of generalisation. This would obviously be a great loss.

[74] H. P. Lovecraft, 'Nyarlathotep', in *The Call of Cthulhu and Other Weird Stories*, ed. by S. T. Joshi (London: Penguin, 2002), pp. 31–3 (p. 33).

I have been arguing that Fantasy operates by iteration; I would also contend that what changes when iteration occurs is what is most important. Fantasies often flirt with general ideals, but in practice, different creators employ very different patterns and value systems that attempts at overarching explanation can disruptively efface. Many fantasies written after World War II were inspired by the schema laid out by Joseph Campbell's *The Hero with a Thousand Faces* (1949), the first paragraph of which shows both the attractions and the grave limitations of his universalising approach:

> WHETHER WE LISTEN with aloof amusement to the dreamlike mumbo jumbo of some red-eyed witch doctor of the Congo, or read with cultivated rapture thin translations from the sonnets of the mystic Lao-tse; now and again crack the hard nutshell of an argument of Aquinas, or catch suddenly the shining meaning of a bizarre Eskimo fairy tale: it will always be the one, shape-shifting yet marvelously constant story that we find, together with a challengingly persistent suggestion of more remaining to be experienced than will ever be known or told.[75]

Leaving aside for a moment the nasty racial stereotyping (to which we will return), we can discern the power of the promise Campbell holds out. His notion of the monomyth suggests that if we can just discern the general pattern, we can find the key to all mythologies. However, general patterns are often among the least interesting things about cultural works. All Jane Austen's novels might be characterised as marriage plots in which the

[75] Joseph Campbell, *The Hero with a Thousand Faces*, Bollingen Series 17, 3rd edition (Novato, CA: New World Library, 2008), p. 1.

heroine overcomes a social disadvantage to make an ostensibly good match, but this tells us very little. What is interesting is not the marriage plot itself, but the way it plays out within a given set of minutely drawn circumstances. If we try to look through what is being said for a single elusive truth, we fail to hear the person speaking. While Campbell's actual writing can be generous and curious, his monomyth is flattening and solipsistic.

General rules can be very effective for bridging people into Fantasy worlds. I have discussed the strong alignment between rules and lore in *Magic*; similarly, the ways that *Dungeons & Dragons* assigns numbers to Fantasy have been fundamental for coding video games. The pleasures of calculation underpin Brandon Sanderson's helpful distinction between hard and soft magic systems. Sanderson believes that 'An author's ability to solve conflict with magic is directly proportional to how well the reader understands said magic.'[76] For this reason, he prefers to treat magic as something more like a science, providing readers with information that will let them understand the limits of enchantment. Sanderson writes that he 'like[s] mystery more than [...] mysticism', and his approach aligns with that of detective fiction, where readers often feel cheated if knowledge necessary to solve the mystery is withheld. However, he is clear that his preference is exactly that, asserting that many of the best Fantasy writers have used softer magic systems extremely effectively to drive character-focused stories. Employing clear rules and loosely defined effects are equally legitimate

[76] Brandon Sanderson, 'Sanderson's First Law', *brandonsanderson.com*, 20 February 2007, www.brandonsanderson.com/sandersons-first-law/.

approaches, and in practice, most fantasies will lie on a spectrum between the two positions.

Maintaining a flexible approach is important because, as N. K. Jemisin writes while pushing back against rule-bound forms of magic, 'systems are remarkably effective at *reinforcing stupid thinking*'.[77] When Jemisin asks for 'mysterious, silly, weird, *utterly cracktastic* magic', she is holding open a space for creativity and critique. Overarching explanations have a nasty habit of eliding difference and codifying prejudice. Campbell's opening paragraph, with its orientalising characterisations of mystical easterners and condescension-worthy Africans, is an unpleasant example of kinds of essentialising that fantasies can also be prone to when they repeat rather than develop. Using travel guides – as Diana Wynne Jones did – to analyse the limitations of systematisation, Roland Barthes decried a tendency to write as if people 'exist only as "types" [. . .] the Basque is an adventurous sailor, the Levantine a light-hearted gardener, the Catalan a clever tradesman and the Cantabrian a sentimental highlander'. He calls this tendency 'a disease of thinking in essences, which is at the bottom of every bourgeois mythology of man'.[78] This is something of which Fantasy is often guilty. One of the early assumptions made in *Dungeons & Dragons* was that Fantasy races have inherently different characteristics that could be reflected in ability score modifiers: elves are fast, dwarves are tough, orcs are

[77] N. K. Jemisin, 'But, but, but — WHY Does Magic Have to Make Sense?', *nkjemisin.com*, 15 June 2012, https://bit.ly/3LctDfv.

[78] Roland Barthes, 'The Blue Guide', translated by Annette Lavers, in *Mythologies* (London: Vintage, 2009), pp. 85–8 (p. 86).

strong and stupid. A work of Fantasy is not the same as the real world, but nevertheless, making racial profiling a founding tenet of a roleplaying system has rightly been seen as deeply problematic.

In *The Dark Fantastic* (2019), Ebony Elizabeth Thomas makes it searingly clear that fantasies often unthinkingly mirror the power dynamics and exclusions of the societies in which they are created, failing imaginatively to accommodate many of those who need them most:

> When readers who are White, middle class, cisgender, heterosexual, and able-bodied enter the fantastic dream, they are empowered and afforded a sense of transcendence that can be elusive within the real world. If this is the case, then readers and hearers of fantastic tales who have been endarkened and Othered by the dominant culture can never be plausible conquering heroes nor prizes to be won in the fantastic.[79]

Similarly, Helen Young has argued that 'Fantasy habitually constructs the Self through Whiteness and Otherness through an array of racist stereotypes, particularly but not exclusively those associated with Blackness.'[80] Campbell seeks to elide difference, presupposing that all stories are ultimately interchangeable. 'Why is mythology everywhere the same,' he writes, 'beneath its varieties of costume?'[81] I would answer this baldly: mythologies are not everywhere the same, and believing that they are

[79] Ebony Elizabeth Thomas, *The Dark Fantastic: Race and the Imagination from Harry Potter to the Hunger Games* (New York: New York University Press, 2019), p. 23.

[80] Helen Young, *Race and Popular Fantasy Literature: Habits of Whiteness* (New York and Abingdon: Routledge, 2016), p. 11.

[81] Campbell, *Hero*, p. 2.

forecloses the possibility of learning from the subtleties of different cultures. Thomas emphasises starkly that unthinkingly perpetuating mythic patterns is likely to reinscribe damaging assumptions:

> From ancient Greece and the classical tradition, to the Christianization of the late Roman Empire and Dark Ages Europe, the emergence of Catholic Europe, and the Crusades against the Islamic world, a nameless and lingering fear of dark-skinned people has been normalized in the popular imagination. Darkness—an antagonist born of this primal fear—is the archetypal monster in much of our literature, media, and culture. Thus, the Dark Other becomes monstrous in our collective imaginations, a shadow creature locked into place and time, imbued with a fixity that is difficult to overcome.[82]

Universalising conceptualisations like Campbell's monomyth thus entrench divisions by denying that these divisions exist. Fantasy's symbols are drawn from the world and are far from value neutral. When employed carelessly or maliciously, they perpetuate closed-minded and harmful attitudes, rather than providing the fresh perspectives that the best fantasies can grant. Iteration can compound, as well as critique.

In building on tropes and ideas that came before, Fantasy communities have a responsibility to acknowledge and rework their problematic elements, reaching towards inclusion and representation. The value of fantasies is ultimately contingent, rather than transcendent. Arguing against purity discourses that create hard borders between things, Alexis Shotwell writes that '*if* we want a world with

82 Thomas, *The Dark Fantastic*, p. 70.

less suffering and more flourishing, it would be useful to perceive complexity and complicity as the constitutive situation of our lives, rather than things we should avoid'.[83] Things are not simple, and this should be seen as an opportunity for Fantasy, rather than a challenge. Jean-Paul Sartre contended that imaginary objects comprise a 'melange of past impressions and recent knowledge'.[84] This seems to me to be a good description of how Fantasy works: blending, hybridising and refashioning the materials of our pasts so they can speak anew to our presents and futures.

[83] Alexis Shotwell, *Against Purity: Living Ethically in Compromised Times* (Minneapolis and London: University of Minnesota Press, 2016), p. 8.
[84] Jean-Paul Sartre, *The Imaginary: A Phenomenological Psychology of the Imagination*, translated by Jonathan Webber (London: Routledge, 2004), p. 90.

3
Root Formations

Reflecting on how she came to write *A Wizard of Earthsea* (1968), Ursula K. Le Guin characterises the book as 'a partial subversion of an accepted, recognized tradition, one I grew up with':

> That is the tradition of fantastic tales and hero stories, which come down to us like a great river from sources high in the mountains of Myth—a confluence of folk and fairy tale, classical epic, medieval and Renaissance and Eastern romance, romantic ballad, Victorian imaginative tale, and twentieth-century book[s] of fantastic adventures such as T. H. White's Arthurian cycle and Tolkien's great book.[1]

Rather than depicting herself as doing something completely new or completely contrary, Le Guin positions the modern fantasies she writes as the coming together of a grand and motley range of earlier modes. Her simile of the river suggests a powerful form of continuity: the various tributaries have their own characters, but eventually they mingle together in a unified flow. In her own work, Le Guin proposes to question certain inherited assumptions – diverting the river's flow somewhat, either *in toto* or by forming a distributary – but she clearly positions her own fiction as joining the moving waters.

[1] Ursula K. Le Guin, *The Books of Earthsea* (London: Gollancz, 2018), p. 128.

Not everyone sees modern Fantasy as being so directly contiguous with older traditions. In *The Encyclopedia of Fantasy* (1997), John Clute suggests that it is best to think of Fantasy as a form that emerged around two hundred and fifty years ago. His discussion of his reasoning is worth quoting at length:

> Only in the last decades of the 18th century, when (at least in the West) a Horizon of Expectations emerged among writers and readers, did a delimitable genre now called Fantasy appear. Before that there were writings which included the Fantastic – and such works can be described as taproot texts. To exemplify: The presence of Ariel and of Prospero's staff in William Shakespeare's *The Tempest* (performed *circa* 1611; 1623) do not make that play a fantasy, according to this criterion; *The Tempest*, however defined generically, may contain elements of the fantastic, but these elements did not govern its audience's sense of its generic nature: it was, first and foremost, a play. On the other hand, Goethe's *Faust, Part One* (1808) clearly reveals its author's consciousness that he is transforming a traditional story containing supernatural elements into a work mediated through – and in a telling sense defined by – those elements. For our purposes, *The Tempest* is best conceived as a [taproot text] and *Faust* as a fantasy.[2]

Clute's argument is based on the idea that Fantasy as a distinctive genre emerged unevenly during the eighteenth century from what Brian Attebery terms the wider fantastic mode.[3] For Clute, a modern Fantasy is a work that

[2] John Clute, 'Taproot Texts', in *The Encyclopedia of Fantasy*, ed. by John Clute and John Grant (London: Orbit, 1997), pp. 921–2. Now available online in a version prepared by David Langford: https://sf-encyclopedia.com/fe/taproot_texts.

[3] In the introduction, I discuss in more detail Attebery's distinctions from *Strategies of Fantasy* in more detail.

employs events and devices its audiences will parse as supernatural or otherworldly as part of its core identity. Clute's definition of Fantasy – like many of those discussed in the introduction – places emphasis on audiences understanding via formal and narrative markers that a text is playing with fictions and fictionality. 'A fantasy text', he writes, 'is a self-coherent narrative. When set in this world, it tells a story which is impossible in the world as we perceive it [. . .] when set in an otherworld, that otherworld will be impossible, though stories set there may be possible in its terms.'[4] Earlier works may be fantastic – in the *Encyclopedia*'s words, 'a general term for all forms of human expression that are not realistic' – but in Clute's view, they are not in any straightforward sense Fantasy, as they were originally viewed through different cultural lenses.[5]

Clute's argument hinges in large part on attempting to preserve a relatively strict fidelity to the perspectives of historical viewers. This is a valuable form of framing, but it is far from the only one possible. Another approach would be to argue that as *The Tempest* moves further from the contexts in which it was first composed, it begins to look increasingly like a work of Fantasy and to operate as such culturally for its audiences. Some of its strong identity as a play has been attenuated as refashionings have made it into other things as well. This began as early as its inclusion in the First Folio of 1623, after which it could be experienced as a reading text alongside or as an alternative

[4] John Clute, 'Fantasy', *Encyclopedia of Fantasy*, p. 338, https://sf-encyclopedia.com/fe/fantasy.

[5] Gary Westfahl, 'Fantastic', *Encyclopedia of Fantasy*, p. 335, https://sf-encyclopedia.com/fe/fantastic.

to performance. The process was taken further as paintings and engravings of the play's characters and scenes and remediated forms of retelling became widely available. The version of *The Tempest* that opens Charles and Mary Lamb's *Tales from Shakespear* (1807) remakes the narrative into a sort of fairy tale. The Lambs' calm scene-setting opening paragraphs can be helpfully contrasted with Shakespeare's dramatic plunge into the storm:

> THERE was a certain island in the sea, the only inhabitants of which were an old man, whose name was Prospero, and his daughter Miranda, a very beautiful young lady. She came to this island so young, that she had no memory of having seen any other human face than her father's.
>
> They lived in a cave or cell, made out of a rock; it was divided into several apartments, one of which Prospero called his study; there he kept his books, which chiefly treated of magic, a study at that time much affected by all learned men; and the knowledge of this art he found very useful to him; for being thrown by a strange chance upon this island, which had been enchanted by a witch called Sycorax, who died there a short time before his arrival, Prospero, by virtue of his art, released many good spirits that Sycorax had imprisoned in the bodies of large trees, because they had refused to execute her wicked commands. These gentle spirits were ever after obedient to the will of Prospero.[6]

Reconfigurations like these imply that in practice *The Tempest* is experienced by changing audiences not as a singular event pinned to the time of its first production but as a living narrative dynamically shaped by shifting

[6] Charles [and Mary] Lamb, 'The Tempest', in *Tales from Shakespear*, 2 vols. (London: Thomas Hodgkins, 1807), 1:1–21 (pp. 1–2).

circumstances of staging, adaptation and mediation. In crossing media to become a film, thereby obtaining the ability to use a wider range of special effects, *The Tempest* often moves further towards the marvellous, whether flashily and slightly disappointingly, as in Julie Taymor's 2010 version, or with lush and overbearing surreality, as in Peter Greenaway's *Prospero's Books* (1991). It would be possible to consider these films – and *Tales from Shakespear*, and *Tempest*-inspired Fantasy stories such as Tad Williams' *Caliban's Hour* (1993) and the final issue of Neil Gaiman's *The Sandman* (1996), and even the First Folio – as derivative works that do not affect the integrity of the play's original identity as a stage drama probably first performed in 1611. This stringent form of historicism would insist that the way *The Tempest* was perceived at the time of its original performance – insofar as we can recreate this – should principally determine how we place and interact with it now. However, we might alternatively assert that *The Tempest* has developed into a complex cultural construct that manifests in a wide range of forms, many of which will be located by modern audiences somewhere within the fuzzy set of Fantasy – not at the centre, perhaps, but certainly in its field of influence.

For me, both these positions have legitimacy. They are also not mutually exclusive. It seems reasonable to assert that *The Tempest*'s fantastic elements may have been received with a kind of knowing wonder in Shakespeare's day, a form of reception that correlates to an extent with the experiences of modern Fantasy audiences. Staging a storm in an early modern theatre might well have evoked something like the form of double consciousness Michael Saler associates with Fantasy's

FIGURE 3.1 Colour plate from a 1926 edition of *The Tempest* with art by Arthur Rackham, a pre-eminent illustrator of fantasies and fairy tales.
Historical Picture Archive/Corbis via Getty Images.

operations, in which we know that something is not real but choose to invest in it as if it is.[7] While 'Fantasy' did not signify as we now understand it to signify when *The Tempest* was first performed, it does not necessarily follow

[7] Saler explores this idea in *As If: Modern Enchantment and the Literary Prehistory of Virtual Reality* (Oxford: Oxford University Press, 2011).

that the concatenation of associations we have gathered within the word never operated until they were named.

However, Clute is certainly correct that *The Tempest* would not have been considered generically as a work of Fantasy in the seventeenth century, and this difference matters when tracing lineages. In considering what Fantasy does, it is worth examining carefully how modern Fantasy is both like and unlike earlier forms that employed the fantastic. Clute's dating a changing horizon of expectation to the late eighteenth century might be disputed in the contexts of different cultures, but I would concur that a sharpened sense of Fantasy emerged in western Europe alongside (and in response to) the conventions of the Enlightenment. The next chapter will explore in detail how influential eighteenth- and nineteenth-century arguments about modernity, rationality, realism, aesthetics and authority positioned themselves against Fantasy, as well as considering the counterarguments developed by advocates of the fantastic. However, it first seems important to acknowledge the upper reaches of Le Guin's river, exploring the influence of ancient tributaries on the flow of more recent fantasies.

In examining older texts and traditions in this chapter, I will follow Le Guin's model, which emphasises forms, rather than Clute's, which ascribes the power of influence principally to extraordinary works. For Clute, a taproot text is one that 'stands out for various reasons – not excepting quality'. '[H]uge quantities of work can be treated as being of backdrop interest only,' he writes, '[but] these titles cannot'.[8] Clute suggests that while a

[8] Clute, 'Taproot Texts', pp. 921–2.

canon of taproot texts would be quite large, it might nevertheless be defined as a discrete set. It is indisputably true that certain older stories have been particularly influential for modern fantasies, but to me it seems that Clute places more weight than necessary on the relatively recent concept of the great individual work of art. Through doing so, he de-emphasises the common modes that broad swathes of artworks share. Fantasies iterate on things that stand out, but they also rework familiar designs. Many Fantasy creators have engaged directly with Snow White, the *Odyssey* or the stories of King Arthur and his knights; however, far more Fantasy creators have employed general forms and patterns drawn from fairy tales, epics or romance.

In this chapter, therefore, I propose to broaden Clute's notion of taproot texts from individual works to types, exploring a selection of the root forms that nourish modern Fantasy. There are many other forms that might be considered – there are, for example, numerous fantasies that draw heavily on the conventions of pastoral, or on comedy and tragedy. However, the forms discussed below have been selected for the pervasiveness of their influence and for the ways in which they have shaped the specifically fantastic qualities of later fantasies. Extending Le Guin's simile, these are examples of the principal underlying currents that lend their force to Fantasy's foaming waters.

* * *

Myth and legend are terms often used interchangeably to characterise many of the earliest narratives we have inherited. Chris Baldick judiciously declines to draw a strong dividing line between the two, writing that 'Legends are sometimes distinguished from myths in that they concern human beings rather than gods, and sometimes in that they have some sort of historical basis whereas myths do not; but these distinctions are difficult to maintain consistently.'[9] For Baldick, a myth is essentially '[a] kind of story or rudimentary narrative sequence, normally traditional and anonymous, through which a given culture ratifies its social customs or accounts for the origins of human and natural phenomena, usually in supernatural or boldly imaginative terms'.[10] Myths (and, by extension, legends) are stories cultures used to tell to explain themselves and the world, drawing people together by positing a shared ethos and understanding. Fantasies are often fascinated by stories of this kind, delighting in their concentrated power and weird sweeps. However, when fantasies restage myths, they tend to question the perceptions and behaviours ratified in earlier tellings, hybridising older generalities with probing specifics.

When we read myths, we are often engaging with rewritings of translations of reworkings of fragments of narratives originally shared orally. As Attebery puts it, 'Most myths come down to us stripped of context. The voices, gesture, rituals, and social interactions that once guided interpretation are gone. Fantasy provides new contexts, and thus inevitably new meanings, for myth.'[11]

[9] Chris Baldick, *The Oxford Dictionary of Literary Terms*, 4th edition (Oxford: Oxford University Press, 2015), p. 199.

[10] Baldick, *Dictionary of Literary Terms*, p. 235.

[11] Brian Attebery, *Stories about Stories: Fantasy and the Remaking of Myth* (Oxford: Oxford University Press, 2014), p. 3.

In Attebery's conception, modern fantasies can never fully understand myths as they were originally understood. However, fantasies can nevertheless revivify myths or forge them anew for different social and cultural contexts. Because myths contain significant gaps when considered from a modern perspective – due to their general brevity, cultural differences and losses during transmission – and because the value systems they seem to extol often align poorly with our own, they provide rich material for modern reconsiderations. When fantasies rework myths, they reframe them as fictions (or impossibilities) rather than as cultural truths. Through doing so, they ask both how older societies made themselves through stories and what sorts of stories we should use to constitute ourselves in the present.

One of the biggest differences between myths, legends and fantasies is how they represent time. In one of the earliest books on the possibilities of the fantastic, Robert Scholes suggests that myths and legends might be distinguished based on their temporality. 'Mythic fictions', he asserts, 'are produced in cultures that lack a concept of historical time. [...] When myths deal with the time between the Beginning and the End, they treat this time as cyclical not as linear.' By contrast, he contends that 'Legendary time has two stages, a "then" and a "now." Then, there were giants in the earth, or a paradise inhabited by men. Now, men are smaller and the conditions of existence are more constricting.'[12] While this

[12] Robert Scholes, *Structural Fabulation: An Essay on the Fiction of the Future* (Notre Dame, IN, and London: University of Notre Dame Press, 1975), p. 12.

might be an overly neat distinction, it is valuable in highlighting how different the basic assumptions of myths, legends and modern narratives are. Many contemporary fantasies enjoy evoking both divine verities and lost golden ages, but they hybridise these with modern models of time and history that diverge considerably from those current in the cultures within which myths and legends originally arose. The relationship between Fantasy and mythology is commonly one of loving criticality that is expressed through temporal lenses. Fantasies test mythic truths, asking to what extent cycles recur and relations remain static; exploring how far meaningfulness has fallen away; and using ancient stories as mirrors and touchstones for contemporary culture.

A good example of a myth subject to numerous fantastic reconfigurations in recent years is the Greek myth of Persephone's abduction by Hades, which usually runs something like this. Hades is the ruler of the afterlife and brother of Zeus, the overbearing monarch of the Olympian gods. Persephone is the daughter of Demeter, the goddess of the harvest. One day, Hades sees Persephone gathering flowers, falls in love (or lust) and sweeps her away down into the underworld. After Hades carries off her daughter, Demeter, in her grief, causes the forms of growth she oversees to cease. Zeus, who had sanctioned the original abduction, requires that Hades allow Persephone to return from the underworld, but Hades tricks (or forces) Persephone into eating pomegranate seeds. Consuming the seeds means that Persephone must spend part of each year with Hades. Demeter's recurring sorrow brings autumn and then winter while Persephone is underground; Persephone's return brings the spring.

In its original context, this was a neat myth to explain the seasons, but it has persisted as a resonant story because it has a wide range of hooks, complexities and problems for writers to work with. Most modern versions elaborate on the mythological narrative by clarifying details, developing the subjectivities of those involved and modifying or interrogating the nature of the abduction. In many ancient versions, Persephone is swept away against her will. Some contemporary versions keep this element and explore it as cruelty, assault or injustice, but other retellings inflect Persephone's connection with Hades differently. Many reimplementations make their relationship a love match of some kind, in keeping with later sensibilities, although its precise nature varies and an element of sourness often remains. The bare bones and strangeness of the myth can be summarised in a few sentences, but its implications can be opened out in a wide variety of directions. In extending the story far beyond the brevity of the forms in which it has been inherited, modern Fantasy writers fill out names and forces into characters, worlds and ethics.

In her musical *Hadestown* (developed in productions between 2006 and 2019), Anaïs Mitchell pairs Hades and Persephone's relationship with another Greek myth, that of Orpheus and Eurydice. Mitchell's musical employs a dustbowl setting that sees Hades transformed into a jaded, gravel-voiced capitalist and Persephone depicted as frequently drunk and somewhat embittered (Figure 3.2). After a raconteurish Hermes and the wider cast lay out the parlous condition of the world, the musical's central thread begins with the sweet courtship and marriage of Orpheus and Eurydice. However, the

Figure 3.2 Amber Gray dances as Anaïs Mitchell's jaded version of Persephone in the 2019 Broadway production of *Hadestown*. Jason Smith/Everett Collection/Alamy.

harshness of their environment conspires to separate them. Rather than dying by snake bite, Eurydice chooses to descend to Hadestown of her own volition, tempted by Hades's promises of safety and security. Eurydice does not abandon Orpheus without regret, but her active decision deliberately deviates from the rather passive figure portrayed in most ancient versions of the story, setting her up as a feisty, practical foil to her rather unworldly partner:

> Orpheus, my heart is yours
> Always was, and will be
> It's my gut I can't ignore
> Orpheus, I'm hungry
> Oh, my heart, it aches to stay
> But the flesh will have its way

Oh, the way is dark and long
I'm already gone... I'm gone[13]

Myths and legends often operate in registers where simple motivators like hunger are taken out of the picture. In Mitchell's telling, Orpheus's lofty goal is to make spring come again, to write a song 'so beautiful / It brings the world back into tune'.[14] Orpheus is god-touched – 'irrationally hopeful', in Mitchell's words.[15] Eurydice has a more realistic sense of how circumstances limit and determine our actions. In George Gissing's novel *New Grub Street* (1891), the protagonist, Jasper Milvain, bemoans the selfishness he perceives in himself, arguing that his ethical potential is limited by his situation. 'If I were rich,' he avers, 'I should be a generous and good man' – an assertion that Gissing's plot to some extent bears out.[16] Infusing Eurydice with a similar awareness of deprivation's dehumanising effects allows Mitchell to make mythic material speak in a context of industrial alienation not a million miles from that of Gissing's novel. While Orpheus (like Gissing's Harold Biffen) seeks to make the art he desires with little regard to circumstances (and suffers as a result), Eurydice, like most of Gissing's other characters, is drawn necessarily into the webs of

[13] Anaïs Mitchell, 'Gone, I'm Gone', as presented in *Working on a Song: The Lyrics of Hadestown* (New York: Plume 2020), p. 120. As the book describes, the lyrics of *Hadestown* have developed iteratively, changing considerably as the shape of Mitchell's story has evolved in dialogue with her collaborators.

[14] Mitchell, 'Come Home with Me', *Working on a Song*, p. 33.

[15] Mitchell, *Working on a Song*, p. 34.

[16] George Gissing, *New Grub Street*, 2nd edition, 3 vols. (London: Smith, Elder, 1891), 1:216.

capital in search of comfort and stability. The cycle here is both a treadmill and the poverty trap.

While the Orpheus and Eurydice plot is being set in motion, we see flashes and fragments of Hades and Persephone. She resents being compelled to take the train back to Hadestown, singing dismissively of the 'neon necropolis' Hades has fashioned, filled with 'Coal cars and oil drums / Warehouse walls and factory floors'.[17] Hurt by her rejection, Hades consoles himself with measurable progress through exploitation and expropriation. Pivoting around the interval, we get two songs that establish their clashing priorities. Hades's Act One closer 'Why We Build the Wall' fetishises control, instructing the citizens (or inmates) of his realm to keep themselves free from the enemies they fear by working to confine themselves. By contrast, Persephone opens Act Two with 'Our Lady of the Underground', holding out the promise that the speakeasy she runs will take the edge off Hadestown's regimented restrictions. However, it is Hades's vision that determines the conditions in the underworld. Eurydice is no longer hungry in Hadestown, but she is trapped in eternal servitude, doomed to forget herself, having signed her life away.

As the myth mandates, Orpheus follows Eurydice down to Hadestown in a desperate attempt to reclaim her. He is received with cold aggression by Hades, but Persephone entreats her husband to allow him to make his case. The song Orpheus sings for Hades – the song of hoped-for healing he has been composing throughout the story – is the story of Hades and Persephone themselves. The song

[17] Mitchell, 'Chant', *Working on a Song*, p. 105.

is called 'Epic', but it does not evoke the fates of heroes and nations. Instead, its beauty lies in its collapse from the vast scales of divine order to the transcendent potential of the deeply personal. Orpheus's lyrics move Hades from being 'King of shadows, king of shades' to being someone 'like me / A man in love with a woman'. In her commentary, Mitchell describes this language as 'almost childish', but in being so, it captures both the powerful equivalence *Hadestown* seeks to draw between its two root myths and the almost naïve connecting power of myth itself, which speaks to us strangely and clearly of things we feel we know.[18] Orpheus's song implores Hades to recall when he saw other beings as people in all their mystery:

> You didn't know how, and you didn't know why
> But you knew you wanted to take her home
> You saw her alone there against the sky
> It was like she was someone you'd always known
> It was like you were holding the world when you
>   held her
> And there were no words for the way that you felt
> So you opened your mouth and you started to sing
> La la la la la la la. . .[19]

In tune with her mythic sources, Mitchell makes expert use of circular motions and reprises. The break into pure sound in this version of 'Epic' is the same beauty that helped seduce Eurydice when Orpheus sang an earlier version for her. The return of songs in different contexts gestures in some respects towards universality and

[18] Mitchell, 'Epic III', *Working on a Song*, pp. 198, 206.
[19] Mitchell, 'Epic III', *Working on a Song*, pp. 198–9.

inevitability, but the changes made to them also hint at the possibility of quiet or radical divergences.

Hades is moved by Orpheus's song, but he is also faced with a dilemma. If he refuses Orpheus's request, he establishes himself as a tyrant. If he accepts, he risks looking weak. In an attempt to wriggle out of this conundrum, Hades sets his famous condition. Eurydice can follow Orpheus out of the underworld, but if Orpheus turns to confirm she walks behind him before they complete their journey, Eurydice must return to Hadestown. This is what happens, of course – while it might be possible to change the heart of the myth, that is not Mitchell's purpose. However, Orpheus's failure is not read through the lens of straightforward fatalism. At the end of the musical, Hermes, who has served as a mentor to Orpheus throughout the story, suggests a more compelling interpretation:

> Cos here's the thing
> To know how it ends
> And still begin
> To sing it again
> As if it might turn out this time
> I learned that from a friend of mine[20]

Hermes' lyric positions the story as one that has happened before, something that is true in several different ways. The gesture acknowledges previous versions of the tale of Orpheus and Eurydice and tips a wink to the nature of theatrical performance. It also speaks more generally to life, to the ability to start again despite previous failures. Mitchell makes a story that usually ends in despair into

[20] Mitchell, 'Road to Hell Reprise', *Working on a Song*, p. 246.

one that can accommodate hope. Orpheus may not have succeeded in rescuing Eurydice, but perhaps he has salved the strained relationship between Hades and Persephone, and perhaps his story has served an inspirational or cathartic function for the audience, hinting at richer alternatives to the emotional logics of capitalism and at ways of going on rather than looping round.[21] *Hadestown* relies in part on the enduring fascination of the myths it intertwines, but it also twists these myths to speak to the experience of making tough choices under duress and tempts the audience to imagine a different set of turns, to 'see how the world could be / In spite of the way that it is'.[22]

In Supergiant's video game *Hades* (2020), the player character, Zagreus, is Hades's son, who has been brought up by Nyx, Mother Night, who maintains the fabric of the underworld. Frustrated by Hades's distant demeanour and acts of passive aggression, Zagreus seeks bullheadedly to escape his father's realm, fighting through its various layers and defeating his father's servants as he attempts to reach the surface. Zagreus is assisted by the Olympian gods, who can make contact briefly to offer advice and boons: Zeus, for example, grants powers related to lightning; Dionysus's gifts relate to wine, hangovers and madness; Hermes speeds things up; Ares enjoys blades and retribution. While Zagreus is the player's avatar, he has a personality and backstory of his own. The game's world is

[21] On capitalism's tendency to monopolise our sense of what is possible or realistic, see Mark Fisher, *Capitalist Realism: Is There No Alternative?* (Winchester: Zero Books, 2009).

[22] Mitchell, 'Road to Hell Reprise', *Working on a Song*, p. 247.

FIGURE 3.3 After another death, Zagreus sardonically greets his sullen father in *Hades* (2020).
© Supergiant Games.

revealed and complicated by means of a vast bank of dialogue that responds to encounters in the game's semi-random environments, to Zagreus's successes and failures, to the player's choices about who to interact with, and to the passing of time.

Unless the player is an action-game expert, it is highly likely that Zagreus will fail repeatedly in his attempts to escape the underworld. Each time he dies, he rises from a pool of blood down the hall from the desk where his father listens to petitioners and makes biting comments about his son's folly (Figure 3.3). However, the game's progression systems mean that each failure makes Zagreus somewhat stronger, allowing him to proceed further through the layers of the underworld and discover more about the denizens of his father's house as he brings back different knowledge and resources. By pivoting from the rush of combat during escape attempts to quieter conversations in the House of Hades with Zagreus's tutor

Achilles; or Dusa, who does the cleaning; or a rather gothic Orpheus, estranged from Eurydice; or the Fury Megaera, who Zagreus must fight to leave Tartarus, the game both satisfyingly varies its rhythms and begins to suggest a larger picture. With his father, Zagreus needles and bickers, but with most of the other characters, he is notably polite and considerate. Each individual interaction is brief, but as Zagreus returns repeatedly to his father's house and encounters the same helpers and opponents in his winding progressions through the underworld, interactions turn into relationships, and mysteries are posited and slowly resolved. The game's combat during runs is deeply satisfying: the fighting is quick and varied, the controls feel punchy, the music is atmospheric, and different semi-random combinations of boons and weapons keep the gameplay fresh. However, much of the game's enjoyment arises from its slower, more incremental forms of progress, an accumulation of both mechanical advantages – as Zagreus unlocks more weapons and abilities – and narrative rewards – as new dialogues flesh out the cast.

If players know Greek mythology, they will anticipate who waits for them in the lush garden overlooking the sea that they encounter when they first manage to escape and wander from the entrance of the underworld along a beautiful cliffside. The reunion is touching but is cut frustratingly short. As a being of the underworld, Zagreus cannot survive for long on the surface, so to rebuild his relationship with his mother, he must repeat the journey again and again, with each success inching forward the game's overarching narrative. Zagreus's interactions with his mother let him slowly understand both her choices and Hades's choices better. As the player and Zagreus learn more about Hades's motivations, his misanthropic, provoking dialogues take on a different colouring. This modified colouring extends both metaphorically and literally to the game's environments and mechanics. *Hadestown* imagines an underworld of 'everlasting overtime' in which nothing changes.[23] By contrast, *Hades* allows the player incrementally to alter the House of Hades and the underworld by selecting new decor, adjusting the game's rules, unlocking new weapons and revealing characters' subtleties. The original myth is a tale of endless cycles, something that is theoretically possible in the gameplay loop *Hades* establishes. However, the incremental forward motion of the narrative pushes back against the idea that circularity is mere repetition, setting mythical materials in a context where persisting through a series of cycles allows for reconciliation and change. Myth provides *Hades* with characters, environments and situations, but Supergiant's writers and designers turn general archetypes into specific instantiations that are mechanically and narratively fascinating enough to encourage the player to persist over a longer term.

While *Hadestown* and *Hades* both imagine a Hades and a Persephone who have grown apart, Rachel Smythe's webtoon *Lore Olympus* (2018–) imagines the early stages of their relationship. *Hadestown* moves aspects of the story into an environment resembling the Depression-era United States, but *Lore Olympus* employs a more forceful form of eclecticism, in which the Greek gods are both fantastical and conceptualised as a business elite in an

[23] Mitchell, 'Way Down Hadestown Reprise', *Working on a Song*, p. 150.

environment resembling contemporary California. Hades rules an underworld in which he is positioned as a powerful CEO. Persephone encounters him as a sheltered ingenue of nineteen in a set-up that initially risks queasily evoking E. L. James's *Fifty Shades of Gray* (2011). However, while Smythe has to pull off some fancy footwork to thread the needle of her core relationship's potential squickiness, she accomplishes this deftly, in part by acknowledging that the mythology she draws on is deeply problematic by modern standards. In keeping with the source material, many of the gods in *Lore Olympus* behave terribly, but while both Hades and Persephone are entangled in toxic relationships with others, their relationship with each other is characterised by decency. Persephone's trust is abused, but not by Hades. The abduction occurs, but not by Hades's choice; instead, it is a result of Aphrodite's jealousy. While Hades has moments in which he is angry, sullen or forbidding, he is quickly humanised through his put-upon awkwardness, his worrying, his seven ridiculous dogs (Cordon Bleu, Mushroom, Russell, J. P., Fudge, Big John and Cerberus) and what Persephone refers to as his 'dorky face'.[24] He is convincingly likeable, but especially so for Persephone, who is unused to anyone seeing her as someone who matters without being smothering and controlling. Smythe treats the Greek myths as what they can seem like to modern readers: a roller-coaster series of bizarre soap-opera twists. The two protagonists are often

[24] Rachel Smythe, 'Episode 9: Gone to the Dogs', *Lore Olympus*, *webtoons.com*, 8 April 2018, https://bit.ly/3LkTzpa; 'Episode 12: Rose Coloured Boy', 29 April 2018, https://bit.ly/3N3NbUp.

drawn damagingly into the intrigues of other deities, but in the moments they are together, they slowly and compassionately open up to one another. In *Lore Olympus*, ancient gods are reframed as modern people. In this context, the cruel and arbitrary aspects of Greek myth become toxic personality traits that are rebuked through the staging of social consequences and alternatives, reflecting the cultural value now placed on the right to self-determination.

So far, we have been looking at how modern fantasies adapt existing myths, but works of Fantasy also commonly incorporate stories designed to feel like myths and legends. In many fantasies, these form a backdrop: they help explain cultures, but their literal truth is either denied or left in doubt. However, the creation of myths that are undeniably real within an imagined world is a major preoccupation of many secondary-world fantasies. Tolkien is one of the most influential examples, although it is mainly in the opening sections of *The Silmarillion* (1977) that he writes in the style of full-blown mythology, with the later sections of that book consisting of legends of the struggles of elves and men. The rhythms of *The Lord of the Rings* (1954–5) take on more of the character of epic or romance, although myths and legends of previous ages return in song and story, and occasionally erupt forcefully into the narrative in forms like the Balrog. Sauron himself is a remnant of the earlier age of myth – as, to a lesser extent, are the elves – and it is thus unsurprising that the Dark Lord's defeat signals a change in the register of Tolkien's world, as the last possessors of mythic power depart from Middle-earth. While Tolkien liked the idea of fabricating myths, he nevertheless framed them as being out of time, with his world reaching a point when they will necessarily be mediated as stories.

Other examples of secondary worlds within which mythologies are literally true are easy to cite. Brandon Sanderson's Cosmere is united by a shared creation myth, the consequences of which continue to resonate across its worlds. In most of Tamora Pierce's Tortall books, the gods are not particularly intrusive, but they definitely exist. In the Elder Scrolls games, the Daedric Princes can be directly encountered. Magic is retreating from the world of Joe Abercrombie's First Law books, but its lingering presence serves to indicate that the myths of Euz banishing demons are substantively true. In these works, myth's literalisation as an order of knowledge is used to stage questions about power, agency and narrative control.

While secondary-world fantasies often imagine a large-scale mythic canvas, fantasies set in our world can tell resonant stories through presenting lingering or recurring mythic presences. Alan Garner's *The Owl Service* (1967) compellingly restages the story of Blodeuwedd in contemporary Wales, exploring generational patterns, class anxieties and adolescent experience. In Silvia Moreno-Garcia's *Gods of Jade and Shadow* (2019), the machinations of Mayan Gods erupt in terrifying and liberating manners into Jazz Age Mexico. In Robert Holdstock's *Mythago Wood* (1984), the titular mythagos ('the image of the idealized form of a myth creature') are rooted both in the deep past and in the psyches of the characters who interact with Ryhope Wood on either side of the Second World War.[25] In stories like these, the irruption of myth disrupts the certainties of a

[25] Robert Holdstock, *Mythago Wood* (London: Gollancz, 2014), p. 40.

realistically rendered present from which it seems fundamentally different, but mythic cycles often turn out to map eerily well onto ostensibly modern circumstances.

A few fantastical works, like Italo Calvino's *Cosmicomics* (1964–5), are comprised principally of constructed myths that stage ethical conceits and artful paradoxes. Lord Dunsany's collection *The Gods of Pegāna* (1905) is an early and revealing example of this style. Echoing genuine mythography, Dunsany assembles a series of stories that are by turns cryptic and parable-like, most of which are very short. To give an impression, I have selected an example from fairly late in *The Gods of Pegāna*. By this point, the divine cast has been introduced and Dunsany has entered a run of stories discussing prophets who suffer more or less misfortunate fates. Contexts given within the story will help with decoding certain characters, but a key might still be useful: Mung is the god of death, Kib is the sender of life, Sish is the god of time's flowing, Yoharneth-Lahai is the god of little dreams and fancies, and Limpang-Tung is the god of mirth and melodious minstrels.

OF THE CALAMITY THAT BEFEL YŪN-ILĀRA BY THE SEA, AND OF THE BUILDING OF THE TOWER OF THE ENDING OF DAYS

When Kabok and his fears had rest the people sought a prophet who should have no fear of Mung, whose hand was against the prophets.

And at last they found Yūn-Ilāra, who tended sheep and had no fear of Mung, and the people brought him to the town that he might be their prophet.

And Yūn-Ilāra builded a tower towards the sea that looked upon the setting of the Sun. And he called it the Tower of the Ending of Days.

And about the ending of the day would Yūn-Ilāra go up to his tower's top and look towards the setting of the Sun to cry his curses against Mung, saying: "O Mung! whose hand is against the Sun, whom men abhor but worship because they fear thee, here stands and speaks a man who fears thee not. Assassin-lord of murder and dark things, abhorrent, merciless, make thou the sign of Mung against me when thou wilt, but until silence settles upon my lips, because of the sign of Mung, I will curse Mung to his face." And the people in the street below would gaze up with wonder towards Yūn-Ilāra, who had no fear of Mung, and brought him gifts; only in their homes after the falling of the night would they pray again with reverence to Mung. But Mung said: "Shall a man curse a god?" And Mung went forth amid the cities to glean the lives of the people.

And still Mung came not nigh to Yūn-Ilāra as he cried his curses against Mung from his tower towards the sea.

And Sish throughout the Worlds hurled Time away, and slew the Hours that had served him well, and called up more out of the timeless waste that lieth beyond the Worlds, and drave them forth to assail all things. And Sish cast a whiteness over the hairs of Yūn-Ilāra, and ivy about his tower, and weariness over his limbs, for Mung passed by him still.

And when Sish became a god less durable to Yūn-Ilāra than ever Mung hath been he ceased at last to cry from his tower's top his curses against Mung whenever the sun went down, till there came the day when weariness of the gift of Kib fell heavily upon Yūn-Ilāra.

Then from the Tower of the Ending of Days did Yūn-Ilāra cry out thus to Mung, crying: "O Mung! O loveliest of the gods! O Mung, most dearly to be desired! thy gift of Death is the heritage of Man, with ease and rest and silence and returning to the Earth. Kib giveth but toil and trouble; and Sish, he sendeth regrets with each of his hours wherewith he assails the World. Yoharneth-Lahai cometh nigh no more.

I can no longer be glad with Limpang-Tung. When the other gods forsake him a man hath only Mung."

But Mung said: "Shall a man curse a god?"

And every day and all night long did Yūn-Ilāra cry aloud: "Ah, now for the hour of the mourning of many, and the pleasant garlands of flowers and the tears, and the moist, dark earth. Ah, for repose down underneath the grass, where the firm feet of the trees grip hold upon the world, where never shall come the wind that now blows through my bones, and the rain shall come warm and trickling, not driven by storm, where is the easeful falling asunder of bone from bone in the dark." Thus prayed Yūn-Ilāra, who had cursed in his folly and youth, while never heeded Mung.

Still from a heap of bones that are Yūn-Ilāra still, lying about the ruined base of the tower that once he builded, goes up a shrill voice with the wind crying out for the mercy of Mung, if any such there be.[26]

Dunsany's theme here is a common one in mythology. There is a clear echo of the Greek myth of Tithonus, who asks for eternal life but not eternal youth and who ends up similarly longing for release. As well as evoking previous myths' content, Dunsany creates an artifice of mythic antiquity through formal means: employing devices such as archaic grammar ('builded'), using phraseology that echoes the cadences of religious texts and imposing some not-entirely-necessary macrons over certain letters as markers of difference. By employing techniques with general resonance to tell his own stories, Dunsany cannily evokes the ways in which myths are often simultaneously

[26] Lord Dunsany, *The Gods of Pegāna* ([London]: Pegana Press, 1911), pp. 57–60.

strangely particular and widely applicable. While the precise experience of Dunsany's Yūn-Ilāra is only possible in a world of myth, the larger point about the shaping power of death's inevitability – and about its potential to come as a mercy – nevertheless carries. This interplay of distance from and closeness to the circumstances of their audiences keeps myths and legends by turns baroquely fascinating and individually resonant.

* * *

In modern parlance, Epic Fantasy is a subgenre that usually deals with large-scale adventures in secondary worlds (or sometimes across vast cosmologies that encompass many worlds). Fantasies of this kind often have roots in both ancient epics and quest romances. The term 'Epic Fantasy' is commonly used interchangeably with 'High Fantasy', a coinage sometimes credited to Lloyd Alexander, the author of *The Chronicles of Prydain* (1964–8), although earlier roots might be traced in the works of Tolkien, who had a fondness both for the word 'high' (which appears more than 350 times in *The Lord of the Rings*) and for registers of high seriousness. Alexander praises High Fantasy as a form that celebrates 'the possibility of effective action. The hero wants to do something, he can do something, and he actually does do something.'[27] By describing the Fantasy hero as 'a doer of deeds', Alexander stresses the importance of meaningful interventions. In traditional epic narratives, when

[27] Lloyd Alexander, 'High Fantasy and Heroic Romance', *The Horn Book*, 16 December 1971. Available online: www.hbook.com/story/high-fantasy-and-heroic-romance.

important things happen, they often occur spectacularly in the world, rather than remaining within the confines of characters' heads. Plots commonly proceed through dramatic, high-stakes conflicts with winners and losers.

The *Oxford English Dictionary*, reflecting older forms of usage, defines an epic as 'A poem, typically derived from ancient oral tradition, which celebrates in the form of a continuous narrative the achievements of one or more heroic characters of history or legend.'[28] While an epic is more likely to have a human protagonist than a myth (although there are some notable exceptions), the principal difference is one of narrative scale. Myths tend to be short; most epics are defiantly not. An epic narrative is relatively unlikely to begin at the beginning (one of the most famous epic techniques is opening *in medias res* – in the middle of things), but it commonly tends to fullness. Epic scale is something that certain forms of Fantasy – the trilogy or series, the extended manga, the multi-instalment franchise – have taken even further, although maintaining a story over an even greater length has required the development of new techniques and hybridisation with other forms – including romance, as we will discuss in a moment.

While epic narratives are usually celebrations of their protagonists, many are rather ambivalent about the conduct of heroes. This is a quality echoed in grimmer modern fantasies by writers such as George R. R. Martin and Joe Abercrombie, which concur that 'heroic' does not necessarily mean 'admirable'. The heroes of ancient epics

[28] 'epic, n. and adj.', *Oxford English Dictionary*, 3rd edition (Oxford: Oxford University Press, 2000-), https://www.oed.com/view/Entry/63237.

and their later imitators are often deeply flawed in certain respects: Gilgamesh begins as a tyrant, Achilles is wrathful, Odysseus overvalues his cleverness, Aeneas betrays Dido, Lucifer is Lucifer. Nevertheless, they generally accomplish significant change, sometimes through cunning, but more often through violence, decorously cloaked or otherwise. An epic is a tale of resonant actions that commonly alter the fate of a society or societies (or, in the case of certain religious epics, a whole cosmic order). Through staging such pivotal moments, epics often claim to express aspects of a society's core identity. This is a quality that modern fantasies, with their deliberate inclusion of impossibility, rarely take on directly, although in representing cultures in particular manners, Fantasy creators knowingly (and less knowingly) perpetuate political positions, both within their works and in terms of how their works resonate with real-world cultures.

While Alexander stresses the importance of epic, his title explicitly pairs High Fantasy with 'Heroic Romance'. Epics have their roots in the ancient world, but romance is often understood to be a more recent form. It is stereotypically associated with medieval European culture, describing stories in poetry and prose that deal principally with 'the exploits of knights, ladies, and noble families seeking honor, love, and adventure'.[29] Epics usually focus on crucial turning points; by contrast, romances often consist of incidents that, while not inconsequential,

[29] Roberta L. Krueger, Introduction to *The Cambridge Companion to Medieval Romance*, ed. by Roberta L. Krueger (Cambridge: Cambridge University Press, 2000), pp. 1–10 (p. 2).

seldom insist on their overwhelming importance to the extent that epic narratives do. Short romances may cover a single incident, while longer romance narratives usually string together a series of happenings. Medieval chivalric romances might present a succession of knightly encounters, or the stages of a relationship, or an interweaving of these two things.

A significant subset of modern Fantasy draws heavily on medieval stereotypes. However, perhaps more importantly, romance exerts a strong formal influence on a vast range of fantasies, which feature quests as a common structuring device and employ the interweaving of incidents as a natural mode for extension and extrapolation. It was not for nothing that William Morris and Tolkien both referred to their works as romances, rather than using the more modern term 'novel'. This is partly performative – both Morris and Tolkien learnt a great deal from more contemporary fictions – but their narratives do have commonalities with romances, which often dispatch their protagonists down strange paths where encounters can conjure wonder through mapping landscapes, cultures and tensions.

Epic and romance are by no means mutually exclusive forms. The stories surrounding King Arthur operate variously in the registers of epic and romance, sometimes separately, sometimes simultaneously. One potential interpretation of the Matter of Britain would be to contend that Arthur's knights often succeed in the register of romance, in which they encounter a series of spurs to great deeds, but the Round Table functions less well once Arthur commits it to the epic pursuit of the Holy Grail. The most biting tragedies in the Arthurian story occur when its focus moves from the personal adventures of the knights to Arthur's aspirations to forge an enduringly just nation, with romance intrigues undermining the possibility of an Arthurian lineage persisting in the world while concurrently securing its narrative resonance.

The affinities between modern fantasies, epic and romance should not blind us to significant divergences. Seeking to define the general shape of American fantasies of the late twentieth and early twenty-first centuries, C. Palmer-Patel contends that 'the narrative structure of Heroic Epic Fantasy is one where the hero realises a messianic duty via a journey, one which results in a spiritual transcendence for the hero along with the salvation of the world by the act of healing or re-creating it, thereby fulfilling their destiny'.[30] This pattern fits a large number of modern Fantasy series, but differs considerably from classical epic. While Virgil glorifies Aeneas as the founder of Rome and the saviour of his people, the stakes of the action in the *Aeneid* do not extend to the messianic scale of something like Stephen R. Donaldson's Chronicles of Thomas Covenant (1977–2013) or Robert Jordan's Wheel of Time (1990–2013). Donaldson and Jordan's works both revolve around a Manichean conflict in which heroes aligned (albeit sometimes ambivalently) with good oppose an unmitigated evil (Lord Foul in Donaldson, the Dark One in Jordan – the naming of such figures is rarely subtle). By contrast, pre-Christian Greek and Roman epics often feature larger divine casts who are less easily

[30] C. Palmer-Patel, *The Shape of Fantasy: Investigating the Structure of American Heroic Epic Fantasy* (New York and Abingdon: Routledge, 2019), p. 1.

defined as moral opposites. The hero who makes sacrifices to save the world is a design heavily influenced by Christianity. Similarly, while modern fantasies draw on romance for archetypes and quest structures, they often place a greater emphasis on learning and growing than traditional romance narratives.

Fantasies thus employ many of the rhythms, character archetypes, and means of representing and managing scale that epics and romances pioneered. However, they are often more cautious about older works' value systems, developing more critical modes of engagement that draw on later, increasingly novelistic understandings even when plots cleave quite closely to epic or romance patternings. In discussing eighteenth- and nineteenth-century epic poetry, Herbert Tucker argues that master narratives in epics have long been a subject of ambivalence, an ambivalence that Fantasy shares:

> Like the Romantics and Victorians we want to belong to the sort of unified community that once embraced epic as its own; and yet that is not what we want at all. We endorse, and we discredit, the thought that our lives acquire meaning through participation in a large, whole and absorbing history, whose collective dimension has an importance that as modern individuals we both covet and mistrust.[31]

In Tucker's view, at its best epic provides a common language that makes us feel like part of something larger. At its worst, it can be a wrongheaded or autocratic form

[31] Herbert Tucker, *Epic: Britain's Heroic Muse 1790–1910* (Oxford: Oxford University Press, 2008), p. 3.

that alienates individuals, divides communities and serves as a tool of aggressive nationalism. Fantasy, as a subcultural inheritor of epic and romance, is acutely aware of this tension, and while some fantasies do universalise in manners that exclude, many are sensitive to the stories that older epics leave out. The principal western epics have focused on the deeds of men, and in older romances, men usually play the most active roles. This is a pattern we can see perpetuated in more traditional modern fantasies, although even these usually reflect changing assumptions to some extent. *The Lord of the Rings* is often criticised for the limited roles that women play, and not without cause, but nevertheless, Tolkien works to contrast more traditionally masculine heroes with the hobbits and creates Éowyn, who boldly refuses to stick to her culture's script. He also takes some care to depict effective alliances in his works, rather than glorifying a single nation, although it is obvious that Gondor is the senior partner in the alliance with Rohan, and the narrative contains several nations whose inhabitants are flat-out demonised.[32]

A more inclusive take on transforming epic and romance conventions might be seen in Michael Dante DiMartino and Bryan Konietzko's animated series *Avatar: The Last Airbender* (2005–8), a show that glories in bringing unexpected subtleties to much-employed conventions. The speech by Katara (Figure 3.4) that opens

[32] I discuss this in more detail in the introduction. See also Dimitra Fimi, *Tolkien, Race and Cultural History: From Fairies to Hobbits* (Basingstoke: Palgrave Macmillan, 2009), especially chapters 9 and 10.

FIGURE 3.4 The initial adventuring party in *Avatar: The Last Airbender* (2005–8): Katara, Aang and Sokka.

most episodes is somewhat unusual in the context of traditional epics in that it allows a woman to frame the narrative, but the situation described has a lot in common with older epics and romances:

Water. Earth. Fire. Air. Long ago, the four nations lived together in harmony. Then, everything changed when the Fire Nation attacked. Only the Avatar, master of all four elements, could stop them, but when the world needed him most, he vanished. A hundred years passed and my brother and I discovered the new Avatar, an airbender named Aang. And although his airbending skills are great, he has a lot to learn before he's ready to save anyone. But I believe Aang can save the world.[33]

Avatar has affinities with epic in basing its story around a longstanding military conflict between nations that is mediated principally through the actions of individuals: while the series includes large-scale battles, they are usually turned by the interventions of accomplished magic users (benders, in the series' parlance). As is common in epics, we join the story at a later stage in a long history. This history is slowly revealed as the narrative proceeds, and it continues to exert a strong influence on the world the central characters navigate. The Fire Nation's military aggression is inspired in part by carefully edited national epics that proclaim its superiority. As a long, episodic adventure narrative, *Avatar* also shares many of the characteristics of romance. Aang himself, as the Avatar, fits Palmer-Patel's formula for Heroic Epic Fantasy pretty well: he is a powerful individual with unique talents, the latest in a long series of reincarnations and the only person with the ability to master all four elements. In line with Palmer-Patel's description, Aang must undertake a gruelling physical and spiritual journey to set the world to rights. The tyrannical Fire Lord Ozai is a relatively straightforward antagonist in the Dark Lord vein, fitting the patterns of more modern Epic Fantasy. His unrepentant villainy veers from some of the more subtle portrayals of opposing forces in older epics, such as the pairing of

33 Used in all the episodes bar the first.

Achilles and Hector in the *Iliad* and John Milton's portrayal of Satan in *Paradise Lost* (1667), a depiction that led William Blake to opine that 'The reason Milton wrote in fetters when he wrote of Angels & God, and at liberty when of Devils & Hell, is because he was a true Poet and of the Devils party without knowing it.'[34] Certain elements of *Avatar* are not that subtle, and the broad brushstrokes of its setup are familiar ones.

However, while *Avatar* obviously draws on patterns from epic and romance, and on previous fantasies' reconfigurations of these forms, the series displays considerable nuance in representing its world and developing its characters. It makes clever use of the affordances of episodic TV, breaking up its story and experimenting with different tones and foci. As the series twists and shifts, Zuko – the banished prince of the Fire Nation who pursues the Avatar in an attempt to restore his honour – proves not to be as implacably opposed to Aang's values as his early actions imply. Key moments in Zuko's development take place in a spotlight episode where his story veers simultaneously into the generic conventions of the western and an extended series of flashbacks.[35] Zuko also comes to some important realisations during a beach episode: an anime cliché that often exposes characters' bodies for their fans, but which in *Avatar* is used to expose the

[34] William Blake, *The Marriage of Heaven and Hell* ([London]: [William Blake], 1790), Plate 6. Accessed via *The William Blake Archive*, https://www.blakearchive.org/.

[35] 'Zuko Alone', directed by Lauren MacMullan, written by Elizabeth Welch Ehasz, *Avatar: The Last Airbender*, Book 2 chapter 7 (Nickelodeon, 2006).

antagonists' histories and neuroses, colouring a format that is usually relatively light and inconsequential with far darker tones.[36] Episodic variation allows *Avatar*'s world-building to deepen as the frames within which characters operate change and the focus falls on different people and places. One of the series' most formally impressive episodes, 'The Tales of Ba Sing Se', could in some respects be considered filler.[37] Only one of the six short stories it includes does much to advance the overall plot. However, they all do important character work: we are reminded of Aang's goofier qualities after a period in which he has been chastened by loss; Sokka's quick thinking is almost sufficient to counteract his cockiness and get him out of a scrape unscathed; Toph and Katara, who have often butted heads, are brought somewhat closer together; and we enjoy seeing Zuko being both gentle and out of his depth as he is inveigled into going on a date. Most powerfully, we see another side of the easy-going former general Iroh. Over the course of the series, we have learnt to care for Iroh through watching him care for his nephew Zuko. After a day in which he is characteristically kind to those he meets, Iroh retreats to a hillside to mourn his son, who died besieging Ba Sing Se while Iroh himself commanded the Fire Nation's armed forces. As a result of this tragedy, Iroh has rejected the

[36] 'The Beach', directed by Joaquim Dos Santos, written by Katie Mattila, *Avatar: The Last Airbender*, Book 3 chapter 5 (Nickelodeon, 2007).

[37] 'The Tales of Ba Sing Se', directed by Ethan Spaulding, written by Joann Estoesta et al., *Avatar: The Last Airbender*, Book 2 chapter 15 (Nickelodeon, 2006).

aggrandising registers associated with epic, instead valuing small pleasures and obligations to others.

In a conventional epic narrative, Iroh might have been presented as the misfortunate loser of a consequential conflict; this is, in fact, how his younger brother Ozai presented him in the chain of incidents that led to Ozai's investiture as Fire Lord. However, *Avatar*'s mixed registers allow us to see Iroh as a figure of heroic generosity, invested in the promotion of mutual understanding. *Avatar* is a show that sets a range of different virtues against the Fire Nation's desire to dominate. While the series does not veer away from the spectacle of magical combat, quieter slice-of-life moments, incidents of playful levity and genuine moral quandaries all serve to prepare its protagonists to remain true to more peaceful and tolerant values. In 'The Beach', we see that the social and emotional growth of the younger Fire Nation characters has been stunted by the unbending expectations of their culture. By contrast, the varied experiences of the Avatar and his companions allow them to acquire the knowledge and skills to overcome the superior strength of the Fire Nation without compromising their principles. The characters' ability to question and laugh lets them – and their writers – strike a balance of elements that both channels the power of older forms and sends them arcing out in satisfying and meaningful new directions.

As *Avatar* demonstrates, works that hew quite closely to established conventions can adroitly incorporate mixed discourses that let them maintain epic stakes while defying epic clichés. Epic Fantasy is sometimes seen as a predictable and conservative form, and this stereotype is not without grounds. Reflecting on her changing perceptions,

N. K. Jemisin records her cautious engagement with Epic Fantasy, which seemed to her to consist of 'stories set in medieval pseudo-England about bookworms or farmboys becoming wealthy, mighty kings and getting the (usually blonde) girl'. 'Epic fantasy', she writes, 'was certainly not black women doing. . .well, anything.' However, she came to realise that the conventions of epic might be reframed to bring a vast range of other stories into the fantastic fold:

> Epic fantasy is not merely what Tolkien made it.
>
> This genre is rooted in the epic — and the truth is that there are plenty of epics out there which feature people like me. Sundiata's badass mother. Dihya, warrior queen of the Amazighs. The Rain Queens. The Mino Warriors. Hatshepsut's reign. Everything Harriet Tubman ever did. And more, so much more, just within the African components of my heritage. I haven't even begun to explore the non-African stuff. So given all these myths, all these examinations of the possible. . .how can I *not* imagine more? How can I not envision an epic set somewhere other than medieval England, about someone other than an awkward white boy?[38]

While Jemisin, like Le Guin, sees epic as a key current in Fantasy's floodwaters, she argues forcefully that it should be seen as encompassing far more than a closed canon consisting principally of European examples. Jemisin's own Broken Earth trilogy (2015–17) is an obvious example of a work that mixes a wide range of source mythologies with its own innovations. *Avatar*, which bases its nations mainly on East Asian cultures, seeks

[38] N. K. Jemisin, 'Dreaming Awake', *nkjemisin.com*, 9 February 2012, https://nkjemisin.com/2012/02/dreaming-awake/.

similarly to diversify the societies and understandings represented in Fantasy. Cognate tasks are undertaken in works ranging from Charles R. Saunders' *Imaro* (1981) and Barry Hughart's *Bridge of Birds* (1984) to G. Willow Wilson's *Alif the Unseen* (2012) and S. A. Chakraborty's Daevabad Trilogy (2017–20). These works all seek to complicate western-centric perspectives by showing how high-stakes heroism manifests differently but unmistakably in fantasies derived from (and which remix) a plethora of cultural influences.

While many Fantasy epics hope to frame novel perspectives, some make the interrogation of traditional framings a key part of their purpose. Sofia Samatar's *The Winged Histories* (2016) is a novel that takes pains to reveal how older forms of epic can excise and exclude. Rather than focusing on a single central protagonist, it tells its story through the memories, reflections and feelings of four women – a soldier, a scholar, a singer and a socialite. A military conflict is a major turning point in the narrative, but this takes place largely off screen. The novel's stories reach back to the characters' histories before the war, winding around the rebellion itself and exploring some of what happens in its aftermath. Each major character sees the world in a very different way. Through sharing all their insights, we follow a chain of actions and reactions, but we also see that imposing a single interpretation would erase perspectives we are encouraged to value.

The book's first narrator is in some respects the most conventional in epic terms. Tavis is an accomplished fighter and an effective leader. However, her gender means that in the lands of Olondria she is seen as a distinct oddity. Consequently, Tavis, like Jemisin, seeks out predecessors. Her section of the novel begins with a passage from her favourite book, *The Swordmaiden's Codex* by Ferelanyi of Bream:

> *The swordmaiden will discover her secret forebears. Maris the Crooked fought for Keliathu in the War of the Tongues. Wounded and left with the high-piled dead, she was rescued before the pyre was lit by the man who most despised her: her second lieutenant, Farod. "Farod," she said to him, "what have you done?" And he answered: "Do not thank me, General. I am like a man who has preserved his enemy's coin; and I am like a man who, having seen his enemy safely submerged among crocodiles, has drawn him out again."*
>
> *The swordmaiden will discover that her forebears are few. There was Maris, and there was Galaron of Nain, and there was the False Countess of Kestenya.*
>
> *Her greatest battle will be waged against oblivion.*[39]

In keeping with this final sentence, one of the first acts depicted in Tavis's story is the burning of Ferelanyi's book by Tavis's aunt Mardith, who, concerned for the reputation of their family, has come to extract Tavis from the army school she has run away to join. Mardith, who we later discover has masterminded a long-gestating scheme to entangle her family with the royal family of Olondria, fails to turn Tavis from her course, and while the burning of the book is hurtful, Tavis finds that she can 'recall the entire *Codex* word for word'.[40] This might sound like Tavis's identity as a soldier and an officer could overwhelm everything else about her. However, Samatar

[39] Sofia Samatar, *The Winged Histories* (Easthampton, MA: Small Beer Press, 2016), p. 3.

[40] Samatar, *The Winged Histories*, p. 9.

also depicts her as a friend, a lover, a sister and a vexed patriot, showing her struggling in the snowy north, awkwardly interacting with fellow nobles while recovering from injury in her childhood home and discovering new aspects of her identity in the deserts of Kestenya.

By mixing its narratives, *The Winged Histories* shows how stories edit out subtleties to create heroes and villains. In her travels, Tavis encounters memories of her grandfather Uskar, known to history as a great traitor, but recalled as an 'excellent dancer' who was 'terrified of wasps'. In tune with the more nuanced picture these quirks suggest, Uskar is described as being 'not [...] a monster or a fool but simply a man of incomplete passions'.[41] Similar recognitions of complexity surface throughout the novel. Its second narrator, Tialon, has led a life dominated by her father Ivrom, the powerful priest of a rising cult. Ivrom's religious practice is based around accurately interpreting the words inscribed on a mysterious stone, but he leaves aside those that do not fit his schema, calling them orphans. Tialon's own interpretations of the past and of her father's life quietly resist such monologic practices, seeking, like Samatar's novel, imaginatively to restore orphan voices:

In the War of the Tongues, the war that established for all time (or so we have always been taught) the superiority and centrality of the Olondrian language, King Thul sacrificed his daughter Solin. He bound her hands behind her back and hurled her from a window in the Tower of Pomegranates. A direct plunge into the placid waters of the Outer Harbour. In the *Vanathul*,

41 Samatar, *The Winged Histories*, p. 70.

Ravhathos creates a touching scene from this historical fragment. The girl begs her father to leave her hands free. "*No*," he answers, weeping, "*for I would have thee suffer little and die swift*."

Alas for the king. Alas.

No one knows what Solin thought, or what she said. We only know that her death was a step on the road to victory.[42]

The protagonist of Samatar's previous book, Jevick, was enthralled by the written literature of Olondria, and Samatar's descriptions make it easy to understand why. However, both *A Stranger in Olondria* (2013) and *The Winged Histories* are determined to think about whose experiences get lost when things are written down and generic conventions are imposed. The third narrative in *The Winged Histories*, 'The History of Music', is dictated to Tavis by her lover Seren, who cannot write and whose voice captures the rhythms of an oral, nomadic culture, built around kinship, traditions and song. The final narrative, 'The History of Flight' (a title whose cleverness slowly reveals itself), is the story of Tavis's sister Siski. Told mainly in the third person, Siski's story depicts the privations that follow the war and returns to the sisters' youth to show secrets that passed Tavis by. The bright flippancy Siski affected in Tavis's account is revealed to have been pasted over darkness. However, in keeping with the ways in which Samatar gently shatters the closed authority of epics and the chain-link forward progressions of romance, Siski is eventually able to embrace the hope that the shadowy legends she has seen flickering back to life may not be as doom-laden as the records claim. The

42 Samatar, *The Winged Histories*, p. 168.

novel's lovely conclusion is tinged with ambiguities, but it is an ending that casts definitively out from the national and imperial lineages Mardith has sought to shape, finding different kinds of meaning in forms of experience that none of Olondria's vaunted literary traditions have ever been able to record.

* * *

Both epic and romance tend to centre on elite individuals, memorialising their deeds and promoting their values. However, stories featuring and told by people in more modest circumstances have also been revivified by creators of Fantasy, who often display a deep awareness of the especial value of such testimonies. Introducing *The Virago Book of Fairy Tales* (1990), Angela Carter – an expert puckish tale-weaver herself – wrote that 'fairy tales, folk tales, stories from the oral tradition, are all of them the most vital connection we have with the imaginations of the ordinary men and women whose labour created our world'.[43] In practice, such stories are often mediated by collectors and literary reworkers, but their strangeness and humour persists, offering glimpses of worldviews very different from those framed by the cosmic scales of myth or the consequential sweeps of epic.

As with the previous forms discussed, there are subtleties and disagreements regarding precisely what 'fairy tale' and 'folk tale' signify. In an excellent introductory volume, Marina Warner offers the following set of definitional propositions:

[43] Angela Carter, introduction to *The Virago Book of Fairy Tales* (London: Virago, 1990), p. ix.

First, 'a fairy tale' is a short narrative, sometimes less than a single page, sometimes running to many more, but the term no longer applies, as it once did, to a novel-length work. Secondly, fairy tales are familiar stories, either verifiably old because they have been passed on down the generations or because the listener or reader is struck by their family resemblance to another story; they can appear pieced and patched, like an identikit photofit. The genre belongs in the general realm of folklore, and many fairy tales are called 'folk tales', and are attributed to oral tradition, and considered anonymous and popular in the sense of originating not among an élite, but among the unlettered, the *Volk* (the people in German, as in 'Volkswagen', the 'People's Car'). The accumulated wisdom of the past has been deposited in them; at least, that is the feeling a fairy tale radiates and the claim the form has made since the first collections. Scholars of fairy tales distinguish between genuine folk tales (*Märchen*) and literary or 'arty' fairy tales (*Kunstmärchen*); the first are customarily anonymous and undatable, the latter signed and dated, but the history of the stories' transmission shows inextricable and fruitful entanglement.[44]

As Warner asserts, a division is often made between folk tales – generally collected as part of efforts to record an oral tradition – and fairy tales, which are more self-conscious fashionings. Fairy tales often evoke older folk tales by imitating aspects of their forms and affects, rather than by directly embellishing an existing narrative. Differentiations like those Warner sketches are not always tightly observed in practice. While the umbrella term 'wonder tales' is sometimes helpfully employed to cover both types of narrative, folk tales are often referred

[44] Marina Warner, *Once Upon a Time: A Short History of Fairy Tale* (Oxford: Oxford University Press, 2014), pp. xvi–xvii.

to as fairy stories, and stories from cultures with no tradition of fairies have nevertheless often been described as fairy tales.

In some respects, this blurring of terms is unsurprising, reflecting the ways in which collections often assemble stories from a range of sources, some original, some fabricated, some reshaped. Most versions of *One Thousand and One Nights* include the frame narrative in which Scheherazade tells a deliberately cascading series of stories to delay her execution by her husband Shahryār (a narrative that sees women as being a great deal more active, clever and creative than most epics, indicating the different kinds of memories that tales can hold). The stories Scheherazade tells draw on Middle Eastern folk tales, but as the collection has crossed cultures, it has swallowed up stories beyond those included in early versions. The story of Aladdin, one of the most familiar to western audiences, was added by Antoine Galland to the first French translation; Galland heard the tale from the Syrian Maronite storyteller Hannā Diyāb.[45] Some might view such processes of accretion as spoiling the purity of a putative original, but wonder tales, both singly and in collections, are by their nature dynamic and various, responding well to changing emphases and new companions. Different people, different communities and different cultures tell them in different ways. While epics seek

[45] For more on this, see Ruth B. Bottigheimer, 'East Meets West: Hannā Diyāb and *The Thousand and One Nights*', *Marvels & Tales*, 28.2 (2014), 302–24 and Paulo Lemos Horta, *Marvellous Thieves: Secret Authors of the Arabian Nights* (Cambridge, MA: Harvard University Press, 2019).

to crystalise master narratives presented as being central to a culture, wonder tales are more resistant and playful.

The multifariousness and adaptability of wonder tales makes them very tempting for Fantasy writers, offering considerable potential for renovation. Carter's project in anthologising fairy tales for Virago was a feminist one, and while she was clear-eyed about stories' outdated standards, she was also keen to highlight people and traditions overlooked in more conventional forms of history. In her own words:

> [Fairy stories] have their roots in the pre-industrialised past, and unreconstructed theories of human nature. In this world, milk comes from the cow, water from the well, and only the intervention of the supernatural can change the relations of women to men, and, above all, of women to their own fertility. I don't offer these stories in a spirit of nostalgia; that past was hard, cruel and especially inimical to women, whatever desperate stratagems we employed to get a little bit of our own way. But I *do* offer them in a valedictory spirit, as a reminder of how wise, clever, perceptive, occasionally lyrical, eccentric, sometimes downright crazy our great grandmothers were, and their great-grandmothers; and of the contributions to literature of Mother Goose and her goslings.[46]

For Carter, to engage with fairy tales is to remember – maybe not perfectly, due to the nature of their transmissions, but perfection is not one of Carter's main interests. Instead, she values fairy tales for their prickliness and peculiarity, for their ability to disrupt and provoke, and for their potential for capturing voices that would otherwise be lost.

[46] Carter, *Virago Book of Fairy Tales*, p. xxii.

As well as anthologising fairy tales, Carter reworked them, most famously in her 1979 collection *The Bloody Chamber.* The collection's title story is Carter's refashioning of 'Blue Beard', commonly known in the version by Charles Perrault. In more traditional tellings, Blue Beard – who does, in fact, have a blue beard – is a man who has been married several times. He persuades another woman to be his bride, luring her with his wealth, which overcomes her reservations about his appearance. When he takes her home, he allows her considerable latitude in taking possession of his property, with only a single exception. In a version published in *The Blue Fairy Book* (1889), Andrew Lang gives Blue Beard's key speech thus:

> 'Here,' said he, 'are the keys of the two great wardrobes, wherein I have my best furniture; these are of my silver and gold plate, which is not every day in use; these open my strong boxes, which hold my money, both gold and silver; these my caskets of jewels; and this is the master-key to all my apartments. But for this little one here, it is the key to the closet at the end of the great gallery on the ground floor. Open them all; go into all and every one of them, except that little closet, which I forbid you, and forbid it in such a manner that, if you happen to open it, there's nothing but what you may expect from my just anger and resentment.'[47]

Of course, the little closet must be opened, and in it, the bride finds that 'the floor was all covered over with clotted blood, on which lay the bodies of several dead women,

[47] Andrew Lang, 'Blue Beard', in *The Blue Fairy Book* (London and New York: Longmans, Green, and Co, 1889), pp. 290–5 (pp. 290–1).

FIGURE 3.5 Harry Clarke's strange, dapper version of Blue Beard, from a 1922 edition of Charles Perrault's fairy tales. The Artchives/Alamy.

ranged against the walls'.[48] These are Blue Beard's previous wives. As Blue Beard's bride scrambles to escape the horror of the murders, the key to the closet becomes stained with blood. This cannot be removed, meaning that what Blue Beard characterises as an unforgiveable trespass cannot be hidden from him. Fortunately, before he can exact retribution, his bride's two brothers arrive to save their sister.

When Charles Perrault presented the story in the late seventeenth century, he included two morals to frame the tale. Maria Tatar translates the first of these thus:

> Curiosity, in spite of its many charms,
> Can bring with it serious regrets;
> You can see a thousand examples of it every day.
> Women succumb, but it's a fleeting pleasure;
> As soon as you satisfy it, it ceases to be.
> And it always proves very, very costly.[49]

Perrault's first moral is, by modern standards, deeply misogynistic, depicting women as weak and seeming to blame Blue Beard's wife for discovering that he is a serial murderer, rather than praising her for her accurate suspicions. For modern readers, the inadequacies of such morals combine with the strange power of the story to invite reversionings that provide more adequate interpretations.

The second of Perrault's morals is a historicising one, positioning the action of the tale he has just recounted safely in the past:

48 Lang, 'Blue Beard', pp. 291–2.

49 Charles Perrault, 'Blue Beard', translated by Maria Tatar, in *The Classic Fairy Tales*, ed. by Maria Tatar, 2nd edition (New York: W. W. Norton, 2017), pp. 188–93 (p. 192).

If you just take a sensible point of view,
And study this grim little story,
You will understand that this tale
Is one that took place many years ago.
No longer are husbands so terrible,
Demanding the impossible,
Acting unhappy and jealous.
With their wives they toe the line;
And whatever color their beards may be,
It's not hard to tell which of the pair is master.[50]

In this moral, Perrault tries to laugh off the grimness of the story by claiming that its precise circumstances no longer obtain, suggesting that modern wives are more likely to oppress their husbands than the other way round. However, many of the story's feminist reworkers have not bought this argument. For them, the story's vision of domestic violence has clear contemporary relevance. The cliché opening for fairy tales is 'Once upon a time': an opening that deflects, but not to a specific place, implying accurately that such tales can be located meaningfully in a wide range of contexts.

Carter's 'The Bloody Chamber' engages with both of Perrault's morals. Her story is set in the late nineteenth century, a form of locating that refutes Perrault's attempts to push the story back into a medieval past. Carter also allows her bride a greater level of psychological complexity. The story is narrated from her perspective, rather than from that of an omniscient narrator, and her motives go beyond simple acquisitiveness and curiosity. Asked by her bold mother whether she is sure that she loves the

[50] Perrault, 'Blue Beard', pp. 192–3.

Marquis (Carter's Blue Beard character), the heroine replies 'I'm sure I want to marry him', making her choice clear, but also shifting the question's terms.[51] While many tellings dodge the issue of sex, Carter is candid about the dynamics of desire. Her heroine likes the Marquis's gifts – he gives her 'a choker of rubies, two inches wide, like an extraordinarily precious slit throat' – and enjoys the way she feels his gaze constructing her:

> I saw myself, suddenly, as he saw me, my pale face, the way the muscles in my neck stuck out like thin wire. I saw how much that cruel necklace became me. And, for the first time in my innocent and confined life, I sensed in myself a potentiality for corruption that took my breath away.[52]

Carter's narrator desires experience, rather than seeking to maintain her innocence. She enjoys thinking about being acted upon, but she also acts herself, first playing a role in the Gothic staging of the romance, and then acting with composure to unwind the castle's mysteries.

While Carter's story plays out roughly along the usual lines, her heroine is smarter, more defiant and more self-aware than the heroines of previous versions, traits that she shares with another family member. Blue Beard's bride is often rescued by her brothers. However, Carter chooses a different saviour:

> You never saw such a wild thing as my mother, her hat seized by the winds and blown out to sea so that her hair was her white mane, her black lisle legs exposed to the thigh, her skirts tucked

[51] Angela Carter, 'The Bloody Chamber', in *The Bloody Chamber and Other Stories* (London: Vintage, 2006), pp. 1–42 (p. 2).

[52] Carter, 'The Bloody Chamber', pp. 6, 6–7.

> round her waist, one hand on the reins of the rearing horse while the other clasped my father's service revolver and, behind her, the breakers of the savage, indifferent sea, like the witnesses of a furious justice. And my husband stood stock-still, as if she had been Medusa, the sword still raised over his head as in those clockwork tableaux of Bluebeard that you see in glass cases at fairs.
>
> And then it was as though a curious child pushed his centime into the slot and set all in motion. The heavy, bearded figure roared out aloud, braying with fury, and, wielding the honourable sword as if it were a matter of death or glory, charged us, all three.
>
> On her eighteenth birthday, my mother had disposed of a man-eating tiger that had ravaged the villages in the hills north of Hanoi. Now, without a moment's hesitation, she raised my father's gun, took aim and put a single, irreproachable bullet through my husband's head.[53]

While Perrault's morals reinscribe patriarchal order, Carter suggests that this order is rotten at the heart. At the end of her story, those in the bloody chamber are laid to rest, the Marquis's wealth is distributed to charities and his castle is turned into a school for the blind. It is not an uncomplicated happy-ever-after, but this is because Carter knows that those are suspensions at best and lies at worst.

Carter's story is considerably longer than Perrault's, and this is a common trend in fantastic refashionings of wonder tales, which often explore what happens when narratives are relocated or given more space. Naomi Novik's *Spinning Silver* (2018) draws on 'Rumplestiltskin', but makes it both a genuine romance and a story that simultaneously records

[53] Carter, 'The Bloody Chamber', pp. 40–41.

and unwrites the persecution of Jewish communities. The Fairy Tale Series edited by Terri Windling similarly questions and deepens. Windling writes that each book 'is based on a specific, often familiar tale—yet each author is free to retell that story in his or her own way, showing the diverse uses a modern storyteller can make of traditional material'.[54] Her authors seize the opportunity to experiment with the forms and settings of their stories as they stretch them into novel-length narratives that often pay keen attention to characters' interiority, an aspect of humanity often elided in traditional fairy tales. In *The Nightingale* (1988), Kara Dalkey situates a tale by Hans Christian Andersen in Heian Japan. Pamela Dean's *Tam Lin* (1991) relocates the border ballad to a college campus in seventies Minnesota. Jane Yolen's *Briar Rose* (1992) sets the tale of Sleeping Beauty in Poland during the Holocaust. Tanith Lee's *White as Snow* (2000) takes a hybrid approach, tangling Snow White with Demeter and Persephone. All combine fidelity and transformation.

Reimaginings like these do not rely on their readers knowing the originals, but for readers aware, however dimly, of previous versions, they accomplish forms of elegant and revealing interplay. Often, this is done implicitly, but sometimes it is brought explicitly into frame, as in Sofia Samatar's 'Selkie Stories are for Losers' (2013), which considers what happens after the common ending of a selkie tale, when the selkie recovers her sealskin, regains her shape-shifting powers and escapes the man who has entrapped her. Samatar's story begins thus:

[54] Terri Windling, introduction to Jane Yolen, *Briar Rose* (New York: Tor, 1993), pp. 1–6 (p. 5).

I hate selkie stories. They're always about how you went up to the attic to look for a book, and you found a disgusting old coat and brought it downstairs between finger and thumb and said 'What's this?', and you never saw your mom again.[55]

Despite its protestations, Samatar's story could be a selkie story, but it is also about a broken home and about people 'stuck on the wrong side of magic'.[56] It is about more than the possibilities of selkie stories, cutting its fairytale elements with small-town realism and queer desire. Samatar's narrator dismisses the overdetermined nature of certain kinds of wonder tale but, like Carter, Samatar herself sees their potential both for exploring resonant patterns and for capturing wildness and discord.

Fairy-tale reworkings often show how the meanings of events can be transformed by small changes and altered logics. Kelly Link's 'Travels with the Snow Queen' (1996) closely follows Hans Christian Andersen's 'The Snow Queen' (1844), but ages up both the protagonist and the stolen man she pursues. Link makes the journey more important than the destination, questioning whether the story's quest is really for a good cause. The unusual second-person voice she employs invites a very particular kind of identification, inserting the reader into the tale as Gerda, who is in painful pursuit of Kay:

Your destination is North. The map that you are using is a mirror. You are always pulling the bits out of your bare feet, the pieces of the map that broke off and fell on the ground as the Snow Queen flew overhead in her sleigh. Where you are,

[55] Sofia Samatar, 'Selkie Stories are for Losers', in *Tender* (Easthampton, MA. Small Beer Press, 2017), pp. 1–9 (p. 1).

[56] Samatar, 'Selkie Stories', p. 9.

> where you are coming from, it is impossible to read a map made of paper. If it were that easy then everyone would be a traveler. You have heard of other travelers whose maps are breadcrumbs, whose maps are stones, whose maps are the four winds, whose maps are yellow bricks laid one after the other. You read your map with your foot, and behind you somewhere there must be another traveler whose map is the bloody footprints that you are leaving behind you.
>
> There is a map of fine white scars on the soles of your feet that tells you where you have been. When you are pulling the shards of the Snow Queen's looking-glass out of your feet, you remind yourself, you tell yourself to imagine how it felt when Kay's eyes, Kay's heart were pierced by shards of the same mirror. Sometimes it is safer to read maps with your feet.[57]

Link follows this lyrical passage with a direct, practical address that sets the tone for the rest of the retelling: 'Ladies. Has it ever occurred to you that fairy tales aren't easy on the feet?' While Andersen's Gerda is protected by her innocence, Link's story is about actions that leave scars. Modern writers are less enamoured with holy purpose as a guiding force than Andersen was, and Link is not alone in questioning and reworking Gerda's motivations. T. Kingfisher's *The Raven and the Reindeer* (2018) retells the Snow Queen story in a style very different from Link's, but with a similar emphasis on the journey expanding Gerta's horizons. Like Link, Kingfisher takes issue with some of the original story's notions regarding sacrifice. In Andersen's tale, Gerda searches for Kay out of pure love, but in Link's telling, all the second-person

[57] Kelly Link, 'Travels with the Snow Queen', in *Stranger Things Happen* (Northampton, MA: Small Beer Press, 2001), pp. 99–120 (p. 100).

protagonist will commit to is having some things to say to him. By the time Kingfisher's Gerta reaches the Snow Queen's palace, she has realised that she is a very different person to the girl she thought she was when she set out, with different talents and different desires. In Andersen's original, the Snow Queen's palace is barred and must be thrown open by angels summoned when Gerda says the Lord's Prayer. In Link's story, you can just walk right in. When Link's Snow Queen finally appears, 'She's not as tall as you—you thought she would be taller. Sure, she's beautiful, you can see why Kay kissed her (although you are beginning to wonder why she kissed him), but her eyes are black and kind, which you didn't expect at all.'[58] The actions Andersen's Gerda takes at the end of her quest are predictable; perhaps those in Link's and Kingfisher's stories are too, once the tales' new moods and premises are established, but the story-logics they employ are wildly dissimilar, proving that the tale's air of wonder and enchantment can be turned effectively to other purposes.

At the end of Link's story, the narrative voice thinks (or says), 'It's nice to see women exploring alternative means of travel.'[59] This is a position that retellings of wonder tales often take. Carter is keen to preserve earlier forms, but she is also keen to remake them so they can speak to modern passions and understandings. Wonder tales have endured because cultures deem them valuable (or amusing, or teachable, or perverse), but they have also changed greatly over time. They are both robust and malleable, accommodating both sweeping Disneyfications and forms of interpretation

[58] Link, 'Travels', p. 118. [59] Link, 'Travels', p. 119.

that insist on keeping them untamed and strange. They sit simultaneously at the hearts of cultures and at their edges, acting as a common fantastic property that can be freely turned to new purposes.

* * *

The foregoing sections have examined taproot forms for Fantasy that modern readers would generally parse as fictions. However, fantasies also draw on forms that make different kinds of truth claim. The following chapter will explore how Fantasy has been shaped through interactions with, among other things, the scientific method, modern history-writing and literary realism. In closing this chapter, though, I want briefly to touch on the ways in which contemporary Fantasy draws both directly and indirectly on religions.

This discussion only needs to be brief for this chapter's purposes because many of the ways that Fantasy uses religious discourses are analogous to how it uses myths and legends. Modern works that use Hades and Persephone draw on aspects of an old religion, and Dunsany's *Gods of Pegāna* imitates both ancient religious texts and the forms of language used in translations of Christian scriptures. Many fantasies use aspects of living religions in similar ways to Dunsany, drawing on resonant forms to vivify and critique.

Fantastic evocations of religion can both align with the tenets of the faiths they evoke and bring heterodox or oppositional discourses into play. The list of historical fighters against darkness in Madeleine L'Engle's *A Wrinkle in Time* (1962) mixes Jesus, Leonardo da

Vinci, Michelangelo, Shakespeare, Bach, Pasteur, Madame Curie, Einstein, Schweitzer, Gandhi, Buddha, Beethoven, Rembrandt, St Francis, Euclid and Copernicus.[60] However, L'Engle's story has dominant strands of unabashed Christianity. At the book's climax, the angelic Mrs Who quotes from 1 Corinthians – '*God hath chosen the foolish things of the world to confound the wise; and God hath chosen the weak things of the world to confound the things that are mighty*'.[61] Her words help lead Meg Murry to a solution based on love and acceptance. By contrast, in Michael Moorcock's *The Warhound and the World's Pain* (1981), Ulrich von Bek is sent on the Grail Quest by Lucifer. The novel concludes with its protagonist arguing that societies urgently need to transcend the dictates of religion: 'I pray, in short, that God exists, that Lucifer brings about his own Redemption and that mankind therefore shall in time be free of them both forever: for until Man makes his own justice according to his own experience, he will never know what true peace can be.'[62] Where L'Engle's fantasy aligns with aspects of a Christian worldview, Moorcock offers a rejoinder. Both, however, rely on the cultural legibility of religious figures and ideas to position their own interventions.

While fantasies, as self-professed fictions, operate according to different social and cultural conventions from those followed by religious texts, this has not prevented hostile responses to Fantasy from certain religious

60 Madeleine L'Engle, *A Wrinkle in Time* (New York: Yearling, 1973), p. 89.

61 L'Engle, *A Wrinkle in Time*, pp. 201–2.

62 Michael Moorcock, *The Warhound and the World's Pain* (New York: Timescape, 1981), p. 182.

communities. These communities often see Fantasy's interventions either as disrespectful or as intruding on forms of meaning-making they would like to reserve for themselves. Discussing the attacks by Christian groups on *Dungeons & Dragons* and other role-playing games in the 1980s, Joseph Laycock argues that 'there is evidence that both religious worldviews and the worlds of fantasy role-playing games are products of a single faculty through which human beings create meaning together'.[63] Laycock considers the forms of framing that religion and role-playing games employ to be clearly distinct, but he also contends that in imagining worlds beyond the world, religion and fantasy can both provide spaces to 'step back and reflect on what reality is'.[64] For groups who zealously promote a single truth, Fantasy represents a means by which religious faith might be corrupted by alternative forms of community and contextualisation. Seeking to ban the Harry Potter books because they depict witchcraft might seem extreme, but it pushes back against the ways in which fantasies can soften distinctions that religion in its more dogmatic forms seeks to keep as hard borders.

Interestingly, lovers of Fantasy have often registered a kind of reverse effect, feeling disappointment when works they read as fantastical reveal themselves to have a religious interpretation. Laura Miller is one of many writers who have recorded a sense of betrayal on being informed

[63] Joseph P. Laycock, *Dangerous Games: What the Moral Panic over Role-Playing Games Says about Play, Religion, and Imagined Worlds* (Oakland: University of California Press, 2015), p. 180.

[64] Laycock, *Dangerous Games*, p. 75.

that C. S. Lewis's *The Lion, the Witch and the Wardrobe* (1950) 'offers a parallel account of the Passion of the Christ':

> I was horrified to discover that the Chronicles of Narnia, the joy of my childhood and the cornerstone of my imaginative life, were really just the doctrines of the Church in disguise. I looked back at my favourite book and found it appallingly transfigured. Of *course*, the self-sacrifice of Aslan to compensate for the treachery of Edmund was exactly like the crucifixion of Christ to pay off the sins of mankind! How *could* I have missed that? I felt angry and humiliated because I had been fooled.[65]

For Miller, the creative potential of Narnia was betrayed when it was revealed as a coded way of retelling a Christian story. This, perhaps, is where we might draw a line between religious forms that seek to communicate a particular moral message and fantasies, which take a more playful approach to meaning-making.

However, in practice that line is less firm than it might seem. Fantasies are perfectly capable of being preachy and didactic if they wish to be, and texts that seek to communicate religious messages say other things too. Miller would not have felt betrayed by Narnia seeming to collapse into the Christian story if she had not experienced something else that she valued on her earlier readings. As she re-engaged, she found that the Christian parallels did not wholly compromise Narnia's strange particularities: 'for me, it had not lost its power or beauty, or at least not entirely'.[66] Aslan's self-sacrifice is not exactly like the

[65] Laura Miller, *The Magician's Book: A Skeptic's Adventures in Narnia* (New York, Boston and London: Back Bay Books, 2008), p. 6.

[66] Miller, *The Magician's Book*, p. 8.

crucifixion, and Lewis's books are not straightforward repetitions of the Bible, but rather creative engagements that point in other directions as well. There is a substantial tradition of Anglophone fantasies that can be read as apologetics – we might consider George MacDonald's *Lilith* (1895) or Charles Williams' *Descent into Hell* (1937) or G. K. Chesterton's *The Man Who Was Thursday* (1908), in which the leader of the Central Anarchist Council, President Sunday, moves in mysterious ways. However, these works are more than simple coded messages where the coding can be discarded once the real meaning has been plumbed. Similarly, while Philip Pullman's His Dark Materials series expresses deep scepticism about religious authority, that is not everything it does. Religious doctrine seeks to lay out determinate truths by which to live. By contrast, the blatant mixing of possibilities and impossibilities in fantasies might suggest morals and insights, but Fantasy remains by its nature constitutionally open to different interpretations.

4
Enlightenment and its Shadows

~

In the essayistic chapters that open the eighteen books of his enduringly popular novel *The History of Tom Jones, a Foundling* (1749), Henry Fielding sought to define what he perceived to be the proper ways for a contemporary author to operate. Many of the practices we would now associate with Fantasy did not meet with his approval. Improbable or magical incidents were to be avoided. 'I think it may very reasonably be required of every writer', he opined, 'that he keeps within the bounds of possibility; and still remembers that what it is not possible for man to perform, it is scarce possible for man to believe he did perform.'[1] For Fielding, the process of writing a novel could be experimental and performative, but it was essential to maintain a level of plausibility. Fielding was writing in an era that was increasingly interested in and confident about defining what was real, and his novel reflected these preoccupations. In *Tom Jones*, he proposed to present '*Human Nature*', something he argued had been lacking in older romances.[2] In Fielding's view, the limitations and excesses of earlier writers had led them repeatedly to miss the mark. Only in his age, with the emergence of works committed to representing things as they really were,

[1] Henry Fielding, *Tom Jones*, ed. by John Bender and Simon Stern (Oxford: Oxford University Press, 2008), p. 346.

[2] Fielding, *Tom Jones*, p. 30.

could a growing middle-class audience begin to receive proper nourishment from culture.

Fielding, like many eighteenth-century novelists, called his novel a history, and while he reserved the right to edit and elaborate, he deliberately echoed documentary and realistic forms. In a 'wonderful long chapter concerning the marvellous', he counselled against using certain commonplaces of older stories, arguing that contemporary audiences no longer had much tolerance for the supernatural, which they were likely to see as artificial or comic:

> The only supernatural agents which can in any manner be allowed to us moderns, are ghosts; but of these I would advise an author to be extremely sparing. These are indeed, like arsenic, and other dangerous drugs in physic, to be used with the utmost caution; nor would I advise the introduction of them at all in those works, or by those authors, to which, or to whom, a horse-laugh in the reader would be any great prejudice or mortification.
>
> As for elves and fairies, and other such mummery, I purposely omit the mention of them, as I should be very unwilling to confine within any bounds those surprising imaginations, for whose vast capacity the limits of human nature are too narrow; whose works are to be considered as a new creation; and who have consequently just right to do what they will with their own.
>
> Man therefore is the highest subject (unless on very extraordinary occasions indeed) which presents itself to the pen of our historian, or of our poet; and, in relating his actions, great care is to be taken that we do not exceed the capacity of the agent we describe.[3]

[3] Fielding, *Tom Jones*, p. 347–8.

In this final assertion, Fielding echoes Alexander Pope's sentiment that 'The proper study of Mankind is Man.'[4] He does not go as far as completely to forbid non-mimetic forms of representation; ghosts might be allowed in particular circumstances, and in the works of individuals who think in self-consciously peculiar ways, elves and fairies might plausibly be acceptable. However, it is clear that Fielding believed the rules of culture were changing to favour forms that imitated proto-scientific processes of empirical observation.

For Fielding and his contemporaries, to move towards more self-consciously realistic forms of writing was to move towards modernity. Older artists and audiences had jumped at and been deceived by shadows. The kinds of discourses later grouped under the heading of Enlightenment sought to dispel these shadows, replacing what they characterised as ignorance, delusion and superstition with genuine knowledge. Proper conclusions were to be arrived at through processes of rational enquiry. Rational enquiries were to be conducted by refining and employing new tools, both actual (scientific instruments, encyclopaedias, periodical publications) and conceptual (the scientific method, documentary realism, political economy). The insights these tools would create would allow old commonplaces to be discarded. In the words of Theodor W. Adorno and Max Horkheimer, 'The programme of the Enlightenment was the disenchantment of the world; the dissolution of myths and the substitution of

[4] Alexander Pope, *An Essay on Man*, Epistle 2, line 2, in *The Poems of Alexander Pope*, ed. by John Butt (London: Methuen, 1963), pp. 501–47 (p. 516).

knowledge for fancy.'[5] It will be immediately apparent that this programme sought to displace many of the modes that fantasies value and draw upon, seeing such modes either as petty distractions or as obstacles to progress.

Oppositions like the one Fielding draws between the modern and the outmoded became increasingly common rhetorical devices over the course of the eighteenth century.[6] Discourses of Enlightenment did not tend to set themselves up as alternatives that could sit alongside existing forms. Instead, they presented themselves as superior systems that explained and ordered the world in ways that were manifestly better. In many fields, there was a certain amount of truth to such claims: I doubt that given the choice between having a malady treated based on sixteenth-century medical knowledge or nineteenth-century medical knowledge, many people would choose sixteenth-century tools and understandings. However, while Enlightenment projects affected to dispel old shadows, they also cast new ones. In their influential critique, Adorno and Horkheimer argue that Enlightenment logics tend towards the tyrannous. 'What men want to learn from nature', they aver, 'is how to use it in order wholly to dominate it and other men.'[7] This, they contend, meant that in practice Enlightenment knowledge and

[5] Theodor W. Adorno and Max Horkheimer, *Dialectic of Enlightenment*, translated by John Cumming (London: Verso, 1997), p. 3.

[6] For a nuanced exploration of how the quarrel of the Ancients and the Moderns informed the shape of the Enlightenment, see Dan Edelstein, *The Enlightenment: A Genealogy* (Chicago, IL: University of Chicago Press, 2010).

[7] Adorno and Horkheimer, *Dialectic*, p. 4.

systems often created or compounded inequalities (in terms of resources, agency or expertise) even when serving ostensibly liberal or democratic ends. Faith in Enlightenment righteousness could lead to diminishment or abuse:

> Men pay for the increase of their power with alienation from that over which they exercise their power. Enlightenment behaves towards things as a dictator toward men. He knows them in so far as he can manipulate them. [...] In this way their potentiality is turned to his own ends.[8]

For Adorno and Horkheimer, certain kinds of Enlightenment thinking had strong consonances with the kinds of covetous, instrumental and despotic motives commonly attributed to Fantasy's psychopathic Dark Lords, reflecting the ways in which a sense of superiority can slip into supremacism. Believing that you accurately understand what is important about the world and that those who understand things differently are backward or deficient almost inevitably leads to inflexibility and intolerance.

When combined with the increasing power of the modern state and the emergence of interconnected capitalist infrastructures, Enlightenment arrogance had far-reaching consequences. The desire for neatness and legibility in the maps that redistributed land in the name of improvement often failed to consider complex situations on the ground. This led to designs that looked reasonable on paper but that were impractical, inefficient or deeply unequal in practice, and which suborned common land

[8] Adorno and Horkheimer, *Dialectic*, p. 8.

and rights to private interests.[9] Explorers, merchants and colonialists who had been taught to consider themselves as being more advanced than the peoples they encountered summarily dismissed Indigenous knowledges from which they might have learnt a great deal about the environments in which they found themselves. Instead, imperial hubris often led to tragedy and violence. Many Enlightenment thinkers believed passionately that the world was improvable. However, progress required sacrifices. One of the less savoury functions of Enlightenment thought was its usefulness for justifying having somebody else make those sacrifices – someone less educated, less advanced, less privileged, less free. This kind of instrumental thinking is often critiqued directly in fantasies that consider colonial or postcolonial societies (as I will discuss later in this chapter) but also in Fantasy more generally through a widespread insistence on the importance of recognising the humanity of others: an insistence epitomised by Granny Weatherwax's assertion in Terry Pratchett's *Carpe Jugulum* (1998) that 'sin [...] is when you treat people as things'.[10]

Enlightenment thought was by no means monolithic. Philosophers, scholars, authors and elites frequently argued with each other, and many maintained a healthy cynicism about the possibility of genuinely bettering the world. While Fielding argued for realism, there were plenty of writers who used fantastic devices to delineate

[9] For more on this, see James C. Scott, *Seeing Like a State: How Certain Schemes to Improve the Human Condition Have Failed* (New Haven, CT: Yale University Press, 2000).

[10] Terry Pratchett, *Carpe Jugulum* (London: Corgi, 2013), p. 302.

human limitations and follies. From the sinister magician and phallic flying chimera in Eliza Haywood's *The Adventures of Eovaai* (1736) to the giants and talking horses of Jonathan Swift's *Gulliver's Travels* (1726) and the fairies of Alexander Pope's *The Rape of the Lock* (1712), there is a significant fantastic current in eighteenth-century literature. This current is particularly prominent in works with critical or satirical purposes. Voltaire is often seen as a paradigmatic figure of rational Enlightenment; nevertheless, the fantastic features prominently in several of his major works. His novella *Le Micromégas* (1752) uses gigantic extraterrestrial visitors to show how scientific and philosophical enquiries can bridge vast differences in scale and understanding, while also demonstrating that such enquiries do not necessarily dispel pettiness and arrogance. *Candide* (1759) parodies philosophical optimism and pessimism through a fast-paced and highly improbable series of adventures, using methods tinged with the fantastic to show a world that is more complicated and less explicable than the philosophers in the story will allow. However, while Voltaire used Fantasy adroitly to articulate humanity's limitations, he also expressed confidence in his own superior understanding. When he asserted that *Candide* was designed to 'bring amusement to a small number of men of wit', he positioned himself as addressing a privileged group with the education and social nous to decode his implications.[11] While he argued that we 'are all steeped in weaknesses and errors' and that consequently we should

[11] Quoted approvingly in Alfred Owen Aldridge, *Voltaire and the Century of Light* (Princeton, NJ: Princeton University Press, 1975), p. 251.

'forgive one another's follies', he nevertheless saw people like himself as possessing an exceptional talent for detecting the errors of others.[12] Follies forgiven are, after all, still follies. They might be tolerated, but it is still better to avoid them.

This brief sketch, when combined with the previous three chapters, should help to explain why the politics of Fantasy became both more distinctive and more vexed as Enlightenment modes of thinking became increasingly prominent. Fantasy's interest in counterfactuals, its commitment to iterative development and its investment in older traditions and mythologies sat awkwardly with the desire to find authoritative and definitive ways of explaining and ordering the world. As fantasies did not subscribe fully to the rational realism that predominated in much Enlightenment discourse, they were often grouped together and condemned as archaic, self-indulgent, childish or deviant. Nevertheless, fantasies continued to be produced in large quantities and varied forms. As the eighteenth and nineteenth centuries progressed, they also found a new purpose as a means of critiquing Enlightenment totalisations. Some fantastic critiques took the form of knee-jerk conservatism, but many sought to show the value of perspectives that Enlightenment opinion side-lined, or to demonstrate how certain toolsets developed by Enlightenment thinkers were less reliable than their fashioners claimed. In her popular Gothic novels, Ann Radcliffe conjured and then dismissed the possibility of supernatural interference as a means of exploring both the psychology of fear and the

12 Voltaire, *Philosophical Dictionary*, ed. and translated by Theodore Besterman (London: Penguin, 1979), p. 387.

implications of malicious forms of patriarchal authority. In the Alice books, Lewis Carroll showed how easily the tools of logic and reason could be employed to produce nonsense. When William Morris turned to Fantasy, it was in part out of a love for medieval aesthetics, but it was also to imagine alternatives to a disenchanted and unequal modern world. Morris was a committed socialist, and while his works are not lacking in knights and monarchs, they also laud societies that value craftsmanship, accountability and responsibility.

Contemporary Fantasy creators have continued to grapple with the legacies of Enlightenment, recognising the value of Enlightenment innovations while refusing to allow these to take up the whole canvas. While modern fantasies adroitly employ techniques derived from the affordances of realism and the scientific method, they also work to hold open a space in which it can be asserted that the discourses of Enlightenment are not sufficient to tell every kind of story. Such fantastic critiques of overreaching systems are a valuable cultural good. Even if we accept the rather blinkered and anthropocentric proposition that 'The proper study of Mankind is Man', it is important to recognise – like Voltaire – that people do not always act rationally, that persistent myths and stories bind us together, and that systems encode the preconceptions and assumptions of their designers – preconceptions and assumptions that are seldom as objective or universally applicable as those designers might like to believe. The kinds of thinking most characteristic of the Enlightenment commonly assume that we can describe and encompass what is true, what is right and what is real. Fantasy is less sure about these propositions, saying with

Hamlet, 'There are more things in heaven and earth, Horatio, / Than are dreamt of in our philosophy.'[13] The ideological difference between these positions is that while Fantasy readily admits the value of realism and rationality, realism and rationality often seek to establish their value by demeaning modes they depict as being suspicious, tawdry and obsolete. Fantasy can both accommodate Enlightenment and posit alternatives to Enlightenment positions. Enlightenment discourses are not as well suited to doing the reverse.

This is in part because advocates of Enlightenment tended to promote personal innovation over collective knowledge. Kathryn Hume, in her important study of Fantasy and mimesis, points to the impact of John Locke's model of the mind as a *tabula rasa*, or blank slate, which emphasises the 'individual and accidental concatenations' of each person's experiences. Hume also considers the far-reaching implications of René Descartes 'finding his ultimate, irreducible point of validation in himself: *cogito ergo sum*'.[14] A focus on individual autonomy derived in part from such positionings is central to Immanuel Kant's influential 1784 essay 'Answering the Question: What Is Enlightenment?'. Kant provides the following answer to his question: '*Enlightenment is the human being's emergence from his self-incurred minority.*'[15] For Kant, new

[13] William Shakespeare, *Hamlet*, ed. by G. R. Hibbard (Oxford: Oxford World's Classics, 2008), p. 195 (I.5.174–5).

[14] Kathryn Hume, *Fantasy and Mimesis: Responses to Reality in Western Literature* (New York and London: Methuen, 1984), pp. 34, 35.

[15] Immanuel Kant, 'Answering the Question: What Is Enlightenment?', in *Practical Philosophy*, ed. and translated by Mary J. Gregor (Cambridge: Cambridge University Press, 1996), pp. 17–22 (p. 17).

ways of thinking provided opportunities to put aside childish things and assert intellectual independence. In setting out his argument, he quotes the Latin motto '*Sapere aude* ', translated variously as 'Dare to know' or 'Dare to be wise': an expression of confidence in the power of the individual mind to reckon with the complexities of the world. Conversely, he has little time for those who rely too much on external influences or cultural truisms:

> It is so comfortable to be a minor! If I have a book that understands for me, a spiritual advisor who has a conscience for me, a doctor who decides upon a regimen for me, and so forth, I need not trouble myself at all. I need not think, if only I can pay; others will readily undertake the irksome business for me.[16]

Kant does not completely dismiss the guidance of experts, but he nevertheless claims that individuals can make great strides beyond inherited truths and thereby effect meaningful change (or, at least, frame meaningful critiques). The model of history Kant endorses is one that believes in ongoing progress, a kind of progress it would be morally indefensible to stop. 'One age,' he writes, 'cannot bind itself and conspire to put the following one into such a condition that it would be impossible for it to enlarge its cognitions [...] and to purify them of errors, and generally make further progress in enlightenment. That would be a crime against human nature.'[17] Kant's Enlightenment is one in which limitations are transcended to birth newly autonomous individuals defined

[16] Kant, 'What Is Enlightenment?', p. 17.
[17] Kant, 'What Is Enlightenment?', p. 20.

by their intellectual freedom. As with Fielding, if older ways of thinking fall short, it is advisable that they be jettisoned.

While there are consonances between the potent independent problem-solvers Kant imagines and the heroes of certain works of Fantasy (with heroic autonomy and omnicompetence occasionally being taken to absurd lengths, as with Richard Cypher in Terry Goodkind's Sword of Truth series (1994–2020)), fantasies tend to be less absolute in valuing independence. Instead, they often model their characters as being necessarily entangled. The Fellowship in *The Lord of the Rings* (1954–5) is an obvious example, but we might think of myriad others: Roland Deschain's ka-tet in Stephen King's Dark Tower series (1982–2012); Terry Pratchett's witches; the seers and spirits in Nalo Hopkinson's *Brown Girl in the Ring* (1998); the Pantheon in Kieron Gillen and Jamie McKelvie's *The Wicked + The Divine* (2014–19); the adventuring parties in thousands of *Dungeons & Dragons* campaigns. In these stories, the abilities of a lone individual are inevitably insufficient. It requires a group of companions – a balanced party – to advance. Individuals grow and change, but they do so in the contexts of relationships that facilitate their intellectual maturity, rather than impeding it. Contra Kant, sometimes the genuinely daring thing to do is to admit that you need to work with and rely upon others to find an answer.

Fantasies, with their depictions of regression, oppression and cultures held in stasis, are also often more cynical than Kant regarding the bright road of progress. In the third volume of his *Book of the New Sun*, *The Sword of the Lictor* (1982), Gene Wolfe depicts his protagonist, the erstwhile torturer Severin, listening to a story of failed knowledge transmission. *The Book of the New Sun* (1980–3) is set in a distant future viewed through a lens more closely resembling Fantasy than Science Fiction. It depicts a world where numerous scientifically oriented orders have risen and declined. The tale Severin hears relates to a period in which beings characterised as intelligent machines are weakening and slipping out of the world:

> And so [the machines] called all who loved them best around them, and for long years taught them all the things their race had put away, and in time they died.
>
> Then all those whom they had loved, and who had loved them, took counsel together as to how their teachings could be preserved, for they well knew their kind would not come again upon Urth. But bitter quarrels broke out among them. They had not learned together, but rather each of them, man or woman, had listened to one of the machines as if there were no one in the world but those two. And because there was so much knowledge and only a few to learn it, the machines had taught each differently.
>
> Thus they divided into parties, and each party into two, and each of those two into two again, until at last every individual stood alone, misunderstood and reviled by all the others and reviling them.[18]

It would be possible to read the people in Wolfe's inset narrative as minors in Kant's terms, too reliant on wisdom derived from their mechanical tutors. However, we might also see Wolfe's story as crystalising a major issue with

[18] Gene Wolfe, *The Sword of the Lictor*, in *The Book of the New Sun*, Volume 2: *Sword and Citadel* (London: Millennium, 2000), pp. 1–310 (p. 53).

Kant's conception: it is now impossible for any one person to be an expert in everything. In an increasingly interconnected world, we necessarily rely on tools made by others and on specialised labour carried out by workers around the globe. The divisions that emerge in the society Wolfe imagines demonstrate how believing that the solution we personally hold is invariably the best can be hugely socially corrosive. If we cannot accept that there are forms of understanding we can only access through others, we risk losing those forms of understanding entirely.

The Book of the New Sun frequently imagines how easy it can be for knowledge to slip away. However, it is also a story about how communications nevertheless occur. The many tales Wolfe's work contains implicitly argue for the enduring efficacy of narrative transmission, but the story also depicts knowledge being passed on through training, inheritances, companions, institutions, technologies, biology and weird forms of grace. Severin regularly (and sometimes unreliably) tells us that he remembers everything, but what he remembers comes from many understandings beyond his own. If Severin was ever a blank slate, by the chronological end of the sequence, from which he narrates his story, he has been written upon by numerous different hands. It is this process of palimpsestic inscription that has made him suitable for what is to come.

* * *

Post-Enlightenment models of worthwhile culture disseminated through a growing network of schools and universities often dismissed Fantasy. However, histories of nineteenth-century British culture that see it as being characterised by realism neglect traditions and works that were hugely popular, including many with long and continuing legacies. We might think of Charles Dickens's *A Christmas Carol* (1843), Bram Stoker's *Dracula* (1897), Mary Shelley's *Frankenstein* (1818), Lewis Carroll's Alice books (1865 and 1871), Sara Coleridge's *Phantasmion* (1837), William Makepeace Thackeray's *The Rose and the Ring* (1854), Christina Rossetti's 'Goblin Market' (1862), Edward Lear's nonsense poems, Alfred Tennyson's Arthurian *Idylls of the Kings* (1859–85), Charles Kingsley's *The Water-Babies* (1862–3), Robert Louis Stevenson's *The Strange Case of Dr Jekyll and Mr Hyde* (1886) and Oscar Wilde's *The Picture of Dorian Gray* (1890), as well as vast swathes of epic poetry, ghost stories, pantomimes, scientific romances, theatrical melodramas and adventure fictions that make considerable creative use of fantasy. Similarly, some of the most treasured Victorian visual art – most notably the works of the Pre-Raphaelites (Figure 4.1) – leans heavily on the fantastic. One way of framing the story of Fantasy in this period would be to describe it as being hidden in plain sight: downplayed by critics but loved both by large audiences and by dreamers and malcontents.

It is certainly true that during the nineteenth century, self-conscious gestures of realism become increasingly important, especially for authors who sought to self-fashion as authoritative commentators. In Kathryn Hume's words, over the course of the eighteenth and nineteenth centuries,

> The function of a traditional literature – to display the ideals for imitation – gives way to a functional model analogous to

FIGURE 4.1 Edward Burne-Jones's painting *The Beguiling of Merlin* (1872–7): an example of a style shaped profoundly by earlier fantastical art that has in turn exerted considerable influence on Fantasy's visual identity. Universal History Archive via Getty Images.

scientific investigation and observation. [Émile] Zola formulated this stance, and may have seemed extreme when he put it forward, but in fact the novel had increasingly been functioning in a quasi-scientific mode – which is to say, it gave the impression of being a presentation of human nature which the audience would watch much as scientists would watch their subjects.[19]

The forms of naturalism and realism that Hume discusses align creativity with a keen eye while simultaneously reserving the spaces of the mind and heart as part of literature's special purview. Conjuring this aesthetic required a delicate balancing act. If an author was to have authority equivalent to that of a scientist, then they should reject that which science has discredited. However, language naturally mixes observation with induction, partial representation, metaphoric association and outright fabrication. Authors needed language to be recognised as a tool that could reveal powerful truths, but they also needed to establish that revealing things through language was a specialist skill. To achieve this, theories emerged that sought to both narrow and heighten conceptions of artistic creativity.

As previous chapters have discussed, Fantasy is deeply invested in a shared commons from which tropes and traditions can be drawn and revivified. The Romantic position, which emerged in the early nineteenth century and became dominant during the 1820s and 1830s, sought to position this kind of iterative creativity as a lower form of art. When Samuel Taylor Coleridge denigrated '*passive* fancy and *mechanical* memory', which in his view had 'no

[19] Hume, *Fantasy and Mimesis*, p. 37.

other counters to play with, but fixities and definites', it was to frame his own creativity as operating in a more impressive manner. His theorisation of the Imagination is rooted in its being 'the living Power and prime Agent of all human Perception'.[20] For Coleridge, the highest form of creative power vests in the self, or as he puts it, in 'a repetition in the finite mind of the eternal act of creation in the infinite I AM'.[21] Coleridge thus positions real creativity as arising not primarily from books, traditions, society or culture, but directly from the artist's being.

In taking this position, Coleridge was iterating a position sketched in the Preface to *Lyrical Ballads*, the volume of poems he had co-produced with William Wordsworth in 1798 and which had been reissued with further compositions and paratexts in 1800 and 1802. The Preface was added in 1800, when Wordsworth's name appeared on the collection's title page for the first time. Expanded in 1802, it made some hefty claims regarding poets. While the Wordsworthian Poet apostrophised in the Preface begins as 'a man speaking to men', as the clauses pile up, he becomes something else altogether:

> a man, it is true, endued with more lively sensibility, more enthusiasm and tenderness, who has a greater knowledge of human nature, and a more comprehensive soul, than are supposed to be common among mankind; a man pleased with his own passions and volitions, and who rejoices more than other men in the spirit of life that is in him; delighting to contemplate similar volitions and passions as manifested in the goings-on of

[20] Samuel Taylor Coleridge, *Biographia Literaria*, 2 vols. (London: Rest Fenner, 1817), 1:104, 296, 295.

[21] Coleridge, *Biographia Literaria*, 1:295–6.

> the Universe, and habitually impelled to create them where he does not find them. To these qualities he has added a disposition to be affected more than other men by absent things as if they were present; an ability of conjuring up in himself passions, which are indeed far from being the same as those produced by real events, yet [. . .] do more nearly resemble the passions produced by real events, than any thing which, from the motions of their own minds merely, other men are accustomed to feel in themselves[.][22]

The Wordsworthian Poet is something of a wizard (at least inside his own skull): someone who possesses the ability to perceive and conjure in manners that are beyond the grasp of most readers. This notion of the sublime transformative power of the individual mind has strongly influenced certain Fantasy magic systems, such as the Will and the Word in David Eddings' Belgariad (1982–4). However, the Wordsworthian model of creativity largely rejects the collaborative, iterative, craft-based practices that contribute powerfully to the making of fantasies. Wordsworthian claims are hard directly to gainsay (as the guarantor is ostensibly the mind of the artist, rather than their works) and their logics tend towards monopolisations of speaking and meaning. The Preface makes it so that poetry is no longer something that anyone can presume to attempt, but rather the preserve of extraordinary people drawing from somewhere mysterious deep within themselves. The characterisation has some consonances with Kant's daring to be wise, but with the strong

[22] William Wordsworth [and Samuel Taylor Coleridge], Preface to *Lyrical Ballads, with Pastoral and Other Poems*, 3rd edition, 2 vols. (London: Longman, 1802), 1:i–lxiv (pp. xxviii–xxix).

implication that for most people, this is an impossible aspiration. The general populace might undertake the mechanical actions Coleridge associates with fancy, but they will never channel capital-I Imagination.

Arguments like this provided means for artists to claim a special place for themselves by diminishing the imagined status of their audiences, mystifying what had previously been teachable forms such as rhetoric and imitation into proprietary forms of art. Such arguments also consolidated a longstanding suspicion of the expanding reading public. One reason why Wordsworth and Coleridge added a preface to *Lyrical Ballads* was to answer initial reviews that were mixed to negative. Their response was to declare that their contemporaries were overwhelmed cultural ignoramuses who lusted after immediate stimulation:

> a multitude of causes, unknown to former times, are now acting with a combined force to blunt the discriminating powers of the mind, and unfitting it for all voluntary exertion, to reduce it to a state of almost savage torpor. The most effective of these causes are the great national events which are daily taking place, and the increasing accumulation of men in cities, where the uniformity of their occupations produces a craving for extraordinary incident, which the rapid communication of intelligence hourly gratifies. To this tendency of life and manners the literature and theatrical exhibitions of the country have conformed themselves. The invaluable works of our elder writers, I had almost said the works of Shakespeare and Milton, are driven into neglect by frantic novels, sickly and stupid German Tragedies, and deluges of idle and extravagant stories in verse.[23]

[23] Wordsworth [and Coleridge], Preface, pp. xv–xvi.

For Wordsworth and Coleridge, the contemporary onrush of news and urbanisation was attenuating people's ability to judge, causing them to seek gaudy forms of delight. In the Preface, claims to discrete individual brilliance are set against a flood of undifferentiated generic writing. This has become a key rhetorical position for denigrating Fantasy. When I or the great authors I respect include impossibilities, the Preface implicitly claims, we do so because we are prompted by our unique genius. When you do similar things, that is servile imitation. What I produce is literature: you should pay careful attention and seek to decode my deep insights regarding human nature. If you do not understand that, and instead admire genre fiction, that is a sure sign of your limited capabilities.

Dismissing readers in general – and genre readers in particular – is a practice that has a long history, and one that dovetails with the rise of realism. Miguel de Cervantes's *Don Quixote* (1605/15) explicitly engages with the perceived failings of earlier books by showing how they mislead a man who genuinely loves them. In Cervantes's opening pages, he describes his hero obsessively reading stories about chivalry (Figure 4.2):

> our gentleman became so caught up in reading that he spent his nights reading from dusk till dawn and his days reading from sunrise to sunset, and so with too little sleep and too much reading his brains dried up, causing him to lose his mind. His fantasy filled with everything he had read in his books, enchantments as well as combats, battles, challenges, wounds, courtings, loves, torments, and other impossible foolishnesses, and he became so convinced in his imagination of the truth of all the countless grandiloquent and

Figure 4.2 Don Quixote reading, surrounded by the characters conjured by his fancy, as depicted by Gustave Doré for an 1863 edition.
DEA/Bibliotheca Ambrosiana via Getty Images.

false inventions that he read that for him no history in the world was truer.[24]

[24] Miguel de Cervantes, *Don Quixote*, translated by Edith Grossman (London: Vintage, 2005), p. 21.

Don Quixote is a man who might be subject to Kant's censure: he allows books to understand for him, or rather, he allows what he reads to rewrite his own understanding in a way that muddies his ability to parse the world accurately. Much of Cervantes's plot revolves around the clash between the romantic notions Don Quixote has internalised and the situations he encounters in the world – situations for which his book-learnt impulses leave him comically poorly equipped. Don Quixote is generally an affable and benign man, an idealist with good intentions. However, he is also a man who upon seeing a windmill finds the most plausible interpretation to be that he is confronting a giant. This leads him to spur his long-suffering horse Rocinante forward to meet the foe in glorious combat. Unsurprisingly, his charge does not end well (Figure 4.3).

Don Quixote was an early example of the credulous reader trope in prose fiction, and the enduring popularity of Cervantes's work contributed to the propagation of the idea that those who read works with far-fetched or fantastical content were likely to be left poorly equipped for understanding the world. The dangers of reading were imagined to be particularly pressing for women and lower-class readers. Works such as Charlotte Lennox's *The Female Quixote* (1752), Sarah Green's *Romance Readers and Romance Writers* (1810) and Eaton Stannard Barrett's *The Heroine* (1813) all feature female protagonists who are misled by the implausible tales they enjoy and who consequently engage in ill-advised ways with the people they encounter. Catherine Morland in Jane Austen's *Northanger Abbey* (1818) might be seen as part of this tradition, although Austen's use of the trope is

FIGURE 4.3 Gustave Doré's rendering of Don Quixote's unfortunate encounter with the windmill.
DEA/Bibliotheca Ambrosiana via Getty Images.

more nuanced. While Catherine is wrong to believe that supernatural activity may be occurring in the precincts of Northanger Abbey, she is wholly justified in feeling concerned about her reception, and she is correct that secrets have been hidden from her. Looking for the fantastic does not provide the right answers in Austen's world, but the desire to look serves as an expression of legitimate anxieties.

However, while Austen allows that certain Gothic novels and devices can be meritorious, her defence of the novel in *Northanger Abbey* takes a position similar to Fielding's. When she argues for the value of novels by Frances Burney and Maria Edgeworth, she does so in part by attacking older writing for its artificiality and implausibility:

> "And what are you reading, Miss———?" "Oh! It is only a novel!" replies the young lady; while she lays down her book with affected indifference, or momentary shame.—"It is only Cecilia, or Camilla, or Belinda;" or, in short, only some work in which the greatest powers of the mind are displayed, in which the most thorough knowledge of human nature, the happiest delineation of its varieties, the liveliest effusions of wit and humour are conveyed to the world in the best chosen language. Now, had the same young lady been engaged with a volume of the Spectator, instead of such a work, how proudly would she have produced the book, and told its name; though the chances must be against her being occupied by any part of that voluminous publication, of which either the matter or manner would not disgust a young person of taste: the substance of its papers so often consisting in the statement of improbable circumstances, unnatural characters, and topics of conversation, which no longer concern anyone living; and their language, too, frequently so coarse as to give no very favourable idea of the age that could endure it.[25]

[25] Jane Austen, *Northanger Abbey*, ed. by Barbara M. Benedict and Deirdre Le Faye (Cambridge: Cambridge University Press, 2006), p. 31.

Austen principally invests in fiction's modern mimetic qualities, as well as its ability to impart taste and teach lessons about human nature and society. In contesting the dismissal of the novel in favour of more respectable non-fictional writings, she charges *The Spectator* (an influential eighteenth-century periodical we will come to in a moment) with being archaic, implausible, abnormal and crude: charges similar to those often levelled at older works that employed the fantastic and at the sorts of Gothic novels Catherine Morland is depicted as enjoying.

When Fielding, Coleridge, Austen and many others represented themselves as producing something better than works of fancy, and when parodies of credulous genre readers began to hit home, it signalled a sea change in how culture was divided up. Audiences' understanding of fantasy began to shift from its being something that might manifest in many places to its being characteristic of specific kinds of writing and art. One of the earliest articulations of Fantasy as a particular aesthetic appears in a 1712 essay by Joseph Addison in *The Spectator*. In anthologising Fantasy criticism, David Sandner gives especial prominence to this essay, which he describes as 'the first coherent critical discussion of the fantastic as a separate form'.[26] Addison's definition of 'the Fairie way of writing' rests heavily on its author's inventiveness:

> THERE is a kind of Writing, wherein the Poet quite loses sight of Nature, and entertains his Reader's Imagination with the Characters and Actions of such Persons as have many of them no Existence, but what he bestows on them. Such are

[26] David Sandner, *Fantastic Literature: A Critical Reader* (Westport, CT: Praeger, 2004), p. 21.

Fairies, Witches, Magicians, Demons, and departed Spirits. This Mr. *[John] Dryden* calls *the Fairie way of Writing*, which is, indeed, more difficult than any other that depends on the Poet's Fancy, because he has no Pattern to follow in it, and must work altogether out of his own Invention.

There is a very odd turn of Thought required for this sort of Writing, and it is impossible for a Poet to succeed in it, who has not a particular Cast of Fancy, and an Imagination naturally fruitful and superstitious. Besides this, he ought to be very well versed in Legends and Fables, antiquated Romances, and the Traditions of Nurses and old Women, that he may fall in with our natural Prejudices, and humour those Notions which we have imbibed in our Infancy. For, otherwise, he will be apt to make his Fairies talk like People of his own Species, and not like other Setts of Beings, who converse with different Objects, and think in a different manner from that of Mankind[.][27]

Addison's depiction has some interesting consonances with Coleridge, but the differences between their positions demonstrate how later thinkers would increasingly seek to marginalise the supernatural. Addison uses fancy and imagination in interrelated manners, whereas Coleridge deliberately makes the two into separate categories, through doing so degrading fancy 'to the status of a lightweight escapist mental epiphenomenon', as Jeffrey Robinson puts it.[28] Addison's claims regarding the Fairie way of writing resemble Coleridge's claims for the primary Imagination in terms of its arising from the creative power of the writer; however, for Addison, working

[27] Joseph Addison, *The Spectator*, No. 419 (1 July 1712).

[28] Jeffrey C. Robinson, *Unfettering Poetry: The Fancy in British Romanticism* (New York: Palgrave Macmillan, 2006), p. 11.

altogether out of one's invention does not preclude drawing on older resources. For Addison, Fantasy relies on a balance between individual creativity and wider knowledges and cultures. Enlightenment arguments dismissing older understandings and Romantic arguments about artists' inherent powers both acted to destabilise such symbiotic models. While Addison characterised the Fairie way of writing as bizarre, entertaining and revealing, later writers positioned it as being just bizarre.

For Sandner, Addison's essay provides 'a working definition of a peculiar, belated, modern, skeptical, uncanny, paradoxical literature of the impossible, the ridiculous and the sublime'.[29] However, early definitions like Addison's represented in many respects false dawns. They began to mark out Fantasy as a distinctive form, but in a manner that proved more useful for dismissing it than for establishing its value. A century later, works with fantastic content were routinely attacked as retrograde, incoherent and unsophisticated. Francis Jeffrey, who would become one of the most respected critics of his age as editor of the influential *Edinburgh Review*, is typically scathing when reviewing Robert Southey's poem *Thalaba the Destroyer* (1801). In *Thalaba*, a group of sorcerers seek to prevent the fulfilment of a prophecy that foretells their doom by acting pre-emptively to kill the title character and his whole family. The predictable result is that their actions lead to the prophecy's coming to pass. Jeffrey was not a fan of Wordsworth and Coleridge – he attacks the Preface to *Lyrical Ballads* in his *Thalaba* review – but he took a similar

[29] David Sandner, *Critical Discourses of the Fantastic, 1712–1831* (Farnham: Ashgate, 2011), p. 14.

position to Wordsworth regarding fantastic extravagance. He has little tolerance for Southey's mages, vampires, quests and enchantments:

> [*Thalaba*] consists altogether of the most wild and extravagant fictions, and openly sets nature and probability at defiance. [. . .] Tales of this sort may amuse children, and interest, for a moment, by the prodigies they exhibit, and the multitude of events they bring together: but the interest expires with the novelty; and attention is frequently exhausted, even before curiosity has been gratified. The pleasure afforded by performances of this sort, is very much akin to that which may be derived from the exhibition of a harlequin farce; where, instead of just imitations of nature and human character, we are entertained with the transformation of cauliflowers and beer-barrels, the apparition of ghosts and devils, and all the other magic of the wooden sword. Those who can prefer this eternal sorcery, to the just and modest representation of human actions and passions will probably take more delight in walking among the holly griffins, and yew sphinxes of the city-gardener, than in ranging among the groves and lawns which have been laid out by a hand that feared to violate nature, as much as it aspired to embellish her; and disdained the easy art of startling by novelties, and surprising by impropriety.[30]

Some of Fielding's arguments return in Jeffrey's critique as established commonplaces. For Jeffrey, Southey's work fails properly to represent the world. *Thalaba* is fundamentally irrational. It might serve to distract the young and impressionable, but it will prove tedious or exhausting for discerning adults. It is tawdry and performative:

30 [Francis Jeffrey], 'Southey's Thalaba', *Edinburgh Review*, 1 (October 1802), 63–83 (pp. 75–6).

essentially a piece of fakery. It is improper and tasteless. It uses magic to make things flashy and exciting, rather than doing the hard work necessary to show people as they really are. Works along these lines might become popular – *Thalaba* was moderately successful – but they would do so based on the admiration of the undiscerning. Writers who sought the approval of respectable people should confine themselves to more realistic prospects.

Dismissals along these lines were common in the nineteenth century, but not universal. The pre-eminent novelist Walter Scott argued for the universality and affective power of Fantasy, writing that 'no mode of exciting the feelings of interest which authors [. . .] desire to produce, seems more directly accessible than the supernatural'. However, he also preached moderation, claiming that the supernatural 'is a powerful spring, but one which is peculiarly subject to be exhausted by coarse handling and repeated pressure'.[31] Reviewing works by the great German talesmith E. T. A. Hoffmann, Scott concludes by stating that while Hoffmann had left behind 'the reputation of a remarkable man', his 'works as they now exist ought to be considered less as models for imitation than as affording a warning how the most fertile fancy may be exhausted by the lavish prodigality of its possessor'.[32] In Scott's view, practising something like Addison's Fairie way of writing had led Hoffmann into Quixote-like circumstances. The implication is that while Fantasy might create interesting one-offs when employed judiciously

[31] [Walter Scott], 'On the Supernatural in Fictitious Composition', *Foreign Quarterly Review*, 1.1 (1827), pp. 60–98 (pp. 60, 62).

[32] [Scott], 'On the Supernatural', p. 98.

and sparingly, too much investment or exposure is likely to lead to error and delusion.

Other writers managed more full-throated defences. Charles Lamb claimed that for him conjured worlds were often more resonant, logical and meaningful than those in ostensibly realistic fictions. For Lamb, confining a narrative to events that could plausibly happen is no guarantee that it will feel naturalistic, solid, tangible or true. He makes his case by contrasting popular society novels published by William Lane's Minerva Press with Edmund Spenser's *The Faerie Queene* (1590/6), asking his reader

> whether he has not found his brain more "betossed," his memory more puzzled, his sense of when and where more confounded, among the improbable events, the incoherent incidents, the inconsistent characters, or no-characters, of some third-rate love intrigue [. . .] than he has felt wandering over all the fairy grounds of Spenser. In the productions we refer to [Lane's publications], nothing but names and places is familiar; the persons are neither of this world nor of any other conceivable one; an endless string of activities without purpose, of purposes destitute of motive:—we meet phantoms in our known walks; *fantasques* only christened. In the poet we have names which announce fiction; and we have absolutely no place at all, for the things and persons of the Fairy Queen prate not of their "whereabout." But in their inner nature, and the law of their speech and actions, we are at home and upon acquainted ground. The one turns life into a dream; the other to the wildest dreams gives the sobrieties of every day occurrences.[33]

[33] Elia [Charles Lamb], 'Popular Fallacies', *New Monthly Magazine*, 16 (January 1826), 519–20 (p. 520).

Discussing reality effects, Roland Barthes notes that 'realism is only fragmentary, erratic, confined to "details"'.[34] The effect Lamb observes might be seen as a consequence of this. Because Fantasy veers from reality, the information it provides takes on a greater degree of significance in guiding readers to conjure worlds in their minds. When reading Fantasy, we cannot rely fully on best-fit assumptions based on our general knowledge (although we do so to a certain extent, while also drawing on our knowledge of generic conventions). Instead, we must actively parse the strange things we are shown to create a world in concert with the work with which we are engaging. In the words of Stephen Prickett, for some nineteenth-century audiences, 'the very unreality of fantasy gave its creations a kind of separate existence, an autonomy, even a "real life" of their own'.[35] While Jeffrey set realism and Fantasy up as opposites, Lamb and others like him saw Fantasy as a serious form of engagement with what it means to be real, one that took fewer of reality's characteristics for granted.

Lamb's contention that Fantasy was a better tool for grasping human nature than its detractors claimed is substantiated by nineteenth-century writers who swung between weaving fantasies and producing works in more documentary forms. Dickens moved adroitly between his generally realist novels and the ghosts, goblins and guardians of his Christmas books. Stevenson and Wilde were

[34] Roland Barthes, 'The Reality Effect', in *The Rustle of Language*, translated by Richard Howard (Berkeley: University of California Press, 1986), pp. 141–8 (p. 147).

[35] Stephen Prickett, *Victorian Fantasy*, revised edition (Waco, TX: Baylor University Press, 2005), p. 6.

also adept pattern switchers, as was George MacDonald, who wrote a considerable number of novels focused on Scottish life and manners, but bracketed his fiction-writing career with *Phantastes* (1858), which he subtitled *A Fairie Romance for Men and Women*, and his heterodox Christian fantasy *Lilith* (1895). MacDonald also wrote numerous fantasies for children, including *At the Back of the North Wind* (serialised in 1868) and *The Princess and the Goblin* (serialised in 1870–1). The latter was a book held up by G. K. Chesterton as 'the most real, the most realistic, in the exact sense of the phrase the most like life.'[36] Like Lamb, Chesterton does not see documentary portrayal as exerting the strongest truth claims. Rather, he looks for works that conjure a resonant sense of reality. This is a quality Wordsworth had reserved for the minds of poets, which, as we have seen, he argued can conjure up passions that 'more nearly resemble the passions produced by real events, than any thing which, from the motions of their own minds merely, other men are accustomed to feel in themselves'.[37] Lamb, Chesterton and those like them translated this quality from authors to their productions, in doing so placing a stronger emphasis on the experience of reading than on the capabilities and intentions of the author.

In his essay 'The Fantastic Imagination' (1893), MacDonald took some clear positions on reality and fidelity in art. This essay is worth spending a little time

[36] G. K. Chesterton, introduction to Greville MacDonald, *George MacDonald and his Wife* (London: Allen and Unwin, 1924), pp. 9–15 (p. 9).

[37] Wordsworth [and Coleridge], Preface, p. xxix.

with, both because it is in direct conversation with Enlightenment and Romantic writings that sought to marginalise Fantasy and because it presents a series of compelling justifications for the fantastic that deeply influenced J. R. R. Tolkien and C. S. Lewis, and through them many modern fantasies. MacDonald's essay sits at a significant inflection point in Fantasy's development, as the modes prevalent during the nineteenth century were alloyed with the world-building practices now seen as being particularly characteristic of fantastic creativity. However, his arguments are less about precise forms and more about the positive reading practices he believes works of Fantasy promote.

As was the case for Tolkien half a century later, fairy tales provided MacDonald with a way in. In opening his essay, he disclaims his own ability to explain what a fairy tale is, contending that definitions and descriptions can only ever be pale shadows of the things they seek to define and describe:

> Were I asked, what is a fairytale? I should reply, *Read Undine: that is a fairytale; then read this and that as well, and you will see what is a fairytale*. Were I further begged to describe the *fairy-tale*, or define what it is, I would make answer, that I should as soon think of describing the abstract human face, or stating what must go to constitute a human being. A fairytale is just a fairytale, as a face is just a face; and of all fairytales I know, I think *Undine* the most beautiful.[38]

[38] George MacDonald, 'The Fantastic Imagination', in *A Dish of Orts*, enlarged edition (London: Sampson Low Marston & Co., 1893), pp. 313–22 (p. 313).

At first glance, MacDonald's position might have consonances with Damon Knight's definition of Science Fiction, contending that a fairy tale is what someone who knows what a fairy tale is points to and says, 'That is a fairy tale.' However, MacDonald is doing something slightly different. Where Knight's definition is a pragmatic one, grounded in social recognition, MacDonald demurs to explain what a fairy tale is because doing so would be necessarily reductive. This is a view with which Tolkien later concurred: 'Faërie cannot be caught in a net of words; for it is one of its qualities to be indescribable, though not imperceptible.'[39] For MacDonald, some questions are better answered by demonstrating than by explaining. In a similar manner to Gertrude Stein's recursive 'Rose is a rose is a rose is a rose', MacDonald's 'fairytale is just a fairytale' asserts that there is something essential and irreducible about the term: it is already the best word for what it describes.[40]

For MacDonald, the richnesses of fantasies will necessarily be different for every person. He reinforces this by imagining a questioner who worries that they will miss the point of one of his works:

["H]ow am I to assure myself that I am not reading my own meaning into it, but yours out of it?"

Why should you be so assured? It may be better that you should read your meaning into it. That may be a higher operation of

[39] J. R. R. Tolkien, 'On Fairy-stories', in *On Fairy-stories*, ed. by Verlyn Flieger and Douglas A. Anderson (London: HarperCollins, 2008), pp. 27–84 (p. 32).

[40] Gertrude Stein, 'Sacred Emily', in *Geography and Plays* (Boston: Four Seas, 1922), pp. 179–88 (p. 187).

your intellect than the mere reading of mine out of it: your meaning may be superior to mine.[41]

There are resonances here with showing rather than telling, although this answer might still apply to more didactic writing that the reader is meant to question. However, the key point is that MacDonald disclaims the notion that art can transmit insights about human nature straightforwardly. Instead, he argues that the artist should encourage audiences to explore for themselves, rather than presuming to think for them. In his view, 'The best thing you can do for your fellow, next to rousing his conscience, is—not to give him things to think about, but to wake things up that are in him; or say, to make him think things for himself.'[42] In some respects, this aligns neatly with Kant's dictum about the value of intellectual autonomy; in refusing to explain, MacDonald requires his readers to interpret. However, MacDonald's version of this paradigm is a more balanced one; writing is important as a stimulus for thoughts and feelings that arise as the reader engages with it. For MacDonald, one of the characteristics of good Fantasy is that it encourages the reader to share in the creation of its effects.

We might illustrate MacDonald's point by looking briefly at Lewis Carroll's poem 'Jabberwocky', which Alice finds written in a book she discovers through the looking glass and which she reads after working out that she needs to hold the book up to a mirror to decipher it:

[41] MacDonald, 'The Fantastic Imagination', pp. 316–17.
[42] MacDonald, 'The Fantastic Imagination', p. 319.

'Twas brillig, and the slithy toves
Did gyre and gimble in the wabe;
All mimsy were the borogoves,
And the mome raths outgrabe.

"Beware the Jabberwock, my son!
The jaws that bite, the claws that catch!
Beware the Jubjub bird, and shun
The frumious Bandersnatch!"

He took his vorpal sword in hand:
Long time the manxome foe he sought—
So rested he by the Tumtum tree,
And stood awhile in thought.

And as in uffish thought he stood,
The Jabberwock, with eyes of flame,
Came whiffling through the tulgey wood,
And burbled as it came!

One, two! One, two! And through and through
The vorpal blade went snicker-snack!
He left it dead, and with its head
He went galumphing back.

"And hast thou slain the Jabberwock?
Come to my arms, my beamish boy!
O frabjous day! Callooh! Callay!"
He chortled in his joy.

'Twas brillig, and the slithy toves
Did gyre and gimble in the wabe;
All mimsy were the borogoves,
And the mome raths outgrabe.[43]

[43] Lewis Carroll, *Through the Looking-Glass, and What Alice Found There* (London: Macmillan, 1872), p. 21–4.

The brilliance of 'Jabberwocky' is that its sounds and its overall arc are clearly evocative even as it resists attempts to define exactly what it means based on received knowledge. After using rational deduction to work out how to read the poem, Alice finds it rather obscure:

> "It seems very pretty," she said when she had finished it, "but it's *rather* hard to understand!" (You see she didn't like to confess, even to herself, that she couldn't make it out at all.) "Somehow it seems to fill my head with ideas——only I don't exactly know what they are! However, *somebody* killed *something*: that's clear, at any rate——"[44]

Like MacDonald's questioner, Alice is unsure what the poem's author intended, but she has already begun her own deciphering, as so many readers would after her. While 'Jabberwocky' includes a considerable number of words that Carroll invented, it both invites and provides contexts for interpretation and reconfiguration. Some of Carroll's words have entered the language convincingly enough for the *Oxford English Dictionary* to include them: it has entries for 'slithy' ('smooth and active') and 'galumph' ('Originally: to march on exultingly with irregular bounding movements. Now usually: to gallop heavily; to bound or move clumsily or noisily').[45] Similarly, vorpal swords have become iconic artefacts in *Dungeons & Dragons*, which parses them based on the action depicted in Carroll's poem: a vorpal blade is one that is enchanted to be exceptionally good at chopping off creatures'

[44] Carroll, *Through the Looking-Glass*, p. 24.

[45] 'slithy, *adj.*' and 'galumph, *v.*', *Oxford English Dictionary*, 3rd edition (Oxford: Oxford University Press, 2000–), www.oed.com/view/Entry/181955 and www.oed.com/view/Entry/76393.

heads.[46] Not everything 'Jabberwocky' contains can be fully decoded using existing resources, but it provides fertile soil, as its many creative interpretations show. In illustrating *Through the Looking-Glass*, John Tenniel and Mervyn Peake drew Jabberwocks that differ considerably (Figures 4.4 and 4.5). Tenniel's is draconic and looming, while Peake's is more avian, but both artists take cues from the poem by giving their creations long, sliceable necks. Both Jabberwocks seem capable of whiffling and burbling (although in Tenniel's illustration the eyes of flame and the claws that catch are more obviously apparent). For both Tenniel and Peake, the poem has worked in MacDonald's terms: they have each read their own meanings into it, filling out its sounds and inferences into visible forms. Tenniel's Jabberwock is perhaps more faithful, Peake's an interesting extrapolation, but both attest to the generative influence of the poem's combination of evocative specifics and constructive ambiguities.

For MacDonald, the most important quality of Fantasy is that it actively creates space for its readers, rather than lulling or deceiving them, as previous critics had argued. Towards the end of his essay, he draws a sharp distinction between writing to communicate information and writing to inspire:

> If a writer's aim be logical conviction, he must spare no logical pains, not merely to be understood, but to escape being misunderstood; where his object is to move by suggestion, to cause to imagine, then let him assail the soul of his reader as the wind assails an æolian harp. If there be music in my reader, I would

[46] For the 5th edition rules, see *Dungeons & Dragons: Dungeon Master's Guide* (Renton, WA: Wizards of the Coast, 2014), p. 209.

Figure 4.4 The Jabberwock through the eyes of John Tenniel: one of the original illustrations for Lewis Carroll's *Through the Looking-Glass* (1871).
Image via New York Public Library.

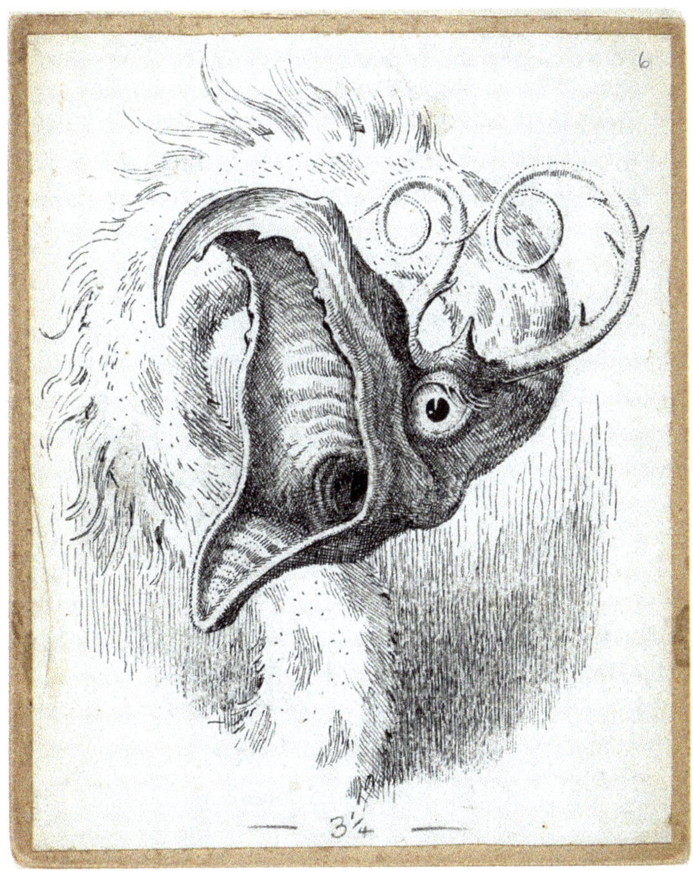

Figure 4.5 The Jabberwock through the eyes of Mervyn Peake, from a series of illustrations he produced for the Alice books in the early 1940s.
British Library Add MS 88931/7/2/2. Courtesy of the Peake Estate.

gladly wake it. Let fairytale of mine go for a firefly that now flashes, now is dark, but may flash again. Caught in a hand which does not love its kind, it will turn to an insignificant ugly thing, that can neither flash nor fly.

The best way with music, I imagine, is not to bring the forces of our intellect to bear upon it, but to be still and let it work on that part of us for whose sake it exists. We spoil countless precious things by intellectual greed.[47]

MacDonald does not suggest a straightforward distinction between realist writing and Fantasy in this passage – in projecting alternative worlds, fantasies often operate in ways that depend deeply on extrapolative logics – but he does provide a powerful argument for the enlivening effects of an encounter with Fantasy. His argument builds on some obvious Romantic inheritances. The æolian harp is famously employed in a poem by Coleridge, in which he ponders the possibility of 'all of animated nature' being 'but organic Harps diversely fram'd'.[48] The evocations of firefly-grasping hands and intellectual greed recall Wordsworth's 'The Tables Turned', in which he writes that 'Our meddling intellect / Mishapes the beauteous forms of things; / —We murder to dissect.'[49] However, MacDonald's positioning of the artist is very different to Wordsworth and Coleridge's. While the Preface exalts the artist and demeans the reader, MacDonald depicts a relationship of mutual apprehension and respect. His argument is deliberately framed in terms that function for art more generally – the workings of the fairy tale are likened both to visual forms and to music – but the nature of his claims gives especial prominence to the fantastic. While other critics found Fantasy wanting by standards that privileged documentary exactitude or the

47 MacDonald, 'The Fantastic Imagination', pp. 321–2.

48 Samuel Taylor Coleridge 'Effusion XXXV' (later titled 'The Eolian Harp'), in *Poems on Various Subjects* (London: Robinsons, 1796), pp. 96–100 (p. 98).

49 William Wordsworth, 'The Tables Turned', in *Lyrical Ballads* (1802), 1:4–6 (p. 6).

performance of individual brilliance, MacDonald argued that strangenesses that require the reader to co-create are paths to liberation from received wisdom and from the limitations of individual authors.

* * *

To summarise the chapter so far: Fantasy became a more distinct cultural mode in the eighteenth and nineteenth centuries, in part due to positive theorisations, but most obviously through attempts to marginalise writings that employed the fantastic. Many critics sought to position fantasies as primitive, premodern or foolish in the context of improved systems and aesthetics. Some of these attack lines have had enduring legacies. Modern works of Fantasy sometimes still have to contend with accusations that they are irrational, escapist, frivolous, derivative, archaic, delusive or inartistic. However, there are plentiful countercriticisms to rebut such charges, which are often driven by agendas that are blinkered, monopolistic, elitist, instrumental, exclusionary or chauvinistic. Powerful positive claims for Fantasy can be made both explicitly – as MacDonald does – and implicitly through the creation of works that employ fantastic conceits to evoke powerful or provoking effects or affects.

This book has already considered several positive arguments for Fantasy, contending that it reveals the constructedness of social conventions while suggesting alternative ways of thinking; that its iterative processes allow communities to develop a cultural commons in concert; and that it that it preserves and refashions invaluable cultural legacies for the modern age. The following two chapters will further explore Fantasy's potential by examining world-building and considering how Fantasy empowers people who other kinds of art consider to be passive audiences, thereby conclusively contradicting the Quixote stereotype. To close this chapter, though, I will consider how fantasies critique Enlightenment narratives that exalt forms of progress without accounting for the harms they cause. This will demonstrate how Fantasy can highlight personal and systemic arrogance and cruelty while making visible perspectives that have been elided, erased or dismissed.

Early in Arthur Machen's weird novella *The Great God Pan* (1894), Dr Raymond proposes to perform brain surgery to accomplish what he characterises as a great scientific feat: piercing the veil that hides true reality from human perception:

> I am perfectly instructed as to the possible functions of those nerve-centres in the scheme of things. With a touch I can bring them into play, with a touch, I say, I can set free the current, with a touch I can complete the communication between this world of sense and —— we shall be able to finish the sentence later on. Yes, the knife is necessary; but think what that knife will effect. It will level utterly the solid wall of sense, and probably, for the first time since man was made, a spirit will gaze on a spirit-world. Clarke, Mary will see the god Pan![50]

Genre-savvy readers will intuit from this speech that Raymond's experiment is risky and abusive. The trope of the scientist clever enough to perform impressive feats but not wise enough to ask whether they should has a

[50] Arthur Machen, *The Great God Pan*, in *The Great God Pan and The Inmost Light*, 2nd edition (London: John Lane, 1895), pp. 1–109 (pp. 4, 7).

history that extends back at least as far as Mary Shelley's *Frankenstein* (1818). Like Victor Frankenstein, Raymond takes pride in pursuing courses of study that others consider doubtful. 'I have devoted myself to transcendental medicine for the last twenty years', he declares, 'I have heard myself called quack and charlatan and impostor, but all the while I knew I was on the right path.'[51] Raymond believes both in the existence of a sublime true reality and that it is acceptable to risk others' minds in its pursuit. When asked about experimental ethics, he dodges the question by claiming dominion over his test subject: 'I rescued Mary from the gutter, and from almost certain starvation, when she was a child; I think her life is mine, to use as I see fit.'[52]

Raymond's Neoplatonic theory of existence and his scientific arrogance combine to set him up for a fall. Ironically, the experiment proves to be even more damaging in succeeding than it would have been had it failed. At the end of the novel, after the calamitous results of his actions have ruined lives across two generations, Raymond talks with his friend Clarke again:

> I broke open the door of the house of life, without knowing or caring what might pass forth and enter in. I recollect your telling me at the time, sharply enough, and rightly too, in one sense, that I had ruined the reason of a human being by a foolish experiment, based on an absurd theory. You did well to blame me, but my theory was not all absurdity. What I said Mary would see she saw, but I forgot that no human eyes could look on such a sight with impunity.[53]

51 Machen, *Great God Pan*, p. 2. 52 Machen, *Great God Pan*, p. 8.
53 Machen, *Great God Pan*, p. 108.

There is some sense of contrition in this passage, as Raymond regrets his lack of understanding. However, even as he does so, hints of his pride at his experiment's monstrous and damaging success creep through. One part of the horror of *The Great God Pan* arises from the depraved actions taken by those whose brains have been irrevocably altered by Raymond's intercessions. However, the story is also horrific in that it is not clear that Raymond would not make the same choice again, his social position having allowed him to abdicate direct responsibility for caring for those affected by his actions.

The Great God Pan presents an extreme example of scientific arrogance run amok, although performing life-ruining experiments on vulnerable or disadvantaged people in the name of progress has unfortunately happened many times outside fiction.[54] However, neither Machen's work nor the Fantasy genre as a whole should be taken as expressing an outright hostility to scientific innovation. While weird fictions like Machen's thrive on dark consequences, there are plenty of fantasies that delight in the excitement of technological progress. Subgenres such as Science Fantasy, Gaslamp Fantasy and Steampunk playfully and productively question the extent to which the affordances of technology are really so different from the imagined powers of magic, showing both to be potential sources of energy, change and enchantment. However, Fantasy is often sceptical of the kinds of techno-utopianism found in certain strands of Science Fiction. While very few fantasies see science and

[54] See, for example, the activities of Unit 731 or the Tuskegee syphilis experiment.

technology as evil in themselves, many see them as tools that can be turned to evil purposes. In *The Lord of the Rings*, Treebeard bemoans Saruman's 'mind of metal and wheels'.[55] In Hayao Miyazaki's *Princess Mononoke* (1997), Iron Town is a refuge for the abused, but also a locus of acquisitive desires that render nature dangerously out of balance. In Joe Abercrombie's Age of Madness trilogy (2019–21), the industrialisation of the Union is depicted as a process that allows those who are already wealthy to make vast profits while the working classes suffer. In a similar vein, the animated series *Arcane* (2021) juxtaposes the excitement of scientific discovery with scenarios that show how easily innovations can be appropriated for violence and oppression.

Arcane is set in two contrasting cities, and it rapidly becomes clear that maintaining the gleaming technological wonderland of Piltover depends on less salubrious conditions obtaining in Zaun. Zaun, referred to suggestively as the undercity, is afflicted by poverty, menaced by smuggling gangs and scarred by pollution arising in part from unfettered experimentation. The residents of Piltover are not necessarily bad people, but to maintain their 'land of progress, equality, innovation', they are prepared to turn a blind eye to the costs of the new technologies they develop to make their lives better (Figure 4.6): an evasion made easier by their outsourcing labour and hazard to Zaun.[56]

[55] J. R. R. Tolkien, *The Lord of the Rings* (London: Grafton, 1992), p. 494.

[56] 'The Base Violence Necessary for Change', directed by Pascal Charrue and Arnaud Delord, written by Ash Brannon, *Arcane*, 1.3 (Fortiche/Riot Games, 2021), 14:28–14:32.

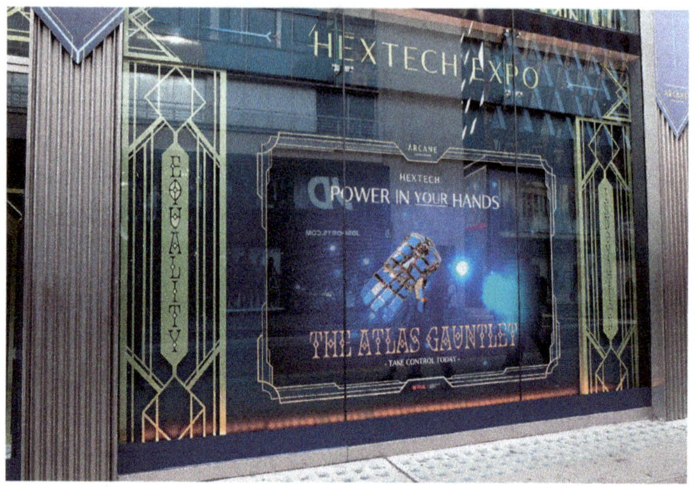

FIGURE 4.6 A Hextech-themed window display on London's Oxford Street, promoting *Arcane* (2021) by displaying the double-edged boosterism of Piltover's rhetoric of scientific progress. Matthew Chattle/Alamy.

In one of the series' major plot threads, the idealistic young scientist Jayce Talis believes he has found a way 'to harness magic through science'. However, his ambition is checked by his mentor, who advises him that 'some [mysteries] are better left unsolved'.[57] This is not a prospect that Jayce is prepared to accept. Jayce begins as a classic figure of scientific hubris. 'We're the champions of discovery', he asserts at one point, 'Why fear it when we can master it?'[58] Jayce's compatriot Viktor agrees to assist with his unsanctioned and potentially dangerous experiments expressing ostensibly similar motivations. 'Scientists

[57] 'Some Mysteries Are Better Left Unsolved', directed by Pascal Charrue and Arnaud Delord, written by Nick Luddington, *Arcane*, 1.2 (Fortiche/Riot Games, 2021), 06:48–06:51, 07:20–07:23.

[58] 'Some Mysteries Are Better Left Unsolved', 16:37–16:41.

seek discoveries', he declares. 'Ways to make the world a better place. This Hextech dream of yours has the potential to do that.'[59]

More blatant story logics would either allow these well-intentioned heroes to succeed or undercut them completely, but *Arcane* is more nuanced, allowing Jayce and Viktor to be correct about their discoveries' transformative potential but then confronting them with consequences. Jayce's status as a celebrated inventor brings him into the corridors of power, making him at first a figurehead for factions and then a callow but sometimes effective reshaper of Piltover's political order. Viktor, originally from Zaun and afflicted with a terminal illness, must decide how far he is willing to go in terms of making shady deals and taking risks to push forward with research that might assist him. Rather than serving as a panacea for social problems, scientific developments exacerbate the inequalities and conflicts between Piltover and Zaun. When Jayce's elite peers suggest that 'We have the knowledge to defend ourselves', he initially resists the weaponisation of his discoveries.[60] However, escalating violence eventually leads him to undertake a poorly conceived retaliation mission that leaves him with blood on his hands and a clear recognition that he has failed to wield the power he has accrued in the interests of the most vulnerable. There are numerous possible interpretations of the title of the first season's final episode, 'The Monster You Created'. It could refer to a considerable number of

59 'The Base Violence Necessary for Change', 08:19–08:28.

60 'The Boy Savior', directed by Pascal Charrue and Arnaud Delord, written by Nick Luddington, *Arcane*, 1.7, 24:30–24:32.

the characters, to the antagonism between the two cities or to Hextech itself, which we see turned violently against its inventor. However, the episode also shows a genuine attempt to broker a difficult compromise that would set the relationship between the cities on a more equitable footing. While science allows for potent actions, it does nothing to guarantee that these actions are fair or beneficial. *Arcane*'s characters are granted increasing personal and political agency through new technologies, but the uses they make of this agency are decidedly mixed.

While the Hextech of *Arcane* blends science and magic, Adrian Tchaikovsky's *Elder Race* (2021) is structured around contrasting a fantastic understanding with a scientific one. At the beginning of the book, we join Lynesse Fourth Daughter, a princess in search of the legendary sorcerer Nyrgoth Elder, who she believes will help her deal with demonic incursions. In the second chapter, we discover that this legendary sorcerer is actually named Nyr Illim Tevitch, 'anthropologist second class of Earth's Explorer Corps [. . .] centuries old and light years from home'.[61] In oscillating between Lynesse (in close third person) and Nyr (in first person), *Elder Race* positions itself self-consciously in a tradition that explores Arthur C. Clarke's axiom that 'Any sufficiently advanced technology is indistinguishable from magic.'[62] *Elder Race* is dedicated to Gene Wolfe, whose *Book of the New Sun* depends on a similar layering of perspectives, and it also

[61] Adrian Tchaikovsky, *Elder Race* (New York: Tom Doherty Associates, 2021), p. 25.

[62] Arthur C. Clarke, 'Hazards of Prophecy: The Failure of Imagination', in *Profiles of the Future: An Enquiry into the Limits of the Possible*, 2nd edition (London: Pan Books, 1973), pp. 30–9 (p. 39).

recalls Iain M. Banks' *Inversions* (1998), in which a world with many of the trappings of Fantasy is subtly manipulated by operatives with access to advanced technology. However, neither of these works strikes contrasts and draws consonances with quite the same clarity as Tchaikovsky's novella.

One strand of *Elder Race* positions magic and science as being effectively synonyms for advanced forms of understanding. When Nyr protests that he is 'just of a people who understand how the world works', the princess's companion, Esha, responds,

> Is that not what magic is? Every wise man, every scholar I have met who pretended to the title of magician, that was their study. They sought to learn how the world worked, so that they could control and master it. That is magic.[63]

Nyr resists Esha's interpretation, arguing that tools are not inherently magical because they make it easier to accomplish tasks. 'Iron is not magic, just because it needs a smith's skill to forge', he insists. 'It is just knowledge.' However, the slippage between process and conceptual framing hints at the larger pattern of the book: while Nyr's access to scientific knowledge lets him achieve things that resemble magic to Lynesse and Esha, Lynesse and Esha possess ways of understanding the world that productively disturb Nyr's investment in methods and standards that have left him feeling inadequate, guilty and alone.

Tchaikovsky does not play down the usefulness of advanced technology, but swiftly unsettles any sense that

[63] Tchaikovsky, *Elder Race*, p. 109.

Nyr's understanding is superior in all respects. Communicating with Lynesse, Nyr employs a translator that renders his personal predicament thus:

"There is a beast that has hounded me down the centuries [. . .] It is always at my back [. . .] and sometimes it grows bold and its teeth are at my throat. It drags me down, and if I did not carry a shield against it, I could not get up from beneath its weight. But perhaps it is the same with you, or some of your people, though maybe they have never told you. Such beasts hunt in secrecy; even their prey are loath to speak of them for fear of showing weakness."[64]

In Nyr's own narration, he describes the same incident like this:

she wanted to know why I looked sad, and I explained it was basically a long-term mental state and it was all under control, but that didn't seem to be what she heard. And of course they don't have a precise word for "clinical depression" or anything like that.[65]

There is obvious slippage between the intensity of Nyr's actual emotions and the feelings he will admit (or is able to admit under the effects of the Dissociative Cognition System that manages his loneliness and ennui). While the precise nature of his diagnosis will not communicate across cultures, the tenor of his mental state is rendered effectively into metaphor by the translation algorithm, which has caught on to his tendency to classify and externalise. Nyr believes that his meaning has miscarried, and to some extent it has, but the translation nevertheless

[64] Tchaikovsky, *Elder Race*, p. 53. [65] Tchaikovsky, *Elder Race*, p. 55.

articulates a sense of his plight to Lynesse and to the reader. While medical language can describe what a condition is, fantastic language can communicate powerfully how it feels. It is no coincidence that much of the language developed by psychoanalysts like Sigmund Freud and Carl Jung draws heavily on the fantastic.

Allowing both descriptions of Nyr's condition legitimacy is typical of Tchaikovsky's approach. The most effective actions of the story arise when Lynesse and Nyr's divergent talents and understandings are successfully aligned. Nyr begins the novella miserable in his isolation, attributing this misery to his own inadequacies. Allowing himself to be touched by a different culture, rather than simply observing it, brings him to an important realisation:

> I am only now, at the wrong end of three centuries after loss of contact, beginning to realise just how broken my own superior culture actually was. They set us here to make exhaustive anthropological notes on the fall of every sparrow. But not to catch a single one of them. To *know*, but very emphatically not to *care*.[66]

Recognising the moral and emotional failings of his social programming lets Nyr see the courage of an approach his intellect tells him is misguided. 'I am sad for Lynesse Fourth Daughter', he thinks, 'trying to be something that never existed in the world, and failing because it's impossible, and trying again.'[67] Lynesse draws her sense of the world from histories that have become stories, stories that Nyr knows to be highly inaccurate. In this sense, she is a female Quixote, although, unlike Cervantes's Quixote, she does not have access to forms of understanding that Nyr

[66] Tchaikovsky, *Elder Race*, p. 148. [67] Tchaikovsky, *Elder Race*, p. 150.

would understand as modern. However, the values Lynesse has learnt from her culture's fantasies allow her to be heroic in ways that Nyr has hitherto been unable to manage. Lynesse ultimately provides the moral example that lets Nyr break out of his slough of despond and allows them together to achieve what she sees as her royal duty: to do impossible things to improve the lot of her people.

Clashing frames like those in *Elder Race* are a device commonly employed in Fantasy to unsettle overbold distinctions between how we were and how we are. Thinking of this sort complicates the kinds of stadial history posited by thinkers such as Adam Ferguson and Adam Smith, which modelled sociocultural progress as a forward motion through distinct phases. Discussing the supposedly rediscovered ancient poetry attributed to the blind bard Ossian, Ian Duncan describes how eighteenth-century thinkers justified the values of the present by claiming definitively to have transcended an increasingly alien past:

> The poems of Ossian unfold the subjective and ontological relation between past and present in the new order of universal history, projected by Smith's science as a succession of distinct cultural stages, each of which cancels the one preceding it – from savage prehistory to civil society, the vantage point of the modern reader. Enlightenment history calls modernity into being upon that obliteration of ancestral worlds which constitutes the imaginary time and space of *Fingal*.[68]

Enlightenment thinkers thus sought to position their own age as superior by staging previous ages as primitive,

[68] Ian Duncan, 'Edinburgh and Lowland Scotland', in *The Cambridge History of English Romantic Literature*, ed. by James Chandler (Cambridge: Cambridge University Press, 2009), pp. 159–81 (p. 160).

ignorant and calamitous. In this respect, they might ostensibly be seen as aligning with James Joyce's Stephen Dedalus, who asserted that 'History [...] is a nightmare from which I am trying to awake.'[69] The 'trying' in that statement is important, however. Stadial models of history play down uneven development, the past's persistence and history's enduring pertinence. As George Santayana puts it, 'Progress, far from consisting in change, depends on retentiveness. [...] Those who cannot remember the past are condemned to repeat it.'[70]

The complex relationship between resonant old traditions and self-consciously modern modes of understanding is one that Susanna Clarke plays with expertly in *Jonathan Strange & Mr Norrell* (2004). Clarke's novel is set in a pastiche version of the early nineteenth century in which stadial notions of history prove to be rather deceptive. In the opening scene, a new member of the society of magicians at York, John Segundus, wishes to know 'why modern magicians were unable to work the magic they wrote about.' As the discussion continues, it becomes clear that there are social reasons why polite York society demurs from practical spellcraft:

> A gentleman could not do magic. Magic was what street sorcerers pretended to do in order to rob children of their pennies. Magic (in the practical sense) was much fallen off. It had low connexions. It was the bosom companion of unshaven faces, gypsies, house-breakers; the frequenter of dingy rooms with

[69] James Joyce, *Ulysses* (Paris: Shakespeare and Company, 1922), p. 34.

[70] George Santayana, *The Life of Reason, or the Phases of Human Progress: Introduction and Reason in Common Sense*, ed. by Marianne S. Wokeck and Martin A. Coleman (Cambridge, MA: MIT Press, 2011), p. 172.

dirty yellow curtains. Oh no! A gentleman could not do magic. A gentleman might study the history of magic (nothing could be nobler) but he could not do any.[71]

Clarke positions the York magicians as fastidious antiquarians: people who will happily collect and catalogue old forms of knowledge, but who do so to locate them as the achievements of a more barbarous age. Their study of magic enforces a stadial model in which the time of true English magic is placed securely in the past. However, over the course of the novel, it becomes clear that magic itself refuses to conform to this model.

A less subtle novelist than Clarke might have set her protagonists against the antiquarian conventions she depicts. However, Mr Norrell, the first person we meet who can obviously do real magic, is if anything even more concerned with decorum than the York society. On determining to 'establish himself in London with all possible haste', he asks his servant Childermass to 'Get me a house that says to those that visit it that magic is a respectable profession – no less than Law and a great deal more so than Medicine.'[72] Norrell's pressing desire for respectability swiftly leads him into considerable acts of hypocrisy. Nor is Jonathan Strange Norrell's opposite in this. As the epigraph to the novel's second book establishes, he can be deeply attentive to social niceties:

"Can a magician kill a man by magic?" Lord Wellington asked Strange. Strange frowned. He seemed to dislike the question.

[71] Susanna Clarke, *Jonathan Strange & Mr Norrell* (London: Bloomsbury, 2005), pp. 4–5.

[72] Clarke, *Jonathan Strange*, p. 51.

"I suppose a magician might," he admitted, "but a gentleman never could."[73]

Strange is a less conventional person than Norrell, but he nevertheless sees himself as a man of honour whose approach to magic is at least initially constrained by codes of polite behaviour. In different ways, both men are keen to be seen as exemplary products of their time, rather than as bearers of an old flame.

Nevertheless, forces of historical subversion are at work in the margins of English society and of Clarke's novel. While Clarke tells the story of Norrell and Strange in the main text, footnotes and allusions slowly allow the Raven King, John Uskglass, to intrude upon the reader's consciousness. Norrell's magic – like that of all modern magicians – is deeply indebted to Uskglass's. However, this is not a debt that Norrell is prepared to acknowledge, even when he is directly confronted with prophesying that channels the Raven King's voice:

["]*I gave magic to England, a valuable inheritance*

But Englishmen have despised my gift

Magic shall be written upon the sky by the rain but they shall not be able to read it;

Magic shall be written on the faces of the stony hills but their minds shall not be able to contain it;

In winter the barren trees shall be a black writing but they shall not understand it..."[74]

73 Clarke, *Jonathan Strange*, p. 263.
74 Clarke, *Jonathan Strange*, pp. 153–4.

Norrell calls these lines 'Mystical ramblings about stones and rain and trees', refusing to countenance older ways of speaking and understanding. Through doing so, he proves the prophecy's point. Much of the modern magic in *Jonathan Strange & Mr Norrell* is bookish, captured between pages and organised into rational formulae by elite men – 'competent and well-educated magicians', in Norrell's terms. However, the intercession of the fairy court and Uskglass's wilder magics both reveal the limitations of modern magicians' understandings, setting the stage for the elevation of women, commoners and servants who those in power had previously ignored and demeaned. Like many histories, the history of magic in Clarke's novel refuses to stay in the past, and while its irruption into the present is shown to be dangerous and disruptive, it is also liberating, authentic and joyous in manners that leave conventional book-magics seeming like pale shadows or small parts of a whole.

Guy Gavriel Kay's literary career might in some respects be seen as a transition from magical paradigms to historical ones. He cut his teeth working on *The Silmarillion* (1977) with Christopher Tolkien, and his early series The Fionavar Tapestry (1984–6) features characters travelling from our world to a high fantasy realm described as being the first world in creation (a conceit similar to Roger Zelazny's Chronicles of Amber (1970–91)). By contrast, Kay's later works closely resemble actual history with just a hint of enchantment, which he often uses to highlight the roles of contingency and chance. The pivot point is *Tigana* (1990), which has a setting with a clear basis in late medieval Europe, but which features acts of magic more blatant than subsequent Kay books would allow. When the book begins, its setting, the Palm – a large peninsula divided into oft-quarrelling provinces – has been occupied by armies led by two sorcerers, Brandin of Ygrath and Alberico of Barbadior. In the most effective defence mounted by one of the provinces, Brandin's beloved son Stevan was killed. Brandin's revenge encompassed destruction and slaughter, but also took the form of a profound attack on the collective identity of those who remained:

> "Brandin of Ygrath [. . .] laid down a spell upon that land such as had never even been conceived before. And with that spell he . . . tore its name away. He stripped that name utterly from the minds of every man and woman who had not been born in that province. It was his deepest curse, his ultimate revenge. He made it as if we had never been. Our deeds, our history, our very name. And then he called us Lower Corte, after the bitterest of our ancient enemies among the provinces. [. . .] He killed a generation, and then *he stripped away our name.*"[75]

Tigana presents a story in which history is unwritten by the victor. When Brandin appears in Kay's narrative, he is in many respects a more reasonable man than Alberico, who has invaded the Palm principally to make himself a viable candidate for an imperial throne and who employs spectacular violence to keep the populace in line. Brandin is prepared to accommodate many of the traditions of the Palm, but he is also someone who has ruthlessly suppressed one of its cultures and who is prepared to take considerable pains to ensure that it can never be known again. His consort Dianora – secretly from Tigana and seeking Brandin's overthrow – recognises that he has stayed

[75] Guy Gavriel Kay, *Tigana* (London: Penguin, 1990), pp. 110–11.

in the Palm and used magic to extend his life principally so he can wait for everyone born in Tigana to die:

> It would truly be gone then. Wiped out. Seventy or eighty years wreaking as comprehensive an obliteration as millennia had on the ancient civilizations no one could now recall. Whole cultures that were now only an awkwardly pronounced name of a place, or a deciphered, pompous title – Emperor of All the Earth – on a broken pottery shard.[76]

Kay uses Brandin's act of epistemological violence to reflect on the trauma of dispossession and on the importance of history for forming identities. Tigana, like most states, was far from perfect. For the few individuals who have slipped through the curse's cracks, Tiganese arrogance is a cliché. While Kay writes Tigana's fugitive heirs as exceptional individuals, he also shows them employing seduction, coercion and compulsion in manners with which they themselves are uncomfortable. However, the crime of taking a people's cultural memory clearly compromises any claims Brandin might have to enlightened rule. While the Palm's many cultures rendered it vulnerable to authoritarian empires, its factions and old magics are shown to be a source of multifarious strength that cannot ultimately be overwritten by monologic histories imposed forcefully by the powerful.

Many fantasies seek to complicate notions of historical inevitability by imagining alternative ways that our world might have gone. Some of these are darkly playful; John Ford's *The Dragon Waiting* (1983) weaves complex webs while imagining a late-fifteenth-century Europe shaped

[76] Kay, *Tigana*, p. 179.

by an enduring Byzantine Empire whose leaders are sustained by blood. Others seek to unsettle the Eurocentrism shared by Enlightenment thought and more traditional neo-medieval fantasies. Kim Stanley Robinson's *The Years of Rice and Salt* (2002) imagines what might have occurred if the Black Death had wiped out nearly the entire population of Europe, combining this with a story of reincarnation that allows him to trace alternative forms of social history as cultures rise, thrive and interact. By imagining a powerful Egyptian state in the early twentieth century, P. Djèlí Clark's *A Master of Djinn* (2021) interrogates imperial histories, showing how these rely on cultural appropriation and the ability to leverage resources and technologies for the purposes of capitalist exploitation.

Seth Dickinson's *The Traitor Baru Cormorant* (2015) is an immersive fantasy, rather than an alternative history, but it shares with *Tigana* and *A Master of Djinn* a keen interest in the elisions and deceptions practised by colonial powers. Dickinson's novel opens by showing Baru's homeland, Taranoke, being slowly suborned by the Imperial Republic of Falcrest via a treaty of federation under the banner of '*Mutual Benefit*'. The Empire of Masks' diplomats seek to establish it as a liberating force. One of its great evangelists, Cairdine Farrier, tells the young Baru that 'in our Imperial Republic, you can be what you desire, if you are disciplined and rigorous in your thoughts'.[77] Baru wants desperately to free Taranoke, but she believes the most effective means of doing so is to take Falcrest at its word, infiltrating its

[77] Seth Dickinson, *The Traitor* [*The Traitor Baru Cormorant* in the United States] (London: Tor, 2015), pp. 10, 17.

supposedly egalitarian institutions. 'They know so much', Baru thinks. 'I must learn it all. I must name every star and sin, find the secrets of treaty-writing and world-changing.' Attending school, she is assured by a Falcresti 'social hygienist' that 'every child of promise will sit the civil service exam, the Empire's great leveler'.[78]

The issue with Baru's infiltration is the extent to which she necessarily ends up internalising values including discipline, rigor and Falcrest's very specific sense of what is sinful. As Sid Jain writes, she cannot wholly resist the ways her education frames 'her island's traditions as primitive compared to the enlightened imperial scholarship'.[79] While her story uncloaks the horrors behind the fastidious technical language of the Imperial Republic – 'Incrastic eugenics', 'corrective conditioning', 'reparatory childbearing' – Baru finds it disarmingly reasonable to justify what she persuades herself is temporary collusion based on her long-term goal.[80] As she later wishes she could tell a fellow subversive, 'It's not what the Masquerade does to you that you should fear [...] It's what the Masquerade convinces you to do to yourself.'[81] Falcrest mixes rhetorics of liberation and rationality, and while Baru realises swiftly that the promise of freedom is a lie, the Masquerade's ability to deliver on promises of knowledge and authority is a powerful temptation. The particular brilliance of the book lies in how neither Baru

78 Dickinson, *The Traitor*, p. 13.

79 Sid Jain, 'Seduced by the Ruler's Gaze: An Indian Perspective on Seth Dickinson's *Masquerade*', *Uncanny Magazine*, 39 (2021), https://bit.ly/41iaONz.

80 Dickinson, *The Traitor*, pp. 30, 155, 175.

81 Dickinson, *The Traitor*, p. 175.

nor the reader is fully aware how the balance between her convictions and the insidious effectiveness of Falcresti indoctrination will play out.

The first major role Baru is given by the Masquerade is that of Imperial Accountant for the Federated Province of Aurdwynn: a clever choice for Dickinson to show the extent to which money serves as an engine of and mask for empire. The idea that free trade creates a rising tide that lifts all boats is one that the Masquerade plays on expertly, refracting arguments such as Adam Smith's evocation of the invisible hand in *The Wealth of Nations* (1776). In Smith's view,

> by directing [. . .] industry in such a manner as its produce may be of the greatest value, [an individual] intends only his own gain, and he is in this, as in many other cases, led by an invisible hand to promote an end which was no part of his intention. Nor is it always the worse for the society that it was not part of it. By pursuing his own interest he frequently promotes that of the society more effectually than when he really intends to promote it.[82]

The invisible-hand metaphor has become overdetermined in twentieth-century commentary, but similar statements elsewhere in his book make it clear that Smith believes that societies work best when individuals are relatively unimpeded in acting to benefit themselves. He has a rather optimistic view of financial self-interest, arguing that this leads to something like the best of all possible worlds Pangloss harps on in *Candide* : 'the private interests and passions of men naturally lead them to divide

[82] Adam Smith, *An Inquiry into the Nature and Causes of the Wealth of Nations*, 2 vols. (London: W. Strahan and T. Cadell, 1776), 2:35.

and distribute the stock of every society [. . .] as nearly as possible in the proportion which is most agreeable to the interests of the whole society'.[83] Arguments like Smith's justify privileging individual property and rights by claiming these to be the most effectual means of promoting collective good.

In practice, though, the equitable division Smith evoked masked less agreeable forms of distribution, as can be seen in the *Wealth of Nations*' consideration of colonialism. When Smith discusses how a 'civilized nation [. . .] takes possession [. . .] of a waste country, or of one so thinly inhabited, that the natives easily give place to the new settlers', his rhetoric of unproductivity and sparseness provides a fig leaf for forms of exploitation very much against the interests of the original inhabitants.[84] Europe's eighteenth- and nineteenth-century flourishing was predicated to a considerable extent on states' ability to expropriate resources from other parts of the world. This was not something Smith appeared to find particularly problematic. He contends that colonists 'carry out with them a knowledge of agriculture and of other useful arts, superior to what can grow up of its own accord over the course of many centuries among savage and barbarous nations'; he also contends that 'among savage and barbarous nations, the natural progress of law and government is still slower than the natural progress of arts'.[85] By arguing that Indigenous peoples are doing civilisation wrong, Smith reinscribes colonial logics that justify taking land and resources for supposedly better uses while defending

[83] Smith, *Wealth of Nations*, 2:241.
[84] Smith, *Wealth of Nations*, 2:407.
[85] Smith, *Wealth of Nations*, 2:157–8.

colonial rule as a means of educating supposedly backward peoples: very similar logics to those that Dickinson depicts as driving Falcrest.

Smith would like the colonies to be places of freedom, opportunity and qualified egalitarianism. He argues that the hard work necessary for establishing new infrastructure means that 'the interest of the two superior orders obliges them to treat the inferior one with more generosity and humanity; at least, when that inferior one is not in a state of slavery'.[86] However, the 'at least' in this sentence is doing a great deal of work to hide truth behind a notional disclaimer. The financial prosperity of Britain was built in considerable part on chattel slavery in some of its colonies, from which British merchants profited both through the direct sale of enslaved people and through the ability to purchase valuable cash crops produced cheaply using slave labour.

Fantasy might initially seem like a strange form to employ to unveil the brutal truths of slavery, but many writers have found its affordances useful both to deal with historical elisions and to rebuke forms of rationalisation and dismissal that allowed societies to minimise slavery's horrors. Discussing her research for writing *Beloved* (1987), Toni Morrison lays out the limitations of drawing on nineteenth-century slave narratives:

> I wouldn't read them for information because I knew that they had to be authenticated by white patrons, that they couldn't say everything they wanted to say because they couldn't alienate their audience; they had to be quiet about certain things. They

[86] Smith, *Wealth of Nations*, 2:158.

were going to be as good as they could be under the circumstances and as revelatory, but they never say how terrible it was. They would just say, Well, you know, it was really awful, but let's abolish slavery so life can go on. Their narratives had to be very understated. So while I looked at documents and felt *familiar* with slavery and overwhelmed by it, I wanted it to be truly felt. I wanted to translate the historical into the personal.[87]

In highlighting how even those who argued for abolition sought to keep the worst sufferings of slaves strategically elided, Morrison emphasises the representational gap that challenges the creation of realist accounts. This gap is not unbridgeable – Morrison discusses how she uncovered the use of bits 'put into the mouth of slaves to punish them and shut them up without preventing them from working' by seeking out obscure sources and piecing together allusions.[88] However, while aspects of *Beloved* are constructed through meticulous research, to 'translate the historical into the personal', Morrison needed to address her sources' limitations in representing both reality and the fullness of the mental and embodied experiences of enslaved people. To achieve this, she made her novel a ghost story. In *Beloved*, Sethe is haunted both literally and figuratively by the daughter she killed to prevent her from being taken by slavers. This haunting isolates Sethe from the community in which she lives, part of the continuing effects of her sufferings at Sweet Home. 'Today is always

[87] Toni Morrison, 'The Art of Fiction', interview by Elissa Schappell and Claudia Brodsky Lacour, in *The Paris Review Interviews Volume* 2, ed. by Philip Gourevitch (Edinburgh: Canongate, 2007), pp. 355–94 (p. 374).

[88] Morrison, 'Art of Fiction', p. 374.

here', Sethe says at one point, 'Tomorrow, never'. At another point, Morrison writes that Sethe's 'brain was not interested in the future. Loaded with the past and hungry for more, it left her no room to imagine, let alone plan for, the next day'.[89] While the haunting is unsettling, it is in some respects a coping mechanism. Sethe's mother, Baby Suggs, tells her devoted congregation that 'the only grace they could have is the grace they could imagine'.[90] Beloved's haunting is both lovingly imagined and harrowingly inflicted, and this entanglement of grace and curse is something the book invites readers to grapple with, denying easy resolutions just as these are denied to Sethe. Fantastic elements create a space where a story can be told, but Morrison's story reminds us insistently that traumatic legacies cannot simply be shaken off.

Morrison's ghosts in *Beloved* are far from the only example of fantastic devices being used to negotiate the legacies of slavery. We might also think of the timeslips in Octavia Butler's *Kindred* (1979), the titular literalisation in Colson Whitehead's *The Underground Railroad* (2016) and the undersea civilisation in Rivers Solomons's *The Deep* (2020). All these fictions make searing use of realism in their depictions of bodies and minds brutalised by slavery, but they also employ the mechanisms of Fantasy to bring home the scope and continuing presence of the histories they seek to reveal. In *Kindred*, Butler's protagonist, Dana, is repeatedly hurled back in time to the Antebellum South for inscrutable reasons that seem to centre around

89 Toni Morrison, *Beloved* (London: Chatto & Windus, 1993), pp. 60, 70.
90 Morrison, *Beloved*, p. 88.

protecting her ancestor Rufus Weylin, but which also force her to reckon with the banalities and horrors of slavery. While Butler was an extremely adept Science Fiction writer, she was not interested in providing a technical explanation for Dana's transportation. '*Kindred* is fantasy', she declared when interviewed. 'Time travel is just a device for getting the character back to confront where she came from.'[91] In entwining Dana with her history, Butler is scathing and sorrowful, evoking horror in part through restraint. When told by Rufus that his father is a fair man, Dana reflects that Tom Weylin 'wasn't the monster he could have been with the power he held over his slaves. He wasn't a monster at all. Just an ordinary man who sometimes did the monstrous things his society said were legal and proper.'[92] In *Kindred*, the scars of slavery run deep. Butler said of her protagonist, 'I couldn't really let her come all the way back. I couldn't let her return to what she was [. . .] Antebellum slavery didn't leave people quite whole.'[93] In showing how Dana's present can be overruled by the past in ways she cannot control, Butler, like Morrison, uses fantasy as a synecdoche for the persistent social and psychological constraints that slavery and its consequences impose.

In an interview, Whitehead asserted that *The Underground Railroad* arose from two 'what if' questions: 'what if the Underground Railroad was an actual railroad?' and 'what if every state our hero went through – as he or she

[91] Randall Kenan, 'An Interview with Octavia E. Butler', *Callaloo*, 14.2 (Spring 1991), 495–504 (p. 495–6).

[92] Octavia E. Butler, *Kindred* (Boston, MA: Beacon, 2004), p. 134.

[93] Kenan, 'Interview', p. 498.

ran North – was a different state of American possibility?'[94] Both of these questions require fantastical extrapolation. Whitehead transforms the clandestine network that helped slaves escape the American South into a literal system of underground transportation, using the fantasy of the railroad to connect a series of environments that depict different ways in which the promise of America has been betrayed. While Morrison and Butler focus on personal stories in particular locations – albeit with far wider implications – Whitehead literalises the metaphor of the Underground Railroad to spin a web across time and space that surfaces the scale and insidiousness of racial oppression. The railroad represents a possibility of hope and connection, a possibility sometimes sustained in specific interactions, but which is also repeatedly belied by its destinations.

Rivers Solomon's novella *The Deep* takes a more expansively fantastic approach. It builds out from a mythology posited by the electronic music duo Drexciya that attempts to address the horrors of the Middle Passage by imagining that death might instead become transformation:

> pregnant America-bound African slaves were thrown overboard by the thousands during labor for being sick and disruptive cargo. Is it possible that they could have given birth at sea to babies that never needed air? Are Drexciyans water-breathing, aquatically-mutated descendants of those unfortunate victims of human greed? Have they been spared by God to teach us or terrorize us?[95]

94 Terry Gross, 'Colson Whitehead's "Underground Railroad" is a Literal Train to Freedom', *Fresh Air*, *NPR*, 8 August 2016, https://bit.ly/409qDEF.

95 Quoted in clipping., Afterword to Rivers Solomon, *The Deep* (London: Hodder & Stoughton, 2020), pp. 157–63 (p. 158).

The reality, of course, is that these women were not spared: the only way to allow them to live on is through a creative process in which the 'murder of enslaved women [is] reimagined as an escape from murderous oppression and the founding of a utopian civilization'.[96] However, both within the Drexciyan corpus and for readers, this utopian vision evokes grief through the wild imagination necessary for its creation and sustenance. In *The Deep*, a historian bears painful ancestral memories on behalf of her people, memories that most of the undersea population only experience at ceremonies of Remembrance. These are presented as sociocultural necessities. As one character puts it:

> One can only go for so long without asking who am I? Where do I come from? What does all this mean? What is being? What came before me and what might come after? Without answers there is only a hole. A hole where a history should be that takes the shape of an endless longing. We are cavities.[97]

The questions here are questions that slavery has often rendered unanswerable. Consequently, fantastic narratives have stepped in to create imagined communities that can both teach and terrorise, providing testimony that renders histories speakable while holding those who would seek to downplay loss and suffering to account.

That life and history do not always feel rational to those experiencing them is something profoundly acknowledged in works of magical realism. In Gabriel García Márquez's *One Hundred Years of Solitude* (1967), the wonders that bind together the misfortunate settlement

[96] clipping., Afterword, p. 158. [97] Solomon, *The Deep*, p. 8.

of Macondo come from community lore set against the encroachments of oppressive states. Isabel Allende's *The House of the Spirits* (1983) mixes the larger-scale movements of politics with a family story that simultaneously intertwines the shaping conditions of prophecy and the potential for personal freedom or change. Both books contend implicitly that history's pretence to rational selection is just that: a pretence. Narratives of improvement often hide inequalities, atrocities and deletions. As one of Whitehead's characters puts it in *The Underground Railroad*, 'Slavery is a sin when whites were put to the yoke, but not the African. All men are created equal, unless we decide you are not a man.'[98] When official histories downplay such contradictions, it can fall to Fantasy to highlight them by providing means for the silenced to speak and alternative cultural imaginaries to flourish. In Isiah Lavender III's terms, fantastic Afrofuturisms, Africanfuturisms and Africanjujuisms '[take] us further into the black-o-sphere—unconfined, if not actualized, emancipatory mindscapes—by using intelligent resistance to negate harmful appropriation that desires to further rewrite an already whitewashed history'.[99]

[98] Colson Whitehead, *The Underground Railroad* (London: Fleet, 2016), p. 182.

[99] Isiah Lavender III, *Afrofuturism Rising: The Literary Prehistory of a Movement* (Columbus: Ohio State University Press, 2019), p. 196. See also Ytasha L. Womack, *Afrofuturism: The World of Black Sci-fi and Fantasy Culture* (Chicago, IL: Lawrence Hill Books, 2013). On Africanfuturism and Africanjujuism, see Nnedi Okorafor, 'Africanfuturism Defined', *Nnedi's Wahala Zone Blog*, 19 October 2019, https://bit.ly/3LfaxFB.

My account in the last part of this chapter has highlighted narratives that resonate with what Ebony Elizabeth Thomas calls 'restorying': a process by which people 'analyze their lived experiences, and then synthesize and recontextualize a multiplicity of stories in forming new narratives'. By '[imagining] themselves into stories', writers can '*reimagine the very stories themselves*' and by doing so challenge the hegemonic and exclusionary implications of certain Enlightenment and Romantic logics.[100] The eighteenth and nineteenth centuries sought to replace older foundational myths with a new one: that of the competent, rational, modern individual. However, many forms of culture have (with good reason) treated this programme with suspicion. A major tendency of the realist novel is to show how misguided those who think themselves competent, rational and modern frequently are. While realist narratives have tended to focus on smaller compasses, the more expansive canvases of Fantasy provide spaces within which the blinkered nature of whole cultures and approaches can be brought into view by positing and platforming alternative perspectives.

This is not to say this is something that all fantasies inevitably do or achieve. Many modern fantasies still lean on paradigms that, as Helen Young and Kavita Mudan Finn write, '[reiterate] centuries of medievalisms that have contributed to, justified, and upheld white power and ideologies'.[101] Fantasies also frequently evoke the

[100] Ebony Elizabeth Thomas, *The Dark Fantastic: Race and the Imagination from* Harry Potter *to the* Hunger Games (New York: New York University Press, 2019), p. 159; see also pp. 159–63.

[101] Helen Young and Kavita Mudan Finn, *Global Medievalism* (Cambridge: Cambridge University Press, 2022), p. 4.

discredited logics of nineteenth- and twentieth-century eugenics by encoding racial difference as a quantifiable taxonomic reality. In some respects, Fantasy's investment in reworking traditions can render its narratives particularly susceptible to thinking and unthinking repetitions. However, Fantasy also manifests an inherent radical potential in its commitment to diverging from conventional understandings of the world. If Enlightenment systems and ideologies of genius seek to pin down how the world is and what art ought to be, Fantasy holds open a space for discussing the limits of definition, considering what the world might become and how art should shift to reflect and question changing times.

5
Fashioning Worlds

Introducing her gawky, confident and fantastical *Description of a New World, Called The Blazing-World* in 1666, Margaret Cavendish, Duchess of Newcastle, wrote that 'although I have neither power, time nor occasion to conquer the world as *Alexander* or *Caesar* did; yet, rather than not be mistress of one, since Fortune and the Fates would give me none, I have made a world of my own: for which no body, I hope, will blame me, since it is in every one's power to do the like.'[1] While modern afficionados would probably use different words to describe the impulse, the attraction of making another world (or of radically extending our own) is something Fantasy lovers recognise as one of the genre's principal lures. World-building has become one of the most common metaphors through which Fantasy creators explain what they do, and the worlds of Fantasy exert fascinations in many cases stronger than those exerted by characters or plots. Oz, Neverland, Hyboria, Elfland, Middle-earth, Narnia, Westeros, the Forgotten Realms, Exandria, the Dreaming, the Stillness, Spyre, the Discworld, Hyrule, the Old World, Earthsea, Equestria, the Cosmere, Thedas, Azeroth, Teyvat, Tékumel, Tortall, Tamriel,

[1] Margaret Cavendish, *The Description of a New World, Called The Blazing World*, in *The Blazing World and Other Writings*, ed. by Kate Lilley (London: Penguin, 2004), pp. 119–225 (p. 124).

Randland, Dominaria, the Circle of the World, the Lands Between – the list doesn't go on because there is limited space in this book, but it certainly could, and for a considerable time.

Fantastic worlds often have commonalities derived from our world and from the conventions they iterate upon, but specific creators are highly various in evoking geographies, politics, societies, magics and cultures. In some respects, imagined worlds reflect consensuses and diversities in our own world; in other ways, they serve as experimental spaces within which divergent alternatives can be imagined and enacted. Depending on their design, they can be expansive or specific, cruel or kind, subject to scrupulous logics or built from wild improvisations. While, like Cavendish, we can make and circulate worlds of our own, processes of harmonious and competitive collaboration have come to play a defining role in much contemporary Fantasy world-building. Worlds, after all, flourish best when they are equitably shared.

Some critics and commentators have used the idea of world-building to draw a line between older fantastical creations and a distinctively modern form of Fantasy, suggesting an additional (or alternative) inflection point to set alongside (or against) John Clute's assertion that we should pay attention to changing horizons of social and generic expectation in the eighteenth century. In Anglophone accounts that stress world-building's importance, William Morris is often the totemic dividing line. In an early study published as part of the Ballantine Adult Fantasy series, Lin Carter claimed that Morris 'invented the imaginary-world novel' in books like *The Wood Beyond the World* (1894), *The Well at the World's End* (1896) and

The Water of the Wondrous Isles (1897), calling him the 'father of modern fantasy'.[2] While Carter acknowledges Morris's precursors, he does not see their works as part of the coherent world-shaping tradition he goes on to construct for post-Morris Fantasy: a tradition into which he drafts figures such as Lord Dunsany, E. R. Eddison, James Branch Cabell and William Hope Hodgson, all of whom serve as waypoints on a path towards J. R. R. Tolkien. Carter's reason for side-lining earlier fantasies – with a few qualified exceptions, including William Beckford's orientalist Gothic novel *Vathek* (1786) and some of George MacDonald's works – is that he does not see their worlds as coherent secondary creations. For Carter, 'a new world should be new all the way, an imaginative invention from the magma up'.[3] This is what he claims Morris and his twentieth-century successors achieve in their works.

Careful readers of previous chapters will have intuited that I am deeply dubious about the idea that Fantasy can – or should want to – create a world that is 'entirely invented' or 'new all the way'. It is telling that Carter's idea of imaginative invention begins from a magmatic base, thus remaining grounded in the geology of our Earth. In practice, like all forms of culture, fantasies always rely to some extent on existing resources of language and understanding. They work towards qualified originality through iteration and extrapolation, rather than by creating worlds out of the void. In considering

2 Lin Carter, *Imaginary Worlds: The Art of Fantasy* (New York: Ballantine Books, 1973), pp. 7–8, 20.

3 Carter, *Imaginary Worlds*, p. 229.

HELP IS TO HAND IN THE WOOD PERILOUS

THE WELL AT THE WORLD'S END
BOOK I. THE ROAD UNTO LOVE

Chapter I. The Sundering of the Ways

LONG AGO there was a little land, over which ruled a regulus or kinglet, who was called King Peter, although his kingdom was but little. He had four sons whose names were Blaise, Hugh, Gregory, and Ralph. Of these Ralph was the youngest whereas he was but of twenty winters & one; and Blaise was the oldest and had seen thirty winters.

NOW it came to this at the last, that to these young men the kingdom of their father seemed strait; and they longed to see the ways of other men, and to strive for life. For though they were king's sons, they had but little world's wealth; save and except good meat & drink, and enough or too much thereof; house-room of the best; fair friends to be merry with, and maidens to kiss, and these also as good as might be; freedom withal to come and go as they would; the heavens above them, the earth to bear them up, & the meadows and acres, the woods & the fair streams, & the little hills of Upmeads, for that was the name of their country and the kingdom of King Peter.

So having nought but this little they longed for much; and that the more because, king's sons as they were, they had but scant dominion save over their horses & dogs: for the men of that country were stubborn & sturdy vavassors, and might not away with masterful doings, but were like to pay back a blow with a blow, and a foul word with a buffet. So that, all things considered, it was little wonder if King Peter's sons found themselves straitened in their little land: wherein was no great merchant city; nor no mighty castle, or noble abbey of monks: nought but fair little halls of yeomen, with here & there a franklin's court or a shield-knight's manor-house; with many a goodly church, & whiles a house of good canons, who knew not the road to Rome, or how to find the door

Figure 5.1 The opening pages of William Morris's lavish Kelmscott Press edition of his *The Well at the World's End* (1896). The frontispiece woodcut is by Edward Burne-Jones; Morris designed the typeface, capitals and borders.
Metropolitan Museum of Art, 17.3.2641(13).

Carter's claims, it is important to recognise that Morris was self-consciously reworking medieval romances in his 1890s fictions. If he was doing something new, it was partly through seeking to transfigure something old. In addition, Carter might be judged to have undersold world-building in earlier epochs. As well as *The Blazing World*, it is easy to name pre-Morris examples of powerfully imagined realms, including Jonathan Swift's Lilliput and Laputa; Dante's Hell, with its nine disturbing circles; and William Blake's complex cosmology. While it might be argued that philosophical domains such as Plato's *Republic* (c. 375 BCE) and Thomas More's *Utopia* (1516) are limited thought experiments, this would serve both to limit world-building to works on a large scale and to deny the extent to which all world-building consists of thought experiments, albeit often in derived, extended or imprecise forms.

However, while the strong version of Carter's argument can be challenged, he is onto something in recognising that world-building has both grown in prominence and changed in its emphases in twentieth- and twenty-first-century Fantasy. James Gifford perceives a similar pattern – 'a nineteenth-century shift from the model of Romance to something new based on the secondary world' – for which 'it is reasonable to look to William Morris as a starting point'.[4] As Mark J. P. Wolf puts it in his influential account of the history, theory and practice of world-building: 'Subcreation and the building of imaginary worlds [have] been around as long as human imagination, but the opening of new media windows during the twentieth century has made them more vivid and concrete, and vastly increased the number of worlds being produced.'[5] We might add other causes to Wolf's new media windows, including increasing generic literacy among readers, the increasing accessibility of culture and leisure time, the speeding up of communications and knowledge transmission, and the development of forms of collective transmedia world-building that include both vast corporate franchises such as Warcraft or Harry Potter and grassroots collaborations among authors, artists and fans.

[4] James Gifford, *A Modernist Fantasy: Modernism, Anarchism, & the Radical Fantastic* (Victoria, BC: ELS Editions, 2018), pp. 7, 93.

[5] Mark J. P. Wolf, *Building Imaginary Worlds: The Theory and History of Subcreation* (New York and London: Routledge, 2012), p. 287.

While a world can be conjured suggestively in a few words – a process I will discuss later in this chapter – the stereotype of Fantasy world-building veers towards the comprehensive, with many creators and audiences placing premiums on scope and depth. This stereotype is strongly influenced by Tolkien's Middle-earth and by the ideas laid out in his touchstone essay 'On Fairy-stories' (1947), which popularised the terms 'secondary world' and 'sub-creation'. For Tolkien, world-building is a high-stakes proposition that plays a profoundly significant role in determining the quality of a reader's investment in a fantastic story:

> Children are capable, of course, of *literary belief*, when the story-maker's art is good enough to produce it. That state of mind has been called 'willing suspension of disbelief'. But this does not seem to me a good description of what happens. What really happens is that the story-maker proves a successful 'sub-creator'. He makes a Secondary World which your mind can enter. Inside it, what he relates is 'true': it accords with the laws of that world. You therefore believe it, while you are, as it were, inside. The moment disbelief arises, the spell is broken; the magic, or rather art, has failed. You are then out in the Primary World again, looking at the little abortive Secondary World from outside.[6]

Tolkien's sense that world-building only really works if it succeeds in enthralling the reader is a clear antecedent for Carter's view that imagined worlds should seek to be wholly new. While these two positions are not in all

[6] J. R. R. Tolkien, 'On Fairy-stories', in *On Fairy-stories*, ed. by Verlyn Flieger and Douglas A. Anderson (London: HarperCollins, 2008), pp. 25–84 (p. 52).

respects aligned, both see the comprehensiveness and coherence of an imagined world as being of paramount importance for its being able to function powerfully. For Tolkien, world-building should engender a kind of faith in the secondary world's integrity that allows its audiences to be trustingly absorbed.

Tolkien's love of being lost in a good book certainly captures part of the attraction of world-building. However, world-building also exerts other forms of enchantment, leading audiences to think critically and work actively to document, extend and refashion the worlds that entice them. Michael Saler has posited a helpful model we might use to supplement Tolkien's, one that sees reflecting on imagined worlds as an important part of the experience:

> On the one hand, imaginary worlds are autonomous from the real world, avowedly fictional spaces that provide an escape from a disenchanted modernity into self-subsistent realms of wonder. On the other hand, these worlds are inextricable from ordinary life and interpersonal engagements. These usually foreground critical reason even in their most outré imaginings. In their virtual instantiations, they provide safe and playful arenas for their inhabitants to reflect on the status of the real and to discuss prospects for effecting concrete personal and social changes. They challenge their inhabitants to see the real world as being, to some degree, an imaginary construct amenable to revision.[7]

We might synthesise Saler and Tolkien's views by aligning the strong enchantment Tolkien imagines with a first reading (or viewing, or playthrough), while the more

[7] Michael Saler, *As If: Modern Enchantment and the Literary Prehistory of Virtual Reality* (Oxford: Oxford University Press, 2011), p. 7.

cerebral responses Saler discusses respond to a powerful feeling of immersion by seeking to recapture, interpret and develop it. While Tolkien values the internal consistency of a secondary world for its own sake, Saler argues that such consistency challenges our world in ways that can lead readers to ask questions or seek change. What Tolkien characterises as a moment of disillusionment when art ceases or fails might be for Saler the point where the enchantment weakens enough for the reader to bring their own values into play, knowingly collaborating in (or resisting) world-building, rather than submitting to it.

For Tolkien, the difficulty of conjuring secondary belief rises markedly as the qualities of a fantastic world diverge further from those of the world with which the reader is familiar:

> it is found in practice that 'the inner consistency of reality' is more difficult to produce, the more unlike are the images and the rearrangements of primary material to the actual arrangements of the Primary World. [...] Anyone inheriting the fantastic device of human language can say *the green sun*. Many can then imagine or picture it. But that is not enough – though it may already be a more potent thing than many a 'thumbnail sketch' or 'transcript of life' that receives literary praise.
>
> To make a Secondary World inside which the green sun will be credible, commanding Secondary Belief, will probably require labour and thought, and will certainly demand a special skill, a kind of elvish craft.[8]

Tolkien's view accords closely with Kathryn Hume's sense that fantasy and mimesis are most usefully viewed

[8] Tolkien, 'On Fairy-stories', pp. 60–1.

as 'the twin impulses behind the creation of literature [. . .] tightly intertwined and not readily separated'.[9] Rather than trying to create completely unreal worlds, Fantasy usually seeks to make worlds that feel differently real.

While Tolkien's metaphors gesture back to older craft forms, Saler argues that 'On Fairy-stories' advances an interpretation that is 'historically specific, mirroring the new ideas about the imagination, imaginary worlds, and the search for specifically modern forms of enchantment prevalent at the turn of the [twentieth] century'. For Saler, the distinctive quality of Tolkien's world-building is that it relies on 'the union of imagination and reality', thereby recognising Enlightenment divisions between fantasy and mimesis, but arguing for the power of synthesis.[10] For Tolkien, the green sun should not be left as a suggestive image, as it might have been in earlier literature or in more abstract forms. Instead, it should be carefully contextualised to make it believable. Tolkien imagines entering a secondary world as a consuming experience for a reader, but this process of absorption depends on a rigorous balancing act on the author's part, a balance described insightfully in the conclusion to C. S. Lewis's review of *The Fellowship of the Ring* (1954), which contends that the book occupies 'the cool middle point between illusion and disillusionment'.[11]

[9] Kathryn Hume, *Fantasy and Mimesis: Responses to Reality in Western Literature* (New York and London: Methuen, 1984), p. 195.

[10] Saler, *As If*, pp. 160, 159.

[11] The text of C. S. Lewis's review is most easily available as part of 'Tolkien's *The Lord of the Rings*', in *On Stories and Other Essays on Literature* (Orlando: Harcourt, 1982), pp. 83–91 (p. 87). Cited in Saler, p. 160.

In identifying a newly self-conscious blending of romance and realism as the defining characteristic of modern Fantasy, Saler suggests a chronology that lines up quite neatly with Carter's sense that a paradigm shift occurred in the late nineteenth century. As Carter and Saler's evocations of *fin de siècle* and Edwardian precursors indicate, Tolkien was not the first person to think of world-building as a balancing act. In 'The Fantastic Imagination' (1893), George MacDonald places a strikingly similar emphasis on ensuring that the laws of a secondary world are harmonious:

> The natural world has its laws, and no man must interfere with them in the way of presentment any more than in the way of use; but they themselves may suggest laws of other kinds, and man may, if he pleases, invent a little world of his own, with its own laws; for there is that in him which delights in calling up new forms—which is the nearest, perhaps, he can come to creation. When such forms are new embodiments of old truths, we call them products of the Imagination; when they are mere inventions, however lovely, I should call them the work of the Fancy: in either case, Law has been diligently at work.[12]

While he does not use the term 'sub-creation', MacDonald's claim that the invention of worlds is probably the closest humans can come to genuine creation *ex nihilo* is clearly in line with Tolkien's argument. The roots of MacDonald's rhetoric can be traced back further; he borrows from Samuel Taylor Coleridge the sense that Imagination is a higher power than Fancy, and he also

[12] George MacDonald, 'The Fantastic Imagination', in *A Dish of Orts*, enlarged edition (London: Sampson Low Marston & Co., 1893), pp. 313–22 (p. 314).

echoes (although possibly not knowingly) Cavendish's sense that imaginative world-making is an expression of individual autonomy that should be available to all. However, the insistence on the importance of Law is more novel, and as MacDonald proceeds, he further prefigures Tolkien in emphasising fidelity to established rules:

> His world once invented, the highest law that comes next into play is, that there shall be harmony between the laws by which the new world has begun to exist; and in the process of his creation, the inventor must hold by those laws. The moment he forgets one of them, he makes the story, by its own postulates, incredible. To be able to live a moment in an imagined world, we must see the laws of its existence obeyed. Those broken, we fall out of it. [. . .] Suppose the gracious creatures of some childlike region of Fairyland talking either cockney or Gascon! Would not the tale, however lovelily begun, sink at once to the level of the Burlesque—of all forms of literature the least worthy?[13]

The sweeping confidence of MacDonald's argument is compelling, but the unequivocal nature of his assertions also highlights an issue that 'The Fantastic Imagination' and 'On Fairy-stories' share. Both Tolkien and MacDonald implicitly assume that it is possible for a writer to predict with a high degree of accuracy what kinds of reality effects will work for their readers. Creators are, of course, likely to have a certain sense of how their audiences might respond, but this can be taken too far. When MacDonald employs the coercive form of

[13] MacDonald, 'The Fantastic Imagination', pp. 314–15.

'we', he elides the fact that not all readers will be appalled by the idea of cockney fairies. For some readers, a Fairyland that only contains creatures who talk in ways that MacDonald would consider elegant might seem rather limited, betraying a prejudice against the less privileged and a level of closed-mindedness about how effectively Fantasy can conjure. In practice, many successful fantasies have given fairies access to a broader range of voices. Rudyard Kipling's Puck in *Puck of Pook's Hill* (1906) has a keen ear for different registers, and the fairies in Hope Mirrlees's *Lud-in-the-Mist* (1926) are far from being straightforwardly gracious. The wave of urban fantasies written in the 1980s and 1990s often juxtapose fairy laws and fairy lore with contemporary city culture. Such works enjoy playing with the clash between expectations and realities. In Emma Bull's *The War for the Oaks* (1987), when the rock musician Eddi is called a 'stupid little beast' by an exasperated fairy interlocutor, her response is precisely to question her tone: '*Is that any way for a great and noble being to talk*?'[14] The sidhe of White Wolf's role-playing setting *Changeling: The Dreaming* (1995) might well speak as MacDonald imagines that fairies should, but this is precisely because in *Changeling*'s cosmos, the sidhe are dreams of honour and arrogance. Fairies born from dreams of technology, travel, passions or home are likely to speak in other voices.[15] MacDonald is right that we may have sociocultural preconceptions about the

[14] Emma Bull, *War for the Oaks* (London: Penguin, 2016), p. 21.

[15] Mark Rein·Hagen, Sam Chupp, Ian Lemke, Joshua Gabriel Timbrook and others, *Changeling: The Dreaming* (Clarkston, CA: White Wolf Publishing, 1995).

FIGURE 5.2 *The Enchanted Forest* by the Victorian artist John Anster Fitzgerald, who specialised in fairy paintings that feature gracious figures who nevertheless seem capable of deeply sinister actions. Fine Art Photographic Library/Corbis via Getty Images.

behaviour of fairies but wrong to suggest that these are necessarily unchanging verities. One of the most powerful functions of world-building can be to highlight our unexamined prejudices.

Tolkien and MacDonald's argument that the reader should be taken in by an imagined world's internal consistency has become something of a truism of Fantasy world-building. However, this paradigm does not account for all the manners in which fantasy might meaningfully manifest. For a contrary view, we might look to Surrealism, which contends that enchantment inheres in moments of incoherence, disruption and wonder. In his 1924 manifesto, André Breton loftily dismisses the 'realistic attitude' as being made up of 'mediocrity, hate, and dull conceit'. By contrast, he argues that 'the marvelous is always beautiful, anything marvelous is beautiful, in fact only the marvelous is beautiful'.[16] While Tolkien and MacDonald seek to alloy the impossible with logics that render it plausible to audiences, Breton desires fantasies that provoke, rather than lull: 'Fear, the attraction of the unusual, chance, the taste for things extravagant are all devices which we can always call upon without fear of deception.'[17] Tolkien worries that readers might be weirded out of a fairy story, placing them irrevocably on the edges of its affective world, but in Breton's view, the most important element of Fantasy is what Tolkien calls 'arresting strangeness'.[18] Rather than settling the reader, Breton looks for devices that unsettle.[19] Concluding his manifesto, he argues for the importance of works that seek radically different forms of feeling and understanding:

> Surrealism is the "invisible ray" which will one day enable us to win out over our opponents. "You are no longer trembling, carcass." This summer the roses are blue; the wood is of glass. The earth, draped in its verdant cloak, makes as little impression upon me as a ghost. It is living and ceasing to live which are imaginary solutions. Existence is elsewhere.[20]

For Breton, blue roses do not need the careful contextualisation of Tolkien's green sun and would fall towards

[16] André Breton, 'Manifesto of Surrealism' (1924), in *Manifestoes of Surrealism*, translated by Richard Seaver and Helen R. Lane (Ann Arbor: University of Michigan Press, 1972), pp. 1–47 (pp. 6, 14).

[17] Breton, 'Manifesto', p. 16.

[18] Tolkien, 'On Fairy-stories', p. 60.

[19] In this respect, Breton's conception of surrealism has a fair amount in common with Tzvetan Todorov's discussion of the fantastic in *The Fantastic: A Structural Approach to a Literary Genre*, translated by Richard Howard (Ithaca, NY: Cornell University Press, 1975).

[20] Breton, 'Manifesto', p.47.

mediocre realism if one was provided. Tolkien has little time for metatheatrical cleverness, arguing that fairy stories 'should be presented as "true"'.[21] Breton, I think, would agree, except that he would see versions of existence that are elsewhere, elsewhen and elsewhy as being artistically true in themselves. Ties back to the familiar are unnecessary to legitimate them, and are likely, in fact, to prove counterproductive.

At this point, it is worth admitting that committed surrealists are not commonly all that interested in sustained world-building. Their works tend to introversion, looking into minds rather than constructing consistently outward. Surrealism is a form that values images and impressions over straightforward narratives or realist profusion. Nevertheless, Breton's arguments about how surrealism works can help us to see that smoothness is not the only virtue in world-building. The shock of difference or estrangement can play an important role in firing an audience's imagination, cuing them to be attentive to meaningful divergences from the reality they know. We might think of first lines like George Orwell's opening to *Nineteen Eighty-Four* (1949), a novel that begins with familiar scene-setting but which adds a sinister twist that quickly puts us on our guard: 'It was a bright cold day in April, and the clocks were striking thirteen.'[22] The prologue of Robin Hobb's *Ship of Magic* (1998) confronts us instantly with a nonhuman presence, setting us the task of deciphering exactly what it is that we are seeing: 'MAULKIN ABRUPTLY HEAVED HIMSELF out of his wallow

[21] Tolkien, 'On Fairy-stories', p. 35.
[22] George Orwell, *Nineteen Eighty-Four* (London: Penguin, 2000), p. 3.

with a wild thrash that left the atmosphere hanging thick with particles.'[23] When J. M. Barrie begins *Peter and Wendy* (1911) with 'All children, except one, grow up', that neat middle pair of words teases us with a provoking exception to the rules we know.[24] When N. K. Jemisin begins *The Fifth Season* (2015) with a question to which we must submit – 'LET'S START WITH THE END of the world, why don't we?' – we are thrown into a collapse we initially have little frame of reference for judging.[25]

In openings like these, the reader is challenged by something they do not have the tools fully to decipher. In many novels, the task of dispelling shock and frisson is taken up quickly. Tolkien's own exam-paper-scribbled beginning – 'In a hole in the ground there lived a hobbit' – has a strangeness that he swiftly seeks to settle: 'Not a nasty, dirty, wet hole, filled with the ends of worms and an oozy smell, nor yet a dry, bare, sandy hole with nothing in it to sit down on or eat: it was a hobbit-hole, and that means comfort.'[26] Nevertheless, readers love that opening sentence for its standalone merits and the marvellous potential it evokes. When we first read it, unfamiliar with hobbits and their ways, we do not know exactly how to parse it, and the memory of wild possibility continues to excite us. The accretion of a world usually employs laws and logics, but the fun for the audience also lies in confronting differences that leave us at least temporarily

[23] Robin Hobb, *Ship of Magic* (London: Harper, 2015), p. xi.
[24] J. M. Barrie, *Peter and Wendy* (London: Hodder & Stoughton, 1911), p. 1.
[25] N. K. Jemisin, *The Fifth Season* (London: Orbit, 2016), p. 1.
[26] J. R. R. Tolkien, *The Hobbit* (London and Sydney: Unwin Paperbacks, 1981), p. 13.

reeling and uncertain. The magic system in Brandon Sanderson's first Mistborn trilogy (2006–8) has defined parameters – in his own terms, it tends towards being a hard magic system, 'where the [author] explicitly describes the rules'.[27] However, the choice to explain only one of his magic's three forms in the first book, with a further form elucidated in each subsequent volume, keeps the reader on their toes. The appearance of things that seem to break established laws is part of the trilogy's fascination. While it can be satisfying to work out how a problem might be solved with magic, it can also be satisfying to be confronted with a mystery that can only be unpicked with further careful investigation.

Some fantasies make things that are undefinable and inexpressible a core aspect of their world-making (or world-breaking). This is particularly true of weird tales. We might think of H. P. Lovecraft's insistence in 'The Call of Cthulhu' (1928) that the titular Great Old One 'cannot be described—there is no language for such abysms of shrieking and immemorial lunacy, such eldritch contradictions of all matter, force, and cosmic order'. Critics sometimes smile at Lovecraft's tendency to describe things he has deemed indescribable, and he does give us a few further specifics, calling Cthulhu 'the green, sticky spawn of the stars' and evoking the destruction caused by his 'flabby claws'.[28] Nevertheless, the sustained uncertainty

[27] Brandon Sanderson, 'Sanderson's First Law', *brandonsanderson.com*, 20 February 2007, www.brandonsanderson.com/sandersons-first-law/.

[28] H. P. Lovecraft, 'The Call of Cthulhu', in *The Call of Cthulhu and Other Weird Stories*, ed. by S. T. Joshi (London: Penguin, 2002), pp. 139–69 (p. 167).

at the heart of his description – what Graham Harman calls a 'de-literalizing gesture' – remains crucial to the story's affect.[29] This refusal to provide concrete detail is an essential element of fantasies that seek to conjure wonder through obscurity, gesturing to the shadowy outlines of forms, rather than filling out logical architectures.

In practice, of course, an equilibrium is struck. While Lovecraft's approach has certain things in common with surrealism's liberating mental play – Lovecraft believed that 'all that a wonder story can ever be is *a vivid picture of a certain type of human mood*' – he saw his stories as juxtaposing cosmic horrors with scrupulous naturalism:

> In writing a weird story I always try very carefully to achieve the right mood and atmosphere, and place the emphasis where it belongs. One cannot, except in immature pulp charlatan-fiction, present an account of impossible, improbable, or inconceivable phenomena as a commonplace narrative of objective acts and conventional emotions. Inconceivable events and conditions have a special handicap to overcome, and this can be accomplished only through the maintenance of a careful realism in every phase of the story *except* that touching on the one given marvel. This marvel must be treated very impressively and deliberately – with a careful emotional "build-up" – else it will seem flat and unconvincing. Being the principal thing in the story, its mere existence should overshadow the characters and events. But the characters and events must be consistent and natural except where they touch the single marvel.[30]

[29] Graham Harman, *Weird Realism: Lovecraft and Philosophy* (Winchester: Zero Books, 2012), p. 24.

[30] H. P. Lovecraft, 'Notes on Writing Weird Fiction', in *Miscellaneous Writings*, ed. by S. T. Joshi (Sauk City, WI: Arkham House, 1995), pp. 113–16 (pp. 115–16).

Lovecraft thus shares with Tolkien a sense that for wondrous things to function credibly, a careful balance must be struck between the familiar and unfamiliar. The nature of this balance differs across Lovecraft's and Tolkien's works; Lovecraft's horrors tend to be difficult or impossible to reconcile with the otherwise relatively quotidian worlds in which his protagonists dwell, while Tolkien can write credible magic into his books because he creates an environment within which wizardry is something we are prepared to accept. However, in both cases world-building employs a mixture of familiar and less familiar registers, with the former helping to bridge audiences into the latter.

In many cases, evocations of the real and marvellous happen in entangled forms. One of Lovecraft's favourite mechanisms for doing this is presenting testimony of the supernatural as a discovered document employing recognisable conventions. At the climax of his late story 'The Haunter of the Dark' (1936), we are presented with the 'final frenzied jottings' of Robert Blake, 'blindly scrawled entries in the diary on the desk':

> "Azathoth have mercy!—the lightning no longer flashes—horrible—I can see everything with a monstrous sense that is not sight—light is dark and dark is light . . . those people on the hill . . . guard . . . candles and charms . . . their priests. . . .
>
> "Sense of distance gone—far is near and near is far. No light—no glass—see that steeple—that tower—window—can hear—Roderick Usher—am mad or going mad—the thing is stirring and fumbling in the tower—I am it and it is I—I want to get out . . . must get out and unify the forces. . . . It knows where I am. . . .
>
> "I am Robert Blake, but I see the tower in the dark. There is a monstrous odour . . . senses transfigured . . . boarding at that tower window cracking and giving way. . . . Iä . . . ngai . . . ygg. . . .

"I see it—coming here—hell-wind—titan blur—black wings —Yog-Sothoth save me—the three-lobed burning eye. . . ."[31]

Lovecraft employs a certain amount of artistic licence in this passage – the text sounds at times more like a voice speaking than a terrified pen scratching – but his careful control of sentence length and the dashes and ellipses that fragment the prose help the reader to believe that this could be a plausible transcription. Textual illusion and elision serve two purposes at the same time, creating a realistic sense of documented distress while also keeping the Haunter's form and motivations shrouded, displaying it (or failing to display it) through Blake's subjective experience, rather than through a more objective narrative lens.

Examples like this remind us that what is left out in world-building can be just as important to as what gets put in. A novel that inserted a multi-page justification every time it mentioned something like a green sun would quickly grow tedious. Audiences enjoy the illusion of wholeness, but are prepared to collaborate in that illusion, working to fill in the gaps. This can, in fact, be a large part of the enjoyment, as shown in Lovecraft's case by the development of the Cthulhu Mythos as a shared universe. In the larger Mythos, crossings-over, reworkings and new writings build on Lovecraft's stories, changing to some extent the nature of the worlds they project. Lovecraftian expansions occurred first through an informal sharing of characters and devices among contemporaries including

[31] H. P. Lovecraft, 'The Haunter of the Dark', in *The Call of Cthulhu and Other Weird Stories*, ed. by S. T. Joshi (London: Penguin, 2002), pp. 336–60 (pp. 359, 358, 359–60).

Robert E. Howard, Clark Ashton Smith and Robert Bloch, and then through codification and extension of Lovecraftian lore in the works of successors like August Derleth and designs such as Sandy Petersen's *Call of Cthulhu* roleplaying game (1981–). In these works, some of Lovecraft's bleakness, delirium and obscurity is replaced by more definite qualities. Derleth arranged many of Lovecraft's inscrutable beings into more recognisable pantheons, and while the early editions of *Call of Cthulhu* are notoriously tough on player characters, they nevertheless assign numerical statistics and specified abilities to creatures that Lovecraft's original stories keep in shadow. While his monstrosities have proliferated across media, Lovecraft's literary techniques have not proved to be infinitely adaptable. Video games, with their focus on player agency, have sometimes struggled to control Lovecraftian enormity and despair, although some, like *Bloodborne* (2015), have drawn effectively on his influence.[32] In building out from Lovecraft's worlds, many of his beings have become familiar, carrying audiences down the path towards the adorable flabby claws of plushie Cthulhu.

This is by no means a solely negative development. There are gains in transformations as well as losses. The Old Gods C'Thun and Yogg-Saron in *World of Warcraft* (2004–) can be defeated by raiding groups of plucky heroes in ways that are anathema to Lovecraft's conception of cosmic horror, but this does not mean that the

[32] For a worthwhile discussion, see NeverKnowsBest, 'An in-depth look at Lovecraftian Video Games', *YouTube.com*, 17 November 2019, https://youtu.be/8CaovqiSPiw.

whisperings and tentacles their designers have drawn from Lovecraft's stories carry no affective charge. The weird tradition is differently alive in games, but vivid transmutation seems wholly in keeping with the aesthetic. Reworkings of Lovecraft have also proactively confronted the reactionary fears that compromise some of his stories by encoding prejudices into horrors. The dedication to Victor LaValle's novella *The Ballad of Black Tom* (2016) reads '*For H.P. Lovecraft, with all my conflicted feelings*'.[33] In his book, LaValle reworks Lovecraft's 'The Horror at Red Hook' (1927), maintaining elements of the plot and of Lovecraft's prose and lore, but centring a black protagonist to expose the naked racism of the original story as its most genuinely disturbing aspect. Similarly, in N. K. Jemisin's *The City We Became* (2020), sinister Lovecraftian intrusions are aligned with hegemonic oppression and gentrification, moving the focus from Lovecraft's fear of the city to New York residents' righteous anger about the subversion of its liberties and diversity. In building out from (and in some cases over) Lovecraft's originals, later creators revivify and redirect the powerful sense of alienation that his aesthetic centres around, allowing elements of the Mythos to embrace new forms and ask new questions.

Lovecraft's predilection for creeping horrors at the edges of our world reminds us that the concept of world-building can be meaningfully employed to discuss many different forms of Fantasy (as well as realist works and works in other genres). In Farah Mendlesohn's terms, world-building is most obviously associated with

[33] Victor LaValle, *The Ballad of Black Tom* (New York: Tor, 2016), [p. 5].

immersive fantasies, which posit Morris-like secondary worlds with no explicit connection to our own. Like Tolkien and MacDonald, Mendlesohn believes that establishing rules and laws is vital for effective immersive storytelling:

> Coherency is crucial to creating the ironic mimesis of the immersive fantasy. It is possible to create a world in which anything can and does happen. But if one does this, then it is impossible to make the characters questioning and *extrapolating* beings. In a fully immersive fantasy, the actors must be able to engage with their world; they must be able to scrape its surface and discover something deeper than a stage set.[34]

Mendlesohn's position on immersive Fantasy has clear resonances with Tolkien's arguments about 'the inner consistency of reality', although she helpfully nuances his view by highlighting the importance of characters for framing this consistency for audiences. Among Mendlesohn's forms, immersive Fantasy is the one that pushes furthest away from the world we know, although in practice there is always a complex interplay between an audience's prior knowledge and the expectations a secondary world meets or subverts.

The other three types of Fantasy Mendlesohn discusses – portal-quests, intrusion fantasies and liminal fantasies – tend to acknowledge the existence of the primary world, but each has its own particular mechanisms for building out into more fantastic realms. In a portal quest, world-building is conducted contrastively as we follow a

[34] Farah Mendlesohn, *Rhetorics of Fantasy* (Middletown, CT: Wesleyan University Press, 2008), p. 63.

character or characters into a strange world, learning the rules alongside them:

> Characteristically, the quest fantasy protagonist goes from a mundane life in which the fantastic, if she is aware of it, is very distant and unknown [...] to direct contact with the fantastic through which she transitions, exploring the world until she or those around her are knowledgeable enough to negotiate with the world via the personal manipulation of the fantastic realm.[35]

This technique bridges the audience into the world more explicitly than an immersive fantasy, but the eventual result can be no less immersive, as the enduring popularity of worlds such as Oz and Narnia attests. As Mendlesohn argues, this is a technique Tolkien himself employs in *The Lord of the Rings*, as we move from the Shire into a deeper, wilder and more alien world along with the hobbits.[36]

Intrusion Fantasy follows a reversed dynamic; rather than a character journeying into an unfamiliar world, characters or parts of an unfamiliar world journey into our own. Intrusion is probably the least Tolkienian dynamic in Mendlesohn's breakdown, as it involves directly destabilising the boundaries of the world we know. However, as we have seen with Lovecraft, this still operates as a kind of world-building, suggesting that our comfortable understandings of how things work are incomplete and that other forms and patternings might impose themselves upon us.

35 Mendlesohn, *Rhetorics of Fantasy*, p. 2.
36 Mendlesohn, *Rhetorics of Fantasy*, pp. 30–8.

Mendlesohn's fourth category, liminal Fantasy, also seems initially to be less amenable to Tolkien's model. Mendlesohn describes liminal fantasies as being dependent on 'recognition of the significance of the doubled world, both mundane and simultaneously a fantasy'.[37] While this could be seen as precluding the development of full-blown secondary belief, we could also see such doubleness as avoiding the moment of disaffection Tolkien fears. If the mundane and the fantastic can be held in perfect balance, this might avoid a collapse back into the primary world, opening the reader's mind to parallel valid interpretations. By superimposing a fantastic world over our own, liminal fantasies directly engage with the fact that our construction of the world is in considerable part a matter of perspective. We could build it other ways.

Mendlesohn's categories thus help to show how widely applicable the world-building metaphor can potentially be. While immersive fantasies posit notionally independent worlds, portal-quest fantasies trace pathways to and through other worlds, intrusion fantasies bleed other worlds into our own, and liminal fantasies hold two worlds in equipoise. The modes of connection differ, but conceptualising a conceivable alternative to or expansion of our familiar world remains a constant.

However, while the world-building metaphor is a powerful one, it is not universally liked or accepted, and those who dislike it have valid reasons for doing so. For many authors, the comprehensiveness and internal consistency associated with world-building are less important

[37] Mendlesohn, *Rhetorics of Fantasy*, p. 195.

than developing characters and narratives. Michael Moorcock – a man often keen to distance himself from Tolkien – writes that the ideals he associates with worldbuilding do not align with his own principal goals in writing fiction:

> I think the notion of worldbuilding is a failure of literary sophistication. Take the Romantic writers of the 19th century, particularly the Brontës. The Brontës loved the idea of depicting weather to suit moods – it's called the pathetic fallacy, where you give inanimate things animate qualities. The point of that style of writing is that it used landscape and weather, all exteriors, to symbolize internal conflict within the individual or within a small group of individuals. I only invent what's necessary to explain the mood of a character. I haven't thought about an imaginary world's social security system; I don't know the gross national product of Melniboné. If worldbuilding is a sophisticated working-out of how a world interacts in and of itself, I don't really have any of that. People interact in my worlds. Weather systems interact. The weather system is always supposed to show what's going on inside the character. That's why I don't see myself as a worldbuilder. The world unfolds in front of the character as the story develops. If the story doesn't need it, it's not there.[38]

For Moorcock, the mechanics of imagined worlds are means, rather than ends, useful only insofar as they facilitate characterisation and narrative growth. Moorcock takes an extreme position, but his sensibilities and priorities are shared by many. Lecturing to aspiring authors,

[38] John Picacio, 'Michael Moorcock: Multiverses' (interview), *Locus*, 21 December 2014, https://locusmag.com/2014/12/michael-moorcock-multiverses/.

Brandon Sanderson – a writer often praised for his ability to tease out the logics of fantastical worlds – plays down the importance of world-building, contending that 'your time is best spent learning how to make engaging and interesting characters, followed by learning how to tell a really good plot, with, in third place, your ability to have a really great setting'. While he argues that a compelling imaginary cosmos can be an asset, he warns against becoming 'so enthralled with building the world of your story that you never finish world-building and never start your story'.[39] Many other writers concur that world-building is best accomplished through careful use of sleights of hand, rather than comprehensive directory-making. In a *Guardian* article surveying novelists on their techniques, Ann Leckie highlights the importance of leaving 'some things unexplained or just referred to, as though the world is much bigger than just this one story and won't all fit in the pages'. M. John Harrison writes that 'you can increase the illusion of depth by leaving plenty of space for the accidental [. . .] But it's important to go back afterwards and wave your magic fauxthenticity wand over the scene of the accident.'[40]

These writers see world-building as a process that involves a certain amount of trickery. They implicitly place greater faith in the reader than Tolkien does, and

39 Brandon Sanderson, 'Lecture #6: Worldbuilding Part Two — Brandon Sanderson on Writing Science Fiction and Fantasy', *YouTube.com*, https://youtu.be/V2KpWOLTXx8, 6:58–7:12, 7:30–7:38.

40 Alastair Reynolds, Nnedi Okorafor, Ann Leckie, Becky Chambers, Kim Stanley Robinson and M. John Harrison, '"If the aliens lay eggs, how does that affect architecture?": Sci-Fi Writers on How They Build Their Worlds', *The Guardian*, 5 January 2021, https://bit.ly/3GWpauE.

greater trust in the kinds of gesture that Breton values, through which 'We really live by our fantasies when we *give free reign to them*.'[41] Wolf describes secondary worlds as 'the *gesamtkunstwerk* that unite all arts', employing a German term usually translated as designating an all-embracing or comprehensive artwork.[42] However, as these writers' testimonies show, the desire to produce a closed totality is not necessarily what drives creators to produce works that feel like worlds. As Leckie notes, constructive ambiguity can be a crucial part of Fantasy world-building. Stories hinted at but not told vivify fantasies in the audience's mind, providing room for imaginative interpolations. It is no coincidence that in many of the Fantasy worlds with the most active fan-fiction communities, much is sketched (backstories, histories) or left unsaid (stereotypically providing scope for interpretation as romantic tension, although fan writers do a great variety of different work in such spaces). In the communities around worlds like these, numerous pens eagerly fill out the possibilities. If certain fantasies might be considered total art, then it is in a more open sense than the term often implies. Their totalities comprise a spectrum of possibilities, rather than a single holistic vision.

Moorcock is in some ways a rather ironic figure to rail against world-building, as his own work conjures intersecting creations on a grand scale. The *Encyclopedia of Fantasy* (1997) credits Moorcock with being one of the earliest users of the term 'multiverse', a conceit he employs to create what John Clute describes as 'an

41 Breton, 'Manifesto', p. 18.
42 Wolf, *Building Imaginary Worlds*, p. 152.

interweaving performance of worlds' that is 'profoundly and multifariously theatrical'.[43] While Moorcock argues that he omits elements unnecessary for his story, his writing builds through its use of parallels, revisions, reconceptualisations, crossovers, paratexts and different forms (story, novel, comic, playscript), forming something Alan Moore calls an 'intertextual and organic whole', albeit one that is shifting and heterogenous.[44] On several occasions, large parts of Moorcock's oeuvre have been assembled into multi-volume retrospective series under the banner *The Tale of the Eternal Champion*. In line with his calling into doubt stricter constructivist views of world-building, Moorcock's multiverse plays out flickering conflicts between Law and Chaos, rather than straightforward battles between good and evil. His oft-hapless central figures are tasked with maintaining balance, rather than achieving ringing victories. His writing tends to cohere around the existential dilemmas of his characters, who he depicts as being trapped in bondage to more powerful forces – able, with effort, to take effective action, but often with unforeseen consequences.

Clute has called Moorcock 'the 20th century's central fantasist about fantasy', a trait apparent in his staging stories in manners that blend metatextual profusion with pulp pragmatism.[45] Take, for example, the prologue to

43 John Clute, 'Moorcock, Michael', in *The Encyclopedia of Fantasy*, ed. by John Clute and John Grant (London: Orbit, 1997), pp. 656–60. Available online in a version prepared by David Langford: https://sf-encyclopedia.com/fe/moorcock_michael.

44 Alan Moore, foreword to Michael Moorcock, *Elric of Melniboné and Other Stories* (London: Gollancz, 2013), pp. 1–7 (p. 7).

45 Clute, 'Moorcock, Michael', p. 660.

Elric of Melniboné (1972), credited in-universe as being part of a text called *The Chronicle of the Black Sword*:

> *This is the tale of Elric before he was called Womanslayer, before the final collapse of Melniboné. This is the tale of his rivalry with his cousin Yyrkoon and his love for his cousin Cymoril, before that rivalry and that love brought Imrryr, the Dreaming City, crashing in flames, raped by the reavers from the Young Kingdoms. This is the tale of the two black swords, Stormbringer and Mournblade, and how they were discovered and what part they played in the destiny of Elric and Melniboné—a destiny which was to shape a larger destiny: that of the world itself. This is the tale of when Elric was a king, the commander of dragons, fleets and all the folk of that half-human race which had ruled the world for ten thousand years.*
>
> *This is a tale of tragedy, this tale of Melniboné, the Dragon Isle. This is a tale of monstrous emotions and high ambitions. This is a tale of sorceries and treacheries and worthy ideals, of agonies and fearful pleasures, of bitter love and sweet hatred. This is the tale of Elric of Melniboné. Much of it Elric himself was to remember only in his nightmares.*[46]

This passage sets the scene in ways that function both thematically – foreshadowing Elric's bonds and doom – and as an *aide-mémoire*. *Elric of Melniboné* was written at quite a late stage in Moorcock's development of the character, so it is likely that this passage was originally encountered by people for whom evoking the fate of Imrryr would serve as a reminder of something they had already read. However, for later readers working through the series in retrospective volumes, there is a good chance this passage will be one of the first they encounter. I dwell

[46] Michael Moorcock, *Elric of Melniboné*, in *Elric of Melniboné and Other Stories* (London: Gollancz, 2013), pp. 175–342 (p. 179).

on this to make the point that the passage works for both audiences in a way that prefigures the handling of complex comics continuities. The Eternal Champion stories, united by crossovers and thematic concerns but various in their settings and the inflections of their protagonists, are an early forebear of the turn superhero comics would take in the 1980s as parallel universes and reboot plotlines proliferated. Rather than building a single consistent world that tells a logical story one way, multiversal forms create a range of possible worlds. Metatextual play in which different laws are tried out might be seen as attenuating the sense of truth that Tolkien considers to be so crucial, but in practice, as Moorcock realises, audiences – and particularly genre-savvy Fantasy audiences – are quite capable of investing in works that occasionally tip them knowing winks. What Angela Carter called the 'teeming, teeming quality of his imagination' inclines Moorcock to enchant his readers not through creating a single intensely designed world, but through a surreal array of instantiations.[47] This makes him a key avatar of the intertextual approaches that Tolkien sought to play down but which power much older fantastic fiction and drive many of the most reflexive and interesting modern fantasies, from the nested worlds of Tad Williams's Otherland (1996–2001) to the flourishings of *isekai* and the metafantasy of Kieron Gillen, Stephanie Hans and Clayton Cowles' comic *Die* (2018–21).

[47] David Pringle, 'Exclusive New Interview with Angela Carter by David Pringle' (conducted 10 August 1979), *Angela Carter Online*, 7 May 2017, https://bit.ly/3mKVREy.

In rejecting unmitigated expansiveness, Moorcock acknowledges something important about how cultural forms reflect upon the world. By implying a depth that is always to some extent an implicit potential, the world-building metaphor can be deceptive regarding comprehensiveness. It can also be deceptive regarding the nature and directionality of fantastic constructions. Writing on *The Left Hand of Darkness* (1969) and *The Dispossessed* (1974), Fredric Jameson argues that Ursula K. Le Guin's work operates

> based on a principle of systematic exclusion, a kind of surgical excision of empirical reality, something like a process of ontological attenuation in which the sheer teeming multiplicity of what exists, of what we call reality, is deliberately thinned and weeded out through an operation of radical abstraction and simplification which we will henceforth term *world-reduction*.[48]

Here, Jameson highlights an important alternative way of thinking about how fantasies create their worlds. Rather than seeing the process as an additive one, in which the writer first says, 'Let there be light', and then builds up layers of complexity, Jameson configures the world-building process as a subtractive one that begins implicitly with our reality and strips away aspects of culture, society and environment to create an alternative world where particular elements are brought into sharp focus. This process accentuates the importance of chosen sets of ideas and relations while allowing others to be left implicit or set aside. For Jameson, this technique has powerful political potential, allowing a writer to 'think Western history

[48] Fredric Jameson, 'World Reduction in Le Guin: The Emergence of Utopian Narrative', *Science Fiction Studies*, 2.3 (1975), 221–30 (p. 223).

without capitalism' by practising a form of 'utopian exclusion'.[49] It should be added that this potential might also be negative or dystopian: by making a world simpler than our own, inequalities and cruelties can be brushed under the carpet, allowing a glittering superstructure to be suspended without imagining the base, leaving any form of ethical projection that world seeks to achieve on dubious foundations.

In a profound sense, all cultural production is really world reduction: rendering the complexities of reality down into comprehensible forms, narratives and juxtapositions. Even the most comprehensive multiform transmedia franchise only contains a tiny fraction of reality's intricacies. World-building is always in practice a process of simplification. However, this is not a bad thing. We already have the real world. When we build unreal worlds, we are looking for somewhere different, whether that be a place of entertainment, escape, reflection, critique, achievement or desire. Our individual control over the real world is very limited. In an imagined world, we can make a difference, or see how a difference could be made.

* * *

Having highlighted some of the complexities of the world-building metaphor and considered how Fantasy creators and critics have approached it, it seems worthwhile to focus on some more specific examples, exploring how different kinds of worlds have been conjured in fantastical works across different media. Looping back to Margaret

[49] Jameson, 'World Reduction', p. 228.

Cavendish's experiments with the Blazing World provides a good starting point. The novelty of world-building in Cavendish's age means that she tends to ruminate interestingly on what she is doing, and her choices leave visible joins that later writers like Tolkien would try and paper over. Cavendish's saying what in later world-building would be the quiet parts out loud both reflects her connections with the utopian tradition and highlights the political and personal stakes of fashioning another world.

The Blazing World opens with its unnamed female protagonist being subjected to a rather perfunctory abduction. The abductors are swiftly killed off and Cavendish gets her central character transported to the Blazing World and made its empress in short order. The protagonist's obtaining this role is accomplished in part by story logics and in part by a form of world reduction in terms of political possibilities:

> [S]he asked, why they preferred the monarchical form of government before any other? They answered, that as it was natural for one body to have but one head, so it was also natural for a politic body to have but one governor; and that a commonwealth, which had many governors was like a monster with many heads: besides, said they, a monarchy is a divine form of government, and agrees most with our religion: for as there is but one God, whom we all unanimously worship and adore with one faith; so we are resolved to have but one Emperor, to whom we all submit with one obedience.[50]

Cavendish was not a disinterested observer on the question of monarchical government. Her husband, William

[50] Cavendish, *The Blazing World*, p. 134. Note that the spelling and formatting in this edition are modernised.

Cavendish, the Duke of Newcastle, had fought for Charles I in the English Civil War, and she had remained in exile with him during the period of the Commonwealth, returning permanently to England only after the Restoration. In making the Blazing World, the Duchess of Newcastle might thus be seen as translating vociferous support for the divine right of kings into her world-building, setting up a system of rulership that had recently been challenged in England as a truth that all the Empress's subjects happily accept.

However, Cavendish is far from alone in focusing her world-building around a powerful monarch. Many modern fantasies centre on a royal family depicted as being both benevolent and righteous, espousing progressive or egalitarian values without necessarily considering the internal contradictions of their positions. There are pragmatic story reasons for using royals. Showing off a world is often more easily accomplished through the lens of someone who either has or obtains power within it, and epic stories often rely on the manipulations of the influential or the marshalling of great forces. However, while Cavendish had clear motivations for espousing the special status of royalty, this is less clearly the case for modern Fantasy creators who employ or literalise the trope that the land and the king are one. As Stefan Ekman points out, many writers are ostensibly inclined to question this trope – asking, with Terry Pratchett's Nanny Ogg, 'One what?', and coming up with a wide range of different answers.[51] Nevertheless, a deep connection between the land and its king is presented

51 Terry Pratchett, *Wyrd Sisters* (London: Corgi, 1989), p. 127. Stefan Ekman examines ruler–realm linkages in detail in chapter 5 of *Here Be*

as existing literally in *Wyrd Sisters* (1988), as Pratchett follows other authors who find that linking rulers tightly to their peoples and realms establishes harmonies or disharmonies that orient audiences swiftly regarding a story's larger stakes. Narrative convenience in world-building can thus potentially inscribe forms of authority (or authoritarianism) that many audience members would be deeply uncomfortable with in a real-world context. This might be a cost worth paying if the focus of world reduction is directed elsewhere or if interrogating power structures forms part of a work's purpose, but it means that many secondary worlds tend to be better at thinking through the psychologies of elites (or artists) than considering the complexities of communities or democracy.

While Cavendish promotes absolute rule, she grants her Empress a diverse panoply of subjects. These include standard humans, but also an extensive range of hybrids and mythological creatures, including bear-men, ape-men, 'syrens', worm-men, fox-men, lice-men, jackdaw-men, satyrs and giants. Cavendish assigns each group particular characteristics and professions. The fox-men are politicians; the bear-men are scientists (experimental philosophers, in Cavendish's parlance) who employ telescopes and microscopes; the lice-men are mathematicians; the jackdaw-men, orators; and the giants, architects.[52] The reader will be able to import existing cultural logics to interpret many of these roles: foxes are presumably suited to be politicians as they are typically thought of as

Dragons: Exploring Fantasy Maps and Settings (Middletown, CT: Wesleyan University Press, 2013), pp. 177–215.

[52] Cavendish, *The Blazing World*, pp. 133–4.

being sly; jackdaws have a distinctive cry; and the large size of giants would presumably be an advantage for certain kinds of surveying. Some of Cavendish's connections are less transparent, perhaps bespeaking a concern about straightforward stereotyping, although this does not prevent her from imagining a society with strict caste roles in the first place. Like employing strong central authorities to represent nations or peoples, imposing broad characterisations by species, race, culture or ethnicity is a tempting form of shorthand in world-building. It is also one that creators often nuance to a greater or lesser extent after beginning with broader brushstrokes – Cavendish does this a little when the Empress speaks with groups of different experts. However, such characterisations risk shading into forms of prejudicial essentialism that can both limit a work's verisimilitude and echo real-world bigotries.

Many modern fantasies explore their worlds by having the characters travel through them. Cavendish employs a different approach, displaying the world through how its inhabitants represent and understand it. A large part of the narrative consists of the Empress asking her subjects questions, allowing Cavendish to show off her natural-philosophical knowledge in the resulting answers. Many of these explanations align with proto-scientific understandings of life on Earth. However, Cavendish also mixes in phenomena specific to the Blazing World. The long lifespans of its rulers are attributed to a kind of plant gum that triggers a visceral regeneration process. This begins with 'vomits of phlegm', followed by vomiting that brings forth 'humours of several colours'. Further humours are expelled through other orifices, albeit 'without any pain or trouble to the patient'. After this purging, the gum 'will make the body break out into a thick scab, and cause both hair, teeth, and nails to come off; which scab being arrived to its full maturity, opens first along the back, and comes off all in a piece like armour'. Following this four-month process, five additional months wrapped in 'cere-cloth' while consuming only 'eagle's-eggs, and hind's-milk' will allow the patient to restore their body to that of a twenty-year old 'both in shape, and strength'.[53] Discussing this gum, Cavendish takes the opportunity implicitly to congratulate herself on her plausible world design:

> [The Empress] had never heard of a medicine that could renew old age, and render it beautiful, vigorous and strong: nor would she have so easily believed it, had it been a medicine prepared by art; for she knew that art, being nature's changeling, was not able to produce such a powerful effect; but being that the gum did grow naturally, she did not so much scruple at it; for she knew that nature's works are so various and wonderful, that no particular creature is able to trace her ways.[54]

While Cavendish attributes the gum's existence to nature's bounty, it is telling how neatly the natural phenomena of the Blazing World align with its political order, allowing monarchs to extend their divine right to rule across centuries. Cavendish's world-building might thus be seen as operating via an extension of the pathetic fallacy Moorcock discusses, with inanimate objects and physical processes validating the statuses of characters. Alternatively, this might be read as a realistic depiction

[53] Cavendish, *The Blazing World*, pp. 155–6.
[54] Cavendish, *The Blazing World*, pp. 156–7.

of the operations of privilege, where the rich can secure advantages unavailable to the populace at large.

Much of Cavendish's examination focuses on the Blazing World's inhabitants, philosophies and social systems, but it is not straightforwardly a separate secondary world. Its future Empress travels into it via the North Pole, and its 'immaterial spirits' know enough of British culture to discourse on John Dee and Edward Kelley's supernatural experiments during the reign of Elizabeth I and their negative depiction in Ben Jonson's play *The Alchemist* (first performed in 1610).[55] However, the most blatant form of connectivity is an authorial self-insert. When the Empress requires a reliable scribe, the spirits recommend Margaret Cavendish, Duchess of Newcastle. The Empress subsequently secures the willing services of Cavendish's soul. The two women – perhaps unsurprisingly – find each other instantly agreeable. In Cavendish's words, 'their meeting did produce such an intimate friendship between them, that they became platonic lovers, although they were both females'.[56] The Duchess later brings the Empress in spirit form to her home and the two women collaborate closely for the rest of the narrative, imaginatively shaping both the Blazing World and our own.

Uncharitable readers might see Cavendish's appearance in the Blazing World as symptomatic of either personal arrogance or deep insecurity. More charitable readers might point out that Cavendish had good reasons to be proud of her talents, and considerable justification for

[55] Cavendish, *The Blazing World*, p. 166.
[56] Cavendish, *The Blazing World*, p. 183.

feeling socially and culturally side-lined. Both would be responding to the ways in which Cavendish frames her world as a personal refuge, providing comfort and control. In her epilogue, Cavendish writes that her world-building choices reflect the fact that she values 'peace before war, wit before policy, honesty before beauty'.[57] Cavendish is far from alone in using an imagined world to express herself and her preferences. Rosemary Jackson has written that 'The fantastic traces the unsaid and unseen of culture: that which has been silenced, covered over and made "absent".'[58] Jackson's view that fantasy is 'a literature of desire' might be applied especially strongly in the context of world-building, in which creators diverge from reality to make a hospitable (or inhospitable) world in which they can imaginatively experiment.

The Blazing World is one of a vast number of realms created as exercises in candid imagination. Glancing at works that initially had private or very limited circulations suggests that using personal modes of world-building to develop literary skills, to build relationships, as a form of shared language, or as a mode of solace is a common activity. The Brontë siblings collaboratively created the worlds of Glass Town, Angria and Gondal; Hartley Coleridge excitedly explained his river-born continent Ejuxria to his brother Derwent; and C. S. Lewis and his brother Warren merged separate imagined worlds into the shared world of Boxen. While these were mostly youthful endeavours, other creators wove worlds throughout their

57 Cavendish, *The Blazing World*, p. 224.

58 Rosemary Jackson, *Fantasy: The Literature of Subversion* (New York and London: Methuen, 1981), p. 2.

FIGURE 5.3 Plate 78 from William Blake's *Jerusalem* (1804–20), which entangles idiosyncratic fantastic imaginaries in poetry and art. Yale Center for British Art, Paul Mellon Collection, B1992.8.1(78).

adult lives without necessarily expecting wide audiences. William Blake's cosmology in his prophetic books was only available to a tiny number of people until long after his death (Figure 5.3). The writer and artist Henry Darger spent a large part of his life creating a fifteen-volume work entitled *In the Realms of the Unreal* with no prospect of publication. Austin Tappan Wright spent a similarly long time creating his quasi-utopian Islandia, a culture characterised by permissive tolerance and possessing four distinct words for kinds of love. These works have now achieved considerable reputations, but can stand as tokens for all the private paracosms, personal portfolios, custom-built roleplaying campaign worlds and drafted maps that the fantastic imaginations of myriad individuals have produced. For every Forgotten Realms (which began as Ed Greenwood's childhood dream space before developing over many years into a hugely popular *Dungeons & Dragons* campaign setting), there must be hundreds of worlds yellowing in old binders and immured in forgotten file structures that once constituted formative experiences in extrapolation and self-expression for their creators.

Thus, while Fantasy worlds can attempt to project a kind of consensus designed to be meaningful to as many people as possible, they can also be idiosyncratic, private and personal. In *The Blazing World*, the immaterial spirits the Empress and Cavendish converse with emphasise the power of world-building for conjuring delight and a sense of individual autonomy:

> every human creature can create an immaterial world fully inhabited by immaterial creatures, and populous of immaterial subjects, such as we are, and all this within the compass of the head or scull; nay, not only so, but he may create a world of what fashion and government he will, and give the creatures thereof such motions, figures, forms, colours, perceptions, etc. as he pleases, and make whirlpools, lights, pressures and reactions, etc. as he thinks best; nay, he may make a world full of

veins, muscles, and nerves, and all these to move by one jolt or stroke: also he may alter that world as often as he pleases, or change it from a natural world, to an artificial; he may make a world of ideas, a world of atoms, a world of lights, or whatsoever his fancy leads him to. And since it is in your power to create such a world, what need you to venture life, reputation and tranquility, to conquer a gross material world?[59]

For Cavendish, an imagined world possesses many advantages over a real one. Its territories can be covered at the speed of thought and are not subject to contestation by others. It can be modified or cast aside without moral scruple. It can also give a sense of mastery or control that would be monstrous to achieve in the real world. For Cavendish, world-building is a source of delight and solace, a means of retreating and reflecting, a way to shape a place that can be structured and comprehended in ways the real world cannot. Cavendish presents these as creatorly pleasures, but they can be pleasures for audiences too, and exploring how other minds play out the possibilities of world-making comprises a large part of Fantasy's fascination.

As previously implied, while Cavendish extols the joy of mental travel, *The Blazing World* is relatively sparing is in its descriptions of geography and environments, and the Empress's will is put into effect with almost comical ease. By contrast, modern fantasies are usually very interested in the frictions of space, time and society. Strong environmental design that can situate and challenge characters is generally seen as a virtue. Consequently, fantasies often seek to establish the lay of the land early on. In the title

[59] Cavendish, *The Blazing World*, p. 185–6.

sequence to *Game of Thrones* (2011–19), we fly across Westeros and Essos, mapping out the territories the episode will straddle. The introduction to each episode of *Avatar: The Last Airbender* (2005–8) includes a map with which to orient ourselves, reminding us briefly of the nations, their powers and their politics. In roleplaying video games, a world map is commonly filled in as locations are discovered, revealing how environments fit together and documenting the player's success in becoming familiar with the land.

Maps in Fantasy television credits and games descend from those in books. In *The Tough Guide to Fantasyland* (1996), Diana Wynne Jones asserts that a map is one of the first things readers will encounter as they leaf through a new Fantasy novel. In practice, this cliché is less prevalent than Jones claims; in a sample of novels surveyed by Stefan Ekman, only 34 per cent contained a map.[60] However, the idea of the Fantasy map remains a powerful one with which to conjure, despite the fact that the maps in Fantasy novels are often cryptic, incomplete and predictable. In Jones's words,

> [The map] will show most of a continent (and sometimes part of another) with a large number of bays, offshore islands, an inland sea or so, and a sprinkle of towns. There will be scribbly snakes that are probably Rivers, and names made of Capital Letters in curved lines that are not quite upsidedown. By bending your neck sideways you will be able to see that they say things like "Ca'ea Purt'wydyn" and "Om Ce'falos." These *may* be names of countries, but since most of the Map is bare it is hard to tell.

[60] Ekman, *Here Be Dragons*, p. 22 (sample documented pp. 225–31).

> These empty inland parts will be sporadically peppered with little molehills, invitingly labeled "Megamort Hills," "Death Mountains," "Hurt Range," and such, with a whole line of molehills near the top called "Great Northern Barrier." Above this will be various warnings of danger. The rest of the Map's space will be sparingly devoted to little tiny feathers called "Wretched Wood" and "Forest of Doom," except for one space that appears to be growing minute hairs. This will be tersely labeled "Marshes."
>
> That is mostly it.

In Jones's view, such maps are of dubious value. 'In short,' she writes, 'the Map is useless, but you are advised to keep consulting it, because it is the only one you will get.'[61] Jones is correct that most Fantasy maps are failures if judged by the standards we might apply to a modern Ordinance Survey map, in which we expect a full and accurate scale representation of the surface and features of an area of land. However, this standard does not really apply to Fantasy maps. They primarily fulfil semantic or gestural roles, establishing a tone and a sensibility. Jones's example is comic, but her description of the map gives a sense that it communicates part of the world's culture (through its use of mysterious language), its dangers (through naming conventions and the depiction of obstacles) and its status as a story space. Jones writes that Fantasy questers usually 'have to visit every single place on [the] Map'.[62] In a realist work, this might be seen as a major flaw. However, a Fantasy map is often principally

[61] Diana Wynne Jones, *The Tough Guide to Fantasyland* (New York: DAW Books, 1996), pp. 10–11.

[62] Jones, *Tough Guide*, p. 11.

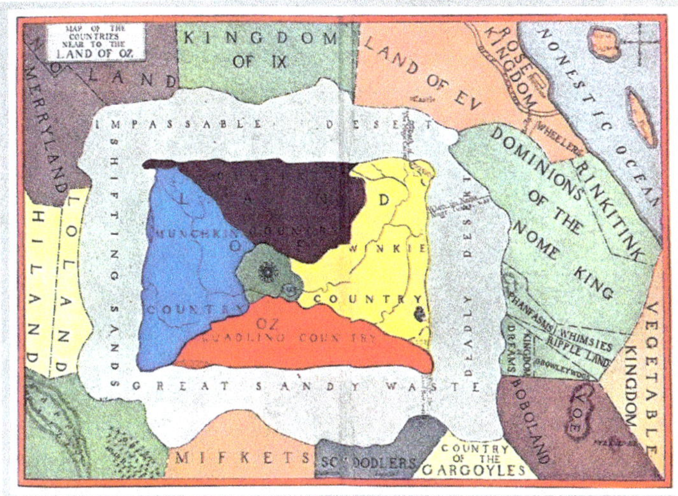

FIGURE 5.4 'Map of the Countries near to the Land of Oz' by John R. Neill: an image of L. Frank Baum's world that demonstrates the level of generalisation Fantasy maps can employ. agefotostock/Alamy.

presented to assist storytelling, rather than for the potentially interesting but rather quixotic purpose of representing accurately a place that does not exist. Fantasy maps can be somewhat frustrating if they include a whole series of interesting-sounding places that do not appear in the story (although for some audiences, this frustration might be generative, leading to the creation of further stories in the form of fanworks). In considering world-building, it is important to be aware that sometimes the land is the way it is simply to give the characters somewhere resonant to stand.

While there are many fantasies set in relatively quotidian environments, it is common for Fantasy world-building to evoke extremes – the grand, the sublime, the horrifying or the wretched. In the central portion of E. R. Eddison's *The Worm Ouroboros* (1922), Juss and Brandoch Daha, two of the Lords of Demonland (who are, slightly counterintuitively, the good guys), set out on a long and involved quest to rescue Juss's abducted brother, Goldry Bluszco. Part of this quest involves traversing a series of improbably enormous mountain ranges of the kind Jones gently mocks. However, Eddison is manifestly a big fan of mountains, and in his writing, they take on a powerful affective charge:

> Suddenly a window opened in the clouds to a space of clean wan wind-swept sky high above the shaggy hills. Surely Juss caught his breath in that moment, to see those deathless ones where they shone pavilioned in the pellucid air, far, vast, and lonely, most like to creatures of unascended heaven, of wind and of fire all compact, too pure to have aught of the gross elements of earth or water. It was as if the rose-red light of sundown had been frozen to crystal and these hewn from it to abide to everlasting, strong and unchangeable amid the welter of earthborn mists below and tumultuous sky above them. The rift ran wider, eastward and westward, opening on more peaks and sunset-kindled snows. And a rainbow leaning to the south was like a sword of glory across the vision.
>
> Motionless, like hawks staring from that high place of prospect, Juss and Brandoch Daha looked on the mountains of their desire.[63]

Juss and Brandoch Daha have a clear goal in their rescue mission, but it is also apparent that they relish conquering heights never before obtained. The desire they feel for

[63] E. R. Eddison, *The Worm Ouroboros* (London: Millennium, 2000), pp. 193–4.

sublime mountains has much to do with their delight in a world that lets them test what the end of the book apostrophises as their 'youth everlasting and unwaning strength and skill in arms'.[64] Heroes cannot be heroic without deeds to do, and the world of *The Worm Ouroboros* is set up by its author's design and its internal logics to provide challenges that bring joy both to the Lords of Demonland and to readers who are drawn into their world. While there is narrative pleasure in the interplay of characters and the forward motion of the plot, there is also pleasure in surveying the world's environments as conjured in Eddison's colour-charged, highly wrought evocations. While such environments may endanger the characters, for audiences, they might be considered 'Sounds and sweet airs, that give delight and hurt not': wonders that grant vicarious access to intense and unfamiliar forms of landscape and emotion, but which readers can experience completely safely.[65] In a similar way, while leaping from a mountaintop in the real world is usually inadvisable, the same experience in a Fantasy video game can be deeply exhilarating, even if the lack or failure of a flight spell ends up mandating a timely reload.

Joy in world-building's representations of extremes can extend to the dark and horrific, as well as the vast and beautiful. The most fell foe that Juss and his compatriots face is the King of Witchland, Gorice, who is reborn in a

[64] Eddison, *The Worm Ouroboros*, p. 512.

[65] William Shakespeare, *The Tempest*, ed. by Virginia Mason Vaughan and Alden T. Vaughan, revised edition (London: Bloomsbury, 2011), 3.2.136 (p. 254).

different form whenever he is killed. After the blustering wrestler Gorice XI is defeated by Goldry Bluszco, he rises again as the formidable necromancer Gorice XII. Eddison's descriptions of the capital of Witchland leave little room for misunderstandings in terms of tone:

> On the southern face of the bluff, monstrous as a mountain in those low sedge-lands, hung square and black the fortress of Carcë. It was built of black marble, roughhewn and unpolished, the outworks enclosing many acres. An inner wall with a tower at each corner formed the main stronghold, in the south-west corner of which was the palace, overhanging the river. And on the south-west corner of the palace, towering sheer from the water's edge seventy cubits and more to the battlements, stood the keep, a round tower lined with iron, bearing on the corbel table beneath its parapet in varying form and untold repetition the sculptured figure of the crab of Witchland. The outer ward of the fortress was dark with cypress trees: black flames burning changelessly to heaven from a billowy sea of gloom. East of the keep was the water-gate, and beside it a bridge and bridgehouse across the river, strongly fortified with turrets and machicolations and commanded from on high by the battlements of the keep. Dismal and fearsome to view was this strong place of Carcë, most like to the embodied soul of dreadful night brooding on the waters of that sluggish river: by day a shadow in broad sunshine, the likeness of pitiless violence sitting in the place of power, darkening the desolation of the mournful fen, by night, a blackness more black than night herself.[66]

In Carcë, Eddison gives his readers an excellent place at which to shudder. At this relatively early stage in the development of modern secondary-world Fantasy, the

[66] Eddison, *The Worm Ouroboros*, pp. 58–9.

fabrics of the Dark Lord's tower had already been fully imported from romance, poetry and the Gothic. Before Mordor, we already have desolate marshes, edifices wrought with black marble and iron, and a shrouding with extreme forms of darkness. Here, as in many works of Fantasy, the location, architecture and design of a significant settlement are indicative of a civilisation's character. Eddison's gothic excesses both foreshadow the scheming and backstabbing that will occur and establish the difficulties that are likely to befall any force that seeks to besiege Carcë. If the great Zimiamvian mountain ranges invite wonder, Carcë instead offers the enjoyment of witnessing awful acts and feeling creeping dread.

The Worm Ouroboros has a few complex and interesting characters – most notably Lord Gro, who is brave, clever, devious and compulsively changeable – but Eddison's use of opposing sides and meaningful landscapes is in many respects quite straightforward (although no less effective for being so). Other Fantasy writers have built more ambivalent and inscrutable worlds for their characters to dwell in, worlds that might be seen more explicitly as shaping their inhabitants, rather than challenging or reflecting them. Mervyn Peake is not given to invoking impossible magics, but he is accorded a high place when Fantasy writers discuss their influences because of how effectively he integrates characters and environments into a world that feels unique, tangible and strange. Opening *Titus Groan* (1946), the first novel of his Gormenghast sequence, Peake confronts the reader immediately with intimidating, crumbling immensity:

Gormenghast, that is, the main massing of the original stone, taken by itself would have displayed a certain ponderous architectural quality were it possible to have ignored the circumfusion of those mean dwellings that swarmed like an epidemic around its outer walls. They sprawled over the sloping earth, each one half way over its neighbour until, held back by the castle ramparts, the innermost of these hovels laid hold on the great walls, clamping themselves thereto like limpets to a rock. These dwellings, by ancient law, were granted this chill intimacy with the stronghold that loomed above them. Over their irregular roofs would fall throughout the seasons, the shadows of time-eaten buttresses, of broken and lofty turrets, and, most enormous of all, the shadow of the Tower of Flints. This tower, patched unevenly with black ivy, arose like a mutilated finger from among the fists of knuckled masonry and pointed blasphemously at heaven. At night the owls made of it an echoing throat; by day it stood voiceless and cast its long shadow.[67]

In some respects, Gormenghast is not so far from Carcë – the sinister Tower of Flints could certainly be exported to Witchland – but where Gorice's palace-fortress is consistently malevolent, the first impression Gormenghast creates is of age, scale and ponderousness. Peake achieves this both through direct description and through the flow of his prose, in which clauses and complex diction pile up into a formidable textual edifice that starts to tell us things about the castle's inhabitants, neighbours and culture as it continues to describe its fabric. We are given hints of a hierarchy and of elites with the power notionally to determine fates, but we are also given our first intimations of the bonds set upon the Earls of Groan, who are

[67] Mervyn Peake, *Titus Groan*, in *The Gormenghast Trilogy* (London: Vintage, 1999), pp. 1–367 (p. 7).

constrained by ancient laws within their vast dwelling: an accumulated megastructure that cannot easily be maintained or encompassed, but which instead sprawls and deteriorates, its vast mysteries both implicitly mocking and rendering understandable the crabbed and constrained lives of those who shuffle and dwell within its precincts.

The lives of Gormenghast's inhabitants are governed by 'iron ritual'. Its denizens' views on ritual differ considerably – some venerate it, others tolerate it, others dislike it, still others seek to resist or subvert it. All, though, are moulded by the castle and the culture it imposes, the Earls of Groan most of all. When Titus's father, Lord Sepulchrave, reflects on Gormenghast, he sees it as something beyond his ability to separate himself from:

> How could he *love* this place? He was a part of it. He could not imagine a world outside it; and the idea of loving Gormenghast would have shocked him. To have asked him of his feelings for his hereditary home would be like asking a man what his feelings were towards his own hand or his own throat.[68]

Gormenghast manifests overwhelmingly, exerting a kind of stifling or enervating pressure on its inhabitants, its vastness demanding that they accord it meaning and significance. In Sepulchrave, who would usually rather be reading, this causes a profound melancholy. From the dolorous servant Flay, the castle draws unwavering loyalty. In the kitchen boy Steerpike, who passes lightly over and through the castle, the reader initially sees someone who appears to resist Gormenghast's gravity. However,

[68] Peake, *Titus Groan*, pp. 41–2.

the potential for power draws Steerpike in, and he eventually becomes as much a creature of the castle as any of its older residents.

While the first volume of the Gormenghast sequence is named for Titus Groan, Gormenghast's ponderousness mandates a deliberate slowing down of the usual conventions of the *bildungsroman* (the novel of growth and education). When the series turns more explicitly to Titus's development in *Gormenghast* (1950), he is shown to be deeply conditioned by the only environment he has ever known:

> He has learned an alphabet of arch and aisle: the language of dim stairs and moth-hung rafters. Great halls are his dim playgrounds: his fields are quadrangles: his trees are pillars.
>
> And he has learned that there are always eyes. Eyes that watch. Feet that follow, and hands to hold him when he struggles, to lift him when he falls. Upon his feet again he stares unsmiling. Tall figures bow. Some in jewellery; some in rags.[69]

This makes Gormenghast sound like an irredeemably gothic place, but Peake's brilliance lies in his depicting his characters as vulnerable, humorous, pathetic and heart-rending, as well as strange and at times monstrous. Titus eventually longs to escape Gormenghast, but there are many examples of weird kindness in his upbringing. To give just one: when Titus has been confined in the Lichen Fort as a punishment for adventuring outside the castle, his benevolent but dubiously effectual headmaster, Professor Bellgrove, dutifully visits him. As is the case in

[69] Mervyn Peake, *Gormenghast*, in *The Gormenghast Trilogy* (London: Vintage, 1999), pp. 369–752 (p. 373).

many of the book's conversations, communication is a struggle, with Bellgrove initially seeking to impart the moral lesson he feels should be expected. However, he is eventually provoked into an anecdote that tells us a great deal about how Gormenghast both seeps into and nurtures its residents:

> although your old headmaster has *been* thirty-seven, long ago, he can't remember a thing about it except that it was somewhere about that time that he bought a bag of glass marbles. O yes he did. And why? Because he became tired of teaching grammar and spelling and arithmetic. O yes, and because he saw how much happier the people were who played marbles than the people were who didn't. That's a bad sentence, my boy. So I used to play in the dark after the other young professors were asleep. We had one of the old Gormenghast tapestry-carpets in the room and I used to light a candle and place my marbles on the corners of patterns in the carpet, and in the middle of crimson and yellow flowers. I can remember the carpet perfectly as though it was here in this old fort, and there, every night by the glow of a candle, I would practise until I could flick a marble along the floor so that when it struck another it spun round and round but stayed exactly where it was, my boy, while the one it had struck shot off like a rocket to land at the other end of the room in the centre of a crimson carpet flower (if I was successful), or if not, near enough to couch itself at the next flick. And the sounds of the glass marbles in the still of the night when they struck was like the sound of tiny crystal vases breaking on stone floors – but I am getting too poetic, my boy, aren't I?[70]

It turns out, of course, that Bellgrove has brought his marbles with him, and while the intrusion of Doctor

[70] Peake, *Gormenghast*, p. 485.

Prunesquallor threatens briefly to destroy what Bellgrove has sought to conjure, Prunesquallor is kind enough to join in with a little moment of playful connection:

For the next hour, the old prison warder, peering through a keyhole the size of a table-spoon, in the inner door, was astounded to see the three figures crawling to and fro across the floor of the prison fort, to hear the high trill of the Doctor develop and strengthen into the cry of a hyena, the deep and wavering voice of the Professor bell forth like an old and happy hound, as his inhibitions waned, and the shrill cries of the child reverberate about the room, splintering like glass on the stone walls while the marbles crashed against one another, spun in their tracks, lodged shuddering in their squares, or skimmed the prison floor like shooting stars.[71]

As well as the vastness of the castle, the Gormenghast that exerts influence is a peculiar, frangible community that is conditioned but not exclusively determined by that vastness. At the end of *Titus Alone* (1959), Titus comes to realise that 'he carried his Gormenghast within him'.[72] He is a product of Gormenghast, but specific experiences have forged him, and he can sift and modify these in memory. In his thriller *Authority*, Jeff VanderMeer's character Whitby borrows the term 'terroir' from wine-making and uses it to describe 'the sum of the effects of a localized environment, inasmuch as they impact the qualities of a particular product'.[73] The peculiar terroir of Gormenghast has moulded both Titus and the reader's

[71] Peake, *Gormenghast*, p. 488.

[72] Mervyn Peake, *Titus Alone*, in *The Gormenghast Trilogy* (London: Vintage, 1999), pp. 753–953 (p. 953).

[73] Jeff VanderMeer, *Authority* (London: Fourth Estate, 2014), p. 40.

FIGURE 5.5 Sketch of Professor Bellgrove and Titus Groan by Mervyn Peake, one of many that he added to his notebooks while he wrote. British Library Add MS 88931/1/3/15 f. 116. Courtesy of the Peake Estate.

experience of his story; nevertheless, in the end, Titus finds that he can be transplanted, letting him grow beyond the shaping presence of his childhood and youth without needing to deny how it has constructed him.

World-building is often associated with Gormenghastly scale, and there is certainly something joyous, involving and revelatory about – for example – haunting Robin Hobb's FitzChivalry Farseer through the nine thick books that describe his life or spending a hundred hours with the cast of *Persona 5* (2016) or dwelling with a manga series created over many years, such as Kentaro Miura's *Berserk* (1989–). However, great world-building can be accomplished in very brief works. Ursula K. Le Guin's story 'The Ones Who Walk Away from Omelas' (1973) is under three thousand words in length, but in that space, she paints the city of the title, its festival customs, the dark secret underpinning its affluence and the means by which those who cannot countenance their prosperity resting on pain remove themselves from the equation. Similarly, a single image or a brief poem can suggest a rich world by firing its audience's minds to extrapolate. We might think of Samuel Taylor Coleridge's 'Kubla Khan' (written around 1797), which creates a powerfully imagined environment in a handful of words:

> In Xanadu did Kubla Khan
> A stately pleasure-dome decree:
> Where Alph, the sacred river, ran
> Through caverns measureless to man
>   Down to a sunless sea.
> So twice five miles of fertile ground
> With walls and towers were girdled round:
> And there were gardens bright with sinuous rills

> Where blossom'd many an incense-bearing tree;
> And here were forests ancient as the hills,
> Enfolding sunny spots of greenery.[74]

Coleridge's world-building depends on intensity of language, rather than on extended or exacting explanation. He provides us with forms and light, gesturing towards ungraspable scale with the unplumbable caverns and giving us a few salient details with which to extend his conjuration if we wish. The reader is left to determine the design of the walls and towers and fill in the colours of the tree blossom if they so choose. World-building always relies on audiences' imaginative collaboration, and in short works, this can be especially important. This is a process Coleridge's poem both recognises and enacts. After he has passed beyond the initial vision, Coleridge dreams of reanimating it by reviving the symphony and song of the damsel's dulcimer, which he imagines will spur him to a new feat of world-recollection when he builds Kubla's dome in air through his own music: a feat he accomplishes in the form of the poem even as he ostensibly defers the possibility.

Brevity asks for different qualities of attention than profusion does. In *The Worm Ouroboros*, Eddison includes a description of a river that distinctly recalls Coleridge's Alph: 'In the depths a carpet of huge tree-tops clothed a vast stretch of country, through the midst of which, seen here and there in a bend of silver among the woods, the Bhavinan bore the waters of a thousand secret mountain

[74] Samuel Taylor Coleridge, 'Kubla Khan: or A Vision in a Dream', in *Christabel: Kubla Khan, A Vision: The Pains of Sleep* (London: John Murray, 1816), pp. 55–8 (pp. 55–6).

solitudes down to an unknown sea.'[75] However, immersed in the larger flow of Eddison's prose, this becomes part of a many-threaded tapestry, rather than a gesture that sets the bounds on a whole creation. Where Eddison gives us many stimuli from which to paint the world his characters travel through, Coleridge creates Xanadu in a tight image. Both techniques can be highly effective, and in practice, many Fantasy creators combine the two. Even in works with a substantial representative canvas, it can be more effective to withhold certain things. Peake never gives us precise dimensions for Gormenghast, and to do so would spoil its mystery. Instead, readers collaborate with Peake, creating the castle from the vastnesses their own minds have known.

In good Fantasy world-building, richness, allusiveness and compression can get a lot done in a limited compass. Nghi Vo's *The Empress of Salt and Fortune* (2020) is a relatively brief novella (just over 100 pages), but one that suggests sweeping complexities through a tight focus on a small cast and a location from which substantial implications can be unspooled. At the beginning of the novella, a cleric and their hoopoe companion are travelling to a former residence of the titular Empress, from which an interdict has recently been lifted following her death. In a couple of early paragraphs, Vo expertly suggests her world's flavour:

> They knew that there was no road there. They had crossed the white pine copse earlier that day, and though they could see the remnants of a road underneath the overgrown bracken and

[75] Eddison, *The Worm Ouroboros*, p. 192.

fallen boughs, it wouldn't have let a dogcart through. Chih suspected that the road had once connected Lake Scarlet to the royal highway, in the days before the lake had been taken off every map and effectively disappeared by a highly dedicated and skilled imperial sorcerer.

There was no road there during the day, but obviously at night, things were different. The road ran as broad as a barge through the trees, and ranged on either side were faded ghosts, the former guardians of Lake Scarlet. Even a few months ago, Chih knew, the ghosts would have fallen on any living thing that crossed their path, tearing them to pieces and then crying because they were still so hungry.[76]

From these paragraphs, we get a sense of the level of technology we might expect from a society that can build road networks and which employs dogcarts and barges. The considerable power wielded by the authorities is clearly established; in this land, rulers can close regions, edit maps and employ powerful sorceries to enforce their will. This is also a world in which things that to us would be supernatural are commonplace enough to be seen as factual. Without complicated explication, Vo swiftly establishes a considerable number of parameters that help bridge the reader into the story's world.

We are briefly introduced to Cleric Chih and their companion in the novella's first hundred words, but Vo introduces them more fully through the first conversation they have with Rabbit, an enigmatic old woman they encounter at their destination. Through this conversation, Vo turns the focus briefly on her focalisers, showing

[76] Nghi Vo, *The Empress of Salt and Fortune* (New York: Tom Doherty, 2020), pp. 10–11.

us the characters whose preoccupations will guide us through the rest of the narrative:

> "Oh, I see I was mistaken. Not a girl at all, but a cleric."
>
> Chih smiled.
>
> "It's an easy mistake, grandmother, but yes. I am Cleric Chih from the Singing Hills abbey. This little feathery menace is Almost Brilliant."
>
> Almost Brilliant whooped in indignation at being so described and showed off her manners by alighting in front of their hostess and tocking the boards in front of her twice with her narrow beak.
>
> "Most honored to make your acquaintance, matriarch," Almost Brilliant said in her grumbling gravelly voice.
>
> "And I yours, Mistress Almost Brilliant. If your cleric is from the Singing Hills, you must be a neixin, are you not?"
>
> Almost Brilliant's feathers fluffed out in pride. "Yes, matriarch. I am descended from the line of Ever Victorious and Always Kind. Our memories go all the way back to the Xun Dynasty."
>
> "What a pleasure. They killed so many of your kind during the reign of Emperor Sung. I was not sure I would ever see another."
>
> "The Singing Hills aviary was torched, but our Divine at the time sent three pairs of nesting couples to their relatives across the Hu River," said Chih. "Among them were Almost Brilliant's great-grandparents. If you know about neixin, grandmother, you must know how they need to have a place and a name for everything."[77]

Vo packs a great deal into this exchange. We are informed that Chih is a non-binary individual, and that this status

[77] Vo, *Empress of Salt and Fortune*, pp. 15–16.

relates to their profession as a cleric. We get a glimpse of Chih's attitude and sense of humour. We learn more about the excellently named Almost Brilliant, and while the word 'neixin' is not glossed directly, the reader can decode at least some of what it implies from the bird's responses. We gather something of society's notions of politeness, and something of the land's past periods of violent conflict. We are given more names, the sounds of which tune us in on China as a probable inspiration for the culture we are observing, but without drawing such direct equivalences that we are asked to decode the novella using particular historical figures or events. The conversation gives us a dense range of referents, hints and information, but, crucially, it retains the appearance of a plausible conversation.

Getting the small details right is important both in Vo's prose and in interpreting the objects that Chih and Almost Brilliant catalogue while Rabbit explains their provenance. In seeking to interrogate the house to which the Empress was exiled, Chih recalls the words of a mentor 'who had always encouraged their acolytes to speak to the florists and the bakers as much as to the warlords and magistrates. *Accuracy above all things. You will never remember the great if you do not remember the small.*'[78] This dictate guides both Chih and Vo, as great events are contextualised through the prism of discarded things and personal reminiscences. As Rabbit tells the stories of inventoried objects, she repeatedly asks Chih whether they understand. Chih usually asserts that they do, but the reader is shown scenes that go beyond what the cleric

[78] Vo, *Empress of Salt and Fortune*, p. 17.

sees. (One story is told first to Almost Brilliant, and while she says she will retell it, we are not shown precisely how this occurs.) Paying attention to the little things holds the key to understanding outcomes in the greater world, but this understanding is predicated on caring for things that others overlook. The scorned Empress's eventual success depends on seeing possibilities and potential her opponents are conditioned not to notice. Vo's story likewise succeeds by making us discern value in details.

As well as happening in different fashions at different scales and durations, world-building necessarily happens very differently across media forms. Both Tolkien and MacDonald have strong predilections for prose fiction, one that Tolkien makes very clear when he argues that the creation of genuine Fantasy is 'a thing best left to words, to true literature'. Conversely, he contends that painted fantasies often tend to 'Silliness or morbidity' and that 'Drama is naturally hostile to Fantasy.'[79] Looking at the plethora of forms in which twenty-first-century fantasies manifest, it is clear that Tolkien's prejudices are not universally shared. As Linda Hutcheon even-handedly puts it, 'each mode, like each medium, *has* its own specificity [...] no one mode is inherently good at doing one thing and not another; but each has at its disposal different means of expression—media and genres—and so can aim at and achieve certain things better than others'.[80]

Examples of this specificity are easy to summon. Lovecraft can blithely write things like 'the *geometry* of

[79] Tolkien, 'On Fairy-stories', p. 61.
[80] Linda Hutcheon with Siobhan O'Flynn, *A Theory of Adaptation*, 2nd edition (London: Routledge, 2013), p. 24.

the dream-place he saw was abnormal, non-Euclidean, and loathsomely redolent of spheres and dimensions apart from ours', relying on the reader to imagine how this might manifest itself.[81] However, a video game artist building an environment based on this description would need to determine what loathsomely redolent non-Euclidean geometry actually looks like. An effect a writer can achieve in a few short sentences might cost millions of pounds to realise on film, and representing certain kinds of feelings and emotions might be implausible in forms that find it harder to get inside characters' heads. Consider, for example, how a film might visualise these few words from N. K. Jemisin's *The Fifth Season*:

> He takes [. . .] the strata and the magma and the people and the power in his imaginary hands. Everything. He holds it. He is not alone. The earth is with him.
>
> Then *he breaks it*.[82]

In animation, conjuring the steam rising from a hot cup of tea can be tricker than creating an erupting volcano; in live-action cinema, the former can be done by making a cup of tea and then carefully filming it, while the latter is likely to be an expensive special effect (now most likely to be achieved using digital technology). A novel using words to tell rather than images to show would find it very difficult to capture the particular creepiness of Doug Jones's movements as the Pale Man in *Pan's Labyrinth* (2006). Prose cannot not strike the eye with everything all at once, in the manner of paintings like Hieronymus Bosch's *The Garden of Earthly Delights* (c. 1503–15) or

[81] Lovecraft, 'Call of Cthulhu', p. 166. [82] Jemisin, *Fifth Season*, p. 7.

FIGURE 5.6 *The Fall of the Rebel Angels* (1562) by Pieter Bruegel the Elder: an example of a fantastic image that is almost impossible to encapsulate briefly in words.
Collection of the Musées royaux des Beaux-Arts de Belgique, Brussels. Fine Art Images/Heritage Images via Getty Images.

Pieter Bruegel the Elder's *The Fall of the Rebel Angels* (1562; Figure 5.6). Novels need time to evoke space. To say this is not to demean them, but rather to point out that Tolkien's preference for words is precisely that: a preference, and one somewhat belied by his use of images at key moments in his own stories.

Media-specific affordances and restrictions can have profound effects on how worlds frame stories (and vice versa). As Katarina O'Dette has discussed, until recently televisual fantasies tended to stay away from quests, as moving through a different landscape each week is expensive and viewers could not necessarily be expected to see every episode in order. The need to produce extensive content that would still work if parts were missed out led Fantasy TV series to develop formats such as monster-of-the-week and conceits that drew fantastic elements to a finite set of locations represented by standing sets:

> Rather than bringing Frodo to Mordor, these series perform their worldbuilding by bringing parts of Mordor to Frodo every episode. *Buffy [the Vampire Slayer]*'s Hellmouth draws mystical forces from various parts of the primary world and linked secondary worlds to Sunnydale. Over seven seasons, viewers accumulate substantial information about the Buffyverse. Viewers learn about the natural realm by encountering the demons and other magical creatures who are pulled to Sunnydale, and the plants needed to cure or combat their spells and potions. Viewers discover the cultural realm by encountering various subcultures within Sunnydale, such as demon poker groups and secret government organizations, as well as factions from outside Sunnydale that are drawn to the town, such as the Order of Taraka, a society of assassins. Viewers learn about the ontological realm through the various types of magic inflicted on Sunnydale by antagonists and employed in its defense by protagonists. They even learn to recategorize elements of the series: earthquakes in the actual world are part of the natural realm, but in the Buffyverse, they can be part of the ontological realm as a magical portent of the apocalypse.[83]

Sunnydale in *Buffy* builds out a larger world through a process that Matt Hills calls hyperdiegesis, 'the creation of a vast and detailed narrative space, only a fraction of which is ever directly seen or encountered within the text,

[83] Katarina O'Dette, 'Fantasy Worlds on the Small Screen: Worldbuilding in Original American Fantasy Television', *Extrapolation*, 62.1 (2021), 37–62 (p. 46).

but which nevertheless appears to operate according to principles of internal logic and extension'.[84] The limitations of episodic television thereby produce a form of world-building through accumulation and suggestion that when employed effectively allows both for a considerable depth of lore and for kinds of playful subversion. Some one-off episodes of *Buffy* might be considered misfires, but the flexibility within its general framework allowed the series to develop its characters by employing a vast range of prisms over the course of its run.

Since *Buffy* struck its careful balance between season-long throughlines and one-off episodic pleasures, televisual Fantasy has been transformed by subscription and streaming models that employ shorter, more tightly interconnected seasons partly designed to be binged. Spearheaded by *Game of Thrones*, high-budget series using modern digital effects have moved closer to the structures of filmic or novelistic fantasies. According to Jason Mittell, such changing formats mandate 'a reconceptualization of the boundary between episodic and serial forms, a heightened degree of self-consciousness in storytelling mechanics, and demands for intensified viewer engagement focused on both diegetic pleasures and formal awareness.'[85] However, while the presumption of sustained viewer attention allows for complex serial storytelling and more intensive and consistent world-building, shorter seasons often jettison effective and pleasurable

[84] Matt Hills, *Fan Cultures* (London and New York: Routledge, 2002), p. 137.

[85] Jason Mittell, 'Narrative Complexity in Contemporary American Television', *The Velvet Light Trap*, 58.1 (2006), 29–40 (p. 39).

episodic rhythms. 'Once More with Feeling' (2001), an experimental musical episode, fits satisfyingly into a twenty-two-episode *Buffy* season, in which writing patterns and contained episodes make mixing tones a natural course of action. Such playful fantastic subversions would be a lot more difficult to accommodate in newer prestige adaptations such as *The Witcher* (2019–) or *The Wheel of Time* (2021–), which aspire to different kinds of immersion. As a result, recent televisual Fantasy has tended to become more visually coherent and convincing while downplaying the mischievous generic experimentation that drove some of the most interesting older series.

Just as the affordances and delivery models of television have profoundly shaped Fantasy worlds on the small screen, so have the requirements of video games mandated more open approaches than in novelistic narratives. While there are experimental exceptions (often with a sinister edge, like *Doki Doki Literature Club* (2017)), many games revolve around letting the player take meaningful actions, presenting the possibility of some kind of failure, but also holding out the prospect of success. Success can be achieved mechanically by overcoming a challenge, narratively by advancing a story, or through the two in combination. While readers of novels or watchers of films are often invited to sympathise with a protagonist, in many games, the player is invited to become them. In some cases, this entails forms of power fantasy, but many games place careful limitations on the player character that serve both as ways of conjuring difference and as a means of bringing the player into alignment with their fantastic context.

In Black Isle Studios' classic roleplaying game *Planescape: Torment* (1999), you play as the forebodingly titled Nameless One. Initially, you are given a limited opportunity to customise your character by placing points in the usual *Dungeons & Dragons* statistics (Strength, Dexterity, Constitution, Intelligence, Wisdom and Charisma). However, you determine little else before you wake up on a slab in a vast Mortuary with no memory of who you are or how you came to be there and only Morte – a floating, talking skull – for company and guidance. The Nameless One's lack of memories would in theory allow him to build himself from the ground up. However, this is not something that the game allows you to do. While the Nameless One cannot remember his own past, his previous incarnations' actions have left scars upon the world, the people he has interacted with and the body he finds himself in. One of the game's first potential interactions is having Morte read the instructions a past self has had tattooed on the Nameless One's back. The player is invited to explore weird environments that blend grimness and exuberance, but they are also constantly reminded that the character they inhabit has a history that predates their experience of guiding (or being) him. Old memories bubble up at opportune and inopportune moments. On the lower floor of the Mortuary, the Nameless One encounters the ghost of Deionarra, a woman devoted to one of his previous incarnations, who asks him bitterly whether he has 'come to see first-hand the misery you have wrought'. She tells him that he cannot die, at a stroke eliminating the most common fail state that video games employ. The Nameless One's journey is not one that balances between death and victory, but rather one about determining what kinds of meaning you will choose to make with a chance to begin in some ways afresh, but in other respects boxed in by a long succession of past choices.

World-building in the Planescape setting combines the physical and the metaphysical. The Great Wheel of the planes is mapped to the points of the alignment compass used in *Dungeons & Dragons* to characterise ethical and moral perspectives. The planes arrayed around the Wheel range from the lawful good paradise of Mount Celestia to the ever-shifting chaotic neutral plane of Limbo to the lawful evil Nine Hells of Baator, in which a strict hierarchy of devils work to tempt and corrupt mortals. At the centre of the setting (at least according to many of its inhabitants) is Sigil, the place where the Nameless One has awoken, known variously as the Cage or the City of Doors. Sigil is riddled with portals to other planes, portals whose keys can be 'almost anything… an emotion, a piece of wood, a dagger of silvered glass, a scrap of cloth, a tune you hum to yourself'. This means that it has become a place that many pass through or fall into accidentally – a city that is mixed and at least in some respects cosmopolitan, but also a place of the lost and exiled, a metropolis within which vastly different ideologies clash. It is a city where reality is somewhat fluid, where belief can change the world and where someone might both find and lose themselves.

The key question of *Planescape: Torment*, articulated by the night hag Ravel Puzzlewell in one of the story's central moments, is 'What can change the nature of a man?' The game's mechanics could be seen as implying that your actions might do this: you begin the game as True Neutral, the centre of the *Dungeons & Dragons* alignment compass, and your deeds can move you towards good or evil along one axis, or towards law or chaos along the other. However, alignment has fairly minor gameplay effects, encouraging the player to engage with the question on a more conceptual level, selecting a truth about how they have come to understand the Nameless One, picking from options including love, power, betrayal, death and regret. Its focus on moments like this has sometimes led *Torment* to be dismissed as a novel disguised as a game. It is certainly accurate to say that much of the gameplay consists of reading dialogue. The combat is adequate but unflashy, with the exception of some enjoyably over-the-top effects for high-level spells. In many cases, fights can be avoided with clever conversation. It is also true that, in keeping with the game's focus on the past's power to constrain, the trail you follow to find answers only leads to one place. However, the nature of the Nameless One who arrives at the game's end is the player's to determine, and the knowledge and options available in the final moments are contingent on the player's curiosity, outlook and investment. Whether the game's ending is tragic, just, a surrender or a triumph ultimately depends on how the player has worked with the stimuli in the game's world to build what goes on inside the Nameless One's head.

Planescape: Torment is somewhat unusual in focusing so intensively on using world-building to explore (or create) an inner world. By contrast, FromSoftware's *Elden Ring* (2022) sets its customisable, largely silent protagonist a relatively conventional video game challenge: overcome decadent demigods, take possession of the titular Elden Ring and use it to determine the future of the world. *Elden Ring* employs many of the world-building techniques discussed previously in this chapter, albeit with a particular emphasis on the player character as the focaliser. The game carefully stages sublime experiences. When a character exits the tutorial area into light, they will quickly glimpse the golden glory of the Erdtree looming over Limgrave. After they fight their way through Stormveil Castle (or bypass it), part of the reward is to crest a rise and see the mists, peaks and vast, strange buildings of Liurnia of the Lakes spread out below. In an unusual twist, the game initially hides the true scale of its map, surprising the player repeatedly with the size, variety and intricacy of its environments.

Elden Ring did not begin with a blank slate. Instead, it expertly iterates on FromSoft's earlier *Dark Souls* series (2011–17), as well as *Bloodborne* (2015) and *Sekiro* (2019). The things reworked range from combat mechanics to very specific elements such as giant wolves awkwardly wielding swords in their mouths, many exciting varieties of poisonous swamp and extremely Pre-Raphaelite women. The world-building in *Elden Ring* is unafraid to play with classic tropes; the dragons in the game are many and various. However, the designers also introduce stranger things, from the character heralded in the bombastic opening cutscene as 'the loathsome Dung Eater' to a race of living jars, represented most memorably by the accident-prone warrior Iron Fist Alexander.

The digital wonderland of the Lands Between is designed to accommodate radically different but equally magical and legitimate forms of engagement. The freedom of the open world, the ability to grind (fight copious weaker enemies) to gain character levels and the spirit-summoning mechanics (which can provide assistance in difficult fights) make the game more accessible for those who previously found FromSoft's trademark action combat intimidating. *Elden Ring* is also sensitive to the interpretive communities that have grown up around FromSoft's games. The oblique storytelling employed in *Dark Souls* created networks of fans dedicated to unpicking the games' lore, which is mostly communicated through environments, item descriptions and the often-cryptic utterances of non-player characters. *Elden Ring*'s huge scale and the intricate design of its world provide a feast for these interpreters. Having commissioned George R. R. Martin to contribute to the narrative, FromSoft might have chosen to put his writing front and centre, but instead Martin's work outlines a past that has fallen away and which is deliberately obfuscated within the game. Players must decode the history of the demigods from the shattered forms they encounter, using statues, snippets of description, voice lines and inferences of location. This means that individual players can feel immersed in a world with a deep and mysterious history, but also acknowledges that for certain fans, the experience of speculating on forums, building and reading wikis, scouring code for cut content, and creating and consuming lore videos is the best part of the game experience. *Elden Ring* thus generously embraces both hardcore investigators and people who will never play the game at all, but who might nevertheless love reading about it or watching it for a while.

Lore theorisers are not the only community who came together swiftly to explore *Elden Ring*'s intricacies. To see the majority of *Elden Ring*'s world might take a relatively completionist player over one hundred hours. The game's

Any% Unrestricted speedrun record at time of writing is under four minutes. Speedrunning is a very particular way of playing, with runners collaboratively optimising an extremely precise route through the game's sprawling world and then competing to execute that route as perfectly as possible. When running Any% Unrestricted, speedrunners skip huge portions of the game using a bewildering portfolio of tricks that break the game's conventional logics. The fact that for portions of *Elden Ring*'s community this is deeply satisfying both to do and to watch speaks powerfully to the ways in which the game's world accommodates different kinds of fantasy.

Some of the earliest run-enabling glitches identified in *Elden Ring* were Wrong Warps, which allow the player to skip areas by tricking the game engine into losing track of the avatar's location. The game then places the avatar in a default location as a fallback, which can be considerably further through the game than the player is supposed to be. This seems like something that FromSoft could have changed if they wanted to, building on experience from previous games in which Wrong Warps were also present, but it is something that brings considerable joy to part of the player base. Players' enjoyment of such glitches may have inspired parts of *Elden Ring*'s design that deliberately allow surprising skips forward. Chests armed with transporter traps, activatable portals and enemies that abduct the player character all provide access to fragments and snippets of areas that the player may not reach legitimately for tens of hours. Wrong Warps feel like doing magic with the game's code. While some might gripe that such forms of play veer from the intended immersive experience, the obvious response is that the possibilities of conventional play are not eliminated, and that accommodating speedruns allows for an additional, parallel kind of fantasy.

With *Elden Ring*, speedrunners found several other major glitches that break the game in ways that have their own kind of magic. Until it was patched, the evocatively named Pegasus glitch allowed the player's spectral steed, Torrent, to fly if a very specific combination of actions was performed. This let players reach unexpected places and clip out of bounds into the underbelly of the game's graphical assets, revealing unintended environments that have a bizarre beauty of their own. The most fruitful glitch for bringing down the speedrun time proved to be zips: near-frame-perfect (or perhaps imperfect) alignments of the blocking and walking animations that allow the player's avatar to teleport forward considerable distances. Careful routing allows zips to facilitate extremely fast progress, avoiding all the game's fights. The code of the game, it turns out, eliminates bosses if the player manages to glitch a significant distance outside their supposedly closed arenas. The Any% Unrestricted run has thus become a bizarre quasi-pacifist route. The avatar runs, then makes strange gestures with its sword before inexplicably teleporting across large distances, performs a few very specific actions of standard play, then begins another exacting series of meticulously planned zips. At this point, the run is a surreal dance, stringing together images and gestures with honed technical precision.

In many ways, the achieved Any% Unrestricted run is less important than the community effort to find and perfect it, with the game's code serving, like its lore, as a powerful focus for collaborative discovery. The Any%

Unrestricted run is also one of many; runners have refined the All Remembrances run (covering a selection of the major bosses), as well as mastery runs including No Hit and Rune Level 1 (where you start as a wretch and never level up). The game thus provides a space within which a whole series of different kinds of interactions – solitary and communal – allow players to enjoy and build upon what its network of creators put in. Alongside wonderful world-building by design – such as the mysteriously long lift ride that builds to an astonishing moment when the amethyst-tinged underground glory of the Siofra River Valley opens up – *Elden Ring* also manifests the trait that characterises much of the best Fantasy world-building: a generosity that allows its audiences to collaborate and share in the joys of discovery, immersion and belonging.

6

Fantastic Communities and Common Ground

~

In a 2019 interview, the speculative fiction writer, poet and reviewer Amal El-Mohtar was asked to name the first book that had a profound impact on her. After giving its title and author – *The Hobbit* by J. R. R. Tolkien – El-Mohtar set out some of the ways in which Tolkien's work had changed her personal horizons of expectation:

> I read it when I was seven years old, and in addition to an engaging, delightful story full of riddles and poems that I could memorize and set to music, it gave me a methodology for becoming a writer. Somewhere in that first copy was a biographical note that explained Tolkien began writing poetry, then moved into short stories, then novels. I thought, "Oh, that's how you become a writer," and set about doing the same thing.[1]

El-Mohtar characterises *The Hobbit* as welcoming and enabling. Reading Tolkien led her to feel that she could participate meaningfully in the world of the work and that guided by its example she might aspire to produce something that could inspire others in turn. *The Hobbit* was not simply a book El-Mohtar read and then put down; it was

[1] Lily Philpott, 'The Pen Ten: An Interview with Amal El-Mohtar', *PEN America*, 19 December 2019, https://pen.org/pen-ten-interview-amal-el-mohtar/.

one that stayed with her and helped her to achieve things she might not otherwise have attempted.

While the facilitative quality El-Mohtar describes is not universal in or unique to works of Fantasy, the testimonies of Fantasy creators and audiences demonstrate that it manifests strongly in many of the genre's most cherished works. These works operate to build lineages and communities that collaborate to celebrate, extend, modify and improve fantasies they care about. A work of Fantasy rarely proclaims, 'I am a thing of such scouring and terrible exactitude that you can scarcely conceive of the shadowy possibility of making anything like me.' Instead, fantasies often include generous tools for further production, providing means for fostering growth, change and development. The interactions with *The Hobbit* El-Mohtar describes are not those of passive admiration; instead, it was a book in which she felt she had the power to intervene, learning by doing so ways of making something new.

The things learnt from interactions like these can be transferred into very different contexts. While El-Mohtar claims that reading Tolkien was a formative experience, nothing she has published thus far is all that similar to *The Hobbit* in any straightforward sense. Her Hugo and Nebula award-winning short story 'Seasons of Glass and Iron' (2016) is in the tradition of the critical fairy tale, resonating with writers such as Terri Windling, Angela Carter and Kelly Link. 'The Truth About Owls' (2015) centres on a character who loves language as Tolkien did, but its examinations of refugee uprootedness and tentative, conflicted self-fashioning are profoundly different from those in Tolkien's legendarium. Her spies-to-kaleidoscopic-lovers novella *This is How You Lose the Time War*

(2019), written in partnership with Max Gladstone, mashes up espionage thriller, epistolary romance, parallel universes, time travel and rebellious desire to create a narrative that is irresistibly itself, but which has only minor resonances with Tolkien's worlds.[2]

To say this is not to deny Tolkien's influence on El-Mohtar, but rather to encourage us to think of forms of influence that go beyond the formal and iterative kinds discussed earlier in this book. The principal value of *The Hobbit* for El-Mohtar was not that it showed her how to write things exactly like itself, but rather that it demonstrated how writing could be deployed in ways that made storytelling matter intensely. As El-Mohtar puts it in an earlier interview, discussing the power of the fantastic:

> I think that telling a story and being told a story are inherently magical acts. When we tell a story, we are changing the world, forcing it to conform to a narrative that is not there until we make it; when we hear a story, we are ourselves being changed as that narrative enters us, and changed again as it leaves us. To use such a profoundly powerful act only mimetically seems to me painfully limiting and mundane. It is amazing that we tell stories; why not tell amazing stories? My interest in the genre definitely began with Tolkien. I read *The Hobbit* when I was seven, and fell completely in love with Tolkien's world, with the ache the songs in that world shook out of me. I wanted my world to be magical the way his was.[3]

[2] At a stretch, perhaps, a conflict between technological and arboreal forces, although Red's Commandant is considerably further through the tech tree than Saruman, and the Garden's motivations as Blue presents them are rather different from those of the ents.

[3] Dominik Parisien, 'An Interview with Amal El-Mohtar', *Postscript to Darkness*, 19 December 2013, https://bit.ly/3GWVQ7q.

The most important thing that El-Mohtar learned from Tolkien was a deep respect for the ways that stories in general – and works of Fantasy in particular – can reveal new worlds of possibilities. A shared belief in this inspirational potential is one of the main things that unites the creators and communities that gather around works of Fantasy to make all manner of things – fan fiction, fan art, cosplay, conventions, games, websites, music, magazines, criticism, memories, affiliations, dissentions, maps, memes and a great deal more besides. This final chapter addresses this wild creativity through exploring the social nature of Fantasy, arguing that the ways in which fantasies and their stakeholders foster an approachable, facilitative and collaborative ethos comprise one of the genre's most important and neglected contributions.

El-Mohtar is far from the only Fantasy creator who feels that they were taught by earlier fantasists. Those working in genre are often happy to position themselves amidst networks of other creatives. In his acknowledgements to *Perdido Street Station* (2000), China Miéville writes that he wants 'to mention two [writers] whose work is a constant source of inspiration and astonishment. Therefore to M. John Harrison, and to the memory of Mervyn Peake, my humble and heartfelt gratitude. I could never have written this book without them.'[4] In a similar vein, Alan Moore has written that Mervyn Peake's Gormenghast novels 'were probably the first books where I began to understand just what you could do with writing: how he could conjure this entire complex environment and these almost fluorescent characters that

[4] China Miéville, *Perdido Street Station* (London: Pan, 2011), p. [viii].

stayed in your mind for ever'.[5] Rather than feeling intimidated by the talents of writers they admired, Miéville and Moore found fantasies that fired them to produce their own innovations. Engagements with the works of others taught them techniques that helped them express both the things inside their heads and the notions and counter-notions latent in the cultures in which they were invested.

Following the chain forward, Neil Gaiman records a more pragmatic mode of instruction a fellow author offered him. He writes that he could never figure out how to get a story onto a comics page until he found out 'by asking someone who wrote comics (it was Alan Moore—one of the best writers ever to work in this medium) and getting him to show me what a script looked like, and how it was laid out. This he did, on one side of notebook paper.'[6] This passage is part of an introduction to one of Gaiman's own comic scripts, printed at the back of *The Sandman: Dream Country* (1991). Gaiman carefully acknowledges the roles his co-creators played in fleshing out the script's skeleton notions, but he displays the bones in the hope they might help others see what lies at the core of comics storytelling as he approaches it. He describes this gesture as offering a glimpse behind the curtain. This was clearly valued by readers; several further scripts were included in later versions of the collected *Sandman*. For those who wanted to go further, Gaiman and Moore both provided glowing endorsements for

[5] Sam Leith, '*Watchmen* Author Alan Moore: 'I'm definitely done with comics'', *The Guardian*, 7 October 2022, https://bit.ly/40lbVL4.

[6] Neil Gaiman et al., *The Sandman*, Volume 3: *Dream Country* (New York: Vertigo/DC Comics, 1995), p. [116].

Scott McCloud's *Understanding Comics* (1993). Gaiman, who is credited in the book for 'editorial advice and selective ego-trimming', described it as opening a 'dialogue on and about what comics are and, more importantly, what comics can be'. Moore claimed that it had 'taken breathtaking leaps towards establishing a critical language that the comic art form can work with and build upon in the future'.[7] Both Moore and Gaiman position the flowering of a language for talking about comics as an important catalyst, seeing the development of a critical vocabulary as part of the iterative work of bringing people together to make meaningful art. While individual and irreducible particularities are involved in fashioning fantasies, creators commonly recognise that many techniques of making can helpfully be discussed and passed on.

A willingness to speak relatively openly and non-prescriptively about process is something that characterises a considerable number of Fantasy authors. An extreme example of this tendency is Gene Wolfe's *The Castle of the Otter* (1982): a whole book that reflects on the process of writing and publishing *The Book of the New Sun* (1980–3). *The Castle of the Otter* is named for an unfortunate (or fortunate?) garbling in *Locus* magazine's announcement for the fourth volume of the tetralogy, *The Citadel of the Autarch* (1983). In his opening essay, Wolfe admits that writing a book about writing other books is a quixotic and somewhat egotistical thing to do, but he quickly provides an explanation:

[7] First edition: Scott McCloud, *Understanding Comics: The Invisible Art* (Northampton, MA: Kitchen Sink Press, 1993). Endorsements as given on various editions and archived on McCloud's website: www.scottmccloud.com/2-print/1-uc/index.html.

> Why do it, then? Out of a sort of blind optimism. Every writer worth his two-cents-a-word hopes, in some little corner of his mind at least, that somewhere out there, there are a few people who will do more than read his book, pitch it away, and reach for the next one—people who will read and reread, study the cover, perhaps in search of some clue, shelve the book and later take it out again, just to hold. There was a time when I could put my hand flat on the front of a tattered paperback called *The Dying Earth* and feel the magic seeping through the cardboard. Turjan of Miir, Liane the Wayfarer, T'sais, Chun the Unavoidable. Nobody I knew had so much as heard of that book, but I knew it was the finest book in the world.[8]

For Wolfe, it was Jack Vance's stories of the Dying Earth, rather than Tolkien or Peake, that revealed the stakes of good Fantasy writing, but the language of inspiration he employs is similar in spirit to that used by Miéville and El-Mohtar. Wolfe found in Vance a lavish stimulus for his imagination. *The Castle of the Otter* seeks to provide a similar kind of facilitative stimulus for others, letting readers into the arcana of stories that Wolfe hopes will fire others' creativity as Vance once fired his.

Wolfe's book is wide-ranging and generous in its inclusions. Some of his essays explore world-building, reflecting on the process of choosing appropriate language, on the forming of names and on why the societies depicted in his tetralogy would still use cavalry despite other technologies being available to them. As its title hints, Wolfe's tone is generally more puckish in *The Castle of the Otter* than in *The Book of the New Sun* itself. Several of the essays

[8] Gene Wolfe, 'The Feast of St Catherine', in *The Castle of the Otter*, in *Castle of Days* (New York: Orb, 1992), pp. 211–16 (p. 211).

provide opportunities for writing exercises that play with characters in ways that the original novels would have found it difficult to incorporate. In one such essay, provoked by his son's complaint that the book does not include enough funny bits, Wolfe imagines how each of the major characters from *The Book of the New Sun* might tell a joke. Some of the jokes are good. Some of them, in keeping with the characters of their tellers, are something else.

The Castle of the Otter also draws back the curtain on the practicalities of being a Fantasy writer in the 1980s. Wolfe discusses his job at *Plant Engineering* magazine, appreciating the ways that it gets him out of the house, makes his writing time precious and provides a secure income. He describes his exchanges with his agent and his publisher (conducted by mail and telephone) and the process of negotiating contracts. He writes about the networks of writers, fans and editors in which he was embedded. In an essay on 'The Rewards of Authorship', he uses a question-and-answer format to give candid, slightly grumpy practical advice on writing courses, specialist programmes, teaching, getting an agent and attending conventions. He provides postal addresses for the Science Fiction Writers of America, World SF and the Authors' Guild. He discusses the arcane implications of the Thor Power Tool Decision for the publishing industry's warehousing practices, highlighting how the pulpy consequences of this legal judgement might affect aspiring authors. Through this shop talk, he seeks to demystify the processes of authorship, just as other parts of the book reveal some of the ways he has worked to craft his writing. Wolfe clearly has strong opinions, but he presents them precisely as opinions. *The Castle of the Otter* is not a how-to guide, demurring from telling its audience exactly what to think. Rather, it is a book that converses with its reader, sharing knowledge, tricks and seeds of enjoyment.

Wolfe's book is a strange and singular thing, but Wolfe is far from alone among Fantasy authors in offering valuable insights into creative processes. Jeff VanderMeer's *Wonderbook* (2013) presents itself more explicitly as a guide for those who aspire to write imaginative fiction, but the guidance it provides is deliberately playful and polyvocal. The book presents the main body of its advice as contingent, setting it alongside alternative viewpoints from both whimsical characters and a diverse range of other writers, including Joe Abercrombie, Rikki Ducornet, Gaiman, Karen Lord, George R. R. Martin, Nnedi Okorafor and Catherynne M. Valente. Like Wolfe, *Wonderbook* seems keen to avoid straightforward didacticism, defending the value of play and experimentation and instantiating these values in its own form. The key attributes for supporting the imagination that VanderMeer proposes – curiosity, receptivity, passion and immediacy – all relate to maintaining kinds of openness he sees as essential for genuine creativity. On curiosity, for example, he writes:

Nothing is more essential to a writer than sustaining an inquisitive nature—being actively interested in the world and the people in it. Curiosity reflects a willingness to be disappointed in a search for knowledge. Curiosity sends out a series of queries that exist for their own sake. [...] The gathering of information—of textures, of anecdotes, of smells, of histories—should be non-judgemental and find pleasure in seemingly disparate, often contradictory elements. From the fusion of the elements comes an essential aspect of creativity. Curiosity is in a sense allied with qualities such as cleverness and with random collection—like a pack rat that accumulates buttons and bottle caps and scraps of paper without caring about the source of such items.[9]

Taking promiscuous joy in words, places and things is at the heart of VanderMeer's approach. He values the unexpected, the surreal and the serendipitous encounter. Consequently, his guide seeks to assist his readers by creating the circumstances for surprising and revealing defamiliarisations. When discussing fictional forms, he animates different kinds of prose as bizarre creatures, describing the short story as an agile life form 'combining dexterity and depth' and the novel as 'the megafauna of the literary world', with an integrity that leaves it subject to 'permanent skeletal and muscular damage' if it is broken up without care into shorter books.[10] Using his novel *Finch* (2009) as an example, he conjures a spectrum of possible beginnings to show how he selected the one he thought best for achieving the effects he sought. He does this to stress the particular importance of openings for guiding readers into a story's world:

A good piece of fiction teaches the reader how to read the narrative from the first paragraph. Think of the beginning as a kind of beneficial restriction or restraint. [...] By the very nature of how words work, the reader cannot receive all of the possible information at once. The limited field of vision means

[9] Jeff VanderMeer, *Wonderbook: The Illustrated Guide to Creating Imaginative Fiction* (New York: Abrams, 2013), p. 13.
[10] VanderMeer, *Wonderbook*, p. 43.

> that what is visible—and invisible—defines the story, and, sometimes, the *type* of story. And the more your story diverges from reality, the more important it is to get those words right, because you are reimagining The Real in the reader's head.[11]

For VanderMeer, creating Fantasy is about choosing to see the world in different ways, playing with ideas, techniques and concepts in a process of trial, error and informed refashioning that seeks to communicate to others a particular and unusual way of perceiving. VanderMeer recognises that such transmissions can often be glitchy and unpredictable. Nevertheless, he argues passionately for the value of experimentation and for channelling such experimentation through forms of craft and refinement that can be developed through practice and in dialogue with others.

Craft is an important concept for many Fantasy creators, discussed in an ever-expanding range of forms, including books, articles, interviews, courses, director's commentaries, blogs, forum posts and serial audio. 2022 saw a monthly podcast series, *Crafting with Ursula*, in which David Naimon discusses Ursula K. Le Guin's works with twelve different writers, each of whom reflects on how aspects of Le Guin's practice inform and resonate with their own.[12] The podcast title acknowledges that 'craft' is one of Le Guin's favourite words for thinking about creation and change-making: a word important both within her stories and in the ethos of the field in

[11] VanderMeer, *Wonderbook*, p. 75.

[12] David Naimon and guests, *Crafting with Ursula*, 12 episodes, *Tin House*, 2022, https://tinhouse.com/th_podcast_cat/crafting-with-ursula/.

which she was embedded. Magic in the Earthsea books is frequently described as a craft. Ged learns 'honest craft' from the witch of Ten Alders, and a wider range of magecraft at the School on Roke.[13] Craft later becomes a key part of his vocabulary of value. Bemoaning the ruin of one of the dyers of Lorbanery by the blight on magic in *The Farthest Shore* (1972), he describes her as having been 'a woman of art and skill, using her craft for the making of the beautiful'.[14] When describing the entanglement of essential things to Yarrow, his friend Vetch's younger sister, craft is one of the key terms Ged reaches for: 'Years and distances, stars and candles, water and wind and wizardry, the craft in a man's hand and the wisdom in a tree's root: they all arise together.'[15] Craft in Earthsea entwines practical and ethical knowledge about how to do things well. This knowledge is learnt and refined through painstaking practice and hard experience, underpinning the kinds of magic that Ged particularly cherishes once he is over his youthful dreams of easy glory.

In valuing craft in this way, Ged reflects his maker. In *Steering the Craft* (1998; revised 2015), Le Guin insists on the importance of developing a keen awareness of different elements and techniques of writing, practising these to find out the multifarious ways in which they can work. While she believes keenly in the power of art, she insists that this can be reached for more reliably by building up a toolkit of skills:

[13] Ursula K. Le Guin, *A Wizard of Earthsea* (London: Puffin, 1971), p. 16.
[14] Ursula K. Le Guin, *The Farthest Shore* (London: Puffin, 1974), p. 97.
[15] Le Guin, *Wizard of Earthsea*, p. 182.

A skill is something you know how to do. Skill in writing frees you to write what you want to write. It may also show you what you want to write. Craft enables art.

There's luck in art. And there's the gift. You can't earn that. But you can learn skill, you can earn it. You can learn to deserve your gift.

I'm not going to discuss writing as self-expression, as therapy, or as spiritual adventure. It can be these things, but first of all – and in the end, too – it is an art, a craft, a making. And that is the joy of it.[16]

Le Guin's insistence that writing Fantasy combines an author's personal perspective with craft forms that can be learnt crystallises the positions expressed by the other Fantasy writers we have been discussing. Fantasy creators balance a belief in the transcendent power of good Fantasy with asserting that this power is not the inscrutable property of a special few, but rather something that Fantasy traditions and communities can help many to wield.

In the chapter so far, I have been arguing that the experience of learning from books (or films or games) that proactively share some of the mysteries of their construction has fostered a Fantasy culture within which debts are often acknowledged freely and in which it is relatively common for practitioners to communicate generously regarding their methods and techniques. In highlighting forms of sharing and openness, I have been writing against conflictual models of literary inspiration

[16] Ursula K. Le Guin, *Steering the Craft: A Twenty-First Century Guide to Sailing the Sea of Story*, revised edition (Boston, MA, and New York: Mariner Books, 2015), p. xiii.

that seek to restrict the credit for genuine creativity to a special few. One of the most famous of these models is Harold Bloom's unabashedly elitist argument about artistic greatness, expressed most powerfully in *The Anxiety of Influence* (1973):

> Poetic history, in this book's argument, is held to be indistinguishable from poetic influence, since strong poets make that history by misreading one another, so as to clear imaginative space for themselves.
>
> My concern is only with strong poets, major figures with the persistence to wrestle with their strong precursors, even to the death. Weaker talents idolise; figures of capable imagination appropriate for themselves. But nothing is got for nothing, and self-appropriation involves the immense anxieties of indebtedness, for what strong maker desires the realisation that he has failed to create himself?[17]

For Bloom – unlike El-Mohtar, Miéville or Wolfe – the works of past authors represent a blocking force that must be broken through or aggressively negotiated to establish an identity of one's own. His framing his argument in terms of strength and weakness and his gendering his 'strong maker' as male speak to the ways in which conservative notions of individual genius propagate a competitive model of culture in which a small number of dominant figures win out, monopolising through doing so what could in other paradigms be conceptualised as a discursive, facilitative space.

Bloom's later book *The Western Canon* (1994) doubles down on this position, seeing great writers as being

[17] Harold Bloom, *The Anxiety of Influence: A Theory of Poetry*, 2nd edition (Oxford: Oxford University Press, 1997), p. 5.

quintessentially different, characterised by aesthetic qualities to which he repeatedly refers, but which he rarely really defines. He sees the authors he calls canonical as functioning necessarily to exclude other writers from their company. Similarly, he believes many readers are likely to recoil from canonical works, writing that 'The strongest poetry is cognitively and imaginatively too difficult to be read deeply by more than a relative few of any social class, gender, race, or ethnic origin.'[18] Bloom appreciated a good number of writers of the fantastic, including in his list of great twentieth-century works fictions by Jorge Luis Borges, Mikhail Bulgakov, Italo Calvino, John Crowley, Ursula Le Guin, Gabriel García Márquez, Mervyn Peake and Amos Tutuola, among others (although notably not Tolkien, whose *Lord of the Rings* he elsewhere called 'inflated, over-written, tendentious, and moralistic in the extreme' and whose style he found 'stiff, false, archaic, overwrought, and finally a real hinderance').[19] However, for Bloom, writers of the fantastic should be valued for their having successfully wrestled with and broken free of tradition. His model has little room for the liberating delight that many of these authors describe when they talk about how the works of their precursors showed them ways to begin and grow.

I dwell on Harold Bloom not because his ideas are now widely accepted in the strong forms in which he articulated them, but because his position represents an extreme

[18] Harold Bloom, *The Western Canon: The Books and School of the Ages* (London: Macmillan, 1995), p. 520.

[19] Harold Bloom, introduction to *J. R. R. Tolkien's The Lord of the Rings*, Bloom's Modern Critical Interpretations, new edition (New York: Infobase, 2008), pp. 1–2 (pp. 1, 2).

version of the ways that several dominant strands of twentieth-century literary studies sought to validate systems of artistic value. Bloom's arguments turn on the exceptional status of a few writers whose works are presented as superior aesthetic achievements and whose relationships to one another are represented as disputatious, rather than associative. He also presents a model of reading that is rather solitary – not, perhaps, in a way that is mournful in his terms, but which might be so in the terms of others. Modifying Gertrude Stein's assertion that 'one [writes] for oneself and for strangers', he contends that his Western Canon 'is there to be read by you and by strangers, so that you and those you will never meet can encounter authentic aesthetic power'.[20] Contra John Donne's assertion that 'No Man is an *Iland*, intire of itselfe; euery man is a peece of the *Continent*, a part of the *maine*', Bloom sees great works and writers as independent monuments, entire in themselves due to their successful struggles for originality, without any real need for others' care or collaboration.[21]

It is easy to see why this paradigm might be attractive to certain kinds of mind: it provides carte blanche to dismiss vast swathes of interesting and meaningful culture as long as proper attention is lavished on the right bits. However, it is equally easy to see that this approach is blinkered and exclusionary, creating a deceptive form of legibility through denying the complex range of things that actually influence writers: overwriting experiences, language,

[20] Bloom, *The Western Canon*, p. 36.

[21] John Donne, '17. Meditation', in *Devotions Upon Emergent Occasions* (London: Thomas Jones, 1624), pp. 410–19 (pp. 415–16).

forms, traditions, training and contingencies with a handful of figures of asserted importance. Despite its pretensions to authenticity and independence, Bloom's position remains irrevocably social. As John Guillory puts it, considering the ideas of Pierre Bourdieu, 'in fact "aesthetic value" is nothing more or other than cultural capital'.[22] In praising a small number of elite writers, Bloom seeks to concentrate credit in a small number of hands, including his own.

For me, the models of artistic community and collective curation emphasised in Fantasy culture present a far more attractive way of thinking about how art works for us than Bloom's monopolising paradigm. While there are Fantasy writers we might identify as being canonically central – Tolkien and Le Guin being the most obvious – these writers do not come into full meaningfulness if they are cut away from Fantasy culture as a whole. Fantasy's complex embeddedness in traditions and communities is one reason why it has often been critically neglected. Works of Fantasy are harder to wrench out of their contexts than works that seek to position themselves as Bloomian originals. Some Fantasy works present islands – Gont, Kalimdor, Laputa, Myst, Neverland, Númenor, Vvardenfell – but these islands are most revealing when considered in the context of the main.

While Fantasy canons can be (and often are) posited, a more flexible model based around traditions invested in playful transmission seems to me to fit the field better. Writers who like Fantasy tend to take delight in

[22] John Guillory, *Cultural Capital: The Problem of Literary Canon Formation* (Chicago, IL: University of Chicago Press, 1993), p. 332.

curious encounters and transformative re-encounters. Borges – who imagined both the endless branchings of the Garden of Forking Paths and the alluring and frustrating infinite shelves of the Library of Babel – returned again and again to the books he loved precisely because they transmuted him in different manners each time: 'I keep on reading the same books I read as a boy. Every time I read them they change. And they're changing me, of course.'[23] When asked what influenced her, Octavia E. Butler displayed a similar openness: 'All sorts of things influence me. I let things influence me. If they catch my interests I let them take hold.'[24] While Bloom imagines his poets as agony-struck, macho wrestlers who see ideas and forms claimed by others as threats to their own essential selfhoods, Borges and Butler are both radically open to being moved.

Genre writers often enjoy a form of what Jonathan Lethain calls the ecstasy of influence (a phrase lifted, with credit, from Richard Dienst). In an essay woven together from acknowledged quotations, Lethem lovingly twists his sources into an anti-Bloomian argument that we should understand art as a means of connection, rather than a form of distinction:

> does our appetite for creative vitality require the violence and exasperation of another avant-garde, with its wearisome killing-the-father imperatives, or might we be better off ratifying the *ecstasy of influence*—and deepening our willingness to

[23] Mark Childress and Charles McNair, '"I'll Be in Another World": A Rediscovered Interview with Jorge Luis Borges', *Los Angeles Review of Books*, 23 August 2021, https://bit.ly/3L9yXA9.

[24] Randall Kenan, 'An Interview with Octavia E. Butler', *Callaloo*, 14.2 (Spring 1991), 495–504 (p. 502).

understand the commonality and timelessness of the methods and motifs available to artists?[25]

Letham's view – as befits an author whose own work glories in generic mixing – is one that aligns pretty well with those of many Fantasy creators. While some Fantasy writers affect to conjure in splendid isolation, many locate themselves comfortably within fields of influence exerted by authors, works, lineages, tropes, fans and communities. Fantasy's methods and motifs are sometimes framed as timeless, but in practice they are time-bound in positive and constructive ways precisely because their commonalities allow them to be reworked and redefined through iterative practices of use.

Patterns of influence and iteration make the reading (or watching, or playing) of Fantasy an active process of engagement and recognition. In the fourth chapter, I discussed the tendency to dismiss readers of genre fiction as myopic, easily pleased or easily deceived. However, the stereotype of the uncritical, easily misled Fantasy reader is precisely that: a stereotype, and one belied by the intelligent and affecting forms of reflexivity that fantasies employ. Fantasy is a form that respects lovers of books and which is often extremely self-aware about its bookishness or, in the case of more recent forms, about its investments in communicative power of media. Fantasy makers know their audiences enjoy thinking creatively about intricacies and are prepared to trust them with considerable agency to interpret. John Crowley, the

[25] Jonathan Letham, 'The Ecstasy of Influence: A Plagiarism', *Harper's Magazine* (February 2007). Available online: https://bit.ly/3mJWyxT.

author of some of Bloom's favourite Fantasy novels, argues that interpolating alternatives to realism creates scope for readers to make active interpretive decisions of their own:

> the kind of fiction that always interested me is stuff that somehow manages to be convincingly actual—in the sense that you believe that truths are being told about the world you live in—and are also somehow connected to the imaginary in some way. If you read [Vladimir Nabokov's] *Pale Fire* you can think either it's a fantasy about some guy who once had a kingdom in some far-off land that he'd lost—or that he's crazy. Because of the way it's written, the book is not going to make that decision for you. I think that's great. I think that is in a certain sense the way the world works, and the way that fiction can model that feeling that there are other worlds, that there are parts of reality and actuality that we don't know.[26]

In Crowley's view, fantastic (im)possibilities evoke the joy of discovery in ways that sharpen imaginative and critical reflexes, rather than dulling them. Fantasies can be means of expressing things we find difficult to say more directly and precisely; we might think of fairy tales, which are often so much wilder and more ambiguous than their starchy moral appendages allow. Fantasies take pride in making their audiences think and interpret. Early in *A Game of Thrones* (1996), Tyrion Lannister tells Jon Snow that 'a mind needs books like a sword needs a whetstone, if it is to keep its edge'.[27] While books in

[26] Ed Halter, 'An Interview with John Crowley', *The Believer*, 62 (May 2009), www.thebeliever.net/an-interview-with-john-crowley/.

[27] George R. R. Martin, *A Game of Thrones* (London: Harper Voyager, 2011), p. 118.

Fantasy are not presented as being without their dangers, the idea that they can challenge and deepen us is a core truism in fantastic forms of representation.

Its investment in bookishness is an aspect of Fantasy's general optimism regarding the transformative, democratic potential of art. One of the attractions of Fantasy is the possibility of reading (or watching, or playing) something that seems to you to be striking and perfect and true, that captures you briefly in what Bloom calls 'the ecstasy of the privileged moment'.[28] However, Bloom leans in to the double-edged nature of the word 'privileged', arguing that such moments are exclusive delights for a gifted few. 'Reading deeply in the Canon will not make one a better or a worse person, a more useful or a more harmful citizen', he writes. 'The mind's dialogue with itself is not primarily a social reality.'[29] Fantasies often take a markedly different line on this issue, arguing that reading meaningfully changes readers and how they relate to the wider world. This might be seen as a rather utopian position, but it is one that reflects Fantasy's belief that stories can build connections as well as serving individuals.

An excellent rebuttal of the trope that Fantasy isolates and deludes can be found in Jo Walton's wonderful novel *Among Others* (2011). In Walton's story, reading Fantasy and Science Fiction helps the traumatised central character, Morgana, to establish a supportive network. There are moments where Morgana glories in Fantasy's ability to serve as a retreat. 'The thing about Tolkien, about *The*

[28] Bloom, *The Western Canon*, p. 446.
[29] Bloom, *The Western Canon*, p. 30.

Lord of the Rings', she enthuses, 'is that it's perfect. It's this whole world, this whole process of immersion, this journey. [...] Reading it changes everything.' However, Tolkien's book also serves as a fruitful means for creating relationships. It formed part of the secret language Morgana shared with her sister, and its relative ubiquity means it can serve as a lingua franca that allows her to establish new friendships. As her appreciation continues, other voices enter in conversation: 'It has everything. (Except lust, Daniel said. But it has *Wormtongue*.)'[30] Morgana certainly wants the experience of being submerged in story, but she wants this for others, as well as for herself. 'When I grow up,' she writes, 'I would like to write something that someone could read sitting on a bench on a day that isn't all that warm and they could sit reading it and totally forget where they were or what time it was so they were more inside the book than inside their own head. I'd like to write like [Samuel R.] Delany or [Robert] Heinlein or Le Guin.'[31] Books for Morgana are about transmission as well as rapture. They can provide practical ideals. She borrows the language she needs for framing the close-knit group of companions she longs to build from Kurt Vonnegut's simultaneously absurdist and deeply serious faux-religion Bokononism, from *Cat's Cradle* (1963). The word *karass* provides a shape for her desires, letting her parlay her love of speculative fiction into a nurturing network of friends. For Morgana, traffic with literature is not one-way, but a form of mutual

[30] Jo Walton, *Among Others* (New York: Tor, 2011), pp. 103, 104.
[31] Walton, *Among Others*, p. 32.

sustaining. 'If you love books enough', she comes to believe, 'books will love you back.'[32]

Bookishness in Fantasy is commonly portrayed as an admirable or lovable quality: more so than in most literary fiction, which often depicts readers and writers as self-absorbed or ineffectual. Fantasy is a genre of emancipated readers, in which books empower people – and often particularly women – to change their worlds. Sometimes bookish Fantasy characters are notionally secondary to a heroic central figure, as is the case with Rupert Giles and Willow Rosenberg in *Buffy the Vampire Slayer* (1997–2003) or Hermione Granger in the Harry Potter universe. However, it is telling that these characters are among those most beloved in their works' respective fandoms, in part because their bookish cleverness enables them to work out what is going on and plan effectively to turn circumstances towards better outcomes. In many works of Fantasy, a propensity for reading is a sign of a powerful latent ability. In Roald Dahl's *Matilda* (1988), the central character's precocious consumption of books is a portent of energies which when they lack other channels eventually result in her developing telekinesis. The public library is Matilda's main source of joy: 'books transported her into new worlds and introduced her to amazing people who lived exciting lives. [. . .] She travelled all over the world while sitting in her little room in an English village.'[33] Matilda's library is one of many bookish places in Fantasy that serve to nurture the imaginations of characters and readers simultaneously – we might also

[32] Walton, *Among Others*, p. 300.

[33] Roald Dahl, *Matilda* (London: Puffin, 2022), pp. 21–2.

think of the Library of the Clayr in Garth Nix's *Lirael* (2001), the library of the Unseen University at the heart of Terry Pratchett's Discworld (1983–2015), the library of the Dreaming in Gaiman's *Sandman* (1989–96), the Great Library of Palanthas in Margaret Weis and Tracy Hickman's Dragonlance universe (1984–), Scott Hawkins' *The Library at Mount Char* (2015), the Archives of the University in Patrick Rothfuss's Kingkiller Chronicle (2007–), and many more. Some of these libraries are welcoming, some forbidding, some sinister, but their shelves and keepers commonly manifest the great potential for transformation that Fantasy sees as residing in books.

One of the fullest endorsements of active reading in Fantasy is Michael Ende's *The Neverending Story* (1979), which begins with a bookshop in which Bastian Balthazar Bux finds the ideal book: one that first inspires him, then responds to him, then consumes him, before finally helping him to find himself again, allowing him to emerge from the story as a kinder, wiser person. Ende offers Bastian's overwhelming passion for stories as the reason why he succumbs to an irresistible temptation to steal from Carl Conrad Coreander's shop:

> *If you have never spent whole afternoons with burning ears and rumpled hair, forgetting the world around you over a book, forgetting cold and hunger –*
>
> *If you have never read secretly under the bedclothes with a flashlight, because your father or mother or some other well-meaning person has switched off the lamp on the plausible ground that it was time to sleep because you had to get up so early –*
>
> *If you have never wept bitter tears because a wonderful story has come to an end and you must take your leave of the characters with whom you have shared so many adventures, whom you have loved and*

admired, for whom you have hoped and feared, and without whose company life seems empty and meaningless –

If such things have not been part of your own experience, you probably won't understand what Bastian did next.[34]

Bastian, like Walton's Morgana, loves the comforts and certainties books offer in part because of the difficulties he faces in other areas of his life. He is dealing with bullying, his sadness after the death of his mother and his father's depression. However, Ende is not interested in presenting a young saint, and Bastian's journey is largely about realising that while books represent an opportunity to judge and be judged differently, engaging with them requires a combination of openness, generosity and discernment. In the first part of the novel, Bastian eagerly devours the story, following Atreyu's quest without fully realising that he is its destination. His self-loathing initially prevents him from taking a role in the narrative, despite the increasingly heavy hints that he is able to do so. Once he is eventually transported into Fantastica, he goes too far in the other direction, with his unwise wishes wreaking havoc both on the realm and on himself. What eventually saves him is the rapport he built up with Atreyu and the potential for benevolence in the storyworld. As in *Among Others*, books prove to be capable of loving their readers back.

As his book's title implies, Ende sees stories not as closed and finite but as presences that continue to live in those who have dwelt with them. At the end of the story, Mr Coreander makes it clear that the magic of books

34 Michael Ende, *The Neverending Story* (London: Puffin, 2014), pp. 8–9.

extends widely: '*There are other such magical books. A lot of people read them without noticing. It all depends on who lays hands on the book.*' In this assertion, Coreander represents attentive readers as an elite group in a way not dissimilar to Bloom. However, he also suggests that books can serve as catalysts for creating friendships, asking Bastian to stop by and share his story: '*I'd appreciate it if you dropped in to see me now and then. We could exchange experiences. There aren't many people one can discuss these things with.*'[35] Coreander's request evokes fannish connections between those who feel particularly deeply that certain kinds of stories have helped form their identities. There are hints of gatekeeping exclusivity, but these sentences also offer an implicit invitation to readers to return to *The Neverending Story* and share its pleasures.

In *The Neverending Story*, the Childlike Empress holds power within Fantastica, but her continuing existence is fundamentally dependent on the linguistic powers of others. This reflects a larger pattern in Fantasy: its tendency to add caveats to the authority of single authors. While works of Fantasy commonly fetishise invention, this is often configured as a collaborative process in which figures who would be considered passive audiences in other paradigms play active creative roles, as Bastian does when called upon to give the Childlike Empress a new name. It is very common in works of Fantasy for written authorities to be incomplete and for supposedly definitive prophecies to go awry. When this happens, it is left to interpreters to choose how to make meanings. In G. Willow Wilson's *The Bird King* (2020), Vikram the

[35] Ende, *The Neverending Story*, p. 510.

Vampire, aiding the consort Fatima and the map-maker Hassan in their flight from the Alhambra, argues that the meanings we make from books are highly reliant on what we bring to them:

> Once a story leaves the hands of its author, it belongs to the reader. And the reader may see any number of things, conflicting things, contradictory things. The author goes silent. If what he *intended* mattered so very much, there would be no need for inquisitions and schisms and wars. But he is silent, silent. The author of the poem is silent, the author of the world is silent. We are left with no intentions but our own.[36]

In this passage, Vikram rehearses in a minor key part of the argument of Roland Barthes's essay 'The Death of the Author', which considers a cultural work to be 'a multi-dimensional space in which a variety of writings, none of them original, blend and clash. The text is a tissue of quotations drawn from the innumerable centres of culture.'[37] For Barthes, this is a liberating prospect. Rather than being unchanging verities, texts live differently in each reader, or in the mind of the same reader at different times, as was the case for Borges when he revisited his childhood reading and found that it had changed. The author's silence is the space in which stories can mutate and flourish. Different states of mind allow for strange new forms of haunting to emerge. Bloom – no friend to Barthes's approaches – nevertheless writes of rereading John Milton's *Paradise Lost* (1667) while trying

[36] G. Willow Wilson, *The Bird King* (London: Grove, 2020), p. 159.

[37] Roland Barthes, 'The Death of the Author', in *Image Music Text*, translated by Stephen Heath (London: Fontana, 1977), pp. 142–8 (p. 146).

to dismiss his existing preconceptions. This experience left him 'curiously shocked, a little alienated, and yet fearfully absorbed [. . .] the peculiar impression it gave me was what I generally ascribe to literary fantasy or science fiction, not to heroic epic'.[38] If Bloom had followed that sense further, he might have argued that the stuff of stories is more malleable, contextual, communal and reader-driven than closed canons readily admit. He might also have been able to drive forward further with the thought that for open-minded readers, the encounter with any text often takes on the liberating air of the fantastic (Figure 6.1).

Many modern forms of Fantasy are avowedly collaborative. Comics are often made by small teams; TV series and films have crews of tens or hundreds or thousands; and while great video games can be made by single individuals, creating the complex gloss of a AAA release or sustaining a massively multiplayer online game (MMO) requires the work of hundreds over numerous years. For many Fantasy forms, therefore, focusing on a single author is deeply deceptive, and something creators themselves often play down. Matthew Mercer – Dungeon Master for *Critical Role* (2015–), the most high-profile *Dungeons & Dragons* livestream, and the person who initially created the world of Exandria – is keen to deny any suggestion that his word should be first and last. In a recorded roundtable session, he described his attitude thus:

[38] Bloom, *The Western Canon*, p. 26.

FIGURE 6.1 One of Gustave Doré's fantastical illustrations for an 1866 edition of John Milton's *Paradise Lost*, blending beasts, birds, waves and light.
Culture Club/Bridgeman via Getty Images.

I despise the auteur theory of world building and creation, in film in general, but in this instance, the idea that one person is the author of a space and kind of domineers over what's right and what's wrong with that. This was, once again, all created kind of out of accident [. . .] nothing has been more fun and more exciting than watching it grow beyond me. I feel like as a person who's not a parent, this is the closest thing I have to a child, is this world. And watching other people become family to it as well, and adding and developing it in their own way, it's really special.[39]

For Mercer, the principal pleasure of having created a Fantasy world is the opportunity to develop it in concert with others. This is something that the role-playing between Mercer and his players naturally allows for, with dice, improvisations and personal quirks shaping the course of Exandria along with plots, plans and conventions. However, as its success has grown, *Critical Role* has extended to incorporate fan collaborations, distinctly different campaigns, a wide range of guest players, other creators running games, artbooks, maps, comics, rulebooks, novels, an animated series, a production studio, a publishing company and a charitable foundation. Mercer's trademark question for his players is 'How do you want to do this?' This has become a form of branding, but it is also a question that fantasies in general often ask as they seek to draw others in to participate in the shaping of works and communities. It is a question that the fans of *Critical Role* have responded to enthusiastically through art, organisation, fashion and feedback (Figure 6.2).

Critical Role is a success story built on digital modes of distribution and connection, but the ways it seeks to

39 Critical Role, 'Game Masters of Exandria Roundtable', *YouTube.com*, 29 June 2022, www.youtube.com/watch?v=LmZSWKPXhZ4, 28:43–29:28. Fan produced transcript available here: https://bit.ly/40KZR66.

Figure 6.2 An excellent cosplay of Vox Machina's Percy (Percival Fredrickstein von Musel Klossowski de Rolo III) from the first *Critical Role* campaign, as worn at New York Comic Con 2022. Alexi Rosenfeld via Getty Images.

empower its audiences have longstanding precedents, displaying consonances with the changing attitudes Clifford Siskin discerns in eighteenth-century print culture. Siskin argues that print culture sought to normalise the technology of writing by both celebrating its power and encouraging people to try to wield it. Discussing the proliferation of periodicals, he writes that 'writing induced a fundamental change in readers—leading them to behave as writers—which, in turn, induced more writing'.[40] Siskin is thinking both of the increasing range of publication venues available and of formal inclusions like letters pages that allowed a broader – although still fairly limited – range of people to see themselves in print. There is a considerable distance between the world Siskin describes and the fan art galleries *Critical Role* screens during its episode breaks or cosplay competitions at conventions, but there are also continuities in the ways that media and communities create spaces through which audiences can become actively involved.

It is not unreasonable to think of the development of genre communities in the twentieth and twenty-first centuries through mass media, fan culture and digital publishing as a vast expansion of the trends and forms that Siskin observed. The story of early-twentieth-century Fantasy and Science Fiction – particularly in the United States – is tied up tightly with the proliferation of magazines, many of which included letters pages in which fans could be included alongside authors they

[40] Clifford Siskin, *The Work of Writing: Literature and Social Change in Britain 1700–1830* (Baltimore, MD: Johns Hopkins University Press, 1998), p. 4.

admired. Alongside professional publications, fanzines quickly came to form an important part of genre culture, recognised by a Hugo Awards category stretching back to 1955. Many writers and artists who became established professionals honed their skills in fan media. In an account of the shaping influence of his early fannish enthusiasms, Roger Ebert asserts that it was 'in the virtual world of science fiction fandom that I started to learn to be a writer and a critic.' Ebert enthuses passionately about interpretive communities that negotiated their standards through letters of comment ('locs'): 'the currency of payment for fanzine contributors; you wrote, and in the next issue got to read about what you had written'. He also argues that the fan culture of the 1950s and 1960s prefigured the rise of the internet:

> we were online before there was online. It is perfectly obvious to me that fanzines were web pages before there was a web, and locs were message threads and bulletin boards before there was cyberspace. Someday an academic will write a study proving that the style, tone, and much of the language of the online world developed in a direct linear fashion from science fiction fandom —not to mention the unorthodox incorporation of ersatz letters and numbers in spelling, later to influence the naming of computer companies and programs. Fanzines acted uncannily like mimeographed versions of Usenet groups, forums, message boards, and web pages—even to such universal design strategies as IYGTFUI (If You've Got the Font, Use It).[41]

[41] Roger Ebert, 'How Propeller-Heads, BNFs, Sercon Geeks, Newbies, Recovering GAFIAtors, and Kids in the Basements Invented the World Wide Web, All Except for the Delivery System', *Asimov's Science Fiction*, 29.1 (2005), 12–17.

While the internet has made genre culture vastly more visible and has hugely reduced barriers to entry, Ebert is right to point out that its conventions arose out of older forms of fannish communication, which it iterated upon and diversified. The written letters and essays Ebert lauds have been joined by author sites, forum threads, review blogs, podcasts, social media and video essays. The limited space of the fanzine page has been expanded into vast digital repositories through which millions of participants can share their stories, artwork and opinions.

Like many stakeholders in art, fans seek both to find spaces for their selves and ideals amidst a constellation of cultural works and to engage with the existences and values of others. The visibility and interconnectedness of modern fan spaces has provided new opportunities for disrupting and renegotiating power relations between creators, publishers, owners and consumers. At a relatively early stage in the roll-out of the internet, Henry Jenkins saw radical potential in how fan writers were reclaiming and reconfiguring cultural works. For Jenkins, this represented the revivification of an older paradigm in which narratives were the shared property of communities, rather than intellectual property to be exploited by those with the status to exert control: 'If you go back, the key stories we told ourselves were stories that were important to everyone and belonged to everyone. [. . .] Fan fiction is a way of the culture repairing the damage done in a system where contemporary myths are owned by corporations instead of owned by the folk.'[42]

[42] Henry Jenkins, quoted in Amy Harmon, 'In TV's Dull Summer Days, Plots Take Wing on the Net', *New York Times*, 18 August 1997, https://bit.ly/3LbZoa3.

More recently, Abigail De Kosnik has considered how fans work together to build rogue digital archives, arguing that these act to 'democratize cultural memory' by expanding in myriad directions on texts that are often grounded in Fantasy.[43] Drawing on Jacques Derrida's sense that democracy must inherently be multiple, De Kosnik argues that online communities let those who have traditionally had little access to the microphones of culture stake their representational claims:

> a great many of the people who take licence with copyrighted cultural products are women and children. As media fans, women and children and queer-identifying people and people of color and people in the Global South and others who have not always been guaranteed enfranchisement, politically or culturally, feel drawn to take liberties, to see what they can do with what they are given. [. . .] [W]e might say that their attention to realizing the potential for multicoloredness and variability in common cultural texts is linked to a "curiosity" about the potential woven into the very concept of democracy for changeability, transformability, recombination.[44]

Prior to the internet, large parts of the audiences for media were generally invisible to creators and to each other. However, in contemporary genre culture, the sorts of personal, creative and critical interrelations that Ebert celebrated have moved decisively into more open fora, allowing for greater participation, coordination, fractiousness and accountability. Fan communities are rarely entirely placid – potential for aggressive gatekeeping and

[43] Abigail De Kosnik, *Rogue Archives: Digital Cultural Memory and Media Fandom* (Cambridge, MA: MIT Press, 2016), p. 2.

[44] De Kosnik, *Rogue Archives*, p. 312.

personal abuse inheres in the kinds of passionate investment they invite – but their visibility and vibrancy make it sharply apparent how fantasies might better serve and reflect the diverse audiences who care deeply about them.

One of the major custodians of fan materials that De Kosnik discusses is the Organization for Transformative Works (OTW). The OTW maintains a range of different meeting places for fans to share their art and reflect on fannish communities. Its largest site, *Archive of Our Own* (*AO3*), contained over ten million fanworks at the end of 2022; its other projects include the *Fanlore* wiki, which contains a crowdsourced history of fandom's conversations, and the open-access scholarly journal *Transformative Works and Cultures.* In maintaining these sites, the OTW espouses a politics along the lines that Jenkins imagined. Its purpose is to support the right to expand upon and modify stories, rather than simply to consume them, arguing that artworks should be seen as an openly available commons that fans can draw from and return things to:

> We envision a future in which all fannish works are recognized as legal and transformative and are accepted as a legitimate creative activity. We are proactive and innovative in protecting and defending our work from commercial exploitation and legal challenge. We preserve our fannish economy, values, and creative expression by protecting and nurturing our fellow fans, our work, our commentary, our history, and our identity while providing the broadest possible access to fannish activity for all fans.[45]

[45] Landing Page, *Organization for Transformative Works*, www.transformativeworks.org/.

The OTW's position is set against traditional kinds of originality claims and the proprietary authority these are commonly invoked to assert. By claiming that culture operates best as a commons or a gift economy, the OTW looks to emancipate fans from feeling that their work is irredeemably secondary. Instead, it argues that everyone should be free to build upon and reconfigure the stories in which they are invested, bringing into play individual perspectives, shared forms and community practices that create new forms of interest and value.

Many of the works that stimulate the most committed fan activity involve Fantasy, in part because Fantasy's iterative techniques and tendency to world-build serve as spurs to creative engagement. A work's general popularity has some bearing on whether it accumulates a fandom, but this is not the principal determining factor. Fan activity thrives on gaps, loose ends and things to rework and subvert. Consequently, fantasies that provoke audiences to imagine how possibilities that are hinted at or denied might play out often foster intense engagement from fans, who extrapolate from what is represented and posit alternatives to it. Tolkien's expansive world-building and the paucity of romance in his world presented both challenges and opportunities for many early online fic (fan fiction) writers inspired by Peter Jackson's film trilogy, and Middle-earth remains an enduringly popular world to develop. The timing of Harry Potter's emergence and its nature as a series that grew up with a key part of its audience conspired to create a massive fan-fictional footprint, stretching from predictive works written in the gaps between the books as they were released to increasingly baroque explorations of romance pairings to vast

Marauders fics focused on the Hogwarts experiences of Harry's parents' generation. Both within individual works and collectively, fan writers have traced back characters encountered relatively briefly as adults in J. K. Rowling's series and fleshed out small references and allusions into a complex chain of branches and possibilities. The scale of fan production often dwarfs the works it draws from. The seven Harry Potter books are collectively around 1.1 million words in length. On *AO3*, there are several individual fics longer than the original series, and counting only Potter fics longer than 100,000 words (less than 2 per cent of those archived) would see the total world count sail easily north of a billion. As Siskin wrote, writing induces more writing as new voices seek to join the conversation. Nor is writing the only kind of proliferation possible through modern media. The emergence of YouTube created the conditions for the enormous success of Team StarKid's *A Very Potter Musical* (2009), originally a student production performed at the University of Michigan but, once posted online, a worldwide phenomenon that spawned two direct sequels, a decade-long series of parody musicals and a whole series of productions inspired by the original (Figure 6.3). The common ground provided by Harry Potter thus provided fertile soil for hundreds of thousands to turn their hands to Fantasy.

Much fan fiction works around the texts it builds upon, either through filling gaps in the original narrative or through positing itself as an alternative universe. Fan fiction can also directly challenge or overwrite, as happened when a substantial section of the Harry Potter fandom rejected the epilogue to the final book and as

FIGURE 6.3 High school students in Texas perform *A Very Potter Musical*, a parody originally created by StarKid Productions (Music and Lyrics: Darren Criss and A. J. Holmes; Book: Matt Lang, Nick Lang and Brian Holden).

occurs routinely when individuals and groups of shippers radically reconfigure the series' web of romances.[46] However, fic's forms of overwriting are less literal than those employed by modders who modify video games' code to make environments more to their liking. The purposes of mods are many and various. Most make quite small adjustments, such as tweaking systems to improve the notional realism of a game's world, adjusting numbers to create new challenges for experienced players or splicing in parts of another property to create surreal juxtapositions. Some have grander ambitions, attempting

[46] A 'ship' (abbreviated from 'relationship') is a romance pairing. The word is also used as a verb and to describe a fannish position – shippers ship pairs of characters.

to realise the potential of games compromised by performance issues on their original releases. Those enraptured by the high points of *Vampire: The Masquerade – Bloodlines* (2004) have worked over many years to improve Troika's ambitious but buggy attempt to bring the beloved roleplaying setting to digital life. The unofficial patch modders have assembled is almost essential for allowing parts of the game to function; it also expands the original by completing cut content latent in the game files and adding new material created by the game's community. While the unofficial *Bloodlines* mod has essentially become the game, other mods are acts of revivification or transformation, turning games into different ones. The *Skywind* mod seeks to recreate the bizarre world of *The Elder Scrolls III: Morrowind* (2002) in the more up-to-date engine of *The Elder Scrolls V: Skyrim* (2011). Thousands of hours have been poured into this act of loving homage by modders keen both to test their skills and to have the chance to start afresh in a place they care about deeply. The mod's team write that they are 'working to renew Vvardenfell's beauty and barbarity, its alien terrains and its mistrustful occupants, its myriad stories, its jealous gods, and its long-fated reborn hero'.[47] While *Skywind* looks back, other total conversion mods work to transform the genre and assumptions of the game on which they iterate. The *Fall From Heaven II* overhaul mod for *Civilization IV* (2005) revamps many of the game's core systems to create a Fantasy world richer and stranger than the original game can accommodate, adding in magic and heroes and warping existing systems to new purposes.

[47] 'What is Skywind?', *TESRSkywind.com*, https://tesrskywind.com/.

Religions in unmodified *Civilization IV* are almost interchangeable. In *Fall From Heaven II*, aligning your civilisation with the Fellowship of Leaves allows a realm's forests to acquire ancient powers, while spreading the tenets of the Ashen Veil mechanically hastens Armageddon, causing hellish terrain to spread and encouraging demonic forces to intrude.

Whole genres of modern games have emerged from modding scenes. *Defence of the Ancients*, a community-created mod for Blizzard's real-time strategy game *Warcraft III: Reign of Chaos* (2002), went on to spawn an entire genre of multiplayer online battle arena games (MOBAs), including two of the most successful esports, *Dota 2* (2013–) and *League of Legends* (2009–). While these games have deliberately swerved away from the world of *Warcraft III* as they have developed, building their own extensive lore, it is still possible to trace many of their champions back to their roots as units in Blizzard's setting.

Modding also facilitates smaller-scale connections. In 2010, Terry Pratchett sent a fan message to Emma, a modder for *The Elder Scrolls IV: Oblivion* (2006), who had developed a companion character called Vilja who he particularly enjoyed. This led to a collaboration in which Pratchett would suggest features and dialogue that let Vilja provide players with new opportunities for peaceful and mischievous interactions. To help support Pratchett in continuing to play *Oblivion* as his Alzheimer's worsened, Emma and her collaborator Charles Cooley added a function that let Vilja guide the player out of dungeons. The collaboration flourished based on a shared desire to deepen the character and render *Oblivion* richer and more enjoyable. As Emma put it in an interview, 'It would be totally unfair to say that I was helping him – he was helping and inspiring me all the time, and I think we both had a lot of fun with figuring out new things for Vilja to say and do.[48] In interactions like this, fantasies provide spaces for people to meet and cooperate, engaging in exchanges of craft that bring mutual delight.

Modding and fan fiction both arise from an impulse to improve something a community cares about, either by expanding it so there is more to love or by reworking it to make it more accommodating to a community's values and requirements. In his book on convergence culture, Henry Jenkins writes that he sees work like this as one of fan culture's most valuable contributions:

> As a utopian, I want to identify possibilities within our culture that might lead towards a better, more just society. My experiences as a fan have changed how I think about media politics, helping me to look for and promote unrealized potentials rather than reject out of hand anything that doesn't rise to my standards. Fandom, after all, is born of a balance between fascination and frustration: if media content didn't fascinate us, there would be no desire to engage with it; but if it didn't frustrate us on some level, there would be no drive to rewrite or remake it.[49]

In this passage, Jenkins highlights how his perspective shifted from one in which he tended to see cultural works

[48] Cian Maher, 'The Story behind the Oblivion Mod Terry Pratchett Worked On', *Eurogamer*, 31 January 2019, https://bit.ly/41lQ87j.

[49] Henry Jenkins, *Convergence Culture: Where Old and New Media Meet*, updated edition (New York: New York University Press, 2008), p. 258.

as completed things to a more process-driven understanding. The love fans feel for the works they engage with is far from blind; instead, fan communities' deep investment positions them to identify flaws and oversights and to work individually and collectively to address these.

While Jenkins examines the balance between fascination and frustration in modern fan culture specifically, the process he describes is part of the engine of genre culture more broadly. In a 2013 blog post, Patricia A. McKillip gave an account of her formative influences that makes clear both how much joy and wisdom she drew from her youthful reading and how she learned to address older works' exclusions in her own writing:

> I grew into reading during the 1950's and the 1960's. I was very lucky to have an older sister who also loved to read. We shared books, comments, and literary allusions from an early age; we stole each other's books, like *The Once and Future King*, when there was only one copy and we couldn't wait for the other to get done with it. Gradually, sometime in our early teenage years, as we read Dumas, Stevenson, Kipling, etc., we both realized we had come up against what was then a commonplace of storytelling: the men had all the adventures. The women only appeared on the last page of the novel to receive a chaste kiss when the hero finally returned from the sea, from exotic lands, from foreign courts, fairytale kingdoms, and the Foreign Legion, to her.
>
> I studied English Literature in the late 60's and early 70's, because I thought the best way to learn to write was to read the best writers I could find. At least 95% of what I read to get my Master's degree was written from a male point of view. (This was before Women's Studies and World Literature came into their own.) I read a great deal and learned a lot about

writing from writers as diverse as William Faulkner, P.G. Wodehouse and J.R.R. Tolkien. But when I sat down to write my first major fantasy, *The Forgotten Beasts of Eld*, I didn't question the point of view that came out of my pen. It seemed very natural to me to wonder why in the world a woman couldn't be a witch or a wizard, or why, if she did, she had to be virginal as well. Or why, if she was powerful and not a virgin, she was probably the evil force the male hero had to overcome. Such was my experience reading about women in fantasy, back then.

So I wrote from the point of view of a powerful female wizard, who, even after she married, was the hero of her own story, and whose decisions, for better and for worse, were her own.[50]

The value of McKillip's new perspective was recognised when *The Forgotten Beasts of Eld* (1974) won the inaugural World Fantasy Award for Best Novel, and her works have continued to be highly regarded by Fantasy readers both for their questioning and for their commitment. Her stories are often quietly subversive, but without making this their only purpose. In a post in which she remembers McKillip by gathering some of her words, Terri Windling recalls McKillip writing that 'Fantasy changes with the changing times, and yet it is still the oldest kind of tale in the world, for it began once upon a time, and we haven't heard the end of it yet.'[51] McKillip clearly sees herself as part of a tradition, but also knows that she has things to add to it, working as a fan of older authors, but also as

50 Patricia A. McKillip, 'Women in SF&F', *Fantasy Cafe*, 15 April 2013, https://bit.ly/3mPKfQQ.

51 Quoted in Terri Windling, 'The Luminous Worlds of Patricia McKillip', *Myth & Moor*, 17 May 2022, www.terriwindling.com/blog/2022/05/pat-mckillip.html.

someone in a position to address the limitations of the works she admires, providing through doing so new tools and inspirations for other Fantasy creators.

One of McKillip's main innovations has been to find ways of writing complex characters without resorting to stark conflicts or artificial tensions. As Julie E. Czerneda puts it, 'Her protagonists are sensible, kind, respectful people.'[52] While earlier works such as the Riddle-Master Trilogy (1976–9) have some roots in Tolkienian fantasy, McKillip seeks to move away from heroic clashes between a clearly delineated light and dark. The principal protagonist of the Riddle-Master Trilogy's first and third books, Prince Morgon, is cleverer with words than with a sword. While conflicts swirl in the world he journeys through, he seeks to solve and understand them, reconsidering his preconceptions through doing so. As Brian Attebery writes, Morgon's 'division of the world into good and evil camps increasingly breaks down as he finds elements of both qualities in himself and his seeming enemies'.[53]

In her later works, McKillip moves even further from the conventional tropes of epic. Considering *The Bards of Bone Plain* (2010), Attebery explores how 'characters and reader are misled by habits of thought' to expect magic to sit far from the common realities of the story's modern day, and to anticipate a climax that takes the form of a conflict against the reimposition of old powers.[54] Instead,

[52] Julie E. Czerneda, 'I Write Fantasy Because of Patricia McKillip's *The Riddlemaster of Hed*', *Tor.com*, 24 September 2021, https://bit.ly/41Fcosj.

[53] Brian Attebery, *Fantasy: How it Works* (Oxford: Oxford University Press, 2022), p. 71.

[54] Attebery, *Fantasy*, p. 72.

McKillip weaves magic through everyday manifestations in language, designs, old buildings and traditions: a synthesis characters come to recognise they have always valued. In *Alphabet of Thorn* (2004), a similar subversion of standard crises occurs. Initially, the spectre of violence seems to haunt the text. Rebellious opponents of the young Queen of Raine are gathering their forces within the Twelve Crowns; simultaneously, research conducted by one of the protagonists uncovers and reifies a threat of unexpected invasion across time and space. However, the narrative principally focuses on the interpersonal relationships formed and sustained within the Royal Library of Raine, the palace above and the nearby Floating School. The ways that people care for each other and for their vocations are given especial narrative weight, a weight that the shape of the story works to validate. At the book's conclusion, a central character's mysterious parentage places them in a position through which they could obtain vast temporal power. However, this character – who has come to like their world as it is – refuses the proffered opportunity. The novel lets its readers understand and empathise with a choice that contradicts the usual logics of epic Fantasy, but which is entirely in keeping with McKillip's more nuanced notions of what is valuable and rewarding.

McKillip's works implicitly critique standard ways of writing Fantasy narratives, developing an alternative style that grew and changed as she continued to experiment. McKillip tended to write standalones, but for writers who return to the same worlds, processes of growth and change can require more explicit forms of engagement. One of Le Guin's many admirable qualities was her ability to modify her worlds in ways that maintained their integrity while addressing earlier oversights. Revisiting the world of *The Left Hand of Darkness* (1969), Le Guin obliquely accepted criticisms levelled by contemporaries including Joanna Russ of her use of male pronouns as the default for her Gethenian characters, who can take on both genders, but who are for most of the month sexually latent androgynes. When interviewed in 2001, she asserted that *The Left Hand of Darkness* 'gives the reader very little opportunity to experience being double-gendered [. . .] Back in 1968, I and most readers needed Genly Ai's [point of view] to mediate the strangeness. I don't think we do, now.'[55] Her later story 'Coming of Age in Karhide' (1995) seems to address Russ's criticism that in the original novel 'child-rearing is left completely in the dark', as well as engaging with some of Russ's points about the surprising conventionality of certain structures of feeling in Gethen's cultures.[56] Le Guin does not disclaim the original book as a failure, but neither does she insist on its perfection in all respects. Instead, she makes her imagined world richer, realer and stranger in light of further reflection.

In a similar fashion, Le Guin boldly reworked her original conception of Earthsea in *Tehanu* (1990), *The Other Wind* (2001) and her later short stories set in the

55 Nick Gevers, 'Driven by a Different Chauffeur: An Interview with Ursula K. Le Guin', *SF Site*, November/December 2001, www.sfsite.com/03a/ul123.htm.

56 Joanna Russ, 'The Image of Women in Science Fiction', in *Images of Women in Fiction: Feminist Perspectives*, ed. by Susan Koppelman Cornillon (Bowling Green, OH: Bowling Green University Popular Press, 1972), pp. 79–94 (p. 90).

world. The three Earthsea books from the late 1960s and early 1970s are brief wonders, deliberately seeking to challenge many of the Fantasy conventions that were standard at the time. Rather than being a continent suspiciously like Europe, Earthsea is an archipelago of many islands inhabited principally by dark-skinned characters. The exceptions in the first book are the Kargs – 'savage people, white-skinned, yellowhaired, and fierce, liking the sight of blood and the smell of burning towns' – although Le Guin nuances this portrayal within the span of *A Wizard of Earthsea* and complicates it further in *The Tombs of Atuan* (1970).[57] While all three books feature journeys with goals, none of them play out as straightforward quests – *Tombs* perhaps comes closest, but Tenar's perspective makes Ged's search for the Ring of Erreth-Akbe a secondary concern. Like McKillip, Le Guin obviously loves Fantasy, but in a clear-eyed manner that allows her to see how she might tweak its affordances and conventions to tell subtle stories of her own.

However, as she reconsidered her Earthsea books in the 1980s, Le Guin came to see them as being in some respects lacking. In 'Earthsea Revisioned' (1992), she testifies to the power and allure of tradition, but also to its potential to constrain:

> The beauty of your own tradition is that it carries you. It flies, and you ride it. Indeed, it's hard not to let it carry you, for it's older and bigger and wiser than you are. It frames your thinking and puts winged words in your mouth. If you refuse to ride, you have to stumble along on your own two feet; if you try to speak your own

[57] Le Guin, *Wizard of Earthsea*, p. 17.

wisdom, you lose that wonderful fluency. You feel like a foreigner in your own country, amazed and troubled by the things you see, not sure of the way, not able to speak with authority.[58]

For Le Guin, the biggest oversight in her original three Earthsea books was accepting the paradigm of male heroism when creating her wizards, with women's magic being perceived folk-culturally on Gont as 'weak' and 'wicked'.[59] When she returned to Earthsea, Le Guin sought to remedy this by thematising the marginalisation of women's magic as resulting from a particular historical prejudice, causing an imbalance that must be rectified for Earthsea fully to prosper. The tools she found for addressing this imbalance were dragons, which are – like traditions – both highly determined and infinitely reconfigurable. As Le Guin puts it, 'The dragon is the stranger, the Other, the not-human: a wild spirit, dangerous, winged, which escapes and destroys the artificial order of oppression. The dragon is the familiar also—our own imagining, a speaking spirit, wise, winged, which imagines a new order of freedom.'[60]

Le Guin was acutely conscious that she was taking a risk by trying to find new ways of telling stories within Earthsea, but she believed this risk to be utterly necessary. In concluding her essay, she deliberately stages her doubt and vulnerability:

When I was writing *Tehanu*, I didn't know where the story was going. I held on, held my breath, closed both eyes, sure I was

[58] Ursula K. Le Guin, 'Earthsea Revisioned', in *The Books of Earthsea* (London: Gollancz, 2018), pp. 981–92 (pp. 983–4).
[59] Le Guin, *Wizard of Earthsea*, p. 15.
[60] Le Guin, 'Earthsea Revisioned', p. 991.

falling. But wings upheld me, and when I dared look, I saw a new world, or maybe only gulfs of sunlit air. The book insisted that it be written outdoors, in the sunlight and the open air. When autumn came and it wasn't done, still it would be written out of doors, so I sat in a coat and scarf, and the rain dripped off the verandah roof, and I flew. If some of the wild freedom of that flight is in the book, that's enough; that's how I wanted, as an old woman, to leave my beloved islands of Earthsea. I didn't want to leave Ged and Tenar and their dragon-child safe. I wanted to leave them free.[61]

Le Guin recognised that what she was doing was trickier than going with the flow of established traditions, with their male-centric biases, but also realised that her values and her position as a respected writer conferred an obligation to use her craft to push back the boundaries of representation in Fantasy, making the world of Earthsea more like the one in which she would wish to live.

In recent years, many Fantasy creators have been thinking carefully about traditions' blind spots and collaborating to address these, both in their own works and through providing guides and reflections. Nisi Shawl and Cynthia Ward's 2005 book *Writing the Other* is explicitly designed to encourage authors to 'learn how to think and write about characters who aren't like you'. The seeds of the book were sown by a comment in a workshop that Shawl and Ward participated in from a writer who felt that 'it was a mistake to write about people of different ethnicities: you might get it wrong'.[62] Shawl and Ward

[61] Le Guin, 'Earthsea Revisioned', p. 992.
[62] Nisi Shawl and Cynthia Ward, *Writing the Other: A Practical Approach* (Seattle, WA: Aqueduct Press, 2005), p. 4.

understand this anxiety, but argue that to give in to it is an abdication of responsibility that forecloses the opportunity to learn. Their advice combines practical strategies and words of encouragement with a sense that working carefully with prose is one of the best means for recognising and addressing biases:

> To think something unpleasant, or to say or publish something thoughtless or uninformed, does not make you now and forever a racist, a sexist, a homophobe, or a garden-variety bigot.
>
> Writing is *considered* speech. It gives you the opportunity to rewrite and revise.[63]

For Shawl and Ward, genre writing should be a productive place to experiment with unwriting our prejudices. Shawl argues that 'as writers it's our job to continually know more', and that those cautious about putting a foot wrong should nevertheless seek to 'welcome the Beautiful Strangers. Don't be afraid to make mistakes with them. Do your best, and you'll avoid the biggest mistake of them all: exclusion.'[64]

Exclusion, of course, is a mistake that has already been made in manners that are encoded in the Fantasy genre's dominant defaults. The increasing interconnectedness of creators and communities has highlighted how forms of representation that many have taken to be neutral or reasonable are in fact loaded and exclusionary. Debates in this area are necessarily ongoing as Fantasy communities change, but they have been marked in recent years

63 Shawl and Ward, *Writing the Other*, p. 8.

64 Nisi Shawl, 'Beautiful Strangers: Transracial Writing for the Sincere', in Nisi Shawl and Cynthia Ward, *Writing the Other: A Practical Approach* (Seattle, WA: Aqueduct Press, 2005), pp. 73–81 (p. 81).

by particular flashpoints. One example is RaceFail, the 2009 controversy described diplomatically by N. K. Jemisin as 'a several-months-long conversation about race in the context of science fiction and fantasy that sprawled across the blogosphere'.[65] While Jemisin's 2010 retrospective blog post recognised RaceFail's bruising effects, she considered it ultimately to have been necessary and worthwhile, creating the momentum for positive change:

> The way I see it, RaceFail was the big thaw for the SFF field. Fans of color, and white fans who were tired of the old ways, literally heated things up with an outpouring of long-pent rage. That fury was *utterly necessary*, because it shocked the whole genre enough to make it pay attention. Without that, SFF would have remained resistant—frozen—against such radical ideas as *why are all these futuristic stories full of white people, when they're already a minority on the planet now?* and *y'know, maybe erasing the brown people from your fantasy continent, or making them allegorical orcs, is a bad idea.*[66]

Ten years later, it is clear that RaceFail and similar conversations have helped to transform how fantasies have been written and valued. Jemisin's unprecedented sequence of Hugo Award wins for the Broken Earth trilogy has been taken as a key sign of change, but her works are part of a larger groundswell seeking to broaden Fantasy out from its medievalist defaults. Writers such as C. L. Clark, Aliette de Bodard, Naseem Jamnia, Fonda Lee, Rebecca Roanhorse, Tasha Suri and Kai Ashante

[65] There is a detailed crowdsourced account on the *Fanlore* wiki: https://fanlore.org/wiki/RaceFail_%2709.

[66] N. K. Jemisin, 'Why I Think RaceFail Was The Bestest Thing Evar for SFF', *nkjemisin.com*, 18 January 2010, https://bit.ly/3mHvteH.

Wilson (along with many others) have brought cultures and forms of experience into Fantasy that have made it vastly richer. New publications and series have been established to broaden the range of voices in Fantasy's conversations. *Samovar*, published by *Strange Horizons*, showcases and promotes translated works and *FIYAH* both publishes and supports speculative fiction by Black creators. Tor.com's highly successful novellas programme has deliberately sought to highlight writing from under-represented populations that veers away from familiar worlds. Fantasy fans and creators have not only displayed an appetite for change but have worked hard to transfigure existing spaces and nurture new ones. As Nalo Hopkinson has put it, 'Fandom is not exempt from the kind of wrongheadedness that humans display every day. But when fans conspire to do a good thing, it is most well done indeed, with verve and enthusiasm.'[67]

Fan culture's changing desires and increasing sophistication have had transformative effects on core Fantasy properties. *Dungeons & Dragons* was developed from the conventions of tabletop war-gaming, and its quintessential 1970s adventures were dungeon crawls in which the party progressed through rooms, dealt with traps, defeated monsters they felt no qualms about slaughtering and gathered conveniently placed treasures: a form of play that inspired board games including *Talisman* (1983) and *HeroQuest* (1989). However, the increasing complexity of Fantasy world-building; the nuancing and development of

[67] Nalo Hopkinson, 'A Reluctant Ambassador from the Planet of Midnight', *Journal of the Fantastic in the Arts*, 21.3 (2010), 339–50 (p. 348).

roleplaying as a form; and the highly visible example of actual play streams, which tend to privilege conversations and interactions over combat for its own sake, have all acted to modify players' core assumptions about what they want from their games. Responding to the *D&D* community in 2020, Wizards of the Coast made a public commitment to inclusivity:

> One of the explicit design goals of 5th edition D&D is to depict humanity in all its beautiful diversity by depicting characters who represent an array of ethnicities, gender identities, sexual orientations, and beliefs. We want everyone to feel at home around the game table and to see positive reflections of themselves within our products.[68]

Statements of this kind have been made about *D&D* before, but in rather different tones. In the Foreword to the 1978 *Advanced Dungeons & Dragons Players Handbook*, Games and Rules Manager Mike Carr described the game's community thus:

> **D&D** players, happily, come in all shapes and sizes, and even a fair number of women are counted among those who regularly play the game—making **DUNGEONS & DRAGONS** somewhat special in this regard. The widespread appeal cuts across many boundaries of interest and background, which means that **D&D** players are marked by a wide range of diversity. In fact, one could easily use the analogy that there are as many *types* of **D&D** players as there are **D&D** monsters[.][69]

[68] Wizards of the Coast, 'Diversity and Dungeons & Dragons', *dnd.wizards.com*, 17 June 2020, https://dnd.wizards.com/news/diversity-and-dnd.

[69] Mike Carr, foreword to Gary Gygax et al., *Advanced Dungeons & Dragons Players Handbook* (Lake Geneva, WI: TSR, 1978), p. 2.

Carr's statement is well intentioned, but it is also complacent, arguing implicitly that *D&D* is already as inclusive as it needs to be. That this was not the case is demonstrated by the gatekeeping argument that *D&D* is special for having female players and by the rather ill-advised analogy between players and monsters. By contrast, the 2020 Wizards of the Coast statement is positioned as part of a continuing dialogue. It commits to substantive change, promising to rework the lore of orcs and drow, both of which have been presented as 'monstrous and evil, using descriptions that are painfully reminiscent of how real-world ethnic groups have been and continue to be denigrated'. In addition, it commits to a new understanding of the relationship between creators and players, in which *Dungeons & Dragons* is seen as a work in progress, developing in dialogue as its stakeholders change: 'That's at the heart of our work—listening to the community, learning what brings you joy, and doing everything we can to provide it in every one of our books.'

Wizards of the Coast obviously has commercial incentives as well as ethical and creative ones for seeking to align its views with *D&D*'s fan base. Nevertheless, alignment remains a worthwhile aspiration that recognises that Fantasy and its audience are continually changing, creating opportunities for new forms of storytelling to join the old. In the recent *D&D* sourcebook *Journeys through the Radiant Citadel* (2022), the central Fantasy city provides a very different gateway from the traditional tavern meeting:

> Against the unending mist and unseen terrors of the Ethereal Plane, the Radiant Citadel stands bright as a bastion of

> hope. It's a living relic of the ingenuity and collaboration of twenty-seven great civilizations. Abandoned and lost for ages, the Citadel was resurrected from its slumber and reclaimed by descendants of those societies, though some peoples remain missing. The city serves as a nexus of diplomacy and trade, a repository of history and secrets, and a thriving sanctuary for those seeking a better life.
>
> [. . .]
>
> Heroes and paupers meet on equal footing in the Radiant Citadel. By common agreements, power and resources are equitably shared. Dignity is afforded to all, and great need is met with great aid.[70]

There is certainly something utopian about the Radiant Citadel – an avowedly collaborative endeavour that has recently been recovered to serve as an egalitarian concourse. As a starting point for adventure, it implies that victory is not to be won by a few plucky heroes overcoming the forces of darkness by force of arms, but rather through understanding histories, negotiating difference and upholding democratic values. In the course of play, the setting can swerve in all sorts of directions, but as presented, it serves as a revealing correlative for contemporary Fantasy communities, in which creativity vests in disparate people coming together to exchange stories, ideas and dreams.

This is not, however, wholly new. While twenty-first century technologies have fundamentally changed the modes of connection available, Fantasy has long been a form fostered in communities. Moving from villagers

70 Ajit A. George, F. Wesley Schneider et al., *Journeys through the Radiant Citadel* (Renton, WA: Wizards of the Coast, 2022), p. 6.

gathered round the fire to tell their grandmothers' tales to podcasters and roleplaying groups is a leap, but one that speaks to the enduring shared currency of crafting narratives and worlds together. Even the Fantasy writers most likely to be exalted as independent geniuses created their works in harmony and disharmony with others. Writing on the Inklings, the Oxford-based circle gathered around C. S. Lewis and Tolkien, Diana Pavlac Glyer took pains to prove that earlier accounts that stressed members' relative independence from one another were inaccurate. For Glyer, their convivial (if sometimes grumpy) interactions were fundamental to the Inklings' work:

> the most common and natural expressions of creativity occur as part of an ongoing dialogue between writers, readers, texts, and contexts. This truth is exemplified by the weekly meetings of the Inklings. It is manifest in their relationships with family, friends, colleagues, and acquaintances. And it is expressed in many of their statements about the creative process. [. . .] Like filaments joined together in a web, writers work as members of larger communities.[71]

Fantasies can be strange and introverted forms that grow in part out of other fantasies. However, what is new in them arises from interactions both with and within the world, and what is valuable in them lies in the wisdom and delight that they synthesise and communicate for others to work with. Stories are nothing without people to care for them, and Fantasy, even more than other cultural forms, seeks to make its audiences into curators.

[71] Diana Pavlac Glyer, *The Company They Keep: C. S. Lewis and J. R. R. Tolkien as Writers in Community* (Kent, OH: Kent State University Press, 2007), p. 226.

Fantasy ultimately works and persists because it persuades people to care about it. Through changing, winding paths, it finds its communities. Even in the most famous cases, these paths can be peculiar ones. In a letter diligently responding to a reader's queries, Tolkien attributed the appearance of the book that made El-Mohtar into a writer to a quixotic chain of associations:

> *The Hobbit* saw the light and made my connexion with [Allen & Unwin] by an accident. It was not known except to my children and to my friend, C. S. Lewis; but I lent it to the Mother Superior of Cherwell Edge to amuse her while recovering from 'flu. It thus came to the notice of a young woman, a student resident in the house or the friend of one, who worked in A & U's office. Thus it passed to the eyes of Stanley Unwin, who tried it on his younger son Rayner, then a small boy. So it was published.[72]

This might seem a thin thread of chance to hang worldwide success upon, but the fact that this thread made its connections speaks to *The Hobbit*'s effectiveness as a work of Fantasy. Through lending his manuscript, Tolkien transformed his story into a gift. That gift flowered in the minds of others, who passed it on to share its pleasures, thus paving the way for Middle-earth to become part of what Tolkien himself might have called a road that goes ever on and on.

[72] Tolkien to Christopher Bretherton, 16 July 1964, Letter 257 in *The Letters of J. R. R. Tolkien*, ed. by Humphrey Carpenter (London: George Allen and Unwin, 1981), pp. 344–9 (p. 346).

Envoi

Opening this book, I contended that defining Fantasy precisely is a thorny proposition, but also one that in many ways misses the point. The introduction surveyed consensuses insofar as these exist while contending that examining what Fantasy does is ultimately more interesting and revealing than trying to draw lines around what it can be. I endorsed a broad-based approach that sees Fantasy as an assemblage of individuals, groups, cultures and ways of thinking, as well as an ever-growing body of texts and artworks.

In the six chapters, I have tried to put this approach into practice while exploring qualities of Fantasy that seem to me particularly important for its creators, audiences and communities. Much of the chapters' interest lies in the particularities of the works and situations they examine, but in closing, it seems worthwhile to distil what I perceive to be their principal contentions. A brief list drawing together the main propositions will serve both as a helpful summation and as a convenient taster for those with limited time. (There are, after all, many worthwhile ways to read beyond beginning at the beginning, going on till you come to the end and then stopping):[1]

1 The King of Hearts, in Lewis Carroll, *Alice's Adventures in Wonderland*, in *Alice's Adventures in Wonderland and Through the Looking-Glass*, ed. by Peter Hunt (Oxford: Oxford University Press, 2009), pp. 3–111 (p. 106).

1. Fantasy arises from languages' ability to represent things that have not happened or do not exist. ('Languages' here can be read as extending to visual representations as well as textual forms). Fantasies love to play with and question the creative potential of language, highlighting its power to generate connections, consensuses and beliefs, but also revealing its fractures, oversights and limitations.
2. Iteration is one of Fantasy's defining techniques. Fantasies take forms, ideas and materials from a shared commons and combine, rework and add to these to fashion new stories that can be iterated upon by others in turn. The iterative practices of fantasies can make them reflexive, engaged and accessible, although when iteration is employed without care, it can also lead to the perpetuation of lazy or harmful stereotypes.
3. Contemporary fantasies have their roots in some of the oldest modes of cultural circulation, including myths, legends, epics, romances and wonder tales. As the self-conscious heirs of such traditions, modern fantasies reanimate and refashion the symbols and patternings of earlier cultures so they can speak old and new truths in the present.
4. Works of Fantasy exist in dialogue with discourses of realism and rationality, mixing in realist and rationalist techniques while holding open spaces for alternative modes of apprehension and understanding. This makes Fantasy an important form for critiquing overreaching forms of Enlightenment systematisation and Romantic hubris, giving voices to those who dominant paradigms have marginalised and damaged.
5. World-building is the prevailing metaphor for discussing modern Fantasy. In practice, world-building is often

conducted in the service of developing characters or plots, relying on inference, suggestion and audience collaboration to provide an illusion of fullness. Nevertheless, the allure of building other worlds is a potent part of Fantasy's attraction, promising both space for individual autonomy and grounds for meaningful connection.

6. Fantasy commonly imagines itself as a form practised in communities, within which creators and audiences frequently switch positions. Rather than simply venerating great artists, Fantasy culture values dialogues about craft and representation that empower many voices to speak. While not immune to being considered as properties, fantasies are often best understood as gifts designed to foster shared understandings.

In keeping with my overall arguments about Fantasy's commitment to entanglement, there is a fair degree of overlap between these six propositions. Iteration comprises one of Fantasy's key modes of interaction with older works; it also underpins the conventions of world-building and resonates with Fantasy creators' investment in sharing their craft. Fantasy's fascination with the power and limits of language plays into its interest in iterating on past language use, its potential for questioning received truths and its knack for sparking dialogues within and between communities. It is no coincidence that fantastic stories are often particularly good at crossing cultural boundaries, their intertwinings of resonant specifics and common experiences comprising some of the most beloved narratives in world literatures.

The claims we can make for Fantasy are interdependent with those we make for other forms, although I would contend that Fantasy has its own identity that intersects with but also differs markedly from other modes and genres. While helping me refine a draft of the first chapter, my friend Robert Maslen remarked that several of the claims I make about Fantasy's alertness to the power of language could be made about literature in general. I think this is true, but also that Fantasy's investments are both intense and particular. Many people learn to love literature through Fantasy. It is in many respects the form of culture that believes most strongly in the wonder of culture itself, delighting in techniques of story-making and image-conjuring. Taking Fantasy seriously can help us better understand what it is that people value in art. The joy Fantasy takes in acknowledging other fantasies and in forms of unpretentious referentiality rebukes more monopolistic and controlling cultural modes that fetishise what they can claim as original. Similarly, the tools that Fantasy and its communities share and the readiness with which these are taken up suggest that people value artworks that welcome them as participants, rather than insisting on separation. Fantasy's generous, generative paradigms are not the only ones that create profound and valuable exchanges through art, but they are potent in ways that we could stand more fully to appreciate.

In an interview conducted at the end of the 1960s, Jorge Luis Borges was asked why he felt particularly drawn to the fantastic. In answering, he argued that while fantasies are not true in a documentary sense, they nevertheless capture deeply meaningful intellectual and emotional realities:

> I think things that we call fantastic may be real, in the sense of being real symbols. If I write a fantastic story, I'm not writing

something willful. On the contrary, I am writing something that stands for my feelings, or for my thoughts. So that, in a sense, a fantastic story is as real and perhaps more real than a mere circumstantial story. Because after all, circumstances come and go, and symbols remain. [...] If I write about a certain street corner in Buenos Aires, that street corner may pass away for all I know. But if I write about mazes, or about mirrors, or about the night, or about evil, and fear, those things are everlasting—I mean they will be always with us.[2]

For Borges, Fantasy is one of our most powerful means of communicating with each other across space and time about the mysteries we struggle with, using symbols through which we render these mysteries if not fully comprehensible, then at least frameable. Fantasy is concerned with making visible the patterns of how we think and feel, with creating shared spaces for communication, collaboration, transformation, critique, sub-creation and community. In Fantasy, common forms lead to uncommon ends. We all know what a wizard is, but a work of Fantasy will develop or subvert that shared understanding, making a particular wizard who will conjure for us in new ways. By beginning from what we share and casting off into impossible worlds, fantasies encourage us to collaborate in thinking differently. Through doing so, they make new realities that expand the possibilities of language, culture and understanding.

[2] Patricia Marx and John Simon, 'An Interview with Jorge Luis Borges: Reality Is Perplexing Enough', *Commonweal Magazine*, 25 October 1968, www.commonwealmagazine.org/interview-jorge-luis-borges.

ACKNOWLEDGEMENTS

This book is dedicated to my grandparents. One of my earliest memories is my grandfather and grandmother reading me *The Hobbit*; their love of books is one of the things that sparked my own love of doing things with words. It has been good to remember them while using the copies of *The Lord of the Rings* and the early Earthsea books they gave me to help write this book.

For sowing the seeds of this *Introduction*, I would like to thank Robert Macfarlane, who supervised my under-graduate dissertation on Fantasy, and Dominic Alessio, who invited me to teach a course on Fantasy literature while I was completing my doctorate. For helping to refine my understanding of Fantasy, I am very grateful to the Let's Enhance Reading Group, Glasgow's Centre for Fantasy and the Fantastic, our fabulous doctoral cohort at Glasgow and the exhibition team I have been working with at the British Library on *Fantasy: Realms of Imagination*. I am particularly grateful for conversations with Marita Arvaniti, Brian Attebery, Tim Barker, Matthew Barr, Francis Butterworth-Parr, Louise Creechan, Joseph Crawford, Matthew Creasy, Sarah Crofton, Maria Damkjær, Taylor Driggers, Gabriel Elvery, Dimitra Fimi, Rachel Foss, Emma French, Sophie Gosling, Lucinda Holdsworth, Kamran Hussain, Tanya Kirk, Jordan Kistler, Alice Jenkins, Oliver Langmead, Christopher Lynch Becherer, Meg MacDonald, Laura Martin, Robert

Maslen, Jon Mee, Katarina O'Dette, Dahlia Porter, Susan Reed, Danielle Schwertner, Mary Shannon, Adrian Streete, Will Tattersdill, Monica Vazquez, Rhys Williams, Hollie Willis and Grace Worm.

Many of the ideas in this book have been honed in dialogue with students on Glasgow's Fantasy MLitt programme: I'd like to thank the Canaries, the Phoenixes, the Ravens, the Merlins, the Owls, the Nightingales, the Sparrowhawks and the Nightjars, and particularly the students who took my 'Fantasy Across Media' course, which strongly influenced much of the discussion here.

At Cambridge University Press, Bethany Thomas and George Laver have been incredibly supportive; thank you for believing in this book, and for all your help in making it a reality. I am also very grateful to the production team, and particularly to Kilmeny MacBride for her meticulousness and care while completing the copy-edit.

Many thanks to the British Library, Lambeth Palace Library, the Peake Estate, Supergiant Games and Wizards of the Coast for granting me permission to reproduce images featured in the book. I would especially like to thank Brenna Lopes for the wonderful cover painting she has created.

SELECT BIBLIOGRAPHY

The following list covers works that are directly quoted or discussed at some length. All links were checked on 19 April 2023.

Addison, Joseph, *The Spectator*, No. 419 (1 July 1712).

Adorno, Theodor W. and Max Horkheimer, *Dialectic of Enlightenment*, translated by John Cumming (London: Verso, 1997).

Aldridge, Alfred Owen, *Voltaire and the Century of Light* (Princeton, NJ: Princeton University Press, 1975).

Alexander, Lloyd, 'High Fantasy and Heroic Romance', *The Horn Book*, 16 December 1971, www.hbook.com/story/high-fantasy-and-heroic-romance.

Arcane, created by Christian Linke, Alex Yee et al. (Fortiche/Riot Games, 2021–).

Attebery, Brian, *Fantasy: How it Works* (Oxford: Oxford University Press, 2022).

Stories about Stories: Fantasy and the Remaking of Myth (Oxford: Oxford University Press, 2014).

Strategies of Fantasy (Bloomington and Indianapolis: Indiana University Press, 1992).

Austen, Jane, *Northanger Abbey*, ed. by Barbara M. Benedict and Deirdre Le Faye (Cambridge: Cambridge University Press, 2006).

Avatar: The Last Airbender, created by Michael Dante DiMartino, Bryan Konietzko et al. (Nickelodeon Animation Studio, 2005–8).

Baldick, Chris, *The Oxford Dictionary of Literary Terms*, 4th edition (Oxford: Oxford University Press, 2015).

Balestrini, Nanni, *Tristano*, translated by Mike Harakis (London: Verso, 2014).

Barrie, J. M., *Peter and Wendy* (London: Hodder & Stoughton, 1911).

Barthes, Roland, 'The Blue Guide', translated by Annette Lavers, in *Mythologies* (London: Vintage, 2009), pp. 85–8.

'The Death of the Author', in *Image Music Text*, translated by Stephen Heath (London: Fontana, 1977), pp. 142–8.

'The Reality Effect', in *The Rustle of Language*, translated by Richard Howard (Berkeley: University of California Press, 1986), pp. 141–8.

Beck, Julie, 'What Fan Fiction Teaches that the Classroom Doesn't', *The Atlantic*, 1 October 2019, https://bit.ly/3A7AgJp.

Bierce, Ambrose, 'An Inhabitant of Carcosa', in *Tales of Soldiers and Civilians* (San Francisco: E. L. G. Steele, 1891), pp. 241–7.

Blake, William, *The Marriage of Heaven and Hell* ([London]: [William Blake], 1790).

Bloom, Harold, *The Anxiety of Influence: A Theory of Poetry*, 2nd edition (Oxford: Oxford University Press, 1997).

Introduction to *J. R. R. Tolkien's The Lord of the Rings*, Bloom's Modern Critical Interpretations, new edition (New York: Infobase, 2008), pp. 1–2.

The Western Canon: The Books and School of the Ages (London: Macmillan, 1995).

Borges, Jorge Luis, 'Tlön, Uqbar, Orbis Tertius', translated by James E. Irby, in *Labyrinths* (London: Penguin, 2000), pp. 27–43.

Bottigheimer, Ruth B., 'East Meets West: Hannā Diyāb and *The Thousand and One Nights*', *Marvels & Tales*, 28.2 (2014), 302–24.

Breton, André, 'Manifesto of Surrealism' (1924), in *Manifestoes of Surrealism*, translated by Richard Seaver and Helen R. Lane (Ann Arbor: University of Michigan Press, 1972), pp. 1–47.

Brooks, Terry, interview by TheOneRing.net, *TheOneRing.net*, 22 May 2000, https://bit.ly/30pgNS3.

'On the Trail of Tolkien', in *Sometimes the Magic Works: Lessons from a Writing Life* (London: Earthlight, 2003), pp. 185–94.

The Sword of Shannara (London: Orbit, 2006).

Buffy the Vampire Slayer, created by Joss Whedon et al. (Mutant Enemy Productions/Sandollar Television/Kuzui Enterprises/20th Century Fox Television, 1997–2003).

Bulgakov, Mikhail, *The Master and Margarita*, translated by Richard Pevear and Larissa Volokhonsky (New York: Penguin, 2016).

Bull, Emma, *War for the Oaks* (London: Penguin, 2016).

Burrow, Colin, *Imitating Authors: Plato to Futurity* (Oxford: Oxford University Press, 2019).

Butler, Octavia E., *Kindred* (Boston, MA: Beacon, 2004).

Campbell, Joseph, *The Hero with a Thousand Faces*, Bollingen Series 17, 3rd edition (Novato, CA: New World Library, 2008).

The Masks of God: Oriental Mythology (New York: Viking Press, 1962).

Carr, Mike, Foreword to Gary Gygax et al., *Advanced Dungeons & Dragons Players Handbook* (Lake Geneva, WI: TSR, 1978).

Carroll, Lewis, *Alice's Adventures in Wonderland*, in *Alice's Adventures in Wonderland and Through the Looking-Glass*, ed. by Peter Hunt (Oxford: Oxford University Press, 2009), pp. 3–111.

Through the Looking-Glass, and What Alice Found There (London: Macmillan, 1872).

Carter, Angela, 'The Bloody Chamber', in *The Bloody Chamber and Other Stories* (London: Vintage, 2006), pp. 1–42.

(ed.), *The Virago Book of Fairy Tales* (London: Virago, 1990).

Carter, Lin, *Imaginary Worlds: The Art of Fantasy* (New York: Ballantine Books, 1973).

The Year's Best Fantasy Stories: 4 (New York: DAW Books, 1978).

Cavendish, Margaret, *The Description of a New World, Called The Blazing World*, in *The Blazing World and Other Writings*, ed. by Kate Lilley (London: Penguin, 2004).

Cecire, Maria Sachiko, *Re-Enchanted: The Rise of Children's Fantasy Literature in the Twentieth Century* (Minneapolis: University of Minnesota Press, 2019).

Cervantes, Miguel de, *Don Quixote*, translated by Edith Grossman (London: Vintage, 2005).

Chesterton, G. K., Introduction to Greville MacDonald, *George MacDonald and his Wife* (London: Allen and Unwin, 1924), pp. 9–15.

Chiang, Ted, 'Story of Your Life', in *Stories of Your Life and Others* (Easthampton, MA: Small Beer Press, 2010), pp. 91–145.

Childress, Mark and Charles McNair, '"I'll Be in Another World": A Rediscovered Interview with Jorge Luis Borges', *Los Angeles Review of Books*, 23 August 2021, https://bit.ly/3L9yXA9.

Cixous, Hélène, 'The Laugh of the Medusa', translated by Keith Cohen and Paula Cohen, *Signs*, 1.4 (1976), 875–93.

Clarke, Arthur C., 'Hazards of Prophecy: The Failure of Imagination', in *Profiles of the Future: An Enquiry into the Limits of the Possible*, 2nd edition (London: Pan Books, 1973), pp. 30–9.

Clarke, Susanna, *Jonathan Strange & Mr Norrell* (London: Bloomsbury, 2005).

clipping., Afterword to Rivers Solomon, *The Deep* (London: Hodder & Stoughton, 2020), pp. 157–63.

Clute, John and John Grant (eds.), *The Encyclopedia of Fantasy* (London: Orbit, 1997), https://sf-encyclopedia.com/fe/.

Cole, Adrian, *Longbore the Inexhaustible*, British Fantasy Society Booklet No. 3 (1978).

Coleridge, Samuel Taylor, *Biographia Literaria*, 2 vols. (London: Rest Fenner, 1817).

'Effusion XXXV' (later titled 'The Eolian Harp'), in *Poems on Various Subjects* (London: Robinsons, 1796), pp. 96–100.

'Kubla Khan: or A Vision in a Dream', in *Christabel: Kubla Khan, A Vision: The Pains of Sleep* (London: John Murray, 1816), pp. 55–8.

Confucius, *The Analects*, translated by D. C. Lau (London: Penguin, 1979).

Crawford, Joseph, *The Twilight of the Gothic?: Vampire Fiction and the Rise of the Paranormal Romance* (Cardiff: University of Wales Press, 2014).

Critical Role, 'Game Masters of Exandria Roundtable', *YouTube.com*, 29 June 2022, www.youtube.com/watch?v=LmZSWKPXhZ4.

Czerneda, Julie E., 'I Write Fantasy Because of Patricia McKillip's *The Riddlemaster of Hed*', *Tor.com*, 24 September 2021, https://bit.ly/41Fcosj.

Dahl, Roald, *Matilda* (London: Puffin, 2022).

Dark Souls (FromSoftware, 2011).

De Kosnik, Abigail, *Rogue Archives: Digital Cultural Memory and Media Fandom* (Cambridge, MA: MIT Press, 2016).

Deleuze, Gilles and Claire Parnet, *Dialogues II*, revised edition, translated by Hugh Tomlinson and Barbara Habberjam (New York: Columbia University Press, 2007).

Derrida, Jacques, *Of Grammatology*, translated by Gayatri Chakravorty Spivak, corrected edition (Baltimore, MD, and London: Johns Hopkins University Press, 1997).

Díaz, Junot, *The Brief Wondrous Life of Oscar Wao* (London: Faber and Faber, 2007).

Dickinson, Seth, *The Traitor* [*The Traitor Baru Cormorant* in the United States] (London: Tor, 2015).

Donne, John, '17. Meditation', in *Devotions Upon Emergent Occasions* (London: Thomas Jones, 1624), pp. 410–19.

Driggers, Taylor, *Queering Faith in Fantasy Literature: Fantastic Incarnations and the Deconstruction of Theology* (London: Bloomsbury Academic, 2022).

Duncan, Ian, 'Edinburgh and Lowland Scotland', in *The Cambridge History of English Romantic Literature*, ed. by James Chandler (Cambridge: Cambridge University Press, 2009), pp. 159–81.

Dungeons & Dragons: Dungeon Master's Guide, 5th edition (Renton, WA: Wizards of the Coast, 2014).

Dungeons & Dragons: Monster Manual, 5th edition (Renton, WA: Wizards of the Coast, 2014).

Lord Dunsany, *The Gods of Pegāna* ([London]: Pegana Press, 1911).

Dyson, H. V. D. and John Butt, *Augustans and Romantics, 1689–1830*, revised edition (London: Cresset Press, 1961).

Ebert, Roger, 'How Propeller-Heads, BNFs, Sercon Geeks, Newbies, Recovering GAFIAtors, and Kids in the Basements Invented the World Wide Web, All Except for the Delivery System', *Asimov's Science Fiction*, 29.1 (2005), 12–17.

Eddison, E. R., *The Worm Ouroboros* (London: Millennium, 2000).

Edelstein, Dan, *The Enlightenment: A Genealogy* (Chicago, IL: University of Chicago Press, 2010).

Ekman, Stefan, *Here Be Dragons: Exploring Fantasy Maps and Settings* (Middletown, CT: Wesleyan University Press, 2013).

Elden Ring (FromSoftware, 2022).

Ende, Michael, *The Neverending Story* (London: Puffin, 2014).

Erikson, Steven, *The Bonehunters*, Malazan Book of the Fallen 6 (London: Bantam, 2007).

Deadhouse Gates, Malazan Book of the Fallen 2 (London: Bantam, 2001).

Memories of Ice, Malazan Book of the Fallen 3 (London: Bantam, 2002).

Fielding, Henry, *Tom Jones*, ed. by John Bender and Simon Stern (Oxford: Oxford University Press, 2008).

Fimi, Dimitra, *Tolkien, Race and Cultural History: From Fairies to Hobbits* (Basingstoke: Palgrave Macmillan, 2009).

Final Fantasy VII (Square, 1997).

Fisher, Mark, *Capitalist Realism: Is There No Alternative?* (Winchester: Zero Books, 2009).

Gaiman, Neil et al., *The Sandman*, Volume 1: *Preludes and Nocturnes* (New York: Vertigo/DC Comics, 1995).

The Sandman, Volume 3: *Dream Country* (New York: Vertigo/DC Comics, 1995).

The Sandman, Volume 7: *Brief Lives* (New York: Vertigo/DC Comics, 1994).

The Sandman, Volume 9: *The Kindly Ones* (New York: Vertigo/DC Comics, 1996).

Game of Thrones, created by David Benioff, D. B. Weiss et al. (HBO, 2011–19).

George, Ajit A., F. Wesley Schneider et al., *Journeys through the Radiant Citadel* (Renton, WA: Wizards of the Coast, 2022).

Gevers, Nick, 'Driven by a Different Chauffeur: An Interview with Ursula K. Le Guin', *SF Site*, November/December 2001, www.sfsite.com/03a/ul123.htm.

Gifford, James, *A Modernist Fantasy: Modernism, Anarchism, & the Radical Fantastic* (Victoria, BC: ELS Editions, 2018).

Gissing, George, *New Grub Street*, 2nd edition, 3 vols. (London: Smith, Elder, 1891).

Glyer, Diana Pavlac, *The Company They Keep: C. S. Lewis and J. R. R. Tolkien as Writers in Community* (Kent: The Ohio State University Press, 2007).

Grahame, Kenneth, 'The Reluctant Dragon', in *Dream Days* (London and New York: John Lane, 1898), pp. 179–245.

Gross, Terry, 'Colson Whitehead's 'Underground Railroad' is a Literal Train to Freedom', *Fresh Air, NPR*, 8 August 2016, https://bit.ly/409qDEF.

Guillory, John, *Cultural Capital: The Problem of Literary Canon Formation* (Chicago, IL: University of Chicago Press, 1993).

Hades (Supergiant, 2020).

Hadestown, created by Anaïs Mitchell et al. (developed 2006–19).

Halter, Ed, 'An Interview with John Crowley', *The Believer*, 62 (May 2009), www.thebeliever.net/an-interview-with-john-crowley/.

Harari, Yuval Noah, *Sapiens: A Brief History of Humankind* (London: Vintage, 2019).

Harman, Graham, *Weird Realism: Lovecraft and Philosophy* (Winchester: Zero Books, 2012).

Harmon, Amy, 'In TV's Dull Summer Days, Plots Take Wing on the Net', *New York Times*, 18 August 1997, https://bit.ly/3LbZoa3.

Headley, Maria Dahvana, *Beowulf: A New Translation* (London: Scribe, 2021).

Heaney, Seamus, *Beowulf* (London: Faber & Faber, 1999).

Hills, Matt, *Fan Cultures* (London and New York: Routledge, 2002).

Hobb, Robin, *Blood of Dragons* (New York: Harper Voyager, 2013).

Ship of Magic (London: Harper, 2015).

Holdstock, Robert, *Mythago Wood* (London: Gollancz, 2014).

Hopkinson, Nalo, 'A Reluctant Ambassador from the Planet of Midnight', *Journal of the Fantastic in the Arts*, 21.3 (2010), 339–50.

Horta, Paulo Lemos, *Marvellous Thieves: Secret Authors of the Arabian Nights* (Cambridge, MA: Harvard University Press, 2019).

Hume, Kathryn, *Fantasy and Mimesis: Responses to Reality in Western Literature* (New York and London: Methuen, 1984).

Hutcheon, Linda with Siobhan O'Flynn, *A Theory of Adaptation*, 2nd edition (London: Routledge, 2013).

Jackson, Rosemary, *Fantasy: The Literature of Subversion* (New York and London: Methuen, 1981).

Jain, Sid, 'Seduced by the Ruler's Gaze: An Indian Perspective on Seth Dickinson's *Masquerade*', *Uncanny Magazine*, 39 (2021), https://bit.ly/41iaONz.

James, Edward and Farah Mendlesohn (eds.), *The Cambridge Companion to Fantasy Literature* (Cambridge: Cambridge University Press, 2012).

Jameson, Fredric, 'World Reduction in Le Guin: The Emergence of Utopian Narrative', *Science Fiction Studies*, 2.3 (1975), 221–30.

[Jeffrey, Francis], 'Southey's Thalaba', *Edinburgh Review*, 1 (October 1802), 63–83.

Jemisin, N. K., 'But, but, but — WHY Does Magic Have to Make Sense?', *nkjemisin.com*, 15 June 2012, https://bit.ly/3LctDfv.

'Character Study: Nahadoth', *nkjemisin.com*, 5 April 2010, https://nkjemisin.com/2010/04/character-study-nahadoth/.

'Dreaming Awake', *nkjemisin.com*, 9 February 2012, https://nkjemisin.com/2012/02/dreaming-awake/.

The Fifth Season (London: Orbit, 2016).

The Hundred Thousand Kingdoms (London: Orbit, 2010).

'Why I Think RaceFail Was The Bestest Thing Evar for SFF', *nkjemisin.com*, 18 January 2010, https://bit.ly/3mHvteH.

Jenkins, Henry, *Convergence Culture: Where Old and New Media Meet*, updated edition (New York: New York University Press, 2008).

'Johns, Norma N.', *Bodoman of Sor*, British Fantasy Society Booklet No. 1 (1977).

Johnson, Catherine, *Telefantasy* (London: BFI, 2005).

Jones, Diana Wynne, *The Dark Lord of Derkholm* (London: HarperCollins, 2013).

The Tough Guide to Fantasyland (New York: DAW Books, 1996).

Joyce, James, *Ulysses* (Paris: Shakespeare and Company, 1922).

Kant, Immanuel, 'Answering the Question: What Is Enlightenment?', in *Practical Philosophy*, ed. and translated by Mary J. Gregor (Cambridge: Cambridge University Press, 1996), pp. 17–22.

Kay, Guy Gavriel, *Tigana* (London: Penguin, 1990).

Kenan, Randall, 'An Interview with Octavia E. Butler', *Callaloo*, 14.2 (Spring 1991), 495–504.

Klaeber's Beowulf, ed. by R. D. Fulk, Robert E. Bjork and John D. Niles, 4th edition (Toronto, Buffalo, NY, and London: University of Toronto Press, 2008).

Knight, Damon, *In Search of Wonder: Essays on Modern Science Fiction* (Chicago, IL: Advent, 1956).

Krueger, Roberta L., Introduction to *The Cambridge Companion to Medieval Romance*, ed. by Roberta L. Krueger (Cambridge: Cambridge University Press, 2000), pp. 1–10.

[Lamb, Charles], 'Popular Fallacies', *New Monthly Magazine*, 16 (January 1826), 519–20.

Lamb, Charles [and Mary Lamb], 'The Tempest', in *Tales from Shakespear*, 2 vols. (London: Thomas Hodgkins, 1807), 1:1–21.

Lang, Andrew, *The Blue Fairy Book* (London and New York: Longmans, Green, and Co, 1889).

LaValle, Victor, *The Ballad of Black Tom* (New York: Tor, 2016).

Lavender III, Isiah, *Afrofuturism Rising: The Literary Prehistory of a Movement* (Columbus: Ohio State University Press, 2019).

Laycock, Joseph P., *Dangerous Games: What the Moral Panic over Role-Playing Games Says about Play, Religion, and Imagined Worlds* (Oakland: University of California Press, 2015).

Le Guin, Ursula K., *The Books of Earthsea* (London: Gollancz, 2018).

'Earthsea Revisioned', in *The Books of Earthsea* (London: Gollancz, 2018), pp. 981–92.

'From Elfland to Poughkeepsie', in *The Language of the Night: Essays on Fantasy and Science Fiction*, ed. by Susan Wood (New York: Putnam, 1979), pp. 83–96.

The Farthest Shore (London: Puffin, 1974).

'It Doesn't Have to Be the Way It Is', in *No Time to Spare: Thinking about What Matters* (Boston and New York: Houghton Mifflin Harcourt, 2017), pp. 80–4.

The Lathe of Heaven (New York: Avon Books, 1971).

Steering the Craft: A Twenty-First Century Guide to Sailing the Sea of Story, revised edition (Boston, MA, and New York: Mariner Books, 2015).

A Wizard of Earthsea (Harmondsworth: Penguin, 1971).

Leckie, Ann, *The Raven Tower* (London: Orbit, 2019).

Leith, Sam, '*Watchmen* Author Alan Moore: 'I'm definitely done with comics'', *The Guardian*, 7 October 2022, https://bit.ly/4olbVL4.

L'Engle, Madeleine, *A Wrinkle in Time* (New York: Yearling, 1973).

Letham, Jonathan, 'The Ecstasy of Influence: A Plagiarism', *Harper's Magazine* (February 2007), https://bit.ly/3mJWyxT.

Lewis, C. S., *The Magician's Nephew* (London: Collins, 2009).

'Tolkien's *The Lord of the Rings*', in *On Stories and Other Essays on Literature* (Orlando, FL: Harcourt, 1982), pp. 83–91.

The Voyage of the Dawn Treader (London: HarperCollins, 2009).

Link, Kelly, 'Magic for Beginners', in *Magic for Beginners* (Northampton, MA: Small Beer Press, 2005), pp. 189–236.

'Travels with the Snow Queen', in *Stanger Things Happen* (Northampton, MA: Small Beer Press, 2001), pp. 99–120.

Lovecraft, H. P., 'The Call of Cthulhu', in *The Call of Cthulhu and Other Weird Stories*, ed. by S. T. Joshi (London: Penguin, 2002), pp. 139–69.

'The Haunter of the Dark', in *The Call of Cthulhu and Other Weird Stories*, ed. by S. T. Joshi (London: Penguin, 2002), pp. 336–60.

'Notes on Writing Weird Fiction', in *Miscellaneous Writings*, ed. by S. T. Joshi (Sauk City, WI: Arkham House, 1995), pp. 113–16.

'Nyarlathotep', in *The Call of Cthulhu and Other Weird Stories*, ed. by S. T. Joshi (London: Penguin, 2002), pp. 31–3.

McCloud, Scott, *Understanding Comics: The Invisible Art* (Northampton, MA: Kitchen Sink Press, 1993).

McCormack, Una, 'Finding Ourselves in the (Un)Mapped Lands: Women's Reparative Readings of *The Lord of the Rings*', in *Perilous and Fair: Women in the Works and Life of J. R. R. Tolkien*, ed. by Janet Brennan Croft and Leslie A. Donovan (Altadena, CA: Mythopoeic Press, 2015), pp. 309–26.

MacDonald, George, 'The Fantastic Imagination', in *A Dish of Orts*, enlarged edition (London: Sampson Low Marston & Co., 1893), pp. 313–22.

McKillip, Patricia A., *Alphabet of Thorn* (New York: Ace Books, 2004).

The Bards of Bone Plain (New York: Ace Books, 2004).

The Forgotten Beasts of Eld (New York: Atheneum Books, 1974).

The Riddle-Master's Game (London: Millennium, 2001).

'Women in SF&F', *Fantasy Cafe*, 15 April 2013, https://bit.ly/3mPKfQQ.

Machen, Arthur, *The Great God Pan*, in *The Great God Pan and The Inmost Light*, 2nd edition (London: John Lane, 1895), pp. 1–109.

Maher, Cian, 'The Story behind the Oblivion Mod Terry Pratchett Worked On', *Eurogamer*, 31 January 2019, https://bit.ly/41lQ87j.

Malory, Thomas, *The Works of Thomas Malory*, ed. by Eugène Vinaver, revised by P. J. C. Field, 3rd edition, 3 vols. (Oxford: Clarendon Press, 1990).

Manlove, C. N., *Modern Fantasy: Five Studies* (Cambridge: Cambridge University Press, 1975).

Martin, George R. R., 'FAQ', *georgerrmartin.com*, https://georgerrmartin.com/for-fans/faq/.

A Game of Thrones (London: Harper Voyager, 2011).

Marx, Karl and Friedrich Engels, *The Communist Manifesto*, ed. by David McLellan (Oxford: Oxford University Press, 2008).

Marx, Patricia and John Simon, 'An Interview with Jorge Luis Borges: Reality Is Perplexing Enough', *Commonweal Magazine*, 25 October 1968, www.commonwealmagazine.org/interview-jorge-luis-borges.

Mendlesohn, Farah, 'Peake and the Fuzzy Set of Fantasy: Some Informal Thoughts', in *Miracle Enough: Papers on the Works of Mervyn Peake*, ed. by G. Peter Winnington (Newcastle-upon-Tyne: Cambridge Scholars Publishing, 2013), pp. 61–74.

Rhetorics of Fantasy (Middletown, CT: Wesleyan University Press, 2008).

Miéville, China, Editorial Introduction to *Symposium: Marxism and Fantasy*, *Historical Materialism*, 10.4 (2002), 39–49.

Perdido Street Station (London: Pan, 2011).

Miller, Laura, *The Magician's Book: A Skeptic's Adventures in Narnia* (New York, Boston, MA, and London: Back Bay Books, 2008).

Mirrlees, Hope, *Lud-in-the-Mist* (London: Gollancz, 2008).

Mitchell, Anaïs, *Working on a Song: The Lyrics of Hadestown* (New York: Plume 2020).

Mittell, Jason, 'Narrative Complexity in Contemporary American Television', *The Velvet Light Trap*, 58.1 (2006), 29–40.

Monléon, José B., *A Specter is Haunting Europe: A Sociohistorical Approach to the Fantastic* (Princeton, NJ: Princeton University Press, 1990),

Moorcock, Michael, *Elric of Melniboné and Other Stories* (London: Gollancz, 2013).

Epic Pooh, British Fantasy Society Booklet No. 4 (February 1978).

The Warhound and the World's Pain (New York: Timescape, 1981).

Moore, Alan, Foreword to Michael Moorcock, *Elric of Melniboné and Other Stories* (London: Gollancz, 2013), pp. 1–7.

Moore, Rosalie, 'Science Fiction and the Main Stream', in *Modern Science Fiction: Its Meaning and its Future*, ed. by Reginald Bretnor (New York: Coward-McCann, 1953), pp. 91–118.

Morrison, Toni, 'The Art of Fiction', interview by Elissa Schappell and Claudia Brodsky Lacour, in *The Paris Review Interviews*, Volume 2, ed. by Philip Gourevitch (Edinburgh: Canongate, 2007), pp. 355–94.

Beloved (London: Chatto & Windus, 1993).

Naimon, David and guests, *Crafting with Ursula*, 12 episodes, *Tin House*, 2022, https://tinhouse.com/th_podcast_cat/crafting-with-ursula/.

NeverKnowsBest, 'An in-depth look at Lovecraftian Video Games', *YouTube.com*, 17 November 2019, https://youtu.be/8CaovqiSPiw.

Newton, Isaac to Robert Hooke, 5 February 1675 [likely actually 1676], Historical Society of Pennsylvania, Box 12/11, Folder 37, https://discover.hsp.org/Record/dc-9792/.

O'Dette, Katarina, 'Fantasy Worlds on the Small Screen: Worldbuilding in Original American Fantasy Television', *Extrapolation*, 62.1 (2021), 37–62.

Okorafor, Nnedi, 'Africanfuturism Defined', *Nnedi's Wahala Zone Blog*, 19 October 2019, https://bit.ly/3LfaxFB.

Orwell, George, *Nineteen Eighty-Four* (London: Penguin, 2000).

Palmer-Patel, C., *The Shape of Fantasy: Investigating the Structure of American Heroic Epic Fantasy* (New York and Abingdon: Routledge, 2019).

Pan's Labyrinth, directed by Guillermo del Toro (Estudios Picasso/ Tequila Gang/Esperanto Filmoj, 2006).

Parisien, Dominik, 'An Interview with Amal El-Mohtar', *Postscript to Darkness*, 19 December 2013, https://bit.ly/3GWVQ7q.

Peake, Mervyn, *Drawings by Mervyn Peake* (London: Gray Walls Press, 1949).

The Gormenghast Trilogy (London: Vintage, 1999).

Perrault, Charles, 'Blue Beard', translated by Maria Tatar, in *The Classic Fairy Tales*, ed. by Maria Tatar, 2nd edition (New York: W. W. Norton, 2017), pp. 188–93.

Philpott, Lily, 'The Pen Ten: An Interview with Amal El-Mohtar', *PEN America*, 19 December 2019, https://pen.org/pen-ten-interview-amal-el-mohtar/.

Picacio, John, 'Michael Moorcock: Multiverses' (interview), *Locus*, 21 December 2014, https://locusmag.com/2014/12/michael-moorcock-multiverses/.

Planescape: Torment (Black Isle Studios, 1999).

Plato, *Republic*, translated by C. D. C Reeve (Indianapolis, IN, and Cambridge: Hackett Publishing, 2004).

Poe, Edgar Allan, 'The Masque of the Red Death', in *Selected Tales*, ed. by David Van Leer (Oxford: Oxford University Press, 2008), pp. 129–34.

Pope, Alexander, *An Essay on Man*, in *The Poems of Alexander Pope*, ed. by John Butt (London: Methuen, 1963), pp. 501–47.

Powell, Manushag N., 'The Legacy of Stage Dragons and the Monstrous Eighteenth Century', *Eighteenth-Century Fiction*, 32.3 (2020), 485–504.

Pratchett, Terry, *Carpe Jugulum* (London: Corgi, 2013).

Hogfather (London: Victor Gollancz, 1996).

Moving Pictures (London: Corgi, 1992).

Sourcery (London: Corgi, 1989).

Wyrd Sisters (London: Corgi, 1989).

Prickett, Stephen, *Victorian Fantasy*, revised edition (Waco, TX: Baylor University Press, 2005).

Pringle, David, 'Exclusive New Interview with Angela Carter by David Pringle' (conducted 10 August 1979), *Angela Carter Online*, 7 May 2017, https://bit.ly/3mKVREy.

Propp, Vladimir, *The Morphology of the Folktale*, 2nd edition, translated by Laurence Scott, revised by Louis A. Wagner (Austin: University of Texas Press, 1968).

Rein·Hagen, Mark, Sam Chupp, Ian Lemke, Joshua Gabriel Timbrook and others, *Changeling: The Dreaming* (Clarkston, CA: White Wolf Publishing, 1995).

Reynolds, Alastair, Nnedi Okorafor, Ann Leckie, Becky Chambers, Kim Stanley Robinson and M. John Harrison, '"If the aliens lay eggs, how does that affect architecture?": Sci-Fi Writers on How They Build Their Worlds', *The Guardian*, 5 January 2021, https://bit.ly/3GWpauE.

Rieder, John, *Science Fiction and the Mass Cultural Genre System* (Middletown, CT: Wesleyan University Press, 2017).

Robinson, Jeffrey C., *Unfettering Poetry: The Fancy in British Romanticism* (New York: Palgrave Macmillan, 2006).

Rosewater, Mark, 'Twenty Years, Twenty Lessons—Part 3', *magic.wizards.com*, 16 June 2016, https://bit.ly/3mUU6oe.

Russ, Joanna, 'The Image of Women in Science Fiction', in *Images of Women in Fiction: Feminist Perspectives*, ed. by Susan Koppelman Cornillon (Bowling Green, OH: Bowling Green University Popular Press, 1972), pp. 79–94.

Sanderson, Brandon, 'Lecture #6: Worldbuilding Part Two: Brandon Sanderson on Writing Science Fiction and Fantasy', *YouTube.com*, https://youtu.be/V2KpWOLTXx8.

'Sanderson's First Law', *brandonsanderson.com*, 20 February 2007, www.brandonsanderson.com/sandersons-first-law/.

Saler, Michael, *As If: Modern Enchantment and the Literary Prehistory of Virtual Reality* (Oxford: Oxford University Press, 2011).

Samatar, Sofia, 'Selkie Stories are for Losers', in *Tender* (Easthampton, MA: Small Beer Press, 2017), pp. 1–9.

The Winged Histories (Easthampton, MA: Small Beer Press, 2016).

Sandner, David, *Critical Discourses of the Fantastic, 1712–1831* (Farnham: Ashgate, 2011).

Fantastic Literature: A Critical Reader (Westport, CT: Praeger, 2004).

Santayana, George, *The Life of Reason, or the Phases of Human Progress: Introduction and Reason in Common Sense*, ed. by Marianne S. Wokeck and Martin A. Coleman (Cambridge, MA: MIT Press, 2011).

Sartre, Jean-Paul, *The Imaginary: A Phenomenological Psychology of the Imagination*, translated by Jonathan Webber (London: Routledge, 2004).

Schlobin, Roger C., *The Literature of Fantasy: A Comprehensive, Annotated Bibliography of Modern Fantasy Fiction* (New York: Garland Publishing, 1979).

Scholes, Robert, *Structural Fabulation: An Essay on the Fiction of the Future* (Notre Dame, IN, and London: University of Notre Dame Press, 1975).

Scott, James C., *Seeing Like a State: How Certain Schemes to Improve the Human Condition Have Failed* (New Haven, CT: Yale University Press, 2000).

[Scott, Walter], 'On the Supernatural in Fictitious Composition', *Foreign Quarterly Review*, 1.1 (1827), 60–98.

The Seventh Seal, directed by Ingmar Bergman (AB Svensk Filmindustri, 1957).

Shakespeare, William, *Hamlet*, ed. by G. R. Hibbard (Oxford: Oxford World's Classics, 2008).

Shakespeare, William, *The Tempest*, ed. by Virginia Mason Vaughan and Alden T. Vaughan, revised edition (London: Bloomsbury, 2011).

Shawl, Nisi and Cynthia Ward, *Writing the Other: A Practical Approach* (Seattle, WA: Aqueduct Press, 2005).

Shepherd, Lucius, 'The Man Who Painted the Dragon Griaule', in *The Dragon Griaule* (London: Gollancz, 2013), pp. 1–30.

Shotwell, Alexis, *Against Purity: Living Ethically in Compromised Times* (Minneapolis and London: University of Minnesota Press, 2016).

Siskin, Clifford, *The Work of Writing: Literature and Social Change in Britain 1700–1830* (Baltimore, MD: Johns Hopkins University Press, 1998).

Smith, Adam, *An Inquiry into the Nature and Causes of the Wealth of Nations*, 2 vols. (London: W. Strahan and T. Cadell, 1776).

Smythe, Rachel, *Lore Olympus*, *webtoons.com*, 2018–, www.webtoons.com/en/romance/lore-olympus/list?title_no=1320.

Solomon, Rivers, *The Deep* (London: Hodder & Stoughton, 2020).

Stein, Gertrude, 'Sacred Emily', in *Geography and Plays* (Boston, MA: Four Seas, 1922), pp. 179–88.

Stevens, Anne H., 'Circulating Libraries as Institutional Creators of Genres', in *Institutions of Literature, 1700–1900*, ed. by Jon Mee and Matthew Sangster (Cambridge: Cambridge University Press, 2022), pp. 120–34.

Sutton, David, 'A History of the BFS: The Early Years: 1970–1984', in *Silver Rhapsody*, ed. by John Carter and Jan Edwards, British Fantasy Society Booklet No. 23 (1996).

(ed.), *William Hope Hodgson: A Centenary Tribute 1877–1977*, British Fantasy Society Booklet No. 2 (1977).

Tchaikovsky, Adrian, *Elder Race* (New York: Tom Doherty Associates, 2021).

Temple, Emily, 'Ten Famous Writers on Loving Buffy the Vampire Slayer', *LitHub*, 10 March 2017, https://bit.ly/41DWq1Y.

Thomas, Ebony Elizabeth, *The Dark Fantastic: Race and the Imagination from Harry Potter to the Hunger Games* (New York: New York University Press, 2019).

Todorov, Tzvetan, *The Fantastic: A Structural Approach to a Literary Genre*, translated by Richard Howard (Ithaca, NY: Cornell University Press 1975).

Tolkien, J. R. R., 'Beowulf: The Monsters and the Critics', in *The Monsters and the Critics and Other Essays*, ed. by Christopher Tolkien (London: HarperCollins, 2006), pp. 5–48.

'On Fairy-stories', in *On Fairy-stories*, ed. by Verlyn Flieger and Douglas A. Anderson (London: HarperCollins, 2008), pp. 25–84.

The Hobbit (London and Sydney: Unwin Paperbacks, 1981).

The Letters of J. R. R. Tolkien, ed. by Humphrey Carpenter (London: George Allen and Unwin, 1981).

The Lord of the Rings (London: Grafton, 1992).

The Silmarillion, ed. by Christopher Tolkien (London: HarperCollins, 1999).

Sir Gawain and the Green Knight, Pearl, and Sir Orfeo (London: George Allen and Unwin, 1975).

Tolkien, J. R. R. and E. V. Gordon (eds.), *Sir Gawain and the Green Knight* (Oxford: Clarendon Press, 1925).

Tucker, Herbert, *Epic: Britain's Heroic Muse 1790–1910* (Oxford: Oxford University Press, 2008).

VanderMeer, Jeff, *Authority* (London: Fourth Estate, 2014).

Wonderbook: The Illustrated Guide to Creating Imaginative Fiction (New York: Abrams, 2013).

Vo, Nghi, *The Empress of Salt and Fortune* (New York: Tom Doherty, 2020).

Voltaire, *Philosophical Dictionary*, ed. and translated by Theodore Besterman (London: Penguin, 1979).

Walpole, Horace, *The Castle of Otranto*, ed. by Nick Groom (Oxford: Oxford University Press, 2014).

Walton, Jo, *Among Others* (New York: Tor, 2011).

The Just City (New York: Tor, 2015).

Warner, Marina, *Once Upon a Time: A Short History of Fairy Tale* (Oxford: Oxford University Press, 2014).

White, Haydon, *Metahistory: The Historical Imagination in Nineteenth-Century Europe* (Baltimore, MD: Johns Hopkins University Press, 1975).

White, T. H., *The Ill-Made Knight*, in *The Once and Future King* (London: Collins, 1958), pp. 325–544.

Whitehead, Colson, *The Underground Railroad* (London: Fleet, 2016).

Williamson, Jamie, *The Evolution of Modern Fantasy: From Antiquarianism to the Ballantine Adult Fantasy Series* (New York: Palgrave Macmillan, 2015).

Wilson, Edmund, 'Oo, Those Awful Orcs!', *The Nation*, 14 April 1956, 326–32.

Wilson, G. Willow, *The Bird King* (London: Grove, 2020).

Windling, Terri, Introduction to Jane Yolen, *Briar Rose* (New York: Tor, 1993), pp. 1–6.

'The Luminous Worlds of Patricia McKillip', *Myth & Moor*, 17 May 2022, www.terriwindling.com/blog/2022/05/pat-mckillip.html.

Wittgenstein, Ludwig, *Tractatus Logico-Philosophicus*, translated by C. K. Ogden with F. P. Ramsey (London: Kegan Paul, Trench, Trubner & Co., 1922).

Wizards of the Coast, 'Diversity and Dungeons & Dragons', *dnd.wizards.com*, 17 June 2020, https://dnd.wizards.com/news/diversity-and-dnd.

Wolf, Mark J. P., *Building Imaginary Worlds: The Theory and History of Subcreation* (New York and London: Routledge, 2012).

Wolfe, Gary K., *Critical Terms for Science Fiction and Fantasy* (New York, Westport, CN, and London: Greenwood Press, 1986).

Wolfe, Gene, *The Castle of the Otter*, in *Castle of Days* (New York: Orb, 1992), pp. 205–309.

The Sword of the Lictor, in *The Book of the New Sun*, Volume 2: *Sword and Citadel* (London: Millennium, 2000), pp. 1–310.

Womack, Ytasha L., *Afrofuturism: The World of Black Sci-fi and Fantasy Culture* (Chicago, IL: Lawrence Hill Books, 2013).

Wordsworth, William, 'The Tables Turned', in *Lyrical Ballads, with Pastoral and Other Poems*, 3rd edition, 2 vols. (London: Longman, 1802), 1:4–6.

Wordsworth, William [and Samuel Taylor Coleridge], Preface to *Lyrical Ballads, with Pastoral and Other Poems*, 3rd edition, 2 vols. (London: Longman, 1802), 1:i–lxiv.

Young, Helen, *Race and Popular Fantasy Literature: Habits of Whiteness* (New York and Abingdon: Routledge, 2016).

Young, Helen and Kavita Mudan Finn, *Global Medievalism* (Cambridge: Cambridge University Press, 2022).

Zaleski, Philip and Carol Zaleski, *The Fellowship: The Literary Lives of the Inklings* (New York: Farrer, Strauss and Giroux, 2016).

INDEX

For EU product safety concerns, contact us at Calle de José Abascal, 56–1°, 28003 Madrid, Spain or eugpsr@cambridge.org.

www.ingramcontent.com/pod-product-compliance
Ingram Content Group UK Ltd.
Pitfield, Milton Keynes, MK11 3LW, UK
UKHW022141080726
473066UK00010B/681

* 9 7 8 1 0 0 9 4 2 9 9 4 8 *